Mom + Dad,

HOW MUCH DOES GOD FOREKNOW?

A COMPREHENSIVE BIBLICAL STUDY

Thanks for all your love & support! I love you both

STEVEN C. ROY

Stev

IVP Academic

An imprint of InterVarsity Press
Downers Grove, Illinois

Apollos
Nottingham, England

InterVarsity Press, USA
P.O. Box 1400, Downers Grove, IL 60515-1426, USA
World Wide Web: www.ivpress.com
Email: email@ivpress.com

APOLLOS (an imprint of Inter-Varsity Press, England)
Norton Street, Nottingham NG7 3HR, England
Website: www.ivpbooks.com
Email: ivp@ivpbooks.com

InterVarsity Press®, USA, is the book-publishing division of InterVarsity Christian Fellowship/USA®, a student movement active on campus at hundreds of universities, colleges and schools of nursing in the United States of America, and a member movement of the International Fellowship of Evangelical Students. For information about local and regional activities, write Public Relations Dept., InterVarsity Christian Fellowship/USA, 6400 Schroeder Rd., P.O. Box 7895, Madison, WI 53707-7895, or visit the IVCF website at <www.intervarsity.org>.

Inter-Varsity Press, England, is closely linked with the Universities and Colleges Christian Fellowship, a student movement connecting Christian Unions in universities and colleges throughout Great Britain, and a member movement of the International Fellowship of Evangelical Students. Website: www.uccf.org.uk.

Design: Cindy Kiple

Images: galaxy of stars: Ian Mckinnell/Getty Images

box: Louie Psihoyos/Getty Images

USA ISBN-10: 0-8308-2759-5
ISBN-13: 978-0-8308-2759-6

UK ISBN-10: 1-84474-144-3
ISBN-13: 978-1-84474-144-1

Printed in the United States of America ∞

Library of Congress Cataloging-in-Publication Data

Roy, Steven C., 1954-
How much does God foreknow?: a comprehensive biblical study /
Steven C. Roy.
p. cm.
Includes bibliographical references and indexes.
ISBN-13: 978-0-8308-2759-6 (pbk.: alk paper)
ISBN-10: 0-8308-2759-5 (pbk.: alk paper)
1. God—Omniscience. I. Title.
BT131.R69 2006
231'.4—dc22

2006013029

British Library Cataloguing in Publication Data

A catalogue record for this book is available from the British Library.

| P | 18 | 17 | 16 | 15 | 14 | 13 | 12 | 11 | 10 | 9 | 8 | 7 | 6 | 5 | 4 | 3 | 2 | 1 |
| Y | 20 | 19 | 18 | 17 | 16 | 15 | 14 | 13 | 12 | 11 | 10 | 09 | 08 | 07 | 06 | | | | |

CONTENTS

Acknowledgments.   7

1 INTRODUCTION   9

2 OLD TESTAMENT EVIDENCE OF DIVINE FOREKNOWLEDGE 27

3 NEW TESTAMENT EVIDENCE OF DIVINE FOREKNOWLEDGE 73

4 A DIFFERENT VIEW OF DIVINE FOREKNOWLEDGE. 125

5 TWO CRITICAL INTERPRETIVE QUESTIONS 195

6 PRACTICAL IMPLICATIONS 229

7 CONCLUSION 279

Bibliography. 283

Name Index 299

Subject Index 303

Scripture Index 306

ACKNOWLEDGMENTS

This study began a long time ago. The earliest phases began when my youngest daughter, Lydia, was in the third grade (she is now a freshman in college). That was when I was starting to consider possible topics for my dissertation research at Trinity Evangelical Divinity School. My ongoing explorations concerning the foreknowledge of God and the contemporary debate concerning its extent convinced me that this was indeed a fruitful topic for further research. This process of study and dialogue culminated in my Ph.D. dissertation, which was mentored by Drs. Bruce Ware and Wayne Grudem. I am grateful to them for their guidance, challenges and encouragement as well as to other faculty members and fellow doctoral students at Trinity. All of you have helped shape me as a Christian and as a theologian, and you have shaped my views on the topic of God's foreknowledge. By the grace of God, I successfully defended my dissertation in January 2001 and graduated in May of that year.

As time has progressed I have continued to reflect on the topic of divine foreknowledge in my teaching at Trinity Evangelical Divinity School. Ongoing interaction with faculty colleagues and students have clarified and sharpened my thinking on this and many other areas of Christian life and doctrine. I am particularly grateful to my colleague Dr. Peter Cha. Many valued conversations with him have significantly shaped the way I think, feel and act at so many levels. I have also participated in discussions on the foreknowledge of God and its implications at several annual meetings of the Evangelical Theological Society. Portions of this study first appeared as papers given at ETS Annual Meetings in 1999 and 2001. Ongoing dialogue and debate with those whose views are similar to mine as well as with those whose views are quite different has been a rich source of growth and insight.

I am grateful to the Board of Regents of Trinity for granting me a sabbatical, during which this project was completed. Special thanks go to Mary Ocasek and others on the library staff of the University of St. Mary of the Lake for their hospitality and gracious assistance to me during my sabbatical. I have appreciated and have profited from my interactions with Gary Deddo of InterVarsity Press throughout the process of writing this work. Thank you for all your help.

I am particularly grateful to my graduate assistant, Daniel Busch, for his assistance with the indexes. Dan, your help in this has been invaluable.

I must express my deepest appreciation to my family. Andrew, Beth and Lydia: you have supported and been patient with your Dad at so many points. Thank you so much. And to Susan, my beloved wife: you have stood with me throughout this project, in both its dissertation and book phases. You have encouraged me and sacrificed for me. I am eternally grateful.

And finally a word to my parents, Curt and Joan Roy: Through your lives and your love, you both have taught me so much about our great and gracious God. To you I dedicate this book with much love and gratitude.

1

INTRODUCTION

God knows the future! His foreknowledge has rightly been prized by Christians of all generations. Much of the confidence, hope and joy of the Christian life traditionally has been based on the conviction that God knows the future. Consider a few of the reasons why.

Intercessory prayer. Christians are regularly encouraged in Scripture to bring their own needs and the needs of others to God in the confidence that he will hear and answer their prayers. This confidence is reflected, for example, in the teaching of Jesus in Matthew 7:7-11.

> Ask and it will be given to you; seek and you will find; knock and the door will be opened to you. For everyone who asks receives; he who seeks finds; and to him who knocks, the door will be opened.
>
> Which of you, if his son asks for bread, will give him a stone? Or if he asks for a fish, will give him a snake? If you, then, though you are evil, know how to give good gifts to your children, how much more will your Father in heaven give good gifts to those who ask him!

Christians, then, are to pray to their heavenly Father with the firm confidence that he will always and only give them good gifts in response to their prayers. Far more than even the best of earthly fathers, our Father will never give us a stone if we ask for bread. And he will never give us a stone even if we, because of our finite knowledge or even our sinful foolishness, ask for the stone itself. But note that this confidence demands that God knows what good gift to give us in response to our prayers, not only now but also in light of our future situation. Thus throughout the various traditions of the church, Christians have taken great comfort in God's response to their prayers precisely because he knows all things perfectly, including all of the future. Indeed in the Sermon on the Mount, Jesus encourages his disciples to a robust life of prayer precisely because "your heavenly Father knows what you need before you ask" (Mt 6:8).

Guidance. Consider more specifically the prayers of Christians asking God to guide them in their lives. Though there are various ways of understanding the guidance of God, Christians of different traditions have regularly sought God's guidance in very specific areas of their lives. Should I marry this particular person? What kind of career should I pursue? Where should I worship and serve? Can I trust God to guide me in such matters? Scripture promises that God will guide us and that such guidance should be pursued in prayer. Think, for example, of Psalm 25, where David prays for God's guidance.

> Show me your ways, O LORD,
>> teach me your paths;
> guide me in your truth and teach me,
>> for you are God my Savior,
>> and my hope is in you all day long. (vv. 4-5)

But Psalm 25 also promises that God will guide his people.

> Good and upright is the LORD;
>> therefore he instructs sinners in his ways.
> He guides the humble in what is right
>> and teaches him his way. . . .
> Who, then, is the man who fears the LORD?
>> He [the LORD] will instruct him in the way chosen for him. (vv. 8-9, 12)

Thus God's promise gives us confidence and hope when we pray for his guidance. But in order for God to fulfill his promise to lead and guide us when we pray, he needs to know the future. Then and only then can he be counted on to give us wise guidance in the way we should go.

Hope. We as Christians are called to live in hope. Specifically, Romans 5:2 calls us to "rejoice in the hope of the glory of God." This divine glory, in which we can hope even in the midst of our suffering, is personal and existential—one day we will see God face to face (1 Cor 13:12) and come to share in his glory as we are conformed to the likeness of Christ (Rom 8:29). God's glory is also cosmic and universal—he will one day fully display it when he consummates all of his purposes of mercy and justice in the new heavens and the new earth (Rev 21—22). But traditionally, this sense of eschatological confidence has been based on God's knowledge of the future. If God does not know the future completely, how will he know what needs to be done to ensure the final and ultimate triumph of his gracious purposes for our own lives, for all of history, and indeed the entire cosmos?[1]

---

[1] The relationship of God's foreknowledge to these practical dimensions of Christian living will be explored in more detail in chap. 6.

But far more goes into the traditional Christian belief in the foreknowledge of God than the these three beliefs. More important is the widespread conviction that this is in fact what the Scripture teaches.

THE OMNISCIENCE OF GOD

Christians have long affirmed the omniscience of God, the infinite perfection of his knowledge. This is an attempt to be faithful to the teaching of Scripture, which describes God's knowledge as being, among other things,

- perfect (cf. Job 37:16, where Elihu describes God as being "perfect in knowledge")

- vast (cf. Ps 139:17-18, "How precious to me are your thoughts, O God! / How vast is the sum of them! / Were I to count them, / they would outnumber the grains of sand")

- limitless (cf. Ps 147:5, "Great is the Lord and mighty in power; / his understanding has no limit")

- all-encompassing (cf. Job 28:24, "[God] views the ends of the earth / and sees everything under the heavens"; 1 Jn 3:20, "God is greater than our hearts, and he knows everything"; Heb 4:13, "Nothing in all creation is hidden from God's sight. Everything is uncovered and laid bare before the eyes of him to whom we must give account")

Because God is altogether holy (i.e., separate from and superior to all that he has made), his knowledge, thoughts and ways are qualitatively greater than ours. Thus Yahweh says in Isaiah 55:8-9:

> "My thoughts are not your thoughts,
>   neither are your ways my ways,"
>   declares the LORD.
> "As the heavens are higher than the earth,
>   so are my ways higher than your ways
>   and my thoughts than your thoughts."

And Paul says in Romans 11:33 that God's knowledge and his wisdom are very deep, very precious, and so vast that they are not fully knowable by us:

> Oh the depth of the riches of the wisdom and knowledge of God!
>   How unsearchable his judgments
>   and his paths beyond tracing out!

Traditionally, Christian theologians have held that God's omniscience in-

cludes his knowledge of the future.[2] Thus the all-encompassing nature of God's
omniscience has been seen to imply that his foreknowledge is exhaustive and
embracing of all things, specifically of the free decisions of human beings. This
exhaustive foreknowledge of God has long been held to be an essential part of
his divine being, without which God would not be God. For example, the
church father Jerome (347-420) said of God's foreknowledge of the fall of Adam
and Eve (an example of God foreknowing free human decisions), "You also
deny His deity when you deny His foreknowledge."[3] The twentieth-century
Christian thinker C. S. Lewis said, "Everyone who believes in God at all, believes
that He knows what you and I are going to do tomorrow."[4] And the great Re-
former Martin Luther argued passionately and eloquently that the practical benefits of faith in the foreknowledge of God come only when his foreknowledge
is viewed exhaustively. Luther wrote:

> How religious, devout, and necessary a thing is it to know [of God's foreknowl-
> edge]. For if these things are not known, there can be neither faith nor any worship
> of God. For that would be ignorance of God, and where there is such ignorance,
> there cannot be salvation, as we know. For if you doubt or disdain to know that
> God foreknows all things, not contingently, but necessarily and immutably, how
> can you believe in his promises and place a sure trust and reliance on them? For
> when he promises anything, you ought to be certain that he knows and is able and
> willing to perform what he promises; otherwise, you will regard him as neither
> truthful nor faithful, and that is impiety and a denial of the Most High God. But
> how will you be certain and sure unless you know that he knows and wills and

---

[2]The future is not the only time dimension that can be used in referring to God's knowledge.
Stephen Charnock, for example, speaks of God's "remembrance" of the past, his "knowledge
of vision" of the present and his "foreknowledge" of the future (*Discourses upon the Existence
and Attributes of God* [1853; reprint, Grand Rapids: Baker, 1996], 1:410). It is beyond the scope
of this book to investigate whether these temporal distinctions relate to God's essential being.
The point for our purposes is that since God's knowledge is, in part at least, of things within
the temporal universe he has created, these temporal categories are helpful and correspond
to biblical usage. See Herman Bavinck, *The Doctrine of God,* ed. and trans. William Hendricksen (Grand Rapids: Baker, 1979), p. 189. For a good introduction to the issues surrounding
the relationship of God and time, see Gregory A. Ganssle, ed. *God and Time: Four Views*
(Downers Grove, Ill.: InterVarsity Press, 2001).

[3]Jerome *The Dialogue Against the Pelagians* 3.6, in *The Fathers of the Church,* trans. John N.
Hritzu (Washington, D.C.: The Catholic University of America Press, 1965), 53:356. Consider
also the words of Augustine (354-430): "To confess that God exists, and at the same time to
deny that he has foreknowledge of future things is the most manifest folly" (*The City of God*
5.9, trans. M. Dods and J. J. Smith, in *The Basic Writings of St. Augustine,* ed. Whitney J. Oates
[Grand Rapids: Baker, 1980], 2:64). Later in the same work, in a discussion of the views of the
Roman philosopher Cicero, Augustine declared that "one who is not prescient of all things is
not God" (ibid., p. 67).

[4]C. S. Lewis, *Mere Christianity* (New York: MacMillan, 1960), p. 148.

will do what he promises, certainly, infallibly, immutably, and necessarily? . . . Therefore, Christian faith is entirely extinguished, the promises of God are completely destroyed, if we teach and believe that it is not for us to know the necessary foreknowledge of God."[5]

THE PROBLEM

But a dilemma arises when this doctrine of God's exhaustive, infallible foreknowledge is combined with an indeterministic, libertarian understanding of human freedom.[6] The following illustration reveals the difficulty. Let's suppose that God infallibly foreknows that next week I will decide to take my wife Susan out to dinner and that when we go she will order shrimp and I will order steak. If this is the case, then when next week comes, can my wife and I do anything other than what God infallibly foreknows that we would choose to do? How could it be otherwise? If either of us chose differently, our decisions would render God's foreknowledge false and mistaken. But that cannot be if God's foreknowledge is not only exhaustive but also infallible. Thus it is certain that I will decide to take Susan out to dinner, that Susan will order shrimp and that I will order steak. Yet if these decisions are certain, are we free in what we choose? Therefore, at various points in the history of the church it has been argued that the exhaustive, infallible foreknowledge of God is logically inconsistent with libertarian human freedom.

RESOLVING THE DILEMMA

Historically, there have been three major ways of seeking to resolve this foreknowledge-freedom dilemma. Some theologians and philosophers have argued that the perceived incompatibility between exhaustive, infallible divine foreknowledge and libertarian human freedom is only on the surface. At the deepest level they are in fact compatible. Both realities can and do exist simultaneously. Within this broad position are several approaches. Some say that though God's exhaustive, infallible foreknowledge and libertarian human freedom are compat-

---

[5]Martin Luther, *The Bondage of the Will,* ed. and trans. Philip S. Watson, in *Luther and Erasmus: Free Will and Salvation,* The Library of Christian Classics 17 (Philadelphia: Westminster, 1969), p. 122.
[6]A helpful discussion of libertarian freedom comes from Bruce Reichenbach: "To say that a person is free means that, given a certain set of circumstances, the person (to put it in the past tense) could have done otherwise than he did. He was not compelled by causes either internal to himself (genetic structure or irresistible drives) or external (other persons, God) to act as he did. Though certain causal conditions are present and indeed are necessary for persons to choose to act, if they are free these causal conditions are not sufficient to cause them to choose or act. The individual is the sufficient condition for the course of action chosen" ("God Limits His Power," in *Predestination and Free Will,* ed. David Basinger and Randall Basinger [Downers Grove, Ill.: InterVarsity Press, 1986], pp. 101-24).

ible, the precise relationship is such a deep mystery that we cannot probe it further.[7] Others argue for ultimate compatibility by affirming that God's foreknowledge does not in fact *determine* anything about future human actions. They affirm that the causal connection goes from the free human actions to God's foreknowledge of it, not vice versa. In other words, God's foreknowledge is like a mirror. It reflects future events that are going to happen. Even though God's foreknowledge is chronologically prior (from a human standpoint at least) to the event in question, its content is caused by that event itself. Since there is no causal influence that comes from God's foreknowledge, it in no way limits or jeopardizes libertarian human freedom.[8] In addition, there are other theologians who argue that God is himself outside of time altogether and so his knowledge is timelessly eternal. Thus he can see every future (to us) human decision in one all-encompassing eternal "present." As a result, they argue, God's timeless knowledge of human actions that are future to us no more causes or determines those actions than does human knowledge of an action in the present.[9] Finally, there are theologians who affirm that God's "middle knowledge" is the key to the compatibility of exhaustive

---

[7]For example, James Arminius says, "I am thoroughly persuaded that God's knowledge is eternal, unchangeable, and infinite, and that it extends to all things as well necessary as contingent, to all things which He himself does mediately or immediately, and which He permits to be done by others. But the mode in which He knows certainly future contingencies, and especially those which appertain to creatures of free will, and which He has decreed to permit, not Himself to do—this I do not comprehend" ("Friendly Conversation of James Arminius with Francis Junius About Predestination," in *The Works of James Arminius,* trans. James Nichols and William Nichols [Grand Rapids: Baker, 1991], p. 64).

[8]This approach was first articulated by Origen (c. 185-254). He argued against Celsus that the fact that God foreknew and predicted Judas's betrayal of Jesus, for example, does not mean he caused it. "Celsus imagines that an event, predicted through foreknowledge, comes to pass because it was predicted; but we do not grant this, maintaining that he who foretold it was not the cause of its happening, because he foretold it would happen; but the future event itself, which would have taken place though not predicted, afforded the occasion to him who was endowed with foreknowledge, of foretelling its occurrence" (*Against Celsus* 2.20, in Ante-Nicene Fathers, ed. Alexander Roberts and James Donaldson [Peabody, Mass.: Hendrickson, 1994], p. 440). Origen's basic principle was: "It is not because God knows that something is going to be that that thing is going to be, but rather it is because it is going to be that it is known by God before it comes to be" (quoted in Luis de Molina, *On Divine Foreknowledge,* trans. Alfred J. Fredosso [Ithaca, N.Y.: Cornell University Press, 1988], p. 182).

[9]This approach was pioneered by the Christian philosopher Boethius (480-524). "If human and divine present may be compared, just as you see certain things in this your present time, so God sees all things in His eternal present. So that this divine foreknowledge does not change the nature and property of things; it simply sees things present to it exactly as they will happen at some time as future events. . . . The divine gaze looks down on all things without disturbing their nature; to Him they are present things, but under the condition of time they are future things. And so it comes about that when God knows that something is going to occur . . . no necessity is imposed on it" (*The Consolation of Philosophy* 5.6, trans. V. E. Watts [New York: Penguin, 1969], pp. 165-66).

divine foreknowledge and libertarian human freedom.[10]

The second major way of seeking to reconcile human freedom and divine foreknowledge involves a different understanding of the nature of human freedom. This is the compatibilist or soft-determinist view, which argues that genuine human freedom and moral responsibility are in fact compatible with divine determinism.[11] According to this understanding, human actions are free if a person is acting voluntarily, according to his or her desires. God can sovereignly determine these free decisions so long as the causal forces he utilizes are non-constraining and do not force the person to choose or act against his or her will. In other words, God actively, decisively and noncoercively shapes human desires, and then the individual freely chooses to act according to those desires.[12]

---

[10]This approach was developed by the sixteenth-century Jesuit theologian Luis de Molina. He defined God's middle knowledge as that aspect of his omniscience whereby he knows, prior to any divine decision of what kind of world he would create, exactly what his creatures would freely choose to do under any hypothetical set of circumstances. Through God's middle knowledge, "in virtue of the most profound and inscrutable comprehension of each faculty of free choice, He saw in His own essence what each such faculty would do with its innate freedom were it to be placed in this or in that or, indeed, in infinitely many orders of things—even though it would really be able, if it so willed, to do the opposite" (*On Divine Foreknowledge,* p. 168). This middle knowledge enables God to know for sure exactly what every free creature will do in those circumstances he chooses to create—without violating the libertarian freedom of his creatures. This view has been adopted and argued for more recently by Alvin Plantinga, *The Nature of Necessity* (Oxford: Oxford University Press, 1974); Jonathan Kvanvig, *The Possibility of an All-Knowing God* (New York: St. Martin's Press, 1986); William Lane Craig, *The Only Wise God* (Grand Rapids: Baker, 1987); and Thomas P. Flint, *Divine Providence: The Molinist Account* (Ithaca, N.Y.: Cornell University Press, 1998).

[11]A classic proponent of this view of human freedom is Jonathan Edwards, "On the Freedom of the Will," in *The Works of Jonathan Edwards* (Carlisle, Penn.: Banner of Truth, 1974), 1:3-93. Contemporary advocates of compatibilist human freedom include John Feinberg, "God Ordains All Things," in *Predestination and Free Will,* ed. David Basinger and Randall Basinger (Downers Grove, Ill.: InterVarsity Press, 1986); D. A. Carson, *Divine Sovereignty and Human Responsibility* (Grand Rapids: Baker, 1995); Paul Helm, *The Providence of God* (Downers Grove, Ill.: InterVarsity Press, 1994); and Bruce Ware, *God's Greater Glory* (Wheaton, Ill.: Crossway, 2004).

[12]Feinberg helpfully describes the compatibilist position by distinguishing between two kinds of causes that influence and determine actions. "On the one hand, there are constraining causes which force an agent to act against his will. On the other hand, there are nonconstraining causes. These are sufficient to bring about an action, but they do not force a person to act against his will, desires, or wishes. According to determinists like myself, an action is free even if causally determined so long as the causes are nonconstraining" ("God Ordains All Things," p. 24). Because compatibilists are *divine* determinists, they believe that the ultimate and sufficient cause for every event is God. God is working noncoercively to shape human desires, preferences and motives so that they align with his sovereign decree. Then human beings freely choose to do what God has determined they would do. Feinberg continues, "God's sovereign decree includes not only God's chosen ends but also the means to such ends. Such means include whatever circumstances and factors are necessary to convince an individual (without constraint) that the act God has decreed is the act she or he wants to do. And, given the sufficient conditions, the person will act" (ibid., p. 26).

But for our purposes, what is important to note is that since this understanding of human freedom is compatible with divine determinism, it is certainly compatible with exhaustive divine foreknowledge. Compatibilists tend to agree that exhaustive divine foreknowledge is incompatible with libertarian human freedom, but it is not incompatible with a compatibilist or soft-determinist understanding of human freedom.

The third way of handling the dilemma involves a different understanding of the extent of God's foreknowledge: God does not foreknow free decisions that will be made by moral agents possessing libertarian freedom. In contemporary evangelical theology this view is known as "open theism" or "the openness of God."[13] While the openness understanding of divine foreknowledge has been a minority position throughout the history of Christian theology, the emergence of the open view within the past decade provides the theological context for this study.[14] And as a result, open theists will be my primary debate partners throughout this book.

THE OPEN VIEW OF DIVINE FOREKNOWLEDGE

Open theism is a variation on classical Arminian theology.[15] This can be seen in

---

[13]This terminology comes from one of the earliest and arguably the most well-known presentation of this position—Clark H. Pinnock et al., *The Openness of God* (Downers Grove, Ill.: InterVarsity Press, 1994).

[14]That the openness view is in the minority is admitted by open theists; see e.g., John Sanders, "Historical Considerations," in *The Openness of God* (Downers Grove, Ill.: InterVarsity Press, 1994), p. 59; Gregory A. Boyd, *God of the Possible* (Grand Rapids: Baker, 2000), p. 22. It is beyond the scope of this work to argue extensively for this conclusion. Helpful overviews of the history of the doctrine of the foreknowledge of God can be found in Benjamin Wirt Farley, *The Providence of God* (Grand Rapids: Baker, 1988), and William Lane Craig, *The Problem of Divine Foreknowledge and Future Contingents from Aristotle to Suarez* (New York: E. J. Brill, 1988). The literature both advocating and opposing open theism in the past decade is voluminous and growing rapidly. Significant works by open theists include Boyd, *God of the Possible;* John Sanders, *The God Who Risks* (Downers Grove, Ill.: InterVarsity Press, 1998); and Clark H. Pinnock, *Most Moved Mover* (Grand Rapids: Baker, 2001). Significant critiques of open theism include Bruce A. Ware, *God's Lesser Glory* (Wheaton, Ill.: Crossway, 2000); John Frame, *No Other God* (Phillipsburg, N.J.: Presbyterian & Reformed, 2001); and John Piper, Justin Taylor, and Paul Kjoss Helseth, eds., *Beyond the Bounds* (Wheaton, Ill.: Crossway, 2002). The latter volume contains a very comprehensive and helpful bibliography compiled by Justin Taylor.

[15]By now the contours of open theism have become quite familiar. One of the best general descriptions comes from David Basinger, who describes five basic characteristics of open theism: "(1) God not only created this world ex nihilo but can (and at times does) intervene unilaterally in earthly affairs. (2) God chose to create us with incompatibilistic (libertarian) freedom—freedom over which he cannot exercise total control. (3) God so values freedom—the moral integrity of free creatures and a world in which such integrity is possible—that he does not normally override such freedom, even if he sees that it is producing undesirable results.

key "control beliefs" that are affirmed by prominent open theists.[16] These include viewing God as personal (as opposed to an absolutist model), significant
(libertarian) human freedom, and the primacy of an initiating and responsive
love as the most important quality we can attribute to God.[17] These control beliefs would be shared by virtually all Arminian theologians. But open theists differ from their classical Arminian brothers and sisters in significant ways. Perhaps
the most important of these differences involves the open view of God's foreknowledge.[18]

Open theists agree with Christians from virtually every theological tradition
in affirming God's essential omniscience. Perhaps the most well-known open

---

(4) God always desires our highest good, both individually and corporately, and thus is affected by what happens in our lives. (5) God does not possess exhaustive knowledge of exactly how we will utilize our freedom, although he may well at times be able to predict with
great accuracy the choices we will freely make" ("Practical Implications," in *The Openness of
God* [Downers Grove, Ill.: InterVarsity Press, 1994], p. 156).

   Arminianism is a deep and rich theological tradition stemming from the writings of Dutch
theologian James Arminius. While it shares much in common with other versions of Reformation theology (e.g., a belief in the ultimate authority of the Bible as the Word of God, jus-
tification by faith alone, and the fall of humanity into sin such that prevenient grace is required for any person to exercise such faith), it differs from Reformed theology in its espousal
of (1) God's conditional predestination, (2) the universal atoning work of Christ, (3) God's
saving grace that can be resisted, and (4) a conditional security of the believer. For a concise
and helpful overview of Arminianism, see J. K. Grider, "Arminianism," in *Evangelical Dictionary of Theology,* ed. Walter A. Elwell (Grand Rapids: Baker, 1984). Fuller expositions of
Arminian thought can be found in Roger Olson, *Arminian Theology* (Downers Grove, Ill.: InterVarsity Press, 2006); Jerry Walls and Joseph B. Dongell, *Why I Am Not a Calvinist* (Downers
Grove, Ill.: InterVarsity Press, 2004); and the anthologies *Grace Unlimited,* ed. Clark H. Pinnock (Minneapolis: Bethany Fellowship, 1975), and *The Grace of God, the Will of Man* (Grand
Rapids: Zondervan, 1989).

[16]Sanders defines *control beliefs* as "those ideas and values that are used as paradigms and ultimate presuppositions to interpret our experiences, recognize problems, and organize information. . . . These paradigms are quite significant because they influence our other beliefs,
values, and actions." As we seek to interpret Scripture, we use these control beliefs "to collect
Scriptures that support our position and to interpret those passages that seem to be against
our views" ("God as Personal," in *The Grace of God, the Will of Man* [Grand Rapids: Zondervan, 1989], p. 168).

[17]Ibid., p. 167; Pinnock, "From Augustine to Arminius," in *The Grace of God, the Will of Man*
(Grand Rapids: Zondervan, 1989), p. 21; and Richard Rice, "Biblical Support for a New Perspective," in *The Openness of God* (Downers Grove, Ill.: InterVarsity Press, 1994), p. 15.

[18]This difference can be seen in comparing the essays by classical Arminian Bruce Reichenbach
("God Limits His Power") and open theist Clark Pinnock ("God Limits His Knowledge") in the
volume *Predestination and Free Will.* It is precisely this difference that moves Richard Rice
to call open theism "consistent Arminianism" ("Divine Foreknowledge and Free-Will Theism"
in *The Grace of God, the Will of Man* [Grand Rapids: Zondervan, 1989], p. 123). This designation stems from Rice's belief that the view of divine foreknowledge advocated by open theism
(or "free will theism") is the only view that is logically consistent with the libertarian freedom
advocated by all forms of Arminianism.

theist, Clark Pinnock, is representative in defining divine omniscience to mean that "God must know all things that can be known and know them truly."[19] But while God's omniscient knowledge rightly includes absolutely everything about the past and the present, it does not include certain elements of the future. Specifically it does not include future free decisions made by moral beings who have been endowed by their Creator with libertarian freedom, nor does it include any element of the future for which free decisions are a causal component.[20] Open theists generally argue for this understanding of divine foreknowledge for three primary reasons.

First, since future free decisions have not yet been made, they do not now exist and therefore cannot be known even by God. For example, John Sanders argues, "Though God's knowledge is coextensive with reality in that God knows all that can be known, the future free actions of free creatures are not yet reality, and so there is nothing to be known."[21] Because the future is in at least part open and indeterminate, it cannot be exhaustively foreknown. Pinnock writes:

> If choices are real and freedom significant, future decisions cannot be exhaustively foreknown. This is because the future is not determinate but shaped in part by human choices. The future is not fixed like the past, which can be known completely. The future does not yet exist and therefore cannot be infallibly anticipated, even by God. Future decisions cannot in every way be foreknown, because they have not yet been made. God knows everything that can be known—but God's foreknowledge does not include the undecided.[22]

But this is not a denial of God's omniscience, which again affirms God's true

---

[19]Clark Pinnock, "Systematic Theology," in *The Openness of God* (Downers Grove, Ill.: InterVarsity Press, 1994), p. 121. Note similar statements by David Basinger: "To say that God is omniscient is to say simply that God knows all that can be known" ("Can an Evangelical Christian Justifiably Deny God's Exhaustive Knowledge of the Future?" *Christian Scholar's Review* 25, no. 2 [1995]: 133); and William Hasker: "God's omniscience entails his knowing, not all true propositions whatsoever, but only those that it is logically possible for him to know" (*God, Time, and Knowledge* [Ithaca, N.Y.: Cornell University Press, 1989], p. 73). This type of definition of God's omniscience is not unique to open theists. For example, nonopenness theologian Millard Erickson defines omniscience as "the ability to know all things that are the proper objects of knowledge" (*God the Father Almighty* [Grand Rapids: Baker, 1998], p. 184).
[20]Sanders calls this view of God's knowledge "presentism," a view that "affirms [God's] omniscience but denies [his] exhaustive foreknowledge" (*God Who Risks*, p. 198). Sanders defines *presentism* as affirming that "God knows all the past and present but there is no exhaustively definite future for God to know" (ibid., p. 129).
[21]Ibid., p. 198.
[22]Pinnock, "Systematic Theology," p. 123.

knowledge of all that can be known. Rather, it is an attempt to be precise as to exactly what can be known.[23]

A second reason for the openness view stems from their conviction that exhaustive divine foreknowledge truly is incompatible with libertarian freedom.[24] Open theists are persuaded that the possession of libertarian free will is an absolutely crucial part of being human. It is a necessary part of being created in the image of the God, who himself possesses libertarian freedom. The ability (and obligation) of human beings to love and trust God demands such significant freedom.[25] And the reality of human sin (and our moral responsibility for such rebellion) proves that such freedom exists.[26] But God's decision in creation to endow human and angelic beings with the gift of libertarian freedom carries with it a freely chosen self-limitation on the extent of his foreknowledge.[27] Richard Swinburne argues that this is a limitation "which results from his own

---

[23]Basinger writes, "Those of us who deny that God has exhaustive foreknowledge of the future do not deny that God knows all that can be known. The debate is over *what it is that can be known*" ("Can an Evangelical Christian Justifiably Deny?" p. 133).

[24]The most detailed argument for the incompatibility of exhaustive divine foreknowledge and libertarian human freedom by an open theist comes from William Hasker in *God, Time, and Knowledge*. He argues extensively that all attempts to demonstrate the ultimate compatibility of exhaustive divine foreknowledge and libertarian human freedom are ultimately unsuccessful. Pinnock agrees with this incompatibility, arguing that if God's foreknowledge were indeed exhaustive, libertarian freedom would not exist. "[God's] omniscience does not mean exhaustive foreknowledge of all future events. If that were its meaning, the future would be fixed and determined, much as is the past. Total knowledge of the future would imply a fixity of events. Nothing in the future would need to be decided. It also would imply that human freedom is an illusion, that we make no difference and are not responsible" ("Systematic Theology," p. 121.)

[25]Open theists insist that genuine love cannot be forced or coerced in any way. Thus Pinnock argues, "Human beings are able to respond (or refuse to) in love to their Creator and enter into partnership with God. By its very nature this covenant relationship cannot be coerced but is something which both parties enter into voluntarily. In the light of this possibility we must conclude that human freedom is significant and real. The response of faith and love cannot be forced" ("God Limits His Knowledge," pp. 147-48). The kind of coercion that is seen to be involved in any form of divine determinism would also violate God's nature as love.

[26]Pinnock writes, "According to the Bible, human beings are creatures who have rejected God's will for them and turned aside from his plan. This is another strong piece of evidence that God made them truly free. Humans are evidently not puppets on a string. They are free even to pit their wills against God's. We have actually deviated from the plan of God in creating us and set ourselves at cross purposes to God. Obviously we are free because we are acting as a race in a way disruptive of God's will and destructive of the values God holds dear for us. It is surely not possible to believe that God secretly planned our rebelling against him. Certainly our rebellion is proof that our actions are not determined but significantly free" (ibid., p. 149).

[27]The vast implications of the libertarian freedom possessed by angelic and especially demonic beings are explored by Gregory A. Boyd, *God at War* (Downers Grove, Ill.: InterVarsity Press, 1997).

choice to create human beings with free will. Choosing to give others freedom,
he limits his own knowledge of what they will do."[28] Pinnock agrees.

> An important implication of this strong definition of freedom is that reality is to an
> extent open and not closed. It means that genuine novelty can appear in history,
> which cannot be predicted even by God. If creatures have been given the ability
> to decide how some things will turn out, then it cannot be known infallibly ahead
> of time how they will turn out. It implies that the future really is open and not avail-
> able to exhaustive foreknowledge, even on the part of God. It is plain that *the bib-
> lical doctrine of creaturely freedom requires us to reconsider the conventional view
> of the omniscience of God.*[29]

The third reason for the open view of the foreknowledge of God stems from
the reflections of open theists on Scripture itself. Openness advocates argue that
many biblical texts actually point to this understanding of divine foreknowledge. They have tended to be underemphasized or even ignored among classical theists, but open theists are seeking to restore them to their proper place in
understanding divine foreknowledge. Among these texts are passages in which
God is said to repent or to change his mind and heart. These include cases
where God is said to repent in response to human sin (Gen 6:6-7; 1 Sam 15:11,
35); in response to human repentance (Jer 18:7-10; Jon 3:9-10); and in response
to intercessory prayer (Ex 32:11-14; 2 Kings 20:1-6; Amos 7:1-6). These texts
raise significant questions about the extent of God's foreknowledge. How can
it be, for example, that God's repentance over the sin of King Saul could be real
and genuine if he infallibly knew from all eternity the exact nature and extent
of Saul's sin? If God foreknew infallibly that the Ninevites would repent at the
preaching of Jonah and that he would relent from his threatened judgment as a

---

[28]Richard Swinburne, *The Coherence of Theism,* rev. ed. (Oxford: Clarendon, 1993), p. 181.
[29]Pinnock, "God Limits His Knowledge," p. 150, italics added. The italicized portion shows the
crucial role that libertarian freedom plays for open theists in determining the extent of divine
foreknowledge. Richard Rice highlights the same crucial role: "*In order to affirm creaturely
freedom,* the open view of God maintains that certain aspects of the future cannot be exhaustive" (*God's Foreknowledge and Man's Free Will* [Minneapolis: Bethany House, 1985], p. 53,
italics added). Rice also says, "Several recent thinkers [including Rice himself] redefine omniscience *in order to allow for a strong sense of creaturely freedom*" ("Divine Foreknowledge
and Free-Will Theism," in *The Grace of God, the Will of Man,* ed. Clark H. Pinnock [Grand
Rapids: Zondervan, 1989], p. 130, italics added). One final example of this comes from the
African American theologian Major Jones. "We believe human actions to be truly free, such
that whereas God's knowledge of the past is total and absolute, God's knowledge of future
events is not yet complete, particularly so far as acts of human freedom are concerned. . . .
God could, of course, preclude uncertainty by determining beforehand what is to be and
what all are to become; the high price he would pay for this, however, would be the freedom of his creatures to develop and grow" (*The Color of God: The Concept of God in Afro-
American Thought* [Macon, Ga.: Mercer University Press, 1987], p. 95).

result, was he being honest when he proclaimed, "Forty more days and Nineveh will be overturned" (Jon 3:4)? Or if God foreknew that Moses would intercede for the nation of Israel after the debacle of the golden calf and that he would refrain from destroying them, was his threatened judgment and promise to build a new nation through Moses (Ex 32:10) genuine and authentic?

Openness advocates would also have us consider a text like Genesis 22:12. After Abraham had demonstrated his willingness to sacrifice his beloved son Isaac in obedience to the command of God, the angel of the Lord told him to stop. Speaking for God himself, the angel said, "Now I know that you fear God, because you have not withheld from me your son, your only son." Shouldn't we infer from the statement "*Now* I know . . ." that God did not know the full extent of Abraham's devotion before this very moment? Isn't God himself saying that until Abraham made the decision to obey, he did not infallibly know what the outcome would be?

One more example. Open theists point us to the words of Yahweh in Jeremiah 3, where he speaks to his prophet:

> Have you seen what faithless Israel has done? She has gone up on every high hill and under every spreading tree and has committed adultery there. *I thought that after she had done all this she would return to me but she did not,* and her unfaithful sister Judah saw it. (Jer 3:6-7, emphasis added)

Similarly, Yahweh speaks to Israel:

> "How gladly would I treat you like sons
> and give you a desirable land,
> the most beautiful inheritance of any nation."
> *I thought you would call me "Father"*
> *and not turn away from following me.*
>
> *But like a woman unfaithful to her husband,*
> *so you have been unfaithful to me, O house of Israel,*
> declares the LORD. (Jer 3:19-20, emphasis added)

These appear to be explicit admissions from Yahweh that his knowledge of the future is not always infallibly accurate. According to the openness interpretation, Yahweh had genuinely thought that Israel would repent. That was his best forecast based on all present and past factors. But through the use of her libertarian freedom, Israel had made an utterly surprising decision—surprising even to God himself. Is this not proof that God's knowledge of the future is not exhaustive and infallible?[30]

---

[30]These and other texts appealed to by open theists in support of their position will be examined more thoroughly in chap. 4.

EVALUATING THE OPENNESS PROPOSAL

How should we evaluate the openness proposal of nonexhaustive divine fore-knowledge? Is it the most faithful construal of the biblical testimony? Is it the most coherent rationally? Is it the most practically helpful?

Both the openness and the classical understandings of divine foreknowledge are theological models. They are conceptual frameworks that guide us in our understanding of this aspect of the character of God. But what makes for a good theological model?

John Sanders helpfully proposes three criteria for evaluating a theological model. The first criterion is "consonance with tradition," which in Christian theology is supremely the revelation of God in Scripture. Sanders says, "If the theological model does not resonate with Scripture overall and with the person and work of Jesus in particular, it cannot, with integrity, be called Christian."[31] Building on this, I propose that a valid theological model must be consonant with Scripture both quantitatively and qualitatively. In other words, we must first ask, does this model deal with *all* relevant biblical data? And second, does it do so fairly, without misreading texts so they serve a prior theological agenda? Admittedly, these quantitative and qualitative criteria are not easy to evaluate. They raise many crucial questions, such as what constitutes relevant biblical data? How is such relevance to be determined? And how do we combine attention to exegetical detail in particular passages with a desire to be synthetic and to integrate this particular passage with the whole of Scripture? But while these questions will not always be answered in the same way, they do point us to important criteria that we cannot ignore. When a proposed theological model is criticized biblically, it will either be because its critics believe that it does not address key biblical passages or that it does not do so fairly and adequately.

The second criterion proposed by Sanders is that of "conceptual intelligibility." For a proposed theological model to be considered valid and worthy of our affirmation, it must make sense in areas such as "internal consistency, coherence with other beliefs we affirm, comprehensiveness in covering the range of relevant considerations, and communicability."[32]

The third criterion affirmed by Sanders is "adequacy for the demands of life." Since all of Scripture is inspired by God to be useful to his people (2 Tim 3:16-17), proposed understandings of its teaching must be examined for just such adequacy. Sanders writes, "The proposed model must be relevant to the real-life

---

[31]Sanders, *God Who Risks,* pp. 16-17.
[32]Ibid.

situations faced by the community. The theological model needs to help us in our relationships with God, others, the creation and ourselves."[33] This adequacy criterion is what prevents the construction of theological models from becoming a purely academic exercise played out in the ivory towers of theological imagination. But the fact that this adequacy criterion is not the only one—there are also criteria that relate to biblical fidelity and rational coherence—guards us from becoming utter pragmatists in doing our theology.

A full evaluation of the classical and open models of the foreknowledge of God would necessitate a thorough investigation of all three areas. That is beyond the scope of this book. My primary goal is much more limited: to evaluate the extent of God's foreknowledge according to Scripture. Specifically, I hope to explore whether the Bible teaches that the foreknowledge of God is exhaustive and infallible. In particular, does Scripture affirm that God foreknows the free decisions of human beings?[34]

I contend that the answer to those questions is yes. I hope to demonstrate that the model of exhaustive divine foreknowledge that embraces all of the future, including free human decisions, is best able to account for the data of Scripture.[35] In seeking to demonstrate this conclusion, I will also endeavor to show the insufficiency of the nonexhaustive model proposed by open theists, both to interpret biblical teaching accurately and to adequately deal with crucial issues of the Christian life. So much in this book could rightly be called polemical. I pray that my critique is fair and not mean-spirited. I am very aware that in recent years, debates about open theism have been highly

---

[33]Ibid., p. 18.

[34]The adequacy of this model for Christian life and ministry will be addressed more briefly in chap. 6.

[35]The model of divine foreknowledge advocated here certainly includes God's knowledge of all hypotheticals, that is, everything that could possibly occur in any given world. Many of these are possibilities that never in fact occur, and thus these are rightly called "counterfactuals" in the strictest sense. Biblical examples of divinely foreknown counterfactuals include 1 Sam 23:10-14 and Mt 11:21-24. Following Molina, many contemporary Molinists see such divine knowledge of hypotheticals as allowing God to have an exhaustive foreknowledge of the actual world God decided to create while allowing humans to possess libertarian freedom within that world. (See note 11 of this introduction). However, an alternative position has been argued recently that sees God's middle knowledge of hypotheticals as functioning together with compatibalistic human freedom rather than libertarian. Advocates of this position include Terence Thiessen, who calls this position "middle knowledge Calvinism" (*Providence and Prayer* [Downers Grove, Ill.: InterVarsity Press, 2000], pp. 289-362), and Bruce A. Ware, who calls his view "compatibilist middle knowledge" (*God's Greater Glory*, pp. 110-30). This latter view is fully consistent with the approach to divine foreknowledge advocated in this book. However, since the focus of this book is primarily on the question of whether God foreknows free human decisions and actions that actually occur in the world, the issue of God's knowledge of hypotheticals will not be addressed.

polarized and emotionally charged on all sides. Many classical theists who share the view of divine foreknowledge I am advocating in this book have engaged in the debate in ways that have been less than charitable. I pray that will not be the case with this book. My goal is to examine Scripture to bring more light than heat to this issue. I understand the debate between classical and open theists to be one that is carried on within the family of God. I view my openness brothers and sisters as fellow believers in Christ, and will endeavor to assume the best about their efforts to understand Scripture on this topic, even when my conclusions differ from theirs. But I do view this issue as an important one—both for our understanding of the nature of God and for our Christian experience. Thus I am convinced that the investigation into biblical teaching on the extent of the foreknowledge of God is warranted. And even though this discussion comes in the context of theological controversy, my ultimate goal is constructive, seeking to promote a positive vision of the exhaustive foreknowledge of God. This, I hope to show, is the model that is most consistent with biblical revelation and that best provides comfort and hope in Christian life and ministry.

It is important for me to stress at this point that this book is not designed to explore every question that is relevant to this topic. In particular, I do not intend to explore the question of *how* God foreknows free human decisions (assuming that our investigation demonstrates that Scripture teaches he does). Many different options have been proposed as to how God foreknows free human decisions. And to explore them all would go far beyond the scope of this book. It is very likely that readers who end up agreeing with the central thesis of this book (that God does infallibly foreknow all free human decisions) will arrive at differing conclusions about how God possesses this foreknowledge (e.g., because of the timeless nature of divine eternity, middle knowledge, divine foreordination, etc.)

A second question that will not be fully explored is the precise nature of human freedom (libertarian or compatibilist). Some will no doubt argue that we must define and defend the nature of human freedom first, before asking whether God foreknows such free human decisions and actions. I take a different approach, however. I will ask whether it can be demonstrated biblically that God foreknows the kind of events that are understood on all sides to be free—even though the definition of the nature of that freedom varies widely. If that can be demonstrated, we may rightly affirm exhaustive divine foreknowledge whether we are libertarians or compatibilists. As the argument of the book proceeds, it will be come evident that I affirm a compatibilist view of human freedom, finding that to be the model of freedom that best accounts for all the evidence of Scripture and experience. And to the extent that some of my arguments are based on the implications of these different views of freedom, they will lay their charge against classical Arminians as well as openness advocates. But even if those who adopt a libertarian model of human freedom are unable to agree with all of my arguments, I trust that they will be able to affirm the central thesis of this book.

A ROADMAP FOR WHAT LIES AHEAD

In seeking to determine whether Scripture teaches that God's foreknowledge includes free human decisions, we will look first to biblical evidence for such a model. Chapter two will examine Old Testament evidence to see whether it supports the model of exhaustive divine foreknowledge, and chapter three will look at New Testament evidence for the same. My conclusion in both chapters is that there is significant and substantive evidence in both Old Testament and New Testament to support an exhaustive model of divine foreknowledge. Then we will ask if there is other biblical evidence that teaches a contrary view. Chapter four will consider the biblical texts claimed by open theists to support a nonexhaustive view of the foreknowledge of God. We will examine these claims, concluding that there are in fact better and more accurate understandings of these texts. Then in chapter five, we will discuss two critical interpretive questions that have been raised against those who argue that Scripture teaches an exhaustive view of the extent of God's foreknowledge. First, has our understanding of the texts we have examined in the previous three chapters been so dominated by a worldview coming primarily from Greek philosophy that we have in fact missed the clear meaning of these texts? The role of Greek philosophy has become a crucial part of the debate and needs to be addressed. Second, can the fixed and foreknown character of the future (argued for from the texts examined in chaps. 2 and 3) and the open character of the future (argued for from the texts examined in chap. 4) both be true? In other words, is it in fact the case that the future is partially fixed and thus foreknown as certain by God, and partially open and thus foreknown by God only as possibilities? Our examination of these questions in chapter five will conclude that an exhaustive understanding of the extent of God's foreknowledge is not primarily the product of Greek philosophical thinking but rather the best understanding of the teaching of Scripture as a whole. And we will see that there is no compelling reason to adopt the partially fixed *and* partially open hypothesis. In chapter six, then, we will ask the crucial "so what" question. What practical value does exhaustive divine foreknowledge actually have for Christian life and ministry? While this assessment of what

Sanders calls the adequacy criterion will necessarily be brief and incomplete, some discussion of these practical considerations is essential for seeing the importance of the issue under investigation. A concluding chapter will follow, which will sum up the conclusions from this study and offer some reflections on where we should go from here.

2

OLD TESTAMENT EVIDENCE
OF DIVINE FOREKNOWLEDGE

The Hebrew language of the Old Testament does not contain a specific word to denote "foreknowledge." God's knowledge is indicated primarily through the verb *yāda'* ("to know"). The temporal relationships involved in God's knowing are then determined by context. When *yāda'* is used with God as subject (123 out of a total of 948 usages in the Old Testament), it has a wide variety of usages.[1] Yet in all of them is that *yāda'* is fundamentally a relational term. At root the verb denotes a relationship between the knower and that which is known.[2] But the relational element of God's knowing does not eliminate a factual element involved in his knowledge. Whenever one person knows another person in an intensely personal relationship, factual knowledge of the other person (knowing his or her hopes, dreams, fears, past history, likes and dislikes, etc.) plays a crucial role. Indeed without significant knowledge of such facts, the relational knowledge would never grow and intensify. God's relational knowing never eliminates the reality of his factual knowledge.

---

[1]Terence Fretheim helpfully summarizes these usages. They include (1) God's special relationship with a person or persons (Gen 18:19; Ex 33:12; Deut 34:10; 2 Sam 7:20; Jer 1:5; Amos 3:2). (2) God's close familiarity with the lives of individuals (Ps 40:9; Jer 17:16; 18:23). God knows how we are made (Ps 103; 14); he knows human thoughts (Gen 20:6), inclinations (Deut 31:21; Ezek 11:5) and words even before they are spoken (Ps 139:4). (3) God's entering into the experience of the nation of Israel (Ex 3:7; Deut 2:7) and the psalmist (Ps 31:7; 69:19; 142:3). (4) God's knowledge that comes as a result of his searching or testing of Israel (Deut 8:2; 13:3; Judg 3:4) or of individuals (Gen 22:1, 12; 2 Chron 32:31; Ps 139:23; Jer 12:3). (5) God's care and protection of his people (Ps 1:6; Hos 13:4-5). This knowledge moves him to saving action on behalf of his people (Jer 29:11) ("*yāda'*," *New International Dictionary of Old Testament Theology and Exegesis*, ed. Willem A. VanGemeren [Grand Rapids: Zondervan, 1997], 2:411-12.)

[2]Fretheim explains, "In the broadest sense, *yāda'* means to take various aspects of the world of one's experience into the self, including the resultant relationship with that which is known. The fundamentally relational character of the knowing (over against a narrow intellectual sense) can be discerned, not least in that both God and human beings can be subject and object of the verb" (ibid., p. 409).

The issue before us in this chapter is the extent to which God's factual knowledge relates to the future. How does the Old Testament portray God's knowledge of the future? Specifically, does God foreknow the free actions of human beings? A good place to begin this inquiry is perhaps the most comprehensive Old Testament meditation on the knowledge of God—Psalm 139.

PSALM 139

Psalm 139 begins with a concerted focus on God's intimate and exhaustive knowledge of David, the psalmist (vv. 1-6). These verses are tied together by a threefold repetition of the verb "to know" (yāda') in verses 1, 2 and 4, and the use of the related noun "knowledge" (da'at) in verse 6. The main point of this section of the psalm is expressed in verse 1, "O LORD, you have searched me and you know me."[3]

The verb "search" (ḥāqar) is used of miners digging into the earth in search of ore (Job 28:3), of explorers spying out a land (Judg 18:2), of judicial investigators conducting a thorough examination of the facts of a legal case (Deut 13:14) and of kings inquiring deeply into an intellectual problem (Prov 25:2). The verb is also used of God's knowledge of the secrets of human hearts (Ps 44:21; Jer 17:10). The thought is that God has conducted an exhaustive and deeply probing search in order to know David thoroughly. But rather than being threatened by the thought of such comprehensive knowledge that God has of him, David joyfully exults in it. It is precisely this kind of knowledge that he calls "wonderful" in verse 6. And his fearless confidence in the exhaustive knowledge of God emboldens David at the end of the psalm to gladly open his heart to such divine scrutiny (vv. 23-24).[4]

But the imagery of God's searching of David raises a crucial question. Does

---

[3]The Hebrew text has no object of the verb "know." The statement is general. It is the context of vv. 2-4 that leads the NIV to supply the object of God's knowing ("you know *me*"). More debated is the question of how to render the tense of the verbs. Leslie C. Allen argues that these verbs should be taken as present in force, as with the other verbs of vv. 2-5 (*Psalms 101-150* [Word Biblical Commentary: Waco, Tex.: Word, 1983], p. 250). E. J. Young, on the other hand, argues that in light of the psalm as a whole, "it is better to translate by the past. David is referring to something that has already occurred. God knows David at the time when the Psalmist speaks to him" (*Psalm 139* [London: Banner of Truth, 1965], p. 14). The NIV's rendering combines both approaches, viewing God's present knowing of David as the result of his past searching. For our purposes, the precise import of these verb tenses is not crucial. Our concern is whether God's knowledge of David relates to his future free actions.

[4]Donald R. Glenn argues that the entire final section of the psalm (vv. 19-24) "are the climax and the key to the whole psalm, expressing in both a negative and positive manner the psalmist's loyalty to the God who knows him so well" ("An Exegetical and Theological Exposition of Psalm 139," in *Tradition and Testament,* ed. John S. Feinberg and Paul D. Feinberg [Chicago: Moody Press, 1981], p. 163).

it imply that God was ignorant of David prior to this examination?[5] Verse 16 seems to indicate no. We will examine verse 16 in more detail below, but for now we note that if all of the days of David's life were ordained by God before one of them came to be, God knew them all in advance. Whether we understand God's knowledge of David's days to be the result of his ordaining them or the cause of such divine ordination, the reality of God's prior knowledge of David's days is strongly implied. And thus we should conclude that God knew David thoroughly and exhaustively before any divine searching took place. E. J. Young argues:

> The language of the Psalm does not mean that God, being ignorant, must remove
> His ignorance by investigation. It means, rather, that God possesses full knowledge
> of David. Indeed what the Psalm presents is only a vivid way of saying that God
> knows all that can be known of David. . . . He who reads the Psalm sympathetically
> will not miss its meaning. He will not entertain any low view of God but will rejoice
> in such a strong declaration of God's great and mighty knowledge.[6]

Indeed it is the effort to read Psalm 139:1 in light of the rest of the psalm (especially v. 16) that warrants this kind of "sympathetic" reading. While Young does not use the term, we could describe his understanding of the imagery of verse 1 as being *anthropomorphic,* a description of God in the language of human experience. We will deal much more with biblical anthropomorphisms and the kind of metaphorical language they are in chapter four. But for now, it is helpful to note the category. Donald Glenn argues that the point of the expression is that "the LORD's knowledge of David is as thorough as though he had conducted a complete investigation of his acts, this thoughts, and his motives."[7]

The rest of this section describes God's knowledge of David—knowledge which David says is "too wonderful" for him to fully comprehend and "too lofty" for him to attain (v. 6). God knows David's external actions. He knows David's sitting and his rising (v. 2), and his going out and his lying down (v. 3). Indeed God knows all his ways (v. 3). God also knows David's inward thoughts, motives and intents (v. 2) and even his words before they are spoken (v. 4). But does this divine knowledge extend to David's future free actions? The evidence of Psalm 139, I argue, strongly indicates that the answer is yes.

---

[5]Note that if this were the case, it would result in a denial of God's exhaustive knowledge of the *present.* What is being discussed in Ps 139:1 is God's knowledge of David as he presently is. If God were ignorant of this until he had searched David, it would be a denial of God's present knowledge (something that is affirmed by both classical and open theists).

[6]Young, *Psalm 139,* pp. 15-16.

[7]Glenn, "Exegetical and Theological Exposition of Psalm 139," p. 171.

Verse 2 indicates that God knows David's outer and the inner life "from afar" (*mērāhôq*). Many interpreters have understood this phrase to refer to God's exalted transcendence, marveling that God can have this intimate knowledge of David while being so transcendently high above him.[8] But others see an alternative interpretation. For example, Raymond C. Ortlund Jr. reads verse 2 in light of verses 7-12, which emphasize God's omnipresent nearness. That being the case, he argues that verse 2 has a temporal meaning.

> In verses 7-12, David makes the point that God is always present with him. The distance in view in verse 2, then, must be not spatial but temporal, as this word is also used in Isaiah 22:11, 25:1 and 37:26. Long before any impulse wells up from within David's psyche, long before David himself knows what his next mood or feeling will be, long before he knows where his train of thought will eventually lead, God perceives it all.[9]

If so, verse 2 would be strong evidence of God's foreknowledge of free human actions.[10]

But while this conclusion with respect to verse 2 may be debated, verse 4 has a much clearer and more unambiguous relationship to God's foreknowledge. David writes, "Before a word is on my tongue, / you know it completely, O LORD." The introductory particle, *kî* (untranslated in the NIV) shows that verse 4 is a specific illustration of the more general principle articulated in verse 3— God's intimate familiarity with all of David's ways. Here in verse 4, David joyfully affirms God's prior knowledge of all the words he will speak. And he strongly affirms the comprehensiveness of this divine knowledge. "Before a word is on my tongue, / you know it *completely*, O LORD." Literally, God knows "all of it" (*kullāh*). E. J. Young explains:

> The last word of the verse may be translated "all of it," and it either means that God knows the words altogether or else He knows every bit of the words that appear upon David's tongue. Whichever of these two renderings we adopt we may see that the language does teach that God knows in their fullness and entirety the

---

[8]Mitchell Dahood, *Psalms III: 101-150,* Anchor Bible (Garden City, N.Y.: Doubleday, 1970), p. 286. See also Allen, *Psalms 101-150,* p. 261.

[9]Raymond C. Ortlund Jr., "The Sovereignty of God: Case Studies in the Old Testament," in *Still Sovereign,* ed. Thomas R. Schreiner and Bruce A. Ware (Grand Rapids: Baker, 2000), p. 29. See also Glenn, "Exegetical and Theological Exposition of Psalm 139," p. 172, and William Lane Craig, *The Only Wise God* (Grand Rapids: Baker, 1987), p. 31.

[10]This is precisely what the Puritan Stephen Charnock argues. He cites Ps 139:2 as an example of God's foreknowledge of free human actions. He says that God knows human thoughts from "as far off as eternity, as some would explain the words, and thoughts are as voluntary as anything" (*Discourses upon the Existence and Attributes of God* [1853; reprint, Grand Rapids: Baker, 1996], 1:445).

words which are upon David's tongue. Certainly God knows every word, but more than that He knows the words in their entirety.[11]

For our purposes it is important to note the freely chosen character of the words David chooses to speak. It is hard to think of actions that are more under the control of a human agent than the words he or she chooses to speak. Whether or not to speak is certainly a free decision, as are the specific words we choose to speak. Yet it is precisely these freely chosen words that God knows in advance.

Open theists have argued that the knowledge spoken of here is not infallible divine foreknowledge. Rather it is a probabilistic prediction based on God's present knowledge of the psalmist (or of any speaker). For example, Sanders says that in Psalm 139:4 the psalmist is expressing in "typical poetical fashion" the idea of "God's knowing the psalmist so well that he can 'predict' what he will say and do."[12] William Hasker agrees, citing this verse as an example of God's ability to know the growing probability of a future choice as the person moves toward the point of decision. He affirms

> God's comprehensive and exact knowledge of the *possibilities* of the future—and of the gradually changing *likelihood* of each of those possibilities being realized. And as the probability of a choice's being made in a certain way gradually increases toward certainty, God knows *that* also: often, no doubt, before the finite agent herself is aware of it. "Even before a word is on my tongue; lo, O LORD, thou knowest it altogether" (Ps 139:4).[13]

But is this an adequate explanation of the text? I think not. The explanation of Sanders and Hasker fails, for it is internally inconsistent. It tries to hold together two realities that open theism argues are fundamentally incompatible: divine predictions about what David will say that have a high enough degree of probability so as to truly constitute divine *knowledge* and the reality and genuineness of David's libertarian freedom. It is a deep commitment to the libertarian freedom of David that leads open theists to "downgrade" God's prior knowledge of the words he will say to the level of probabilistic forecasts. But it is the explicit language of the text that speaks of God's *knowing* David's words completely in advance that makes them argue that the probability of God's beliefs rises as David approaches the point of decision until it reaches "certainty." And that level of certainty would still need to be reached in advance of David's de-

[11]Young, *Psalm 139*, pp. 31-32.
[12]John Sanders, *The God Who Risks* (Downers Grove, Ill.: InterVarsity Press, 1998), p. 130.
[13]William Hasker, *God, Time, and Knowledge* (Ithaca, N.Y.: Cornell University Press, 1989), p. 189.

cision to speak in order to do justice to the temporal language of the text ("*Before* a word is on my tongue . . ."). But it is precisely that level of certainty in God's foreknowledge that open theists argue would rule out genuine libertarian freedom (see chap. 1).

I believe that in open theism there is ultimately an inverse relationship between the two realities in question. The higher the probability of God's predictions of the content of David's words, the less libertarian freedom he enjoys in deciding when and how and what to say; and the greater the libertarian freedom that David exercises, the more potentially fallible are God's beliefs concerning his words. This inverse relationship could be described in the following way: If human decisions about which words we will speak are indeed free in a libertarian sense, then according to open theists they cannot be infallibly known in advance. God can only have probabilistic beliefs concerning them. But since we are all capable of saying surprising things (surprising even to ourselves), not even God's perfect knowledge of all past and present factors concerning a person could lead him to predict with complete and total accuracy the words he or she will speak next. Thus while God's beliefs concerning our future words would undoubtedly be very accurate predictions, they would nonetheless be at least potentially fallible. And if this is the case, how can David's words be *known* by God in advance, as Psalm 139:4 so clearly affirms?[14] But on the other hand, if the probability of a person choosing to speak a particular word or words rises to the point of sufficient certainty that God could be said truly to *know* them in advance, then the content of their words would be fixed. Therefore, the decision to speak them would no longer be free in the libertarian sense. It would no longer be possible to decide not to use that particular word.

Yet Psalm 139:4 clearly speaks of God's *knowledge* of David's words before they are on his tongue. Thus this verse explicitly affirms what may possibly be understood from verse 2. God's knowledge of David does include his future free decisions.[15]

---

[14]See Bruce A. Ware, *God's Lesser Glory* (Wheaton, Ill.: Crossway, 2000), p. 123.

[15]Terence Fretheim argues that it is "doubtful" that Ps 139 can support the view of exhaustive divine foreknowledge, for it makes only "limited claims" about God's knowledge of the future. "God has so 'searched and known' (v. 1, cf. vv. 23-24) the psalmist that there is a thorough acquaintance with him and his ways (vv. 2-3), even to such an extent that his thoughts are known before they issue in speech (v. 4). Such divine knowledge is indeed wonderful, unattainable by the human (v. 6), but not necessarily limitless with respect to the future" (*The Suffering God* [Philadelphia: Fortress, 1984], p. 57). Fretheim's statement is not strictly accurate with regard to v. 4. The text does not just say that God knows in advance David's *thoughts* before they issue in speech, but rather he knows the words themselves. In addition, it is hard for me to see what limitations to God's knowledge of the future David is trying to retain—especially in light of v. 16.

Psalm 139:16 also speaks to God's knowledge of David's future. After rejoicing in God's omnipresent nearness and his inescapable presence in verses 7-12, David turns to God's marvelous work of creating him. He affirms that God created his body in his mother's womb (vv. 13, 15). In addition, God formed, planned and ordained the life David would live (v. 16). The Hebrew of verse 16 is wooden, stating literally that "all of them" *(kullām)* were written in God's book before even one of them came to be.[16]

But if "all of them" were written in God's book, we must ask, All of what? The KJV looks back to David's "unformed substance" that God saw while fashioning his body in his mother's womb. Thus it renders verse 16, "in thy [God's] book all my members were written."[17] However, many other English translations (NIV, NASB, NRSV, ESV) look ahead to the "days" that were "formed" or "ordained."[18] These translations consider all the days that God had formed and ordained to be written in his book before one of them came to be (e.g., the NIV's "All the days ordained for me / were written in your book / before one of them came to be").

This latter translation has the advantage of the grammatical agreement of the plural ("all of *them*") with the plural "days." And Glenn argues that interpreting verse 16 as referring to the foreordination of David's life best fits the broader context of verses 1-12 as well as the connection of verse 16 with verses 17-18 that follow.

> The reason David can affirm that the LORD knows his every thought, word, and action (and knows them beforehand—verse 2b), and the reason he cannot escape from this knowledge and consequent control is because the LORD formed him and foreordained the course of his life. Likewise, the reason that in verses 17-18 David responds with such awe about the LORD's thought and purposes is that the LORD's

---

[16]Ulrich Becker argues that in the Old Testament, God's "book" is "a picture of God's eternal purposes for the future of his people, his world, or his creatures. . . . [It is] always an expression of the sovereign will and work of God in history" ("βίβλιος," in *New International Dictionary of New Testament Theology,* ed. Colin Brown [Grand Rapids: Zondervan, 1986], 1:243). Glenn argues on the basis of both Old Testament and ancient near eastern usage that God's book refers to his foreordination, that is "something [that] is as known and designed beforehand as if it had been detailed in a book" ("Psalm 139," p. 176).

[17]Boyd agrees with the KJV in translating Ps 139:16: "Though the wording is a bit awkward, it has the advantage of being consistent with the rest of this psalm and especially with the immediate context of this verse. . . . The verses immediately preceding v. 16 describe the formation of the psalmist's body in the womb" (Gregory A. Boyd, *God of the Possible* [Grand Rapids: Baker, 2000], p. 41).

[18]Francis Brown, S. R. Driver, Charles A. Briggs, *Hebrew and English Lexicon* (New York: Oxford University Press, 1976), pp. 427-28, 2b. Boyd suggests the possibility of a weaker rendering—"planned" (*God of the Possible*, p. 41).

foreordination of his life proves how precious and constant are the LORD's thoughts about him.[19]

If we adopt this interpretation, as I think we should for both grammatical and contextual reasons, the implications for our current discussion are very profound. If all the days of David's life were so formed, planned and ordained that they were written by God in his book, then certainly God knew all of those days.[20] He knew not only how many days there would be in David's earthly life, but also the character of those days as well. And clearly the character and content of the days of David's life were determined in innumerable respects by his own choices and decisions. Thus Psalm 139:16 confirms the teaching of verses 2 and 4, that God's intimate and exhaustive knowledge of David extends to his future free decisions.

PREDICTIVE PROPHECY

God's exhaustive knowledge of future free human decision is also displayed in predictive prophecies that run throughout the Old Testament (and the New Testament). This is no small phenomenon in Scripture. Walter Kaiser says that approximately 27 percent of Scripture involves such prophecy.[21] In my own research I have identified 4,017 predictive prophecies in canonical Scripture. Of that number, 2,323 of them relate in one way or another to free human decisions.[22]

But not only are these predictive prophecies numerically abundant, they also play a crucial part of the story line of Scripture itself. Robert C. Newman says, "The message of the Bible [is that] God has intervened in history to rescue people from sin and futility through Jesus his Messiah, and this was predicted far in advance by the prophets sent to his people Israel."[23]

---

[19]Glenn, "Psalm 139," pp. 176-77.

[20]Boyd suggests that in light of other texts which suggest that what is written in God's book of life can be changed (e.g., Ex 32:33; Rev 3:5) and Yahweh's addition of fifteen years to Hezekiah's life (Is 38:1-5), it is better to understand God's book to be filled with his plans and intentions at the time of the psalmist's fetal development rather than with his unalterable decrees (*God of the Possible*, p. 42). The texts Boyd cites will be examined further in chaps. 3 and 4, but I don't think that they overturn the interpretation of Ps 139:16 that I am arguing for.

[21]Walter C. Kaiser Jr., *The Messiah in the Old Testament* (Grand Rapids: Zondervan, 1995), p. 235.

[22]These 2,323 prophecies are listed by reference in Steven C. Roy, "How Much Does God Foreknow? An Evangelical Assessment of the Doctrine of the Extent of the Foreknowledge of God in Light of the Teaching of Open Theism," (Ph.D. diss., Trinity International University, 2001), pp. 400-407.

[23]Robert C. Newman, "Fulfilled Prophecy as Miracle," in *In Defense of Miracles*, ed. R. Douglas Geivett and Gary R. Habermas (Downers Grove, Ill.: InterVarsity Press, 1997), p. 214. See also Craig, *Only Wise God*, p. 27.

Kaiser sees the predictive activity of God and the divine foreknowledge that it represents to be so central to the biblical portrayal of God that "it can almost be described as an attribute of God himself."[24] Thus predictive prophecies form a persuasive argument that Yahweh alone is God and is the Lord of history.[25] This is an especially significant argument, as we will see, in Isaiah 40—48. And as such, the reality of God's predictive prophecies and their fulfillment forms a source of comfort and assurance for believers in times of distress.

I will argue that the massive reality of predictive prophecy in Scripture has decisive implications for our understanding of the extent of God's foreknowledge. We will examine three broad categories of Old Testament predictive prophecies. Together they form a strong case for affirming that God does indeed possess exhaustive foreknowledge of free human decisions.

The promise and fulfillment motif of 1-2 Kings. The books of 1 and 2 Kings trace the outworking of the Davidic Covenant throughout the history of the monarchy in Israel. This covenant was originally articulated by God to David through the prophet Nathan in 2 Samuel 7:5-16. And the central promises of this covenant were reiterated to Solomon by David on his deathbed (1 Kings 2:2-4) and by God himself (1 Kings 9:5). Solomon himself recounts them in 1 Kings 8:19-20. These foundational promises are then worked out in history in the events recounted in 1-2 Kings.[26]

A prominent motif of these books is Yahweh's covenant faithfulness as exhibited by the fulfillment of predictive promises uttered by his spokespersons.[27] There are twenty different examples of this pattern in the two books, many of which utilize an explicit fulfillment formula (e.g., this particular event occurred "according to the word of Yahweh"). These fulfillment formulas call explicit attention to the fact that this particular event had formerly been predicted by God

---

[24]Walter C. Kaiser Jr., *Back to the Future* (Grand Rapids: Baker, 1989), pp. 17-18.

[25]Newman argues that fulfilled prophecies can legitimately function as evidence for the reality of God and his sovereign control over history when four criteria are met: (1) the prophecy in its oral or written form clearly envisions the sort of event alleged to be the fulfillment, (2) the prophecy was made well ahead of the event predicted, (3) the prediction actually came true, and (4) the event predicted could not have been staged by anyone but God. In addition, the case is greatly enhanced if (5) the event itself is so unusual that the apparent fulfillment cannot plausibly be explained as just a good guess ("Fulfilled Prophecy as Miracle," pp. 215-24).

[26]Gerhard von Rad argues that the author of 1-2 Kings "sets the whole complex [of events narrated in these books] in the shadow of the Nathan prophecy (2 Sam 7)" (*Old Testament Theology*, trans. D. M. G. Stalker [New York: Harper & Row, 1962] 1:342).

[27]See O. Palmer Robertson, *The Christ of the Covenants* (Phillipsburg, N.J.: Presbyterian & Reformed, 1980), pp. 252-69. Robertson calls this promise and fulfillment motif "the architectonic structure of the books of Kings" (p. 267).

through his prophets.[28] Gerhard von Rad argues that the author of these books

> gave the historical course of events which he describes its inner rhythm and its
> theological proof precisely by means of a whole structure of constantly promul-
> gated prophetic predictions and their corresponding fulfillments, of which exact
> note is generally made. . . . The history of Israel is a course of events which receives
> its own peculiar dramatic quality from the tension between constantly promulgated
> prophecies and their corresponding fulfillment.[29]

Von Rad continues on to say that the author's repeated use of the promise
and fulfillment motif has "practically hammered into the reader" the thesis that
"it is by his word that Jahweh directs history." Thus, he argues, the divine guidance of history "is established beyond all doubt."[30]

Especially important for our purposes are those occurrences of the promise
and fulfillment pattern that involve free human decisions. The following eight
examples include some kind of fulfillment formula.

A promise to Jeroboam. In 1 Kings 11:34-37 Yahweh speaks through his
prophet Ahijah to Jeroboam, the future king of the northern kingdom of Israel.
He promises Jeroboam:

> I will not take the whole kingdom out of Solomon's hand; I have made him ruler
> all the days of his life for the sake of David my servant. . . . I will take the kingdom
> from his son's hands and give you ten tribes. I will give one tribe to his son so that
> David my servant may always have a lamp before me in Jerusalem, the city where
> I chose to set my Name. However, as for you, I will take you, and you will rule
> over all that your heart desires; you will be king over Israel.

This promise finds fulfillment in the free decisions of the ten northern tribes
to make Jeroboam their king and of the tribe of Judah to remain loyal to the
Davidic monarchy: "When all the Israelites heard that Jeroboam had returned,
they sent and called him to the assembly and made him king over all Israel.
Only the tribe of Judah remained loyal to the house of David" (1 Kings 12:20).
And God's preservation of the tribe of Judah to be ruled by the sons of David
is explicitly described as a fulfillment of God's promise recounted in 1 Kings 11,
a specific example of his covenant faithfulness. "Nevertheless, for the sake of

---

[28]Robertson sees a threefold pattern recurring throughout 1-2 Kings: "First, God's word experiences *particularization* so that a specific application of the broader word concerning the
Davidic covenant is made evident. Then the particularized word of God finds *verification* in
the history of Israel. Finally the author of Kings pointedly calls attention to the fulfillment of
God's word through *formularization*" (ibid., p. 256).
[29]Von Rad, *Old Testament Theology,* 1:340.
[30]Ibid., 1:342.

his servant David, the LORD was not willing to destroy Judah. *He had promised to maintain a lamp for David and his descendants forever*" (2 Kings 8:19, emphasis added).

A promise concerning Josiah. In 1 Kings 13:2, an unnamed "man of God" from Judah came to the altar at Bethel as Jeroboam was making an offering. He cried out "by the word of the LORD: O altar, altar! This is what the LORD says, 'A son named Josiah will be born to the house of David. On you he will sacrifice the priests of the high places who now make offerings here, and human bones will be burned on you.'"

Clearly free decisions are involved here, for the prophecy identifies the future king of Judah by name, Josiah.[31] Charnock comments, "What is more contingent, or is more the effect of the liberty of man's will, than the names of their children?"[32] And the decision of the future King Josiah to desecrate the altar by burning the bones of pagan priests on it is clearly free as well.

In the providence of God, it was over three hundred years before Josiah, the son of Amon, would become king of Judah (2 Kings 21:26). During his reign the Book of the Law was rediscovered in the temple (2 Kings 22:8-13). In accordance with God's law, Josiah renewed the covenant of the Lord (2 Kings 23:3). He sought to root out idolatry from the land. And in his efforts to do so, he freely fulfilled the earlier prophecy of 1 Kings 13:2.

---

[31]The mention of the future King Josiah by name over three hundred years before his birth has caused problems for some commentators. For example, John Gray affirms that "the naming of reforming King Josiah is a *vaticinium post eventum* [prediction after the event]. . . . The sequel with its literal fulfillment in the Josianic reformation (2 Kings 23:16-18) suggests that the original tradition was reshaped in light of later events" (*I and II Kings* [Philadelphia: Westminster, 1963], p. 296). See also Gwilym H. Jones, *1 and 2 Kings,* New Century Bible Commentary (Grand Rapids: Eerdmans, 1984), 1:262. Yet the Josiah prediction is no more specific than the prediction of the exact price that will be charged for a seah of flour the next day in 2 Kings 7:2 or the specific location of the predicted death of Ahab (1 Kings 21:19) or of Jezebel (2 Kings 9:10). If God can predict these specific things, there is no a priori reason why God cannot predict by name the future king Josiah (and later the Persian king Cyrus—Is 44:28; 45:1). Only a naturalistic worldview that by definition would utterly rule out the possibility of supernatural prophecy would prevent that. See R. D. Patterson, *1 and 2 Kings,* Expositor's Bible Commentary 4 (Grand Rapids: Zondervan, 1988), p. 121.

[32]Charnock, *Discourses upon the Existence and Attributes of God,* p. 441. Charnock also cites Yahweh's prediction of the Persian king Cyrus by name and that he would help to rebuild Jerusalem (Is 44:28). John Piper also links this prediction of Josiah with that of Cyrus in Is 44:28, marveling that "God foreknew this human choice of Cyrus' and Josiah's parents [of what to name their children], not to mention their own choices to do what God had predicted they would do" (*The Pleasures of God* [Portland, Ore.: Multnomah Press, 1991], p. 72, n. 6). Boyd argues that the prediction of 1 Kings 13:2-3 implies that "for providential reasons the Lord determined that he would exert whatever influence was necessary to accomplish these tasks." And so the libertarian freedom of Josiah and his parents was restricted in these cases (*Satan and the Problem of Evil* [Downers Grove, Ill.: InterVarsity Press, 2001], p. 121, n. 7).

Even the altar at Bethel, the high place made by Jeroboam son of Nebat, who had
caused Israel to sin—even that altar and high place he [Josiah] demolished. . . .
Then Josiah looked around, and when he saw the tombs that were on the hillside,
he had the bones removed from them and burned on the altar to defile it, *in accordance with the word of the LORD proclaimed by the man of God who foretold
these things.* (2 Kings 23:15-16, emphasis added)

A prophecy against Baasha. In 1 Kings 16:2-4, the prophet Jehu prophesied
against Baasha, king of Israel:

[Yahweh] lifted you up from the dust and made you leader of my people Israel, but
you walked in the ways of Jeroboam and caused my people Israel to sin and to
provoke me to anger by their sins. So I am about to consume Baasha and his house,
and I will make your house like that of Jeroboam son of Nebat. Dogs will eat those
belonging to Baasha who die in the city, and the birds of the air will feed on those
who die in the country.

First Kings 16:11-12 records the fulfillment of this prophecy through Zimri,
who killed Elah, the son of Baasha, and succeeded him as king. "As soon as
[Zimri] began to reign and was seated on the throne, he killed off Baasha's
whole family. He did not spare a single male, whether relative or friend. So
Zimri destroyed the whole family of Baasha, *in accordance with the word of the
LORD spoken against Baasha through the prophet Jehu"* [emphasis added].

A promise from Elijah to the widow of Zeraphath. In 1 Kings 17:9 Yahweh told
his prophet Elijah to go to Zeraphath because the Lord had commanded a widow
in that region to supply him with food during the drought. Elijah did so, and even
though the widow had only a handful of flour and a little oil, he told her

Don't be afraid. Go home and do as you have said. But first make a small cake of
bread for me from what you have and bring it to me, and then make something
for yourself and your son. For this is what the LORD, the God of Israel, says: 'The
jar of flour will not be used up and the jug of oil will not run dry until the day the
LORD gives rain on the land. (1 Kings 17:13-14).

And Yahweh's promise was fulfilled: "She went away and did as Elijah had
told her. So there was food every day for Elijah and for the woman and her family. For the jar of flour was not used up and the jug of oil did not run dry, *in
keeping with the word of the LORD spoken by Elijah* (1 Kings 17:15-16, emphasis
added).

Now clearly God worked miraculously to cause the widow's supply of flour
and oil to continue throughout the drought. But still the woman had to trust the
promise enough to risk using the flour and oil to cook each day's food. Those
were daily free decisions on her part. Here too the promise of God reflected his

foreknowledge of the free decisions of this widow.

A prophecy against Ahab. In 1 Kings 21:19 Elijah said to King Ahab of Israel: "This is what the LORD says: Have you not murdered a man and seized his property? . . . In the place where dogs licked up Naboth's blood, dogs will lick up your blood—yes, yours!" 1 Kings 22:29-38 records the death of Ahab at Ramoth Gilead at the hands of the army of the king of Aram. Verses 37-38 record the specific fulfillment of the prophecy uttered by Elijah: "So the king [Ahab] died and was brought to Samaria, and they buried him there. They washed the chariot at the pool in Samaria (where the prostitutes bathed), and the dogs licked up his blood, *as the word of the LORD had declared*" (emphasis added).

A prophecy against Jezebel and the house of Ahab. Elijah's prophetic word continued on in 1 Kings 21:23 with a word concerning Ahab's wife, Jezebel: "And also concerning Jezebel the LORD says: 'Dogs will devour Jezebel by the wall of Jezreel.'" This prophetic word was reiterated to Jehu by Elisha, after he had anointed Jehu as king of Israel and had given him a mandate to destroy the house of Ahab.

> This is what the LORD, the God of Israel, says: "I anoint you king over the LORD's people Israel. You are to destroy the house of Ahab your master, and I will avenge the blood of my servants the prophets and the blood of all the LORD's servants shed by Jezebel. The whole house of Ahab will perish. I will cut off from Ahab every last male in Israel—slave or free. I will make the house of Ahab like the house of Jeroboam son of Nebat and like the house of Baasha son of Ahijah. As for Jezebel, dogs will devour her on the plot of ground at Jezreel, and no one will bury her." (2 Kings 9:6-10)

In obedience to this divine word, Jehu confronted Jezebel in the city of Jezreel and demanded that the inhabitants of the city throw her down from the gate. They did, and Jezebel was trampled by horses. Jehu then instructed that Jezebel be buried there. But we read: "When they went out to bury her, they found nothing except her skull, her feet and her hands. They went back and told Jehu, who said, *"This is the word of the LORD that he spoke through his servant Elijah the Tishbite: On the plot of ground at Jezreel dogs will devour Jezebel's flesh*" (2 Kings 9:35-36, emphasis added).

And in chapter 10 we read of the fulfillment of Elisha's mandate to Jehu to destroy the house of Ahab: "When Jehu came to Samaria, he killed all who were left there of Ahab's family; he destroyed them, *according to the word of the LORD spoken to Elijah*" (2 Kings 10:17, emphasis added).[33]

---

[33]The mandate Elisha gave to Jehu in 2 Kings 9:6-9 to destroy the house of Ahab reflects the commission Yahweh gave to Elijah in 1 Kings 19:16-17.

A promise concerning the price of flour. When the city of Samaria was being besieged by Ben-Hadad, king of Aram, and the resulting famine was so great that the inhabitants of Samaria were forced to resort to cannibalism (2 Kings 6:24-29), Elisha prophesied an end to the famine. He said to the king of Israel,

> "Hear the word of the LORD. This is what the LORD says: About this time tomorrow, a seah of flour will sell for a shekel and two seahs of barley for a shekel at the gate of Samaria."
>
> The officer on whose arm the king was leaning said to the man of God, "Look, even if the LORD should open the floodgates of the heavens, could this happen?"
>
> "You will see it with your own eyes," answered Elisha, "but you will not eat any of it." (2 Kings 7:1-2)

After four lepers went over to the Aramean camp to surrender and beg for mercy, they found the camp abandoned. Yahweh had caused the Arameans to hear the sounds of chariots and of a great army, and as a result they had fled in panic, leaving all their supplies and plunder behind (2 Kings 7:6-7). The lepers told the city gatekeepers this good news, and after it was verified, we read

> Then the people went out and plundered the camp of the Arameans. So a seah of flour sold for a shekel, and two seahs of barley sold for a shekel, *as the LORD had said.*
>
> Now the king had put the officer on whose arm he leaned in charge of the gate, and the people trampled him in the gateway, and he died, *just as the man of God had foretold when the king came down to his house. It happened as the man of God had said to the king:* "About this time tomorrow, a seah of flour will sell for a shekel and two seahs of barley for a shekel at the gate of Samaria."
>
> The officer had said to the man of God, "Look even if the LORD should open the floodgates of the heavens, could this happen?" The man of God had replied, "You will see it with your own eyes, but you will not eat any of it." *And that is exactly what happened to him,* for the people trampled him in the gateway, and he died. (2 Kings 7:16-20, emphasis added)

Once again Yahweh brought about these events by miraculous means (causing the Arameans to hear what they thought were chariots and a great army, enticing them to flee). But there were also many free human decisions involved in the fulfillment of this prophecy. These include the decision of the four lepers to go over to the Aramean camp, their decision to report what they found to the gatekeepers of Samaria, the willingness of the king to investigate, the plundering of the camp by the inhabitants of Samaria, and the rush of people through the gate such that the official was trampled to death. Thus the divine foreknowledge expressed through the prophetic word of Elisha included many free decisions.

A prophecy of judgment given to Hezekiah. In 2 Kings 20:17-18, the Lord spoke to Hezekiah, king of Judah, through the prophet Isaiah:

> The time will surely come when everything in your palace, and all that your fathers have stored up until this day, will be carried off to Babylon. Nothing will be left, says the LORD. And some of your descendants, your own flesh and blood, that will be born to you, will be taken away, and they will become eunuchs in the palace of the king of Babylon.

We find the fulfillment of this prophecy in 2 Kings 24:12-14.

> In the eighth year of the reign of the king of Babylon, he took Jehoiachin prisoner. *As the LORD had declared,* Nebuchadnezzar removed all the treasures from the temple of the LORD and from the royal palace, and took away all the gold articles that Solomon king of Israel had made for the temple of the LORD. He carried into exile all Jerusalem: all the officers and fighting men; and all the craftsmen and artisans— a total of ten thousand. Only the poorest people of the land were left.

Additional examples of the promise and fulfillment motif. In addition to these eight, there are six other examples in 1-2 Kings in which a fulfillment formula is used, but they do not explicitly refer to free human decisions.

- 1 Kings 13:5 speaks of Yahweh's action to confirm that the prediction of the man of God from Judah about Josiah would be fulfilled. "The altar was split apart and its ashes poured out *according to the sign given by the man of God by the word of the Lord*" (emphasis added).
- 1 Kings 16:34, presented as a fulfillment of the promise of Joshua 6:26 (that anyone who seeks to rebuild Jericho will suffer the loss of his firstborn or youngest sons).
- 2 Kings 1:16, Elijah's promise to Ahaziah that he would not recover but die, is fulfilled in 2 Kings 1:17 ("according to the word of the LORD that Elijah had spoken").
- 2 Kings 2:21, Elisha's promise that the water he had "healed" would never again cause death, is fulfilled in 2 Kings 2:22 ("according to the word Elisha had spoken").
- 2 Kings 4:43, Elisha's promise that a hundred men will eat from twenty loaves and have some left over, is fulfilled in 2 Kings 4:44 ("according to the word of the LORD").
- 2 Kings 10:30, the LORD's promise to Jehu that his descendants will sit on the throne of Israel to the fourth generation, is fulfilled in 2 Kings 15:12 ("So the word of the LORD spoken to Jehu was fulfilled").

While there is no explicit mention of free human decisions in these examples, they do reinforce the promise and fulfillment motif throughout 1-2 Kings and testify to the divine foreknowledge that underlies such predictive prophecies.

Finally, and also very important for our purposes, are examples of predictive prophecies concerning free human decisions that are made and fulfilled in 1-2 Kings, but for which there is no explicit fulfillment formula. The following six examples fall into this category.

- 1 Kings 14:5: Yahweh says to Ahijah, "Jeroboam's wife is coming to ask you about her son, for he is ill and you are to give her such and such answer. When she arrives, she will pretend to be someone else." And that is exactly what happened according to 1 Kings 14:6.

- 1 Kings 20:22: a prophet says to the king of Israel, "Strengthen your position and see what must be done, because next spring the king of Aram will attack you again." And that is precisely what happened. "The next spring Ben-Hadad mustered the Arameans and went up to Aphek to fight against Israel" (1 Kings 20:26).

- 1 Kings 22:22: Yahweh tells a lying spirit that he will succeed in enticing Ahab to attack Ramoth Gilead and go to his death there. The prophet Micaiah speaks the promise to Ahab directly: "If you ever return safely, the LORD has not spoken through me" (1 Kings 22:28). That promise was fulfilled. Ahab did in fact decide to attack Ramoth Gilead, and he was killed there (1 Kings 22:29-40).[34]

- 2 Kings 3:18-19: Elisha says to Jehoshaphat and Joram, "[The LORD] will also hand Moab over to you. You will overthrow every fortified city and every major town. You will cut down every good tree, stop up all the springs, and ruin every good field with stones." That is exactly what happened. We read in 2 Kings 3:24-25: "When the Moabites came to the camp of Israel, the Israelites rose up and fought them until they fled. And the Israelites invaded the land and slaughtered the Moabites. They destroyed the towns, and each man threw a stone on every good field until it was covered. They stopped up all the springs and cut down every good tree."

- 2 Kings 8:13: Elisha tells Hazael that the LORD had shown him that Hazael would become king of Aram. And verse 15 records that Hazael kills Ben-Hadad by spreading a thick cloth soaked in water over the king's face. "Then Hazael succeeded him as king."

---

[34]According to 1 Kings 22:34, the arrow that ultimately killed Ahab was shot at random. Such is the sovereign control of Yahweh, that even randomly shot arrows fulfill his word of predictive promise.

- 2 Kings 19:32-34: Yahweh tells Hezekiah through Isaiah the prophet that Sennacherib, the king of Assyria "will not enter this city [Jerusalem]. . . . By the way he came he will return; / he will not enter this city. / . . . I will defend this city and save it, / for my sake and the sake of David my servant." And that very night Yahweh fulfilled his promise. "That night the angel of the LORD went out and put to death a hundred and eighty-five thousand men in the Assyrian camp. When the people got up the next morning—there were all the dead bodies! So Sennacherib king of Assyria broke camp and withdrew. He returned to Nineveh and stayed there." (2 Kings 19:35-36).

It is hard to imagine a stronger or more convincing case to demonstrate that God knows all of the future, including the free decisions of human beings. The sheer volume of examples strongly points to this conclusion, as does the variety embodied in the various predictions. These predictions, made by prophets of Yahweh and fulfilled according to his word, are widely varied. They vary with respect to time—from a prediction fulfilled "that night" (2 Kings 19) to one fulfilled the next day (2 Kings 7) to those fulfilled "next spring" (1 Kings 20) and throughout the remainder of a three year drought (1 Kings 17) to a prediction made over three hundred years before it would be fulfilled (1 Kings 13/2 Kings 23). These predictions involve the people of God and people from the surrounding nations. They involve matters of life and death, war and peace, the provision of food and water, and randomly shot arrows and planned deception.

The point, I trust, is abundantly clear. These numerous and widely varied examples from 1-2 Kings convincingly demonstrate that the prophets of Israel are indeed predictors of the future. They can do so as spokespersons of Yahweh, precisely because Yahweh does in fact know both the near and distant future. And he knows all of the future, including the future free decisions of human beings. Thus to be true to the overwhelming teaching of 1-2 Kings, we must affirm that the foreknowledge of Yahweh is truly exhaustive.

Divine foreknowledge in Isaiah 40—48. A dominant theme of Isaiah 40—48 is the utter and complete superiority of Yahweh over all the gods of the pagan nations that surrounded Israel. This polemic frequently takes the literary form of a "trial speech." Most commentators see six trial speeches in these chapters (Is 41:2-5, 21-29; 42:18-25; 43:8-13; 44:6-20; 45:20-25).[35] John Oswalt describes the nature of these trial speeches:

God calls the gods and their representatives, the nations, into council to present

---

[35]See, e.g., Claus Westermann, *Isaiah 40-66,* trans. David M. G. Stalker (Philadelphia: Westminster Press, 1969), p. 63.

evidence as to who is God. Israel is the intended audience. There is no sense in which this is a formal trial with the outcome in doubt until some sovereign jurist hands down a judgment. God is judge and jury, bailiff and prosecutor. He summons the court, makes the case, and declares the verdict. The scenes are a device whereby the prophet can make the logic of God's transcendent monotheism both clear and compelling.[36]

The key evidence called for in these trial speeches is the ability to predict historical events in advance.[37] The pagan gods cannot do this. But Yahweh can. And his foreknowledge is supremely seen in the predictions of Cyrus and the deliverance he will bring the Israelites (especially in Is 44:28—45:1, where Cyrus is predicted by name).[38] Thus the gods are shown to be "less than nothing" (Is 41:24),

---

[36]John N. Oswalt, *The Book of Isaiah: Chapters 40-66*, New International Commentary on the Old Testament (Grand Rapids: Eerdmans, 1998), p. 79.

[37]Oswalt rightly notes that in these chapters the superiority of Yahweh over the pagan gods is also shown by the fact that he alone is the Creator (Is 43:1; 44:1, 24; 45:18-19). But still the primary emphasis in these chapters, and especially in the trial speeches is on the demonstration of the absolute superiority of Yahweh through his foretelling of the exile in Babylon and of his mighty deliverance of his people through Cyrus (*The Book of Isaiah: Chapters 1-39*, New International Commentary on the Old Testament [Grand Rapids: Eerdmans, 1986], p. 49).

[38]The specificity of these predictions is a major reason why many scholars adopt a late date for Second Isaiah. John L. McKenzie is representative: "The most striking feature of Second Isaiah is the two occurrences of the name of Cyrus (44:28 and 45:1). That Isaiah of Jerusalem (First Isaiah) could use the name of a king, in a language unknown to him, who ruled in a kingdom which did not exist in the eighth century B.C., taxes probability too far. It is not a question of placing limits to the vision of prophecy but of the limits of intelligibility; even if the name were by hypothesis meaningful to the prophet, it could not be meaningful to his readers or listeners. Yet Cyrus is introduced without any explanation of his identity, or of why he should be an anchor of hope to the Israelites whom the prophet addresses" (*Second Isaiah*, Anchor Bible [Garden City, N.J.: Doubleday, 1968], p. xvi). In my view, the question of whether such specific prophecy "taxes probability too far" is primarily one of worldview. If the supernatural God of the Bible actually exists and if he is able to reveal himself through his prophets, then such prophecies are not at all improbable. And in light of the purpose of God's predictions of the future, including his predictions of Cyrus (i.e., to validate his claim to deity and to give his people reason to trust and obey him), it is necessary that these predictions involve events specific enough and far enough into the future that only God could predict them. This function of divine predictions demands a date of writing prior to the events foretold. Robert Vasholz argues, "Whether one holds to the unity of the book of Isaiah or not, Isaiah 40—48 is ludicrous if one assumes that the prophet of these chapters feels he is speaking *vaticinia ex eventu* or *vaticinia post eventu*. Such a position completely undermines all that the prophet stands for in Isaiah 40—48. It reduces Yahweh to a status inferior to 'the gods.' The book becomes a self-contradiction. The citations concerning Cyrus and his deliverance of Judah (Is 44:28—45:6), to make sense, must be considered as prophetic, not present or past history, reinforced by a prophet who has a record that he is Yahweh's spokesman. The prophecies about Cyrus and Israel's new exodus are told way in advance ('you have not heard of them before') to demonstrate Yahweh's decisive supremacy over 'the gods' and to prove anew the futility of worshiping them" ("Isaiah vs. 'The Gods': A Case for Unity," *Westminster Theological Journal* 42 [1980], 393-94).

and Yahweh is convincingly shown to be the one and only true and living God.

A very clear example of such a trial speech comes in Isaiah 41:21-29. It begins with a challenge from Yahweh to the foreign gods:

"Present your case," says the LORD.
  "Set forth your arguments," says Jacob's King.
"Bring in your idols to tell us
  what is going to happen.
Tell us what the former things were,
  so that we may consider them
  and know their final outcome.
Or declare to us the things to come,
  tell us what the future holds,
  so we may know that you are gods.
Do something, whether good or bad,
  so that we will be dismayed and filled with fear." (Is 41:21-23)[39]

The gods cannot do this. Thus Yahweh pronounces his verdict.

But you are less than nothing
  and your works are utterly worthless;
  he who chooses you is detestable. (Is 41:24)

Yahweh then proceeds to display his own credentials. He can know and foretell the future. And so Yahweh predicts something no other god could predict—the coming deliverance of his people through Cyrus (though not yet identifying the deliverer by name).

I have stirred up one from the north, and he comes—
  one from the rising sun who calls on my name.
He treads on rulers as if there were mortar,
  as if he were a potter treading the clay.
Who told of this from the beginning, so we could know,
  or beforehand, so we could say "He was right"?
No one told of this,
  no one foretold it,
  no one heard any words from you.

---

[39]We need not be detained by the exegetical debate as to whether "the former things" and "the things to come" are both future (relating to the near future and the far-distant future) or whether "the former things" are past and "the things to come" are future. For representative arguments on both sides, see E. J. Young, *The Book of Isaiah* (Grand Rapids: Eerdmans, 1972), 3:96-97, and Oswalt, *Isaiah: Chapters 40-66,* p. 101. Simply note that on both interpretations Yahweh is demanding that the foreign gods—and proving that he himself can—predict future events, events that as we will see involve free human decisions.

I was the first to tell Zion, "Look, here they are!"
   I gave to Jerusalem a messenger of good tidings.
I look but there is no one—
   no one among them to give counsel,
     no one to give answer when I ask them. (Is 41:25-28)[40]

And given the inability of the gods to do what Yahweh can do, his devastating verdict on the gods is pronounced again.

See, they are all false!
   Their deeds amount to nothing;
     their images are but wind and confusion. (Is 41:29)

Commenting on this trial speech, Stephen Charnock writes:

> Such a foreknowledge of things to come is here ascribed to God by God himself, as a distinction of him from all false gods; such a knowledge, that if any could prove that they were possessors of it, he would acknowledge them gods as well as himself. . . . He puts his Deity to stand or fall upon this account, and this should be the point which should decide the controversy, whether he or the heathen idols were the true God; the dispute is managed by this medium—he that knows things to come, is God; I know things to come, *ergo,* I am God; the idols know not things to come; therefore they are not gods. God submits the being of his Deity to this trial.[41]

The crucial importance that God himself places on his unique ability to know and to declare the future (which, according to v. 25, includes the freely chosen actions of Cyrus) cannot be overstressed. God declares this to be the criterion by which his claim to absolute and unique deity is to be evaluated. Clearly this divine foreknowledge is no small thing.

But it is the glory of Yahweh that he can know and predict the future. So he argues once again in Isaiah 42:8-9:

I am the LORD; that is my name!
   I will not give my glory to another
   or my praise to idols.
See the former things have taken place,
   and new things I declare;

---

[40]Regarding the "one from the rising sun" of v. 25, this description recalls Is 41:2 ("who has stirred up one from the east, calling him in righteousness to his service?"). Oswalt takes both passages to refer to Cyrus, saying that the one described in 41:25 "is almost certainly the Persian emperor Cyrus, who, although hailing from the east, came on Babylon from the north" (*Isaiah: Chapters 40-66,* p. 103).

[41]Charnock, *Discourses upon the Existence and Attributes of God,* 1:431.

before they spring into being
    I announce them to you.

Two elements of this text are of special importance for our discussion. First, God declares that he can and will announce the "new things" well in advance— "before they spring into being." In this verse, God likens future events (which include events like those decided on and carried out by Cyrus) to seeds planted in the ground. Even before they sprout and become visible, God can know them and declare them through his prophet.[42] This understanding of God's knowledge of future events is different than that promoted by open theism. Open theists claim that before future events "spring into being," they do not exist and so cannot be known, even by God. But according to Isaiah 42:9, before they spring into being, they are known by God and can be declared by him.

Second, note the explicit link that Yahweh makes between his ability to know and announce future events (before they spring into being) and his glory. God's sovereign determination to not give his glory to idols is linked to his determination to declare and even to boast in his ability to know and to foretell the future (including free human decisions). Indeed, this is a distinguishing mark of Yahweh's divine glory.[43]

Again and again, Yahweh contrasts himself with pagan idols, because he alone can know and declare the future. This makes Yahweh the absolutely unique God.

"Which of them foretold this
    and proclaimed to us the former things?
Let them bring in their witnesses to prove they were right,
    so that others may hear and say, 'It is true.'
"You are my witnesses," declares the LORD,
    "and my servant whom I have chosen,
so that you may know and believe me
    and understand that I am he.
Before me no god was formed,
    nor will there be one after me.
I, even I, am the LORD,
    and apart from me there is no savior.
I have revealed and saved and proclaimed—
    I, and not some foreign god among you. (Is 43:9-12)

---

[42]Young, *Isaiah*, 3:124.
[43]See John Piper, "Why the Glory of God Is at Stake in the 'Foreknowledge' Debate," *Modern Reformation* 8, no. 5 (1999): 41.

Who then is like me? Let him proclaim it.
    Let him declare and lay out before me
what has happened since I established my ancient people,
    and what is yet to come—
    yes, let him foretell what will come.
Do not tremble; do not be afraid.
    Did I not proclaim this and foretell it long ago?
You are my witnesses. Is there any God besides me?
    No, there is no other Rock; I know not one. (Is 44:7-8)

The supreme example of God's ability to know and predict the future comes
in his specific prediction of the future deliverer Cyrus.[44] In Isaiah 44:26—45:6,
Yahweh identifies himself as the one

who says of Jerusalem, "It shall be inhabited,"
    of the towns of Judah, "They shall be built,"
    and of their ruins, "I will restore them."
who says to the watery deep, "Be dry,
    and I will dry up your streams,"
who says of Cyrus, "He is my shepherd
    and will accomplish all that I please;
    he will say of Jerusalem, 'Let it be rebuilt,'
    and of the temple, 'Let its foundations be laid.' "
This is what the LORD says to his anointed,
    to Cyrus, whose right hand I take hold of
to subdue nations before him
    and to strip kings of their armor,
to open doors before him
    so that gates will not be shut:
I will go before you
    and will level the mountains;
I will break down gates of bronze
    and cut through bars of iron.
I will give you the treasures of darkness,
    riches stored in secret places,
so that you may know that I am the LORD,

---

[44]R. K. Harrison suggests that the two mentions of Cyrus's name (Is 44:28; 45:1) may well be later glosses added after the actual name of the predicted deliverer had become known (*Introduction to the Old Testament* [Grand Rapids: Eerdmans, 1969], 794-95). Oswalt says that while this could possibly be the case in 45:1, it is more difficult to see this possibility with respect to 44:28. Yet even if the name itself were a later gloss, the identity of the one predicted is still very specific (*Isaiah: Chapters 40-66*, pp. 196-97, n. 99).

the God of Israel, who summons you by name.
For the sake of Jacob my servant,
of Israel my chosen,
I summon you by name
and bestow on you a title of honor,
though you do not acknowledge me.
I am the LORD, and there is no other;
apart from me there is no God.
I will strengthen you,
though you have not acknowledged me,
so that from the rising of the sun
to the place of its setting
men may know that there is none beside me.
I am the LORD and there is no other.[45]

This passage describes Cyrus in fascinating ways. This Persian ruler, who does not acknowledge Yahweh (45:4), is nonetheless designated as Yahweh's "shepherd," who will accomplish all that he pleases (44:28). And even more surprisingly (and more shockingly to Isaiah's readers), Cyrus is explicitly called Yahweh's "anointed" (45:1). Both *shepherd* and *anointed* are royal designations. But the crucial element is the use of personal pronouns. Yahweh says that Cyrus is "*my* shepherd." John D. W. Watts notes the implication. By calling Cyrus "my shepherd," Yahweh makes it clear that "Cyrus is Yahweh's tool (not the reverse). . . . Cyrus is employed to do what Yahweh wants for Israel."[46] Oswalt notes that when Yahweh speaks of "*his* anointed" in Isaiah 45:1, the point is what Isaiah has been pointing to all along.

> God is not the Lord of Israel alone; he is the God of the whole world. Israel's election is not for itself, and thus neither is its deliverance necessarily to be effected by itself. It is this sense in which *anointed* is used here: Cyrus has been especially chosen and empowered to carry out the purposes of God. In this sense he typifies the Messiah: he is God's chosen instrument through whom God's gracious purposes will be accomplished, especially as through him God is revealed to the world.[47]

---

[45]Westermann understands Yahweh's word to the deep (Is 44:27) to refer to his act of creation (cf. Is 44:24). Thus he argues that the coupling of God's word to the deep (Is 44:27) and his word to Cyrus (Is 44:28) points to Yahweh as Lord both of creation and of history (*Isaiah*, p. 155). Oswalt argues, on the other hand, that the drying up of the deep refers to the exodus. Thus both v. 27 and v. 28 refer to God's acts in history—v. 27 referring to past history and v. 28 to an event yet in the future that Yahweh will accomplish as Lord of history (*Isaiah: Chapters 40-66*, p. 196).

[46]John D. W. Watts, *Isaiah 34-66*, Word Biblical Commentary (Waco, Tex.: Word, 1987), p. 156.

[47]Oswalt, *Isaiah: Chapters 40-66*, pp. 200-201. Young also points to the typological role played by Cyrus (*Isaiah*, 3:195).

This passage also makes clear why God raised up Cyrus. In these verses he gives three reasons for anointing and using Cyrus to accomplish his redemptive purposes. All three are explicitly God-centered and relate to God's passion that he might be known, trusted and followed as the only true and living God. Why will Yahweh raise up Cyrus and announce the fact in advance? (1) So that Cyrus himself would know that he is the LORD (45:3), (2) so that Israel might truly know their God (45:4), and (3) so that the world might know that Yahweh is God and that there is no other (45:6). Again we see how closely God ties the display of his glory to his predictions of future free human actions of people like Cyrus.[48]

The most important thing for us to note is the crucial role that God's fore-knowledge of the decisions and the work of Cyrus plays in the overall narrative of these chapters. It serves as the lynchpin of Isaiah's argument for the unique deity of Yahweh and his worthiness of being trusted and worshiped alone. Oswalt captures this emphasis rightly:

> The centerpiece of the whole argument against the idols is that they cannot declare the future. . . . But God not only has done so in the past, he does so now. . . . Three of the four references to Cyrus (41:25; 44:28; 46:11) are directly connected to this argument, and the other (41:2) is connected by implication because it opens a statement that concludes with the argument of 41:21-29. These facts cannot mean anything else but that the person or persons responsible for the final form of the book wish us to believe that the specific predictions of Cyrus were given far enough in advance that they could not have been part of any normal process of forecasting future events. The Cyrus predictions are thus made the specific evidence that God can and does tell the future. As such they are made the very fulcrum on which the whole argument for God's uniqueness turns.[49]

Once again it is this recognition of the crucial use that God makes of his fore-knowledge of free human actions that makes it such a significant thing.

Isaiah is not finished with his polemic against the idols. Because Yahweh can announce Cyrus in advance, he is absolutely unique.

Gather together and come;
   assemble, you fugitives from the nations.

---

[48]While the verb "know" is not used in v. 4, which simply says that God has summoned Cyrus "for the sake of Jacob my servant, of Israel, my chosen," Oswalt argues persuasively that in the larger context of these chapters (e.g., 40:28; 43:10; 48:8), Israel's problem is that it really does not know God. And thus Yahweh's larger purpose in the return from exile is to reveal himself to his people in all his power and grace so that they might know and trust him (*Isaiah: Chapters 40-66*, p. 203, n. 24).

[49]Ibid., p. 196.

Ignorant are those who carry about idols of wood,
>   who pray to gods that cannot save.
Declare what is to be, present it—
>   let them take counsel together.
Who foretold this long ago,
>   who declared it from the distant past?
Was it not I, the LORD?
>   And there is no God apart from me,
a righteous God and a Savior;
>   there is none like me. (Is 45:20-21)

Oswalt argues that in this passage, Isaiah "is looking forward to the time when the judgments associated with Cyrus (45:1-3, 14, 16) have already occurred." Thus the "fugitives from the nations" are those who remain alive after those judgments have occurred. In this passage, they are invited by Yahweh to gather together to present the strongest possible case concerning the identity of the one true God. Once again, the key piece of evidence cited is Yahweh's ability to predict the future. Oswalt understands the "this" that was foretold to be "the specific prophecy of Cyrus and the Babylonian overthrow."[50]

Two elements of this prophecy are crucial for its functioning in this trial speech. The first is the specificity of the prediction. A fairly generic promise could not support the claim that its fulfillment was proof of the unique deity of Yahweh.[51] Second, and equally important, is the fact that this prediction was made "long ago" *(miqqedem)* and in "the distant past" *(mē'āz)*. While there is scholarly debate about how distant this past is, I would argue that for the prediction to function as it does in Isaiah's trial speech, it must have been made

---

[50]Ibid., pp. 221-22. J. Alec Motyer offers a different understanding. He sees Is 45:20-21 in the context of Is 45:9—46:13, a section in which, he argues, Cyrus has dropped into the background and Isaiah's primary concern is to help Israel see God's larger redemptive purposes, which include the salvation of the Gentiles. "Unless we are to divorce vv. 20-21 from this context, then the *fugitives* are those who have come to Israel to find the Lord, thus escaping the fate that awaits idolaters, and *this* refers to the Lord's determination to take a world-wide people for himself" (*The Prophecy of Isaiah* [Downers Grove, Ill.: InterVarsity Press, 1993], p. 365). It is in this sense, Motyer argues, that Yahweh describes himself as a "Savior" (v. 21). Intriguing as this suggestion is, I am not convinced that it is the best interpretation. It is not at all clear that Cyrus has faded into the background, especially in light of 46:11. And second, I question whether predictions of God's redemptive intention to save Gentiles would have been sufficiently specific and fulfilled in a sufficiently clear way to function in the trial as the prediction of 45:21 does.

[51]Oswalt contrasts the specificity of this promise with the suggestion of Pieper that the reference is to generic promises such as Gen 22:17. Oswalt says, "The promise would surely have had to be more specific than that to support the stupendous claim that its fulfillment was conclusive proof of the Lord's sole godhead" (*Isaiah: Chapters 40-66*, p. 222).

sufficiently far in the past to serve as evidence of the truly divine character of Yahweh.[52] Oswalt brings together both the future orientation and the specificity of the prediction as follows:

> I suggest that this passage itself is the prophecy and the fulfillment. If the words were first spoken by Isaiah about 700 B.C. and only came to fufillment in 539 B.C., then they certainly were from of old by the time they were fulfilled. At the same time, they are sufficiently specific for the Jew of 539 B.C. to recognize them as indicating that God does indeed know the future.[53]

In Isaiah 46:9-11. Isaiah continues this theme, citing the exultant words of Yahweh:

> Remember the former things, those of long ago;
>   I am God, and there is no other;
>   I am God, and there is none like me.
> I make known the end from the beginning,
>   from ancient times what is still to come.
> I say: My purpose will stand,
>   and I will do all that I please.
> From the east I summon a bird of prey;
>   from a far-off land, a man to fulfill my purpose.
> What I have said, that will I bring about;
>   what I have planned, that will I do.

Once again, Isaiah uses the Hebrew word *miqqedem* to describe the time frame of Yahweh's predictions. He declares what is still to come "from ancient times *(miqqedem)*." And he makes known the end "from the beginning *[mērē'šit]*." While the word *rē'šit* is a general one, referring to the beginning of any kind of process (e.g., the gaining of wisdom [Prov 1:7], sin [Mic 1:13], a quarrel [Prov 17:14] or creation itself [Gen 1:1]), the parallelism Isaiah employs between *mērē'šit* and *miqqedem* points to the future orientation. And as Young points out, "the greater the time between the utterance of the prophecy and its fulfillment, the more efficacious the proof of the divine transcendence will be."[54]

The point is clear. Yahweh's unique deity ("I am God and there is no other; / I am God, and there is none like me") is clearly evidenced by his ability to know and predict the future. But what elements of the future? Virtually all commentators are agreed that the bird of prey, whom Yahweh summons to do his

---

[52]Ibid., p. 222, n. 6. Note the contrasting view of C. R. North, *Second Isaiah* (Oxford: Clarendon, 1964), p. 160.

[53]Oswalt, *Isaiah: Chapters 40-66*, p. 222.

[54]Young, *Isaiah*, 3:227, n. 9.

purpose in verse 11, is a reference to Cyrus.[55] This makes Yahweh's pronouncement in verse 10 that he alone can declare the end from the beginning and what is still to come from ancient times all the more significant. The future that Yahweh knows, declares from the beginning and says he will accomplish includes the free decisions of Cyrus to bring about the predicted outcome.

This observation counters the most common interpretation of Isaiah 46:10-11 proposed by open theists. John Sanders, for example, argues that this passage affirms that what God knows of the future involves those things that "God is going to do irrespective of creaturely decisions," things that "God can bring about on his own."[56] Yet given the clear identification of the future God knows and declares in advance as involving the decisions of Cyrus (v. 11), it is hard to see how this is an example of God acting "*irrespective of creaturely decisions.*" Rather, this seems to be a clear illustration of God foreknowing free human decisions and sovereignly accomplishing his purposes through them.

The theme we have been tracing, that God alone can predict the future, is repeated once again in Isaiah 48:3-5. Here Yahweh gives yet another reason for this divine activity.

> I foretold the former things long ago,
>   my mouth announced them and I made them known;
>   then suddenly I acted, and they came to pass.
> For I knew how stubborn you were;
>   the sinews of your neck were iron,
>   your forehead was bronze.
> Therefore I told you these things long ago;

---

[55]An exception is Norman Snaith, who takes v. 11 to refer to the returning exiles ("Studies in the Second Part of Isaiah," in H. M. Orlinsky and Norman Snaith, *Studies on the Second Part of the Book of Isaiah,* Vetus Testamentum Supplements 14 [Leiden: Brill, 1967], pp. 186-87).

[56]Sanders, *God Who Risks,* p. 130. Richard Rice argues on the basis of this text that "if God's will is the only condition required for something to happen, if human cooperation is not involved, then God can unilaterally guarantee its fulfillment, and he can announce it ahead of time" ("Biblical Support for a New Perspective," in *Openness of God* [Downers Grove, Ill.: InterVarsity Press, 1994], p. 51). Yet in light of the specific reference to Cyrus, it is hard to see how Is 46:9-10 is a case in which "human cooperation is not involved." Gregory Boyd argues that in Is 46:9-10 God "is appealing to *his own intentions* about the future. He foreknows that certain things are going to take place because he knows *his own purpose and intention* to bring these events about" (*God of the Possible* [Grand Rapids: Baker, 2000], p. 30). In a later work, Boyd admits that the unilateral divine activity pointed to in this passage does end up restricting Cyrus's libertarian freedom. But this does not imply that everything about Cyrus was settled ahead of time (*Satan and the Problem of Evil,* p. 121, n.7). Yet when we consider the myriad of human decisions involved in the birth and naming of Cyrus, in his rise to kingship in Persia, and in his allowing the Jews to return to Jerusalem, we must recognize what a massive restriction on libertarian human freedom is involved here.

before they happened I announced them to you
so that you could not say,
    "My idols did them;
    my wooden image and metal god ordained them."

In the past ("long ago"—*mēʾāz*), Yahweh did things that no idol or pagan god could do—foretell what will happen in the future and then decisively act so that the predicted events actually did come to pass. Oswalt cites the prediction of Genesis 15:13-14 about Israel's slavery in Egypt for four hundred years and subsequent exodus as one example. But the focus of Isaiah 48, he argues, is not any one particular prediction. The point is that Yahweh regularly did such things.[57] And Yahweh's stated reason for doing so involves the sinful rebelliousness of his people. Yahweh predicts the future and acts to bring it about precisely so that no Israelite might be tempted to attribute these mighty acts (and indeed the entire course of history) to anyone other than the true and living God.

When Yahweh turns his attention from his past predictions to predictions of events yet to come, his concern remains the same. Yahweh is jealous for his own glory above all. So when he predicts "new things," he does so in a way that ensures that the Israelites will not be able to presumptively attribute such foreknowledge to themselves.

From now on I will tell you of new things,
    of hidden things unknown to you.
They were created now, and not long ago;
    you have not heard of them before today.
So you cannot say,
    "Yes, I knew of them."
You have neither heard nor understood;
    from of old your ear has not been open.
Well do I know how treacherous you are;
    you were called a rebel from birth.
For my own name's sake I delay my wrath;
    for the sake of my praise I hold it back from you,
    so as not to cut you off.
See, I have refined you, though not as silver;
    I have tested you in the furnace of affliction.
For my own sake, for my own sake, I do this.
    How can I let myself be defamed?
    I will not yield my glory to another. (Is 48:6-11)

---

[57]Oswalt, *Isaiah: Chapters 40-66*, pp. 261-62.

The point of this passage is the repeated emphasis that we find throughout Isaiah 40—48: Yahweh glorifies himself as the only true God by means of his foreknowledge. He and he alone can know and declare the future. And a God who displays such knowledge warrants the exclusive worship of his people.

In conclusion, we might say that Isaiah 40—48 provides us with both a quantitative and a qualitative argument for God's exhaustive foreknowledge. Quantitatively, the sheer number of references to Yahweh's knowledge of the future (41:21-29; 42:8-9; 43:9-12; 44:7-8; 44:24—45:6; 45:20-21; 46:9-11; 48:3-5; 48:6-11) is very significant. But even more powerful is the qualitative argument, stemming from the purpose for which Yahweh appeals to his foreknowledge. Time and time again, he appeals to his ability to know and to predict future historical events—including those which involve free human decisions (e.g., Cyrus)—as the conclusive proof of his unique deity. That is the crucial truth repeated throughout these chapters: Yahweh knows and thus is able to predict the future—including future free human decisions. And thus joyfully affirming this truth is of monumental importance for the people of God.

Old Testament messianic prophecies. A central theme throughout the Old Testament is God's promise to redeem and to bless his covenant people through his coming Messiah. Kaiser sees this promise to be at the heart of God's redemptive plan; it constitutes the "center" of the Scriptures. He writes, "It [the promise plan of God] is a center that is personal in that it focuses on God's Son the Messiah. But it is also dynamically historical in nature, for it involves a larger plan that took its distinctive shape in history and a plethora of provisions that embraced the whole of biblical revelation."[58]

One of the ways we can see the prominence of the Messiah to God's plan for history is in the quantity of messianic prophetic predictions found in Scripture. J. Barton Payne cites 574 verses in the Old Testament that contain direct, personal messianic foretellings.[59] Kaiser is more moderate, citing sixty-five direct messianic predictions. Of these, twenty-seven are quoted or clearly alluded to as being fulfilled in the New Testament in fifty-three verses or passages.[60]

Particularly important for our purposes is the fact that many of these messianic prophecies involve free human decisions, either of Christ himself or others around him. Space constraints limit our discussion to two examples, one relating to the birth of Christ and one to his death.

---

[58]Kaiser, *Messiah in the Old Testament*, p. 233.
[59]J. Barton Payne, *Encyclopedia of Biblical Prophecy* (New York: Harper & Row, 1973), pp. 667-68.
[60]Kaiser, *Messiah in the Old Testament*, pp. 240-42, 237-39.

Micah 5:2. In Micah 5:2, the prophet Micah predicts, among other things, the birthplace of the Messiah—Bethlehem, the city of David.[61] This verse is quoted in Matthew 2:6 and alluded to in John 7:42. Micah writes:

> But you, Bethlehem, Ephratha,
>> though you are small among the clans of Judah,
> out of you will come for me
>> one who will be ruler over Israel,
> whose origins are from of old,
>> from ancient times. (Mic 5:2)

This verse follows a description of Israel's present distress (Mic 4:11-13) and the humiliating and degrading insult given to the king of Judah (Mic 5:1), thus making the future greatness of Bethlehem's role in Israel's salvation all the more striking. The city is personified and addressed directly with the dual designation, "Bethlehem, Ephratha." Bruce Waltke notes that the meanings of these designations—Bethlehem (house of bread) and Ephratha (fruitful)— "pregnantly portend Messiah's career."[62] The key contrast within the verse itself is between the smallness and relative insignificance of Bethlehem as a town and the greatness of its future role as the birthplace of the Messiah.[63] Waltke writes, "The focal point in redemptive history is none other than the insignificant town of Bethlehem, showing that Israel's greatness does not depend on a great human king but on divine intervention to bring greatness out of nothing."[64]

---

[61]2 Sam 7:12 and Is 11:1 also link the Messiah's origins with David. See Bruce K. Waltke, "Micah," in *The Minor Prophets,* ed. Thomas E. McComiskey (Grand Rapids: Baker, 1993), 2:704.

[62]Waltke, "Micah," p. 703.

[63]Matthew inserts a strong negative *(oudamōs)* into his quotation of Mic 5:2 in Mt 2:6 ("But you, Bethlehem, in the land of Judah, are *by no means* least among the rulers of Judah"). This seems to contradict the Masoretic Text of Mic 5:2. D. A. Carson argues that the contradiction is merely formal for the following reasons: (1) the Masoretic Text does implicitly imply the greatness of Bethlehem: "though you are small among the clans (which refers to the great clans into which the tribes were subdivided, cf. Judg 6:15; 1 Sam 10:19; 23:23; Is 60:22) of Judah" sets the stage for the future greatness that would flow from Bethlehem; and (2) Matthew's formulation assumes that apart from being the birthplace of the Messiah, Bethlehem is indeed of little importance. Carson concludes, "though the second line of Micah 5:2 formally contradicts the second line of Mt 2:6, a wholistic reading of the verses shows the contradiction to be merely formal. Mt 2:6 has perhaps a slightly greater emphasis on the one factor that makes Bethlehem great" (*Matthew, Expositor's Bible Commentary* 8 [Grand Rapids: Zondervan, 1984], pp. 87-88).

[64]Waltke, "Micah," p. 704. He also notes how God's election of lowly Bethlehem is suggestive of the lowliness and humility of the Messiah. Thus both David's town and his greater Son are brought from lowly humility to exalted greatness only by supernatural divine intervention.

For our purposes it is important to note that the fulfillment of the prophecy of Micah 5:2 in the birth of Jesus was brought about by a myriad of free human decisions. These include, among others, the decision of Caesar Augustus to issue his decree to tax his entire empire (Lk 2:1-3) and Joseph's decision to obey the decree and to travel with pregnant Mary from Nazareth to Bethlehem, where the birth of Jesus occurred (Lk 2:4-7). Now it might be argued that all Micah 5:2 explicitly affirms is that the Messiah would be born in Bethlehem and that it says nothing explicitly about how this would take place. Thus it could be argued that no conclusions can be drawn from the prediction and its fulfillment about God's foreknowledge of Caesar's decree and so forth. This, of course, is true as far as it goes. But it is hard for me to conceive of God making the prediction of Micah 5:2 based on nothing more than a strong estimate of probability and deciding to incarnate his Son, the Messiah, in the womb of a young virgin living in Nazareth with no more than a strong suspicion that Mary and Joseph would make their way to Bethlehem for the birth of their son. It is far more likely that God would not utter this widely understood messianic prophecy (cf. Mt 2:4-6) without the sure knowledge that it would be fulfilled and without a strong commitment to sovereignly act so as to ensure its fulfillment.[65]

That Micah 5:2 points to God's foreknowledge of his Messiah, the place of his birth and all the circumstances that brought about that birth in that particular place is made more likely by the reference at the end of the verse to Messiah's origins being "from of old, from ancient times" *(miqqedem mîmê ʿôlām)*. There has been considerable debate over whether these phrases refer to the eternal nature of the Messiah or to his antiquity in time.[66] But under each understanding, these terms do denote God's foreknowledge and foreplanning of his Messiah. Waltke, who adopts a temporal understanding of this point, argues, "Messiah's lineage derives from the very beginning of David's house, in the loins of Jesse. Messiah is no upstart or afterthought in God's program. His origins began when God chose David in the first place."[67]

Psalm 22:18. Psalm 22 can very naturally be divided into two sections: a la-

---

[65]God's sovereign work in and through a pagan ruler to insure that his redemptive purposes are accomplished is not without precedent (e.g., God's moving of Cyrus's heart to issue his proclamation allowing the exiled Jews to return to Jerusalem—Ezra 1:1; cf. Is 44:28; 45:1). See also Prov 21:1.

[66]Kaiser, for example, takes ʿôlām to refer to eternity, arguing that since the temporal birth of the Messiah is presented as being future, his "going forth" presented here must refer to his eternal generation (*Messiah in the Old Testament*, p. 154). Waltke, on the other hand, understands both *miqqedem* and *mîmê ʿôlām* to be temporal designations of the distant past ("Micah," pp. 704-5).

[67]Waltke, "Micah," p. 705.

ment (vv. 1-21) and an expression of praise and thanksgiving (vv. 22-31).[68] The psalm is an individual lament, yet the individual sufferer, convinced of God's help, vows to give thanks in the midst of the congregation (vv. 25-26), thus bringing a corporate component to the psalm.[69] Peter Craigie argues that the psalm was likely used in Israel for any individual who was severely sick or threatened by death in any way. The worshiper would participate in the liturgy in the midst of the congregation, hoping for a favorable priestly oracle in response to his plea.[70]

The superscription of the psalm attributes it to David. And the use of the first person throughout the psalm has led many to believe that David was first and foremost writing about himself as an innocent sufferer.[71] Yet because the sufferings described seem to surpass that which David personally suffered, whether in a single experience or his sufferings as a whole, the psalm has been widely interpreted as pointing beyond David to the suffering of his greater Son, Jesus Christ—especially in his crucifixion. For example, John Calvin writes, "Although David here bewails his own distresses, this psalm was composed under the influence of the Spirit of prophecy concerning David's King and Lord."[72] And Derek Kidner writes:

> No incident recorded of David can begin to account for this. As A. Bentzen points out, it is "not a description of an illness, but of an execution," and while David was once threatened with stoning (1 Sam 30:6), this is a very different scene. . . . Whatever the initial stimulus, the language of the psalm defies a naturalistic explanation; the best account is in the terms used by Peter concerning another psalm of David: "Being therefore a prophet, . . . he foresaw and spoke of . . . the Christ" (Acts 2:30f.).[73]

This messianic interpretation of Psalm 22 is also pointed to by the extensive New Testament usage of the psalm. John H. Reumann cites twelve quotations

---

[68]Peter C. Craigie, *Psalms 1-50,* Word Biblical Commentary 19 (Waco, Tex.: Word, 1983), p. 197. See also Willem A. VanGemeren, *Psalms, Expositor's Bible Commentary* 5 (Grand Rapids: Zondervan, 1981), p. 198.

[69]Mitchell Dahood, *Psalms I: 1-50,* Anchor Bible (Garden City, N.J.: Doubleday, 1965), p. 138.

[70]Craigie, *Psalms 1-50,* p. 198.

[71]E.g., Delitzsch, *Psalms,* pp. 303-5.

[72]John Calvin, *Commentary on the Book of Psalms,* trans. James Anderson (Grand Rapids: Eerdmans, 1948), 1:362.

[73]Derek Kidner, *Psalms 1-72,* Tyndale Old Testament Commentary (Downers Grove, Ill.: InterVarsity Press, 1973), p. 105. Kidner quotes A. Bentzen, *King and Messiah* (London: Lutterworth, 1955), 94, n. 40. See also E. W. Hengstenberg, *Christology of the Old Testament,* trans. Reuel Keith and abridg. Thomas K. Arnold (Grand Rapids: Kregel, 1970), pp. 78-90; and Kaiser, *Messiah in the Old Testament,* pp. 111-18.

of and eight allusions to Psalm 22 in the New Testament.[74]

In the lament portion of the psalm the psalmist declares that he (1) is forsaken by God (vv. 1-5),[75] (2) is despised by his fellow human beings (vv. 6-10), (3) prays for help (v. 11), (4) is surrounded by trouble (vv. 12-18), and (5) prays again for deliverance (vv. 19-21).[76] Our concern is with the fourth section, "the most intense description of the suffering" of the psalmist.[77] His enemies are likened to "strong bulls" (v. 12), "roaring lions tearing their prey" (v. 13) and vicious wild dogs that prowl the streets (v. 16). The suffering psalmist feels exhausted, "poured out like water" (v. 14). His bones are "out of joint" (v. 14); his heart has turned to wax and melted away (v. 14); his thirst is raging (v. 15). He is near to dying (v. 15). His hands and feet are pierced (v. 16). His skin has become so taut that his bones stick out (v. 17). He watches helplessly as his enemies gamble for his garments (v. 18).

This last verse is our special focus here. VanGemeren argues that verse 18 continues the thought of verse 15 ("you lay me in the dust of death"). Both expressions speak to the severity of the situation described by the psalmist. "The psalmist feels as if he is about to die; therefore the wicked are waiting to swoop down on him like vultures. The 'garments' ('clothing') are divided up like the spoils from battle."[78]

Each of the Synoptic Gospels records the dividing of Jesus' clothes through the casting of lots as he was being crucified (Mt 27:35; Mk 15:24; Lk 23:34). John, however, gives the most detailed account, and he specifically states that what happened at Calvary on that day was in fulfillment of Psalm 22:18.

> When the soldiers crucified Jesus, they took his clothes, dividing them into four shares, one for each of them, with the undergarment remaining. This garment was seamless, woven in one piece from top to bottom.
>
> "Let's not tear it," they said to one another. "Let's decide by lot who will get it."
>
> This happened that the scripture might be fulfilled which said,

---

[74]John H. Reumann, "Psalm 22 at the Cross: Lament and Thanksgiving for Jesus Christ," *Interpretation* 28, no. 1 (1974): 41. The quotations cited by Reumann are Mt 27:46/Mk 15:34, quoting Ps 22:1; Rom 5:5, quoting Ps 22:5; Mt 27:39/Mk 15:29, quoting Ps 22:7; Mt 27:43/Lk 23:35, quoting Ps 22:8; Mt 27:35/Mark 15:24/Luke 23:34/John 19:24, quoting Ps 22:18; and Heb 2:12, quoting Ps 22:22. The allusions he cites are 1 Pet 1:11, alluding to the whole psalm; Mk 9:12; Acts 13:29; Lk 24:27; Mark 14:21, all alluding to Ps 22:1-18; 1 Pet 5:8, alluding to Ps 22:13b; Jn 19:28, alluding to Ps 22:15; 2 Tim 4:17, alluding to Ps 22:17.

[75]The most well-known portion of this segment is v. 1, in which the psalmist expresses his horrifying sense of being forsaken by God. These agonizing words ("My God, my God, why have you forsaken me?") were uttered by Jesus on the cross (Mt 27:46; Mk 15:34).

[76]Craigie, *Psalms 1-50*, p. 198.

[77]Kaiser, *Messiah in the Old Testament*, p. 115.

[78]VanGemeren, *Psalms*, p. 207. Craigie agrees, saying that even though the sufferer "is not yet dead, they are already dividing up his clothes as if he were deceased" (*Psalms 1-50*, p. 200).

> "They divided my garments among them
> and cast lots for my clothing."
> So this is what the soldiers did. (Jn 19:23-24)

John sees an ultimately christological focus of Psalm 22, stemming from his view of David as a type of Christ and from Jesus' own use of the words of Psalm 22:1 as he hung on the cross. Carson writes:

> The psalmist is afflicted by both physical distress and the mockery of his opponents, and apparently uses the symbolism of an execution scene, in which the executioners distribute the victim's clothes, to elaborate the depth of his sense of abandonment. Davidic typology, a central motif in early Christianity, assures that this will have final reference to Christ, a connection made all the easier in this instance by the fact that Jesus himself drew attention to the relevance of Psalm 22 by citing the first verse on the cross: "My God, my God, why have you forsaken me?" (Matt 27:46; Mark 15:34).[79]

This christological focus leads John to see in the actions of the soldiers around the cross a fulfillment of Psalm 22:18 as he cites the LXX rendering of that verse.

However, the way John uses Psalm 22:18 has generated much controversy. Some have argued that he misuses the Old Testament text, for the parallelism of the Hebrew poetry makes it probable that the "my garments" in the first line refer to the same thing as the "my clothing" of the second line. Yet John seems to distinguish them, with the first expression referring to the clothes apart from the tunic, which the soldiers divided into four shares, one for each of them, and the second referring to the tunic, for which the soldiers cast lots.[80] Yet this problem may be a false one, for two reasons. First, the Hebrew parallelism may not be so tight as to disallow a different referent. E. C. Hoskyns points out that the LXX switches from the plural "clothes" in the first line of Psalm 22:18 to the singular form of the noun in the second line. This might allow distinctive references to the outer clothing and to the inner tunic of Jesus respectively.[81] Second, if the Hebrew parallel is very tight so that both expressions refer to the same inner tunic, then the parallelism would also demand that the verbs ("they divided" and "they cast lots") refer to the same action as well. In other words, the entirety of Psalm 22:18 would refer only to the second portion of what the soldiers did at the foot of the

---

[79]D. A. Carson, *The Gospel According to John* (Grand Rapids: Eerdmans, 1991), p. 613.
[80]E.g., C. K. Barrett asserts that it seems likely John's distinction "arose out of a failure to understand that in the parallel form of Hebrew verse, *himatia* ('clothes') and *chitōna* ('tunic') are to be regarded as synonyms, and not to be distinguished" (*The Gospel According to St John*, 2nd ed. [Philadelphia: Westminster Press, 1978], p. 550).
[81]E. C. Hoskyns, *The Fourth Gospel*, ed. F. N. Davey (London: Faber & Faber, 1947), p. 629.

cross.[82] In either case, John's use of Psalm 22:18 need not be viewed as inaccurate.

The primary interest of John, however, is in viewing the division of Jesus' clothes as the fulfillment of Scripture. He says that the soldiers acted "that the Scripture might be fulfilled." Carson says:

> However customary this merciless bit of byplay was at ancient executions, in the case of Jesus' death it was nothing less than the fulfillment of prophecy: it occurred *that the scripture might be fulfilled*. This does not mean that the soldiers wittingly complied with Scripture, but that God's mysterious sovereignty so operated in the event that it occurred, and occurred just this way, in order to fulfill Scripture.[83]

And in order to give additional emphasis to this point, John follows his quotation of Psalm 22:18 with the statement "So this is what the soldiers did." The combination of the purposive *that* preceding and the resultative *so* following the quotation of Psalm 22:18 shows how clearly the apostle believed that the soldiers' actions truly fulfilled the Old Testament prediction. Regarding this Leon Morris says, "[John] stresses that this is the reason for the soldiers' action. Once again we see his master-thought that God was over all that was done, so directing things that His will was accomplished and not that of puny men. It was because of this that the soldiers acted as they did."[84]

But this emphasis on the fulfillment of Scripture in no way made the actions of the soldiers any less free or any less morally responsible. They acted as they freely chose, and John, under the inspiration of the Holy Spirit, saw their actions as the fulfillment of what God had foreknown and predicted through David the psalmist in Psalm 22:18. Here then is another example of an Old Testament prophetic prediction of the future free actions of human beings.

While Micah 5:2 and Psalm 22:18 and their respective New Testament fulfillments cannot in and of themselves make an airtight case for exhaustive divine foreknowledge of free human actions, I believe they are most plausibly interpreted in light of this model. Thus these and other Old Testament messianic predictions do make a significant contribution to the composite biblical argument for God's foreknowledge of free human actions.

EXCURSUS: PREDICTIVE PROPHECY IN OPEN THEISM

It should be clear from the preceding discussion that the matter of predictive prophecy in Scripture is absolutely crucial in determining the extent of God's

---

[82]Carson, *John,* pp. 613-14.
[83]Ibid., p. 612.
[84]Leon Morris, *The Gospel of John,* New International Commentary on the New Testament (Grand Rapids: Eerdmans, 1971), pp. 809-10.

foreknowledge. It is crucial both because of the massive amount of predictive prophecies found in the Bible and also because of the use that is made in Scripture of predictive prophecies of free human decisions. Especially in Isaiah 40—48 such predictive prophecies are put forward as the supreme evidence of the God-ness and glory of Yahweh. Thus we must ask, How is the phenomenon of predictive prophecy in Scripture accounted for in open theism, with its distinctive denial of God's infallible and exhaustive foreknowledge of free human decisions?

John Sanders begins his treatment of this issue by citing the work of his own doctoral mentor, South African theologian Adrio König. König distinguishes between biblical prophecies (or promises) and biblical predictions (or forecasts), and he articulates two major differences between them.[85]

First of all, predictions or forecasts are very specific with respect to their referent, and thus they either come true or they do not. They come to an end; they are not at all open-ended. And because of this, "these predictions have a limited value, exerting no particular influence on salvation history." Prophecies or promises, on the other hand, are very different. They are fulfilled repeatedly, in ways that exert a decisive influence on redemptive history.[86]

A second difference between prophecies/promises and predictions/forecasts has to do with the nature of their respective fulfillments. Predictions, being specific, come true "in a literal and exact way," while God's prophecies are fulfilled in a "freer manner." We are not able to know in advance the exact form that the fulfillment of a prophecy will take, but we should never naively assume that Old Testament prophecies/promises must literally come true. God is free and is often surprising in the way he fulfills them.[87]

---

[85]Adrio König, *The Eclipse of Christ in Eschatology* (Grand Rapids: Eerdmans, 1989), pp. 183-89. Sanders's treatment of König is found in *God Who Risks,* pp. 125-27.

[86]König writes, "In salvation history, a whole series of 'new' things develop along the lines laid down by repeatedly fulfilled promises. . . . They maintain their energy and character as promises, pointing us decisively to the future. . . . It seems that prophecies cannot be fulfilled completely in this imperfect world. Again and again fulfillment is incomplete, so that the preliminary fulfillment becomes a promise of a yet more glorious fulfillment" (*Eclipse of Christ,* pp. 183-85).

[87]König says, "Predictions come true in a literal and exact way, so that it is possible to say beforehand exactly what should happen. Predicting is a form of history-in-advance. . . . [Prophecies] are fulfilled in a freer manner. No one can deduce from prophecy exactly what shape events will take. In fact, it is not even possible to recognize prophecy's fulfillment without faith in Christ. This is why the Jews could not see Old Testament promises fulfilled in Jesus, even though he fulfilled the entire compass of Old Testament promises. . . . God reserves the prerogative of giving us a fundamental surprise, when he fulfills his promise. . . . Prophecy remains open and that God is free to take us by surprise. The openness of prophecy and its surprising fulfillments fit admirably with the idea of the God of the promises, who places neither himself nor his promises at our disposal. He alone rules over his promises and so over history" (ibid., pp. 185-87).

Sanders agrees, arguing that "prophecies allow room for God to fulfill them in a variety of ways—ways that we cannot anticipate."[88] For example, Old Testament messianic prophecies were fulfilled in the kind of Messiah that no one anticipated. While Peter claims that the Old Testament promise of God's outpouring of the Spirit on the day of the Lord in Joel 2:28-32 was fulfilled at Pentecost, it was fulfilled without many of the specific signs mentioned by Joel (e.g., the moon turning to blood). Amos 9:11-12 is cited by James as being fulfilled in Acts 15:15-18, even though Israel was not literally ruling over Edom. Rather, in a very surprising divine fulfillment, James understands that this promise is fulfilled in the inclusion of the Gentiles into the people of God through faith in Christ. Thus Israel will "rule" over the Gentiles through faith in Jesus. And finally, according to Sanders, the Old Testament promises God made to Abraham concerning a land, a seed and a blessing to the Gentiles are qualified and universalized in the New Testament so that through Jesus, the true seed of Abraham (Gal 3:16), Gentiles can become children of God through faith (Gal 3:29) and can look forward to inheriting a "new earth" and a "new Jerusalem" (Rev 21:1-2).[89] Sanders concludes:

> Clearly God is sovereign over his prophecies and can bring them to fruition in the way he deems best fitted to the particular historical circumstances. [Thus] the promises of God should be understood as part of the divine project rather than as some eternal blueprint, a project in which God has not scripted the way everything in human history will go. God has a goal, but the routes remain open. . . . God is working in the world according to covenant, rather than to a meticulous plan.[90]

These open routes that could possibly lead to the accomplishment of God's goal points to the inherent openness of the future that, according to Sanders and other open theists, can be surprising even to God himself.

I find myself in basic agreement with König and Sanders that God's promises are open to multiple fulfillments and that God is free to surprise us by fulfilling them in ways unanticipated by us. But whether the fulfillment that is surprising to *us* will also be surprising to *God* is another question altogether. The clear implication from Sanders's statement that God has not scripted the way everything in human history will go and that the routes to the accomplishment of that goal remain open is that God himself does not know the specifics of the future completely and exhaustively. And in this Sanders is going well beyond what is necessarily implied by König's analysis of predictions and prophecies. At issue for

---

[88]Sanders, *God Who Risks,* p. 126.
[89]Ibid., pp. 126-27.
[90]Ibid., p. 127.

us is whether the future events of human history, including both those unanticipated and surprising [to us] fulfillments of divine promises and the specific fulfillments of divine predictions, are known in advance by God.[91]

So how does Sanders understand biblical predictions and prophecies? He acknowledges that he follows the thinking of Richard Rice, who argues that biblical prophecy is "a subtle and varied phenomenon," one for which no simple
and uniform model suffices.[92] Indeed, Rice argues that there are three possible
ways to understand biblical predictions.

1. Some biblical predictions are statements of what God intends to do in the
future. God can predict that certain things will happen because he intends to
take direct and unilateral action to make them happen.[93] But this kind of prediction is possible only if God intends to do something "irrespective of creaturely decisions."[94] Rice argues, "If God's will is the only condition required for
something to happen, if human cooperation is not involved, then God can unilaterally guarantee its fulfillment and he can announce it ahead of time."[95]

This is how many open theists understand God's claim in Isaiah 46:10 to
be able to declare the end from the beginning. Rice, for example, argues that
Isaiah 46:11 ("What I have said, that will I bring about; / what I have planned,
that will I do") makes it clear that God's predictions relate to his own activity
(presumably without human cooperation).[96] According to Sanders, these pre-

---

[91]Among the examples of biblical predictions that König cites are 1 Kings 11:29-30 (fulfilled in
1 Kings 12:15-20), 1 Kings 13:1-2 (fulfilled in 2 Kings 23:15-20), 1 Kings 14:1-6 (fulfilled in
1 Kings 14:18; 15:19), 1 Kings 16:1-4 (fulfilled in 1 Kings 16:11-12), 1 Kings 21:17-24 (fulfilled
in 2 Kings 9—10), and 1 Kings 22:17 (fulfilled in 1 Kings 22:29-37). (*Eclipse of Christ*, p. 193).
It should be noted that these predictions are all predictions of freely chosen human actions.
How then could God predict them if he does not possess foreknowledge of them? Thus,
König seems to allow for a kind of divine foreknowledge that Sanders and other open theists
would not.
[92]Rice, "Biblical Support for a New Perspective," p. 51. Rice is not following here the distinction
of König and Sanders between prophecy and prediction. He is using these two terms inter-
changeably. Pinnock also argues that biblical prophecy "is a complex phenomenon," one that
does not necessarily entail exhaustive divine foreknowledge (*Most Moved Mover,* p. 50).
[93]Richard Rice, *God's Foreknowledge and Man's Free Will* (Minneapolis: Bethany House, 1985),
p. 78.
[94]Sanders, *God Who Risks,* p. 130.
[95]Rice, "Biblical Support for a New Perspective," p. 51.
[96]Rice also cites Is 48:3 ("I foretold the former things long ago . . . / I made them known; / then
suddenly I acted, and they came to pass") to argue the same point (*God's Foreknowledge and
Man's Free Will,* p. 78). Pinnock cites these same two texts (Is 46:11; 48:3) to argue for his
contention that "some prophecies announce what God is planning to do and what he will
bring to pass" (*Most Moved Mover,* p. 50). Boyd argues that the scope of Is 46:9-10 is very
limited—speaking of Yahweh's intention to bring the Jews back to their homeland. And so
he argues "we outrun what the passages warrant if we universalize them" (*Satan and the
Problem of Evil,* p. 93).

dictions "do not require [divine] foreknowledge, only the ability [of God] to do it."[97]

2. Rice's second kind of biblical prediction expresses

> God's knowledge of what will occur in the future as the inevitable consequence of factors already present (e.g., Jer 37:6-10). Since God's knowledge of the present is exhaustive, his knowledge of the future must be unimaginably extensive. . . . A skilled physician can predict the death of a seemingly healthy individual because he perceives symptoms that escape the untrained eye. Likewise God may describe apparently unlikely events in the relatively remote future because He knows and understands the present exhaustively.[98]

This is the way Rice understands, for example, God's prediction that Pharaoh would not let the Israelites go when Moses asked him to. Sanders agrees, although he is not nearly as confident as Rice about how certain or "inevitable" Pharaoh's obstinance or the future occurrence of any event so predicted will be.

> Given the depth and breadth of God's knowledge of the present situation, God forecasts what he thinks will happen. . . . God's ability to predict the future in this way is far more accurate than any human forecaster's, however, since God has exhaustive access to all past and present knowledge. . . . Nonetheless, this does leave open the possibility that God might be "mistaken" about some points, as the biblical record acknowledges.[99]

As examples of these "mistaken" predictions, Sanders cites Exodus 3:16—4:9, in which God states his belief that the elders of Israel would listen to Moses. Yet as the conversation goes on, God acknowledges that Moses is correct in suggesting the possibility that they may not believe in him. Sanders also cites Jeremiah 3:6-7 and Jeremiah 19—20, in which God says that he thought the Israelites of Jeremiah's day would return to him but they did not.[100] But Sanders goes on to explain that because these predictions are in fact conditional, they are not in fact "mistakes" in the strict sense of God infallibly declaring that something would come to pass when in fact it did not. It is only

---

[97]Sanders, *God Who Risks,* p. 130. While it is clear that the fulfillment of these kinds of predictions do require that God possess the ability to bring about what he has announced, it is nevertheless hard to see how God's prediction of his own activity in advance does not require at least some kind of divine foreknowledge.

[98]Rice, *God's Foreknowledge and Man's Free Will,* p. 78. Rice's later statement is even stronger: "A prophecy may also express God's knowledge that something will happen because the necessary conditions for it have been fulfilled *and nothing could conceivably prevent it*" ("Biblical Support for a New Perspective," p. 51, emphasis added).

[99]Sanders, *God Who Risks,* pp. 131-32.

[100]Ibid., p. 132. These passages will be examined in chap. 4.

in a secondary, looser sense that God's beliefs about the future could be considered mistaken.[101]

Pinnock declines to use the adjective *mistaken*. Rather, he speaks in the language of precision, claiming that predictions of this type are

> imprecise prophetic forecasts based on present situations, as when Jesus predicts the fall of Jerusalem. Such prophecies are rooted in present situations, for example when God says through Isaiah that Egypt and Assyria will become his people in the future. It is a promise in general terms more than it is a precise prediction. It is often claimed that Ezekiel's prophecy of the destruction of Tyre was fulfilled in detail (Ezek 26:1-21), but that is not so according to Ezek 29:17-20. The city continued to be inhabited right up until Jesus' own day. Nebuchadnezzar did not do to Tyre exactly what Ezekiel had predicted. We have no right to make a prophecy more precise than it is.[102]

Rice acknowledges the possibility of a particular prophecy combining categories 1 and 2. Such is the case, he argues, with the Cyrus prediction of Isaiah 44:28—45:4. It expresses both God's knowledge of what will happen based on present and past factors, and his intention of what he himself will bring about.

> God may have perceived factors that indicated the decline of Babylon and the rise of Persia a hundred years ahead. He also must have known the ancestors of Cyrus and foreseen the possibility of his birth. In addition, God may have been actively involved in bringing events to the place where this prophecy would be fulfilled.[103]

3. The third and final category of biblical predictions involves conditional prophecies. They "express God's intention to act in a certain way if a particular course of action obtains or if people behave a certain way. . . . Their fulfillment depends—or is conditional—upon the way their recipients respond to them."[104] Perhaps the most commonly cited example of a conditional prophecy (cited by

---

[101]Ibid., pp. 132-33.
[102]Pinnock, *Most Moved Mover*, pp. 50-51. In addition, Pinnock cites other examples of prophecies that go unfulfilled: "Joseph's parents never bowed to him (Gen 38:9-10); the Assyrians did not destroy Jerusalem in the eighth century (Mic 3:9-12); despite Isaiah, Israel's return did not usher in a golden age (Is 41:14-20); despite Ezekiel, Nebuchadnezzar did not conquer the city of Tyre; despite the Baptist, Jesus did not cast the wicked into fire; contrary to Paul, the second coming was not just around the corner (1 Thess 4:17); despite Jesus, in the destruction of the temple, some stones were left one on the other (Mt 24:2). God is free in the manner of fulfilling prophecy and is not bound to a script, even his own" (ibid., p. 51, n. 66).
[103]Rice, *God's Foreknowledge and Man's Free Will*, pp. 78-79. But if God declares in Is 46:10-11 that he will summon Cyrus as the bird of prey from the east, then God must know more than just the "possibility" of his birth, and he definitely was actively involved (not just "may have been actively involved") in bringing about the fulfillment of this prophecy.
[104]Ibid., p. 79.

both open theists and classical theists alike) is Jonah's announcement that Nineveh would be destroyed in forty days (Jon 3:4). Yet the promised destruction did not occur because the city's inhabitants repented in response to Jonah's message (Jon 3:10). But open theists argue that the category of conditional prophecies applies more broadly.

> Even "successful" predictions may have been conditional also. It is common for proponents of foreknowledge to apply the category of conditional prophecy *only* to failed predictions and to view all fulfilled predictions as manifestations of exhaustive foreknowledge. But some divine statements regarding the future that came to pass were just as conditional—just as dependent on human response—as those that were unfulfilled.[105]

Open theists argue that the genuineness and integrity of such conditional prophecies would be eliminated if God possessed exhaustive foreknowledge. Sanders asks, "How can a conditional promise be genuine if God already foreknows the human response and so foreknows that he will, in fact, never fulfill the promise?[106] But on the other hand

> If it is true that creaturely decisions are not foreknowable and that reality is open to some extent, then conditional prophecies acquire new integrity. They express genuine divine intentions. They represent invitations to actually change the course of events. At face value, conditional prophecies indicate a real interaction between God and the creaturely world. They imply that what men and women do is indefinite to a significant extent and therefore unknowable until these decisions are made. In contrast, the concept of absolute foreknowledge removes the "if" from (so-called) conditional prophecies. . . . As a result, they detract from the dramatic portrait of God's interaction with the world which the Bible provides.[107]

How should we evaluate these three ways of understanding biblical predictions

---

[105]Sanders, *God Who Risks*, p. 131. For another openness statement about conditional prophecies, see Rice, "Biblical Support for a New Perspective," p. 52. Rice cites fulfilled predictions about Cyrus's aid to the Jews and the destruction of Jerusalem by the Babylonians (e.g., Jer 32:4; 52:12-14) as examples of fulfilled conditional prophecies.

[106]Sanders, *God Who Risks*, p. 131.

[107]Rice, *God's Foreknowledge and Man's Free Will*, p. 80. Rice argues that God's conditional prophecy of the destruction of Nineveh was intended to move the Ninevites to repentance. "Indeed this is the only way to make sense out of it. For if God intends simply to destroy Nineveh, willy-nilly, there was no reason to send Jonah with his announcement. What would that have accomplished? If, however, God intended to destroy Nineveh only if its citizens failed to change their ways, then Jonah's mission becomes intelligible. God wanted to enable and encourage the Ninevites to avert their impending destruction" (ibid., pp. 79-80). The same argument is made by nonopenness authors William Lane Craig, *Only Wise God*, pp. 41-44, and Wayne Grudem, *Systematic Theology* (Grand Rapids: Zondervan, 1994), pp. 164-65.

that are affirmed by Rice, Sanders and other open theists? While many of the
texts cited by open theists will not be examined until chapter four of this book
and so my evaluative comments here will of necessity be provisional, it is my
opinion that given the theological commitments of open theism, none of these
three options, alone or in combination, is adequate to explain the full scope of
biblical prophecy.[108] Let me explain.

Consider Rice's first category of biblical prophecy—God's prior announcements of what he intends to do. Two questions must be raised at this point for
open theists. First, what if something utterly unexpected happens in the future
that would cause God to change his mind about what he had originally intended
to do?[109] Because the God of open theism cannot infallibly know the future free
decisions of humans, the possibility of an utterly unexpected (to God) event or
events always exists. And if God is indeed genuinely responsive to human beings in the give and take of their real relationship, then in principle it is impossible for God to know infallibly what he will do in the future. It is always possible for an unforeseen occurrence to lead God to reconsider his previously
planned and previously announced course of action. And should it occur, it is
certainly possible that a genuinely responsive God would decide to change his
plan. That is, after all, what happened in Nineveh when God reconsidered his
previously announced intention to destroy the city after the Ninevites had repented. God's statement of his intention to bring about judgment included an
implicit, though unstated, condition. But how do we know that other statements
of God's intended future actions are not equally conditional? What about God's
predictions of his Son's first coming? What about his predictions of his second
coming, of final judgment, of the establishment of the new heavens and the new
earth and of the final glorification of all believers? Are these predictions conditional as well? The point I'm trying to make is that the mere statement of the
God of open theism that he will most assuredly do something in the future is
no guarantee that the announced divine action will actually take place. There is

---

[108]For example, Pinnock writes, "A very high percentage of prophecy can be accounted for by
    one of three factors: the announcement ahead of time of what God intends to do, conditional
    prophecies which leave the outcome open, and predictions based on God's exhaustive
    knowledge of the past and the present" ("God Limits His Knowledge," in *Predestination and
    Free Will,* ed. David Basinger and Randall Basinger [Downers Grove, Ill.: InterVarsity Press,
    1986], p. 158). An obvious question for Pinnock is: If "a very high percentage" of prophecy
    can be accounted for in one of these three ways, what is true of the rest? What kind of pre-
    dictions are they? How are they to be accounted for?
[109]We will examine biblical texts in which God is said to have changed his mind in considerable
    detail in chap. 4. For now, it is sufficient to note that this divine repentance or change of
    mind is a crucial part of the openness understanding of God.

always the possibility that an unforeseen event in the future would move this genuinely responsive God to reconsider and do things differently. Thus even God's knowledge of his own future actions is at best probabilistic. There can be no certain predictive prophecies based on the first category.

Second, if the predictions of what God intends to do in the future includes free human decisions (as is the case with the predictions of Cyrus in Isaiah 46:11 and of the birth of the Messiah in Bethlehem announced in Micah 5:2 and so many others) and if God wants to guarantee that he will in fact do what he says he will do, he will have to overrule libertarian freedom to ensure that the future event will take place just as God announced it would. Open theists do affirm that God retains the right to do this and does this on very rare occasions to ensure that his ultimate purposes are accomplished. But if God does overrule libertarian human freedom only very rarely, then category one does not operate very often at all, and thus it is of little help in trying to come to grips with the massive amount of predictive prophecies that involve free human decisions. But if category one does operate frequently enough to help us deal with the volume of biblical prophecies, it does so at the cost of a significant diminishing of libertarian freedom (and consequently, according to open theists, of moral responsibility).

With respect to the second category—viewing biblical prophecies as God's forecasts based on his exhaustive knowledge of the past and the present—another question must be asked. How accurate are God's forecasts? If they are truly accurate (as seems to be implied by Rice), then the future God accurately and truly forecasts is just as fixed and just as certain as it would be if God had infallible foreknowledge.[110] And if the future is fixed and certain, there is no room for libertarian freedom. This problem is exacerbated by Rice's statements of the necessity of those things that God accurately forecasts because the inevitable causal connection between present and past factors (which God exhaustively knows) and the future event. He describes this second category of biblical prophecies, you remember, as being based on "God's knowledge of what will occur in the future as the *inevitable* consequence of factors already present."[111] In his chapter in *The Openness of God,* Rice sharpens this statement even more when he speaks of prophecies that express "God's knowledge of something that will happen because the necessary conditions for it have been fulfilled and *nothing could conceivably prevent it.*"[112] This would certainly account for the ac-

---

[110]John Feinberg, "Response to Clark Pinnock," in *Predestination and Free Will,* ed. David Basinger and Randall Basinger (Downers Grove, Ill.: InterVarsity Press, 1986), p. 168.

[111]Rice, *God's Foreknowledge and Man's Free Will,* p. 77, emphasis added.

[112]Rice, "Biblical Support for a New Perspective," p. 51, emphasis added.

curacy of forecasts made by God. But once again it does so at the cost of the libertarian freedom of a person, which affirms that he or she could always have chosen differently, even in exactly the same set of circumstances. If, in fact, nothing could conceivably prevent an action from occurring, that action most certainly would not be free in a libertarian sense. And if God can so accurately anticipate and predict future human decisions on the basis of his knowledge of the present and the past, doesn't this suggest that the future grows out of the present and the past? Isn't there a latent form of determinism in that understanding?[113] If so, there is no problem with God's knowing and predicting the future. But we would be left, at significant points at least, with a compatibilist rather than a libertarian understanding of human freedom.

Often times, however, to insure that the future is not definite and fixed in such a way as to drastically minimize or even eliminate libertarian human freedom, open theists downgrade God's category-two predictions of the future to beliefs and anticipations about the future that are potentially fallible. By pointing to texts like Jeremiah 3:6-7 and Jeremiah 18—19 Sanders and others affirm that God's beliefs about the future are at times mistaken.[114] This potential fallibility of God's beliefs, anticipations and forecasts of the future does in fact serve to protect the libertarian freedom of human beings and the open character of the future. But these kinds of forecasts hardly seem to match the character of biblical predictive prophecy on which God based his claim to be the only true and living God in Isaiah 40—48. It is hard for me to understand that God would stake his claim to unique deity based on potentially fallible probabilistic forecasts of the future. In reality there is, I would argue, an inverse relationship between the certainty and the functioning of biblical prophecy on the one hand and the openness of the future and the indeterminate character of human freedom on the other. To the extent one is elevated, the other is diminished. Open theists cannot have both in full measure.

Third, consider the case of conditional prophecies. All sides in the foreknowledge debate affirm that this reality exists. But a question must be asked of open theists here as well. If the outcome of a conditional prophecy is truly left open and if God himself does not know what the individuals involved will choose and thus does not know what the outcome of his prediction will be, in what sense can this legitimately be called a prophecy of the future? Isn't it rather God's statement of his best estimate based on his best information of the time?

---

[113]Feinberg, "Response to Clark Pinnock," p. 168.

[114]See Sanders, *God Who Risks,* pp. 74, 205; Boyd, *God of the Possible,* p. 60; Fretheim, *Suffering God,* p. 46. Jer 3 will be examined in more detail in chap. 4.

In other words, isn't this another example of a category-two divine forecast? Or if there is another divine purpose in God's conditional statement (e.g., a divine plea to the Ninevites to repent), why is this necessarily inconsistent with God's full and infallible knowledge of the future response?

My purpose in this discussion is to point out the problems that remain with openness efforts to explain predictive prophecy in Scripture in the absence of God's exhaustive foreknowledge. Three factors are put forward to account for this biblical phenomenon. But given the theological commitments of open theists, I have argued that they are insufficient to explain the massive reality of predictive prophecy in Scripture.

CONCLUSION

In this chapter we have examined Old Testament evidence for exhaustive divine foreknowledge. After beginning with a brief survey of the wide variety of usages of the *yāda ͨ*, the most common Hebrew verb for God's knowledge, we turned our attention to the primary question of this book: *Does God's knowledge of the future involve free human decisions?*

We began to explore this question by looking at Psalm 139. And we saw that God's knowledge extolled in the psalm is indeed vast and rich, and too wonderful for David to fully put into words. And particularly from Psalm 139:4, 16, we saw that God's knowledge does indeed include David's future free decisions. He knows the very words David will speak before they are on his tongue, and he knows the number and the character of all the days of his life before even one of them came to be.

We then turned our attention to a massive feature of the Old Testament portrayal of God—that he is a God who predicts the future. We looked at three categories of predictive prophecy to illustrate this Old Testament theme. First, we looked at a vast and important prediction and fulfillment motif in 1-2 Kings. Both the quantity and the variety of examples of this motif in these books give pervasive evidence to the fact that Yahweh is indeed the Lord of history, the God who announces his purposes in advance and then acts to bring about his will. Second, we looked at the theme of God's foreknowledge and his ability to predict the future in Isaiah 40—48. We saw Yahweh point again and again to his unique ability to do this as conclusive evidence of his "God-ness" over against the pagan gods. The supreme example of God's predictive abilities comes in his predictions of Cyrus (including identifying him by name in Is 44:28—45:1) and the deliverance of the Jewish people that Yahweh would bring about through him. Thus it is clear that God's foreknowledge, to which he appeals so strongly in these chapters, does include his foreknowledge of free hu-

man decisions. It is impossible to stress too highly how important God's foreknowledge of free human decisions is to the argument of Isaiah 40—48. It is
ultimately Yahweh's foreknowledge that show him to be the one true God in
distinction from the idols of the surrounding nations. Finally we looked at the
phenomenon of Old Testament messianic prophecies and focused specifically
on Micah 5:2 and Psalm 22:18. Our examination of these two messianic prophecies revealed that they too embrace a vast number of free human decisions that
are encompassed in their fulfillments at the birth of Jesus the Messiah and at his
death on the cross.

Finally, we looked at the openness understanding of the phenomenon of
biblical prophecy in the absence of God's exhaustive foreknowledge. We examined the three primary ways open theists understand such biblical predictions
and concluded that neither individually nor collectively are these categories of
understanding sufficient to explain biblical prophecy.

The conclusion we have drawn from this chapter is that the Old Testament
presents to us God "who knows" (1 Sam 2:3), who is "perfect in knowledge"
(Job 37:16) and whose "understanding has no limit" (Ps 147:5). This God does
indeed foreknow free human decisions.

The next question before us involves the New Testament. Does the evidence
from the New Testament similarly support the model of exhaustive divine foreknowledge? This is our subject in chapter three.

3

NEW TESTAMENT EVIDENCE
OF DIVINE FOREKNOWLEDGE

W e begin our examination of New Testament evidence concerning the extent of the foreknowledge of God by looking at the specific language of foreknowledge.

THE NEW TESTAMENT LANGUAGE OF FOREKNOWLEDGE

These specific terms are used relatively rarely in the New Testament. The key words for our purposes are the verb *proginōskō* (to foreknow) and the related noun *prognōsis* (foreknowledge).[1] The verb is used five time times in the New Testament. Three of these usages relate to the foreknowledge of God.[2] Twice Scripture speaks of God's foreknowledge of his people—of Israel (Rom 11:2) and the church (Rom 8:29), while the third usage speaks of God's Son, the Lord Jesus Christ, who is the Lamb of God foreknown by the Father before the creation of the world (1 Pet 1:20). Similarly the noun *prognōsis* is used twice to speak of the foreknowledge of God. In 1 Peter 1:2, it speaks of God the Father's foreknowledge of his elect people. And in Acts 2:23 the noun describes God's

---

[1]In addition to these two primary words, two other related verbs deserve brief mention. The verb *prooizō* (to decide beforehand, predestine, preordain) is used six times in the New Testament, in each case with God being the subject (Acts 4:28; Rom 8:29-30 [2x]; 1 Cor 2:7; Eph 1:5, 11). The verb *prooraō* (to see previously [looking back], to foresee or see in advance or, in the middle voice, to see before oneself) is used four times in the New Testament (Acts 2:25, 31; 21:29; Gal 3:8). It is important to note for our purposes that the Gal 3:8 usage, in which Paul says that God's gospel promise to Abraham in Gen 1:23 ["All nations will be blessed through you"] was the result of the Scripture foreseeing *[prooraō]* that God would justify the Gentiles by faith, presupposes that this divine foresight includes not only God's redemptive plan in Christ, but also the free decisions of men and women from all nations to trust Christ and his gospel.
[2]The other two usages of *proginōskō* deal with human knowledge of people and truths that has been known in advance. In Acts 26:5, Paul states at his trial before Agrippa that his Jewish adversaries had for a long time known him and his former pharisaic lifestyle. And in 2 Pet 3:7, Peter says that his readers have already known that the Lord's patience in delaying the second coming of Christ is for the sake of the salvation of those who have yet to believe.

foreknowledge of the handing over of Jesus to death. These final five references to divine foreknowledge are clearly the most relevant for our discussion. They will be the focus of the investigation that follows.

These passages concerning divine foreknowledge have long been a point of contention between Calvinists and Arminians. Our discussion of these texts will enter into that debate at points. But remember, our primary concern is whether or not the extent of God's foreknowledge includes free human decisions.

God's foreknowledge in Acts 2:23. In Peter's Pentecost sermon, he spoke of the death of Christ, saying, "This man was handed over to you by God's set purpose and foreknowledge *[prognōsis]*, and you, with the help of wicked men, put him to death by nailing him to the cross."

What exactly was foreknown by God? Peter says that it was the handing over of Jesus Christ to death. But how did that come about? It is crucial to note what Acts 2:23 affirms—the handing over of Jesus to death is the result of both human sin (note the description of those who put Jesus to death as "wicked") and God's sovereign, redemptive purpose (his "set purpose and foreknowledge").[3] This dual reality has been seen and affirmed by numerous commentators on this passage. For example, John Stott argues that in this text "the same event, the death of Jesus, is attributed simultaneously both to the purpose of God and to the wickedness of men."[4] And I. Howard Marshall says that in Acts 2

> nothing is said to minimize the fact of Jewish guilt in crucifying Jesus (v. 36). Nevertheless, at the same time the crucifixion took place according to the plan and purpose of God (4:28). Here we have the paradox of divine predestination and human freewill in its strongest form. Even in putting Jesus to death, the Jews were simply

---

[3]This dual responsibility for the handing over of Jesus to death can also be seen in biblical texts that use the verb "hand over" *[paradidōmi]*. The gospels point to three individuals or groups that have special responsibility for handing Jesus over to be crucified: Pilate (Mt 27:26), the Jewish religious leaders (Mt 27:18) and Judas Iscariot (Mt 26:14-16). John Stott summarizes: "First, Judas 'handed him over' to the priests (out of greed). Next, the priests 'handed him over' to Pilate (out of envy). Then Pilate 'handed him over' to the soldiers (out of cowardice), and they crucified him" (*The Cross of Christ* [Downers Grove, Ill.: InterVarsity Press, 1986], p. 58). Yet God was not passive and uninvolved in the handing over of his Son to death. Rom 8:32 says that God the Father "did not spare his own Son but gave him up *[paradidōmi]* for us all." Thus it was the will of the Father to surrender him over to death "for us all." And this was as well the voluntary self-surrender of God the Son. In Gal 2:20, Paul speaks of Jesus Christ as "the Son of God who loved me and gave *[paradidōmi]* himself for me."
[4]John R. W. Stott, *The Spirit, the Church, and the World* (Downers Grove, Ill.: InterVarsity Press, 1990), p. 75. See also John B. Polhill, *Acts,* New American Commentary 26 (Nashville: Broadman, 1992), p. 112. Polhill notes that these two themes run throughout Luke-Acts: "On the one hand, Jesus' death follows the divine purpose: Lk 9:22; 17:25; 22:37; 24:26, 44, 46; Acts 17:3. On the other, the guilt of the people is strongly emphasized in the passion narrative: Luke 23:2, 4-5, 20-23, 25, 51" (ibid., n. 111).

fulfilling what God had already determined must take place and indeed had foretold in the prophetic writings.[5]

The key point for our purposes is that the dual assignment of responsibility
for the death of Christ implies that God's foreknowledge in Acts 2:23 includes
both his own redemptive purposes through the death of Christ and the human
sin that was involved in bringing it about.

Much debated is the relationship in Acts 2:23 between God's foreknowledge
and his "set purpose." It is clear that Luke intends us to understand a relationship because he uses one definite article to govern two nouns. But the question
is, what is the nature of that linkage?

Classical Arminian theologians affirm that God's set purpose is formulated in response to free and undetermined actions that he foreknew rather than understanding God's foreknowledge of the death of Christ to occur because he ordained it to
come to pass. For example, Roger T. Forster and V. Paul Marston argue that "God
made his plans in light of what He knew would happen. God's plan to deliver up
His Son to them was made in the knowledge that they would crucify him."[6]

Classical Calvinist theologians, on the other hand, see divine foreordination
in the phrase "set purpose." The noun "purpose" *(boulē)* emphasizes the deliberation and planning undertaken by the one who purposes.[7] When used of
God, *boulē* can refer to God's revealed will and purpose (e.g., Lk 7:30; Acts
20:27) or to his sovereign will (e.g., Eph 1:11, which speaks of God doing all
things according to the *boulē* of his will). The fact that God's *boulē* is "set"
(hōrismenē) in Acts 2:23 points to God's determined resolve to hand over his
Son to death for the redemption of his people. When put together with God's
foreknowledge, the meaning is intensified. Thus G. Schrenk argues that the entire expression ("set purpose and foreknowledge") implies that "this counsel is
predetermined and inflexible. Both phrases emphasize the resolute and deter-
minateness of the decree."[8]

---

[5]I. Howard Marshall, *The Acts of the Apostles,* Tyndale New Testamant Commentary (Grand Rapids: Eerdmans, 1986), p. 75. See also Acts 3:17-18, where Peter attributes the death of Christ
both to the culpable ignorance of the Jews and to God's work of fulfilling prophecy. "Now,
brothers, I know that you acted in ignorance, as did your leaders. But this is how God fulfilled
what he had foretold through all the prophets, saying that his Christ would suffer."

[6]Roger T. Forster and V. Paul Marston, *God's Strategy in Human History* (Wheaton, Ill.: Tyndale
House, 1973), p. 192.

[7]S. M. Baugh cites Acts 27:12, 42; Lk 23:51 in which *boulē* is used to refer to a plan designed
with deliberation to meet a specific problem ("The Meaning of Foreknowledge," in *Still Sovereign,* ed. Thomas R. Schreiner and Bruce A. Ware [Grand Rapids: Baker, 2000], p. 189, n. 31).

[8]G. Schrenk, "βουλή" *Theological Dictionary of the New Testament,* ed. Gerhard Kittel and Gerhard Friedrich, trans. Geoffrey W. Bromiley (Grand Rapids: Eerdmans, 1981), 1:635.

This latter understanding seems to be confirmed by Acts 4:27-28. In their prayer after Peter and John had been released from prison, the believers in Jerusalem affirm:

> Indeed Herod and Pontius Pilate met together with the Gentiles and the people of Israel in this city to conspire against your holy servant Jesus, whom you anointed. They did what your power and will [boulē] decided beforehand [proorizō] should happen.

Again we find the death of Jesus attributed both to human sin (the unholy conspiracy of Herod and Pilate together with the Gentiles and the people of Israel) and to God's foreordaining will. Significant for our purposes is the fact that Luke uses in the same verse both the term *boulē* to describe God's will and the verb *proorizō* to describe the action of his *boulē*. This verb is formed by adding the temporal prefix *pro-* to the verb *horizō*, the verb from which the participle *hōrismenē* in Acts 2:23 is derived. Schrenk draws out the implications of this fact: "Here [Acts 4:28] the *horizō* and *prognōsis,* separated in 2:23, are combined in a single word, thus showing that Luke wishes to emphasize the elements both of impregnability and foreordination."[9] And these linguistic observations must be joined together with the explicit teaching of Acts 4:28 that the very acts of Herod, Pilate, the Gentiles and the Jews to conspire against Jesus and put him to death were *themselves* what God's "power and will decided beforehand should happen." Together these observations from Acts 4:28 confirm the understanding of Acts 2:23 that the events of the death of Jesus Christ, including the sinful actions of handing Jesus over to be killed and conspiring against him, are not outside the sovereign, ordaining purpose of God.[10] This is the "set purpose" of God that Peter links together with God's foreknowledge in Acts 2:23. S. M. Baugh expresses this understanding of the linkage and its implications for the extent of divine foreknowledge:

> We can conclusively infer from Peter's remark that Christ "was delivered over by God's fixed purpose and foreknowledge," that God had clear prescience of all that surrounded Christ's death, not through mere foresight of decisions beyond his control, but because he had determined to bring it about. God's foreknowledge is joined to his will.[11]

---

[9]Ibid.

[10]F. F. Bruce cites Acts 3:18 in addition to Acts 2:23 and Acts 4:28 to indicate "the divinely foreordained character of the death of Christ . . . (its foreordination was attested in prophetic scripture)" (*The Acts of the Apostles*, 3rd ed. [Grand Rapids: Eerdmans, 1990], p. 159). The precise relationship between the sovereign, ordaining purpose of God (which Peter links with the foreknowledge of God) and the sinful acts of human beings is filled with mystery, as is acknowledged by theologians on all sides. For more on this mystery, see chap. 6.

[11]Baugh, "Meaning of Foreknowledge," p. 189.

I find this line of argument convincing, even in light of the difficult and perplexing questions it raises about the relationship of God's sovereign will to sin and evil.[12] But note that Luke, the inspired author of Scripture, is content to affirm the sovereign control of God over the events surrounding the crucifixion of Jesus without precisely describing the nature of that sovereign control or its relationship to the problem of evil. And at the same time, it is very important for our purposes to stress that those who, like Forster and Marston, see the linkage of God's foreknowledge with his set purpose in a very different way still affirm that God foreknew that the opponents of Jesus would crucify him. His foreknowledge includes these free decisions.

Open theists, however, go further in opposing the interpretation I favor. Boyd argues that while the fact of the crucifixion of Christ was foreknown and predestined, the individuals involved and their actions were not.[13]

> While Scripture portrays the crucifixion as a predetermined event, it never suggests that the individuals who participated in this event were predestined to do so or foreknown as doing so. It was certain that Jesus would be crucified, but it was not certain from eternity that Pilate, Herod or Caiaphas would play the roles they played in the crucifixion. They participated in Christ's death of their own free will.[14]

John Sanders also argues that the foreknowledge referred to in Acts 2:23 was not infallible or linked with God's determining will. Rather, it was his anticipation of the freely chosen responses of those individuals into whose hands God delivered his Son.

> It was God's definite purpose (*hōrismenē boulē,* a boundary setting will) to deliver the Son into the hands of those who had a long track record of resisting God's work. Their rejection did not catch God off guard, however, for he anticipated their response and so walked onto the scene with an excellent prognosis (foreknowl-

---

[12]These questions will be discussed further as we go along, especially in chap. 6.

[13]A similar view was set forward in the nineteenth century by the American Methodist theologian, L. D. McCabe. He argued that while the death of Jesus to atone for sin was foreordained by God, the method of crucifixion was not. The choice of that horrific and shameful method of execution was the result of free and sinful decisions of human agents (*The Foreknowledge of God and Cognate Themes in Theology and Philosophy* [1887; reprint, North St. Paul, Minn.: American Reformation Project, 1987], p. 103).

[14]Gregory A. Boyd, *God of the Possible* (Grand Rapids: Baker, 2000), p. 45. See also Boyd's *Satan and the Problem of Evil* (Downers Grove, Ill.: InterVarsity Press, 2001), p. 121. That the individuals involved in the death of Christ participated freely is assumed by the assignment of moral responsibility to them in both Acts 2:23 and 4:27-28. But left unanswered is the nature of that freedom. Boyd clearly assumes that it is libertarian freedom. But in light of the teaching of these texts that God sovereignly determined these actions, I would argue that a compatibilist understanding of human freedom best does justice to these passages.

edge, *prognōsis*) of what would happen. The crucifixion could not have occurred to Jesus unless somehow it fit into the boundaries of what God willed (*boulē*, Acts 2:23, 4:28). But this does not mean that humans cannot resist the divine will. Luke says that the Jewish leaders "rejected God's purpose *(boulēn)* for themselves" (Luke 7:30). God sovereignly established limits within which humans decide how they will respond to God. In this sense God determined that the Son would suffer and die and sent him into a setting in which this result, given the history and character of the covenant people, was quite assured.[15]

But we need to ask, how assured was the death of Christ? Sanders says it was "quite assured," because of the "long track record of resisting God's work" of those involved. But if these individuals possessed libertarian freedom and were not predetermined to act in a certain way, they were free to act contrary to that long track record. They could continue to resist God's will, but they could also decide to follow his will, even if their track record made such obedience unlikely. So again we must ask, how accurate was God's anticipation of their response? How "excellent" was his "prognosis" of what would happen? If it was perfectly accurate and excellent, we once again run into the problem of the fixity of the future that such a divine prognosis would imply, and its impact on libertarian free will. But if God's anticipation was not perfect, and Jesus could have been exonerated and set free by the Jewish and Roman authorities, it is hard to see how this qualifies as divine *prognōsis*.

But Sanders also affirms that God's "fore-anticipation," however accurate it may have been, did not exist far in advance. He argues that Jesus' prayer in Gethsemane that if possible the Father would take this cup from him (Mt 26:39) demonstrates that the future was indeed open to both Jesus and the Father. Prior to Jesus' decision to submit to the will of the Father, no final decision had been made. Christ's death on the cross was not inevitable and certainly not foreknown or planned in advance by the Father. Sanders explains:

> Jesus wrestles with God's will because he does not believe that everything must happen according to a predetermined plan. Even the Son of God must search and seek for the Father's will, for the Son is not following a script but is living in dynamic relationship with the Father. Together they determine what the will of God is for this historical situation. Although Scripture attests that the incarnation was planned from the creation of the world, this is not so with the cross. The path of the cross comes about only through God's interactions with humans in history. Until this moment in history other routes were, perhaps, open. . . . In Gethsemane

---

[15]John Sanders, *The God Who Risks* (Downers Grove, Ill.: InterVarsity Press, 1998), pp. 103-4. In an endnote (p. 301, n. 46) on this point, Sanders cites the view of McCabe, which I have cited in n. 12 of this chap.

Jesus wonders whether there is another way. But Father and Son, in seeking to accomplish the project, both come to understand that there is no other way.[16]

This is a significant revision to the historic Christian understanding of the relationship of the death of Christ to the plan and purpose of God. And I believe that this proposed revision is unsuccessful. It removes from the divine *prognōsis* of Acts 2:23 any meaningful temporal understanding. It leaves the *prognōsis* of God separated and detached from his *hōrismenē boulē* (Acts 2:23) and from its predetermining work (Acts 4:28). It does not take into account the fact that the death of Christ was clearly prophesied in the Old Testament (e.g., Ps 22; Is 53). And finally, it fails to do justice to texts like 2 Timothy 1:9, 1 Peter 1:19-20 and Rev 13:8, all of which argue persuasively that the death of Jesus as the Lamb of God was not only foreknown but foreordained from before the creation of the world.

In summary, we have argued that God's foreknowledge in Acts 2:23 includes his handing his Son over to death and all the events (even those involving free decisions) that were involved in his death on the cross. And God's foreknowledge is effectively linked with his determining will in such as way that the events God foreknew are indeed certain to occur.

God's foreknowledge in Romans 8:29; 11:1. In Romans 8:28-30 Paul says:

And we know that in all things God works for the good of those who love him, who have been called according to his purpose. For those God foreknew *[proginōskō]* he also predestined to be conformed to the likeness of his Son, that he might be the firstborn among many brothers. And those he predestined, he also called; those he called, he also justified; those he justified, he also glorified.

Here we are faced with a different context for the foreknowledge of God. In Acts 2:23 the objects of God's foreknowing are historical events accomplished through both divine and human agency. But in Romans 8:29 the objects of God's foreknowledge are personal ("*those* he foreknew"). And so we are forced to ask, In what sense does God foreknow these people (those who have also been predestined, called, justified and will be glorified). Is this divine foreknowledge factual only?[17] Or does it include a relational dimension as well?

---

[16]Ibid., pp. 100-101.

[17]A purely cognitive, factual understanding of God's foreknowledge in Rom 8:29 would create problems for both classical and open theists. On a nonuniversalist understanding of the text (which I affirm but will not argue for), Rom 8:29 says that God only foreknows certain people (those who are predestined, called, justified and glorified). But classical theists argue that God would have cognitive foreknowledge of everyone. And under openness, presentist understandings, God does not foreknow any person's free decision to trust Christ or not. Neither understanding accounts for what we find in Rom 8—God foreknowing a portion of humanity but not the entire race.

Jack Cottrell's understanding is representative of a classical Arminian approach. He affirms that God's foreknowledge (which Cottrell defines as real cognition of something that actually happens in history) is the means by which God determines which individuals will be conformed to the likeness of his Son.[18] Cottrell argues that the basic condition for being elected is our being in Christ (Eph 1:4). But that comes through faith and similar related conditions (e.g., repentance and baptism). And "having set forth these conditions for being in Christ, God foreknows from the beginning who will and who will not meet them. Those whom he foresees as meeting them are predestined to salvation."[19] Thus what God foreknows is human faith in Christ and which persons will freely choose to exercise such faith. This is clearly a case of God foreknowing free human decisions.

A different and, I would argue, preferable understanding is put forward by Douglas Moo. He argues for a relational understanding of divine foreknowledge in this context, one that includes elements of distinguishing divine choice. Moo sees three primary reasons for his view.

1. It is suggested by the New Testament usage of *proginōskō* and *prognōsis*. Of the four New Testament usages with God as subject (excluding Rom 8:29), Moo argues that all refer to more than prior intellectual cognition. Rather they mean "to enter into relationship with before" or "to choose or determine before" (Acts 2:23; Rom 11:2; 1 Pet 1:2, 20).[20] This usage flows out of the LXX's use of *ginōskō* to translate the Hebrew verb *yāda'* (to know), "when it denotes intimate relationship."[21]

2. Moo notes that the object of the verb is the personal pronoun *hous* ("*those* God foreknew"). Paul is affirming here that God foreknows people, not merely certain facts about them (i.e., whether or not they would trust in Christ at some future point in time). "Paul does not say that God knew anything *about us,* but that he knew *us,* and this is reminiscent of the Old Testament sense of 'know'."[22]

---

[18]Jack Cottrell, "Conditional Election," in *Grace Unlimited,* ed. Clark H. Pinnock (Minneapolis: Bethany House, 1975), pp. 58-59.

[19]Ibid., p. 61.

[20]Douglas J. Moo, *The Epistle to the Romans,* New International Commentary on the New Testament (Grand Rapids: Eerdmans, 1996), p. 532. Previously I argued that God's *prognōsis* does include his prescience of historical events. But, as Moo rightly argues, the connection of God's *prognōsis* with his *hōrismenē boulē* demonstrates that his foreknowledge should be understood to include his "determining before."

[21]Ibid., p. 532, n. 140. In support of this relational sense of *yāda'* Moo cites Gen 18:19, Jer 1:5 and Amos 3:2 as "outstanding examples." Thomas Schreiner concurs, arguing that in these contexts *yāda'* refers to "[God's] covenantal love in which he sets his affection on those whom he has chosen" (*Romans,* Baker Exegetical Commentary on the New Testament [Grand Rapids: Baker, 1998], p. 452).

[22]Moo, *Romans,* pp. 532-33. See John Murray, *The Epistle to the Romans,* New International Commentary on the New Testament (Grand Rapids: Eerdmans, 1968), 1:316-17; Schreiner, *Romans,* p. 452.

3. Moo notes that only some individuals are foreknown by God in Romans 8:29—that is, those who are also predestined, called, justified and glorified by God. Thus there must be a distinguishing characteristic to God's foreknowledge in this sense. If God's foreknowledge does in fact mean "know intimately" or "have regard for," then "this must be a knowledge or love that is unique to believers and that leads to their being predestined. This being the case, the difference between 'know or love beforehand' and 'choose beforehand' virtually ceases to exist."[23]

Yet the verbs *proegnō* ("he foreknew") and *proōrisen* ("he predestined") in Romans 8:29 are not totally identical. Thomas Schreiner notes, "The latter term stressed the preordained plan of God that will certainly come to pass (Acts 4:28; 1 Cor 2:7; Eph 1:5, 11) in accordance with his will. . . . The former has a different nuance in that it highlights his covenantal love and affection for those whom he has chosen."[24]

This understanding of *proginōskō* in Romans 8:29 is confirmed, I believe, by Paul's use of the same verb in Romans 11:2. There the apostle writes, "Did God reject his people? By no means! I am an Israelite myself, a descendent of Abraham, from the tribe of Benjamin. God did not reject his people, whom he foreknew [*proegnō*]."

Here again the objects of divine foreknowledge are personal (God's people, the Israelites). And the context makes clear that God's foreknowledge is not merely precognition of facts about them. Paul contrasts God's foreknowledge of his people (Rom 11:2) with his rejection of them (v. 1). Thus, as Baugh argues, the issue is not ignorance versus previous cognition of God's people but rather absolute rejection versus "a prior, personal commitment to them."[25]

---

[23]Moo, *Romans*, p. 533.

[24]Schreiner, *Romans*, p. 453. Schreiner concludes, "In Rom 8:29, the point is that God has predestined those upon whom he set his covenant affection" (ibid., p. 452). Note the similar conclusion of John Murray. He argues that the phrase *he foreknew* in Rom 8:29 "means 'whom he set regard on' or 'whom he knew from eternity with distinguishing affection and delight' and is virtually equivalent to 'whom he foreloved.' . . . [God's foreknowledge in Rom 8:29] is not the foresight of difference but the foreknowledge that makes differences to exist, not a foresight that recognizes existence but the foreknowledge that determined existence" (*Romans*, 1:317-18). Other interpreters coming to the same basic conclusion include Rudolf Bultmann, who interprets God's foreknowledge here as "an election or foreordination of his people" ("προγινώσκω," *Theological Dictionary of the New Testament*, ed. Gerhard Kittel and Gerhard Friedrich, trans. Geoffrey W. Bromiley [Grand Rapids: Eerdmans, 1981], 1:715), and Judith M. Gundry Volf, who says that "*proginōskein* denotes God's prior choice, not prior knowledge" (*Paul and Perseverance* [Tübingen: J. C. B. Mohr, 1990], p. 9).

[25]Baugh, "Meaning of Foreknowledge," p. 195. Schreiner argues that the immediate context of Rom 11:1-2 confirms that the usage of *proginōskein* is similar to that of Rom 8:29. Both uses do "not merely connote foreknowledge but also implies foreordination, with the emphasis being on God's covenantal love for his people (cf. Amos 3:2; 1 Cor 8:3; Gal 4:9; 2 Tim 2:19)" (*Romans*, p. 580).

In addition, Schreiner argues for a meaning of "selected" for the verb *proegnō* from other factors in the context of Romans 11. These include:

1. Paul's quotation from 1 Kings 19 in Romans 11:2-4. This is Paul's reason for his statement that God had not rejected his people whom he foreknew. He concludes his citation of 1 Kings 19 with the statement "I [God] have reserved for myself seven thousand who have not bowed the knee to Baal." Thus in Elijah's day, God's action is the decisive reason that a remnant is preserved. "So, too, the preservation of Israel in Paul's day is ascribed to God's covenantal foreknowledge, which secures a people for his name."[26]

2. In Romans 11:5, Paul argues that the remnant has been "chosen by grace," which Schreiner says is "merely another way of saying that God has foreknown his people."[27]

3. The wording of Romans 11:2 ("God did not reject his people") is derived from the Old Testament—from Psalm 94:14 and 1 Samuel 12:22. The context of 1 Samuel 12:22 in particular supports an identification of Paul's view of divine foreknowledge with God's election.

> The promise [in 1 Sam 12:22] that God will not forsake his people is grounded in God's election of his people, which is expressed in the words, "because it pleased the LORD to make you a people for himself" (RSV). The idea of the verse [Rom 11:2], then, is that God has not rejected those upon whom he has set his covenantal love. Such an idea is unthinkable and indeed impossible.[28]

All of these reasons strongly argue for a relational understanding of God's foreknowledge in Romans 8:29 and Romans 11:2, one that involves God's choice. But an understanding of divine foreknowledge in this context as involving God's prior intimate, covenant love does not preclude his factual knowledge of his people. If God's foreknowledge is linked to his predestination (Rom 8:29) that his people come to faith in Christ and are ultimately conformed to his image, God's relational foreknowledge also includes his factual foreknowledge of them and their decisions and actions.

Among openness interpreters, Gregory Boyd also adopts a personal and intimate rather than a merely cognitive understanding of God's foreknowledge in

---

[26]Schriener, *Romans*, p. 580.

[27]Ibid.

[28]Ibid., pp. 580-81. Gundry Volf comes to a similar conclusion: "Israel's relationship to God as 'his people' makes their rejection unthinkable. For to be God's people is to be 'foreknown' by God (11:2). Divine foreknowledge refers to God's election in eternity of a people to be set apart for God" (*Paul and Perseverance*, p. 167). Moo also argues that "the 'know' in the verb 'foreknow' refers to God's election. . . . How could God reject a people whom he in a gracious act of choice had made his own?" (*Romans*, p. 674).

Romans 8:29. "In customary Semitic fashion, Paul seems to be using the word *know* to mean 'intimately love.'"[29] But Boyd argues that God's intimately loving foreknowledge is corporate rather than individual.

> We must notice that Paul doesn't specify that God foreknew certain individuals would believe. He simply says, "those whom [God] foreknew he also predestined." In Rom 8:29 Paul is saying that the church as a corporate whole was in God's heart long before the church was birthed. But this doesn't imply that he knew who would and would not be in this church ahead of time. He predestined that all who choose to receive Christ would grow to be in the image of his Son. But whether particular individuals receive Christ and thus acquire this predestined image depends on their free will.[30]

This corporate rather than individual view certainly fits Boyd's openness understanding of the extent of the foreknowledge of God. Individualized foreknowledge of specific persons would be impossible for the God of open theism, given the myriad of free human decisions involved in the birth and ongoing lives of such persons. Under open theism, God could not even know precisely *who* would exist in five, ten, a hundred or a thousand years.

It should be noted that this corporate understanding of God's foreknowledge and predestination is also argued for by scholars who do not hold to an openness position, such as Karl Barth, Robert Shank and William Klein.[31]

So what should we say in response to this "corporate only" view of divine foreknowledge/election in Romans 8:29 and Romans 11:2? Clearly there is, in the broader biblical witness, abundant evidence of God's election of the nation of Israel and of the church as corporate bodies (e.g., Deut 7:7-8; 1 Pet 2:9). But I believe that there are strong reasons to conclude that God's election is not corporate *only,* with no specific individuals foreknown and predestined by God. Consider the following lines of evidence:

---

[29]Boyd, *God of the Possible*, p. 48.

[30]Ibid., pp. 47-48. See also Boyd, *Satan and the Problem of Evil*, pp. 118-19. The corporate understanding of God's election and predestination is also argued for by Richard Rice, "Biblical Support for a New Perspective," in *Openness of God* (Downers Grove, Ill.: InterVarsity Press, 1992), pp. 56-57; Sanders, *God Who Risks*, pp. 101-2, 120-23; and Clark Pinnock, "From Augustine to Arminius," in *Grace of God, the Will of Man* (Grand Rapids: Zondervan, 1989), p. 20.

[31]Barth writes, "An elect man is in any case elect in and with the community of Jesus Christ. . . . The people of Israel is elect in its Messiah, Jesus, and the Church in its Lord, Jesus. Thus every election of individuals is an election in the sphere of the community—on the basis of the fact that this sphere is both established and marked out in the election of Jesus Christ" (Karl Barth, *Church Dogmatics* 2/2, trans. Geoffrey W. Bromiley [Edinburgh: T & T Clark, 1957], p. 410). See also Robert Shank, *Elect in the Son* (Springfield, Mo.: Westcott, 1970), pp. 45-55, 154-55), and most recently William W. Klein, *The New Chosen People* (Grand Rapids: Zondervan, 1990).

1. With regard to Romans 8:29-39, the plural pronouns in these verses (*hous*, "those whom") are easily explained by the fact that Paul was writing this letter to a church, a corporate entity. But this corporate entity was made up of individual believers, to whom Paul wanted to provide confidence and assurance, even as Paul derived such confidence for himself in Rom 8:38-39. Moo says rightly of the corporate view, "Whatever might be said about this interpretation elsewhere, it does not fit Rom 8:28-29 very well. Not only is there nothing said here about 'in Christ' or the church, but the purpose of Paul is to assure individual believers—not the church as a whole—that God is working for *their* good and will glorify *them*."[32]

2. It is clearly true that in Romans 9, Paul uses two Old Testament quotations to support his argument for God's election of his people that in their original contexts are explicitly corporate (Gen 25:22, quoted in Rom 9:12; and Mal 1:2-3, quoted in Rom 9:13). But this chapter also contains many textual pointers to the reality of an individual election by God along with his corporate election. These pointers include Paul's ongoing use of singular pronouns, nouns and participles in Romans 9:15, 16, 18, 19 and 21 to denote specific individuals whom he has chosen and on whom he has mercy.[33] In addition, Paul stresses in Romans 9:6-9 that God has selected some out of the larger elect body of corporate Israel. This is the crux of the argument Paul gives in Romans 9:6-29 for his thesis that God's salvific word of promise had not failed (v. 6). If Paul was only concerned with the corporate election of Israel, without any regard to the individuals within that chosen group, the logic of his argument fails completely. To be sure, the "spiritual" Israel (v. 6), "Abraham's children" (v. 7) and "the children of the promise" who are in fact "God's children" (v. 8) are all designations of a smaller group chosen out of a larger group. This is also true of the "remnant chosen by grace" (Rom 11:5). But the fact that Paul identifies himself as a mem-

---

[32]Moo, *Romans*, p. 533.

[33]In Rom 9:15, Paul uses singular pronouns in his quotation of Ex 33:19: "I will have mercy on whom (*hon*) I will have mercy and I will have compassion on whom (*hon*) I will have compassion." Rom 9:16 also contains the singular. God's mercy does not depend on "the man who wills (*tou thelontos*) or the man who runs (*tou trechontos*) but on God who has mercy" (NASB). Rom 9:18 once again uses the singular, "Therefore God has mercy on whom (*hon*) he wants to have mercy, and he hardens whom (*hon*) he wants to harden." So also Rom 9:19, "One of you will say to me: 'Then why does God still blame us? For who (*tis*) resists his will?'" And finally, in Rom 9:21, Paul continues his relentless use of the singular when he speaks of God making one vessel (*skeuos*) for honorable use and another for common use. Looking at this abundant evidence, Schreiner concludes, "Those who say that Paul is referring only to corporate groups do not have an adequate explanation as to why Paul uses the singular again and again in Romans 9 ("Does Romans 9 Teach Individual Election unto Salvation?" in *Still Sovereign*, ed. Thomas R. Schreiner and Bruce A. Ware [Grand Rapids: Baker, 2000], p. 99).

ber of the remnant that has been saved (Rom 11:1) shows that he is not thinking of corporate groups only. Paul is an individual who is part of the faithful remnant who experiences God's salvation in Jesus. Schreiner concludes, "The election of the remnant to salvation and the election of the individuals who make up that remnant are not mutually exclusive. They belong together."[34]

3. With respect to Romans 11:2, the context of this verse demands that the object of God's foreknowledge is the nation of Israel as a whole. It is the national entity whose spiritual status has been called into question by Romans 9:30—10:21. It is the nation about whom Paul asks, "Did God reject his people?" (Rom 11:1). And it is the nation of Israel as a whole that is the object of God's election in Romans 11:28.[35] Yet the corporate election pointed to in these verses stands side by side, in Paul's thought, with his election of specific Jews (and Gentiles) for salvation (Rom 9:6-29). For Paul, the relationship of corporate and individual election is not either-or but rather both-and. This is evidenced once again by Paul's reference to himself in Romans 11:1 as an individual Israelite who is a believer in Jesus and thus constitutes part of the elect remnant.[36]

4. With regard to the related passage Ephesians 1:4-5, openness theologian Richard Rice writes, "God elects Christians by virtue of their connection to Jesus, the principle object of election."[37] In this he is following Barth's view of election as primarily Christocentric, that God elects his Son, the Lord Jesus, first and foremost and then the corporate body of those who are in him.[38] But it is important to note that the text does not say that God chose Christ. Rather it says that God chose "us" *(hēmas)* in him before the creation of the world. The verse thus stresses the election of people in Christ rather than the election of Christ himself. And in addition I would argue that the "corporate only" understanding of the election of Ephesians 1—the election of all those who are in Christ, with the factor determining whether any particular individual is a part of that group being his or her undetermined faith—goes against the specific teaching of Ephesians 1:5 (which says that Christians have been predestined to be adopted as

[34]Ibid.
[35]C. E. B. Cranfield, *A Critical and Exegetical Commentary on the Epistle to the Romans* (Edinburgh: T & T Clark, 1975), p. 545. See also Schreiner, *Romans*, p. 626; Moo, *Romans*, pp. 674-75; Gundry Volf, *Paul and Perseverance*, pp. 169-70.
[36]On the dual reality of God's election of Israel as a whole, which guarantees national blessings and benefits but not necessarily the salvation of every individual within that nation, and his election of specific Israelites (and specific Gentiles) that guarantees their salvation, see Calvin *Institutes* 3.21.5-7.
[37]Rice, *God's Foreknowledge and Man's Free Will*, p. 91.
[38]Karl Barth, *Church Dogmatics* 2/2, p. 117. For a helpful critique of Barth's view, see Paul K. Jewett, *Election and Predestination* (Grand Rapids: Eerdmans, 1985), pp. 47-56.

God's children "in accordance with *his* pleasure and will" rather than in accordance with our faith) and Ephesians 1:11 (which says that we have been chosen and predestined "according to the plan of *him* who works out everything in conformity with the purpose of *his* will").

In conclusion, Paul's teaching on divine foreknowledge in Romans centers on God's intimate, personal, electing, covenantal knowledge of his people. The context determines whether Paul is thinking primarily corporately (Rom 11:2) or individually (Rom 8:29). But when the corporate emphasis exists, it does not eliminate the individual emphasis or vice versa. The two emphases stand together. The link that Paul makes between God's foreknowledge and his predestination in Romans 8:29 is reminiscent of the connection Peter makes between God's set purpose and his foreknowledge in Acts 2:23. And while God's foreknowledge in Romans is personal rather than being purely factual, it certainly includes his prior factual knowledge of the kind we saw to be evidenced in Acts 2:23.[39]

God's foreknowledge in 1 Peter. Peter speaks of God's foreknowledge two times in 1 Peter 1. He uses the noun *prognōsis* in 1 Peter 1:2 to describe his readers. They are God's elect, strangers who are dispersed throughout Asia Minor "who have been chosen according to the foreknowledge *[prognōsin]* of God the Father, through the sanctifying work of the Spirit, for obedience to Jesus Christ and sprinkling by his blood."

First Peter 1:2 is very similar to Romans 8:29 in that the objects of God's foreknowledge are persons, his chosen people, and that God's foreknowledge is seen to be the basis *(kata)* of his electing choice.[40] Often Arminian interpreters understand this verse to mean that God's choice of an individual to be saved is based on his foresight of that person's faith.[41] This is the same understanding of God's foreknowledge and its relationship to his election and predestination that Arminian interpreters affirm in Romans 8:29. And many of the same arguments against such an understanding of God's foreknowledge that we have already surveyed are applicable here as well. Perhaps most to the point in 1 Peter 1:2 is that human faith is best seen here as part of our "obedience to Jesus

---

[39]Baugh is surely correct when he argues, "This . . . is not to say that God's foreknowledge is devoid of intellectual content; to have a personal relation with someone, such as a marriage relation, includes knowledge about that person" ("The Meaning of Foreknowledge," p. 194).

[40]Murray J. Harris, "Prepositions and Theology in the Greek New Testament," *New International Dictionary of New Testament Theology,* ed. Colin Brown (Grand Rapids: Zondervan, 1986), 3:1201. Harris renders 1 Pet 1:2 as saying that God's election of his people is "based on *(kata)* the foreknowledge of God, is effected by *(en)* the sanctifying work of the Spirit, and aims at or achieves *(eis)* obedience and the constant sprinkling of the blood of Jesus Christ."

[41]See Forster and Marston, *God's Strategy,* pp. 195-204; and Cottrell, "Conditional Election," pp. 57-62.

Christ."[42] And Peter says that we were chosen for *(eis)* such obedience, not because of it.

Later, in 1 Peter 1:19-20, Peter uses the verb *proginōskō*. He says that Jesus Christ, "a lamb without blemish or defect," whose precious blood has redeemed his people, "was chosen [lit. foreknown] before the creation of the world, but was revealed in these last times for your sake."[43] Once again the object of God's foreknowledge is personal, in this case his eternal Son.[44] This foreknowledge could hardly be understood as prior cognition of Christ's faith or any other action or attribute of his. Rather, as is the case in Pauline usage, the divine foreknowledge refers to a previous loving commitment (between members of the Trinity) and the Father's predetermination to bring redemption to his people through his Son.[45] Wayne Grudem says:

> In this context, it would make little sense to say merely that God *knew* Christ before the creation of the world. Rather, the immediately preceding context with its emphasis on Christ's redeeming death suggests that it is as *a suffering Savior* that God "foreknew" or thought of the Son before the creation of the world. These considerations combine to indicate that the "foreknowledge" was really an act of God in eternity past whereby he determined that his Son would come as the Savior of mankind.[46]

These factors lead us to understand God's *prognōsis* of his chosen people in 1 Peter 1:2 in the same way we did in Romans 8:29 and Romans 11:2. God's foreknowledge is lovingly personal and can be described in the words of Baugh as his "eternal commitment to individuals[47] as part of his determination to bring

---

[42]Michaels understands "obedience" in 1 Pet 1:2 to have a similar meaning to the Pauline phrase "the obedience of faith" in Rom 1:5; 16:26 (J. Ramsey Michaels, *1 Peter*, Word Biblical Commentary [Waco, Tex.: Word, 1988], p. 11).

[43]In addition to the NIV, note the translations of the NRSV ("he was destined"), the AV ("foreordained") and the NEB ("predestined").

[44]While the subject of the foreknowledge of Christ is not explicitly mentioned by Peter, it must be God the Father since Christ was foreknown "before the creation of the world."

[45]Baugh says that "this foreknowledge expresses a loving committed relationship between the members of the Trinity, and is given in vs. 20 to emphasize the precious character of the redeeming blood and its efficacy to bring us to faith" ("Meaning of Foreknowledge," p. 196).

[46]Wayne Grudem, *1 Peter*, Tyndale New Testament Commentary (Grand Rapids: Eerdmans, 1990), p. 85.

[47]Robert Shank understands God's foreknowledge in 1 Pet 1:2 to comprehend individuals, "but only within the context of the corporate election of the Israel of God" (*Elect in the Son*, 1 p. 53). The corporate dimension of God's election is clearly evident in 1 Peter (e.g., 1 Pet 2:9). But as in Romans, the reality of corporate foreknowledge/election does not eliminate the possibility of individual foreknowledge/election. 1 Pet 2:7-8 seems to point to God's individual election and predestination, both of those who believe and those who do not. In addition, Jack Cottrell sees the specific geographic locations of these elect believers identified in 1 Pet 1:1 to indicate that God's foreknowledge/election of them is individual. ("Conditional Election," p. 58).

them to faith and to all the glories and benefits of Christ's work."[48] Leonhard Goppelt highlights the predetermination inherent in God's foreknowledge here when he says that it is "not knowledge beforehand but predetermination, which is effective as election."[49]

Conclusion. Our survey of the New Testament use of the language of divine foreknowledge has shown us that this is a multifaceted reality. Three strands of meaning stand out. First, God's foreknowledge of his people (Rom 8:29; 11:2; 1 Pet 1:2) and of Christ (1 Pet 1:20) is intensely personal, involving his covenant commitment of love to them from before the creation of the world. Second, God's foreknowledge is so connected with his omnipotent will that the future occurrence of what he foreknows—both historical events brought about by divine and human agency (Acts 2:23) and the destiny of his people (Rom 8:29; 11:2; 1 Pet 1:2) and of Christ (1 Pet 1:20)—is assured. Acts 2:23 specifically links God's foreknowledge with his set purpose, and Romans 8:29 links this divine foreknowledge with his predestination. Thus in these contexts, what God foreknows will most assuredly occur. Third, while God's loving, personal foreknowledge of his people certainly involves far more than prior cognitive awareness of them, it does in fact have factual content. This is certainly part of his overall relationship with his people. Acts 2:23 specifically speaks of God's foreknowledge of the sinful actions involved in the death of Christ. Thus in the New Testament, as in the Old Testament, God's foreknowledge does in fact embrace free human choices.[50]

DIVINE FOREKNOWLEDGE AND PRAYER

Two times in Matthew 6, Jesus refers to the knowledge of God the Father in his exhortations to his disciples to pray. In Matthew 6:31-32, we read "So do not worry, saying 'What shall we eat?' or 'What shall we drink?' or 'What shall we wear?' For the pagans run after all these things, and your heavenly Father knows that you need them."

---

[48]Baugh, "Meaning of Foreknowledge," p. 196. Note the conclusion of Edmund Clowney, "The expression *foreknowledge* does not mean that God had information in advance about Christ, or about his elect. Rather it means that both Christ and his people were the objects of God's loving concern for all eternity" (*Message of 1 Peter* [Downers Grove, Ill.: InterVarsity Press, 1989], p. 33).

[49]Leonhard Goppelt, *A Commentary on 1 Peter,* ed. Ferdinand Hahn, trans John E. Alsup (Grand Rapids: Eerdmans, 1993), p. 73. J. N. D. Kelly says that for Peter, "God's foreknowledge is much more than knowing what will happen in the future; it includes . . . his effective choice" (*A Commentary on the Epistles of Peter and Jude,* Black's New Testament Commentaries [London: Adam and Charles Black, 1969], p. 42-43). See also Edwin Blum, *1 Peter,* Expositor's Bible Commentary 12 (Grand Rapids: Zondervan, 1981), p. 219.

[50]This threefold understanding of God's foreknowledge was initially suggested to me by a student at Trinity Evangelical Divinity School, Paul Alexander.

In this passage Jesus gives two reasons why his disciples should not be filled with anxiety and worry. The first reason is that obsessive worry about food, drink, clothing and the like is pagan ("for the pagans run after all these things).[51] Gentiles, who are outside the family of God, and thus cannot look to a heavenly Father to provide for them, must seek to provide all these things by their own effort and out of their own resources. Thus worry is natural for them.[52] But this should not be the case with the children of God. For they have a heavenly Father, and he knows what they need. This is the second reason Jesus gives. Thus ongoing attitudes of worry are "an affront to God who knows the needs of his people."[53] And when this divine knowledge of our needs is combined with the sovereign grace and mercy of our heavenly Father, and if the logic of Jesus' previous argument (from lesser to greater) holds, then our anxious worry "can only result from lack of genuine belief in God's goodness and mercy."[54] When Jesus' disciples give themselves over to anxious worry about the necessities of life, they are acting no differently than godless pagans, not at all reflecting their true status as children of the all-knowing heavenly Father.

In Matthew 6:7-8 the nature of God's knowledge of our needs is clarified. Jesus says to his disciples, "And when you pray, do not keep on babbling like pagans, for they think they will be heard because of their many words. Do not be like them, for your Father knows what you need before you ask him." Again the Father's knowledge of our needs is emphasized, grounding Jesus' efforts to motivate his disciples to pray simply and sincerely to God. He contrasts this kind of prayer with that of the pagans, who believe that the value of their prayers is in direct relationship with the volume of words they utter.[55] This is not to be the case with disciples of Jesus. They are to pray with confidence to their all-knowing heavenly Father. Just as our heavenly Father's lov-

---

[51]D. A. Carson notes that the verb translated "run after" *(epizētousin)* is a strengthened form of the verb translated "seek" *(zēteō)* in v. 33 ("seek first [God's] kingdom and his righteousness"), perhaps denoting an intensification of their pursuit into an anxious obsession (*Matthew*, Expositor's Bible Commentary 8 [Grand Rapids: Zondervan, 1984], p. 181).

[52]Leon Morris, *The Gospel According to Matthew* (Grand Rapids: Eerdmans, 1992), p. 163.

[53]Carson, *Matthew*, p. 181.

[54]Craig Blomberg, *Matthew*, New American Commentary 22 (Nashville: Broadman, 1992), p. 126.

[55]As an example, see 1 Kings 18:26-29. Morris writes, "The Gentiles think of prayer as effective only if long. They agree that God hears and answers prayer, but hold that he does so in proportion to their wordiness" (*Matthew*, p. 142). Robert Gundry says that this pagan babbling "may denote meaningless or repetitive speech, as in the extensive listing of divine names by pagans. They hoped that at least one of the names might prove effective for an answer. (It was thought that knowing the name of a god and pronouncing it correctly gave a certain power to manipulate the god)" (*Matthew*, 2nd ed. [Grand Rapids: Eerdmans, 1994], pp. 103-4).

ing desire to give good gifts to his children is meant to motivate us to pray (Mt 7:7-11), so here the fact that our Father already knows our needs before we ask is to motivate and shape our praying. As Morris comments, "Before [Jesus' disciples] offer any prayer, he knows exactly what their need is. They pray, not to inform the Father on matters of which he is ignorant, but to worship him."[56] Thus their prayer is "an expression of trust in a Father who already knows one's needs and merely waits for his children to express their dependence on him."[57]

Note the future orientation of this divine knowledge. Jesus says that the Father knows our needs *before* we ask him. Thus Gundry says it is "the Father's *foreknowledge* of the disciples' needs [that] makes wordiness unnecessary."[58]

But some might object to understanding God's knowledge here to be foreknowledge. All that Jesus says is that the Father knows our needs before we ask. But our needs may very well exist before we ask God to meet them (or even know of them ourselves). Thus it could be the case that what God knows are needs that we currently have before we bring them to God in prayer. In that case, his would be a marvelously comprehensive knowledge of the present circumstances of his children, but not foreknowledge.

In response, I believe that the context of Matthew 6 does not support the elimination of a future aspect to God's knowledge. Jesus' affirmation of the Father's knowledge is meant to move his disciples to prayer, and, especially in Matthew 6:32, to turn to prayer as an antidote to anxiety. But what are we *not* to worry about? Matthew 6:25, 31 specify things like food, drink and clothing. But are these only present concerns? The parallel command in Matthew 6:34 ("Do not worry about tomorrow") puts a future orientation to the issue of worry versus prayer for the disciples of Jesus. Certainly we are not to worry but rather to pray about our present needs and concerns (cf. Mt 6:11, "Give us today our

---

[56]Morris, *Matthew*, p. 142. Note the comment of John Calvin, "Believers do not pray with the view of informing God about things unknown to him, or of exciting him to do his duty, they pray in order that they may arouse themselves to seek him, that they may exercise their faith in meditating on his promises, that they may relieve themselves from their anxieties by pouring them into his bosom; in a word, that they may declare that from him alone they hope and expect, both for themselves and for others, all good things" (*Commentary on a Harmony of the Evangelists* [1558; reprint, Grand Rapids: Baker, 1979], 1:314).

[57]Craig S. Keener, *A Commentary on the Gospel of Matthew* (Grand Rapids: Eerdmans, 1999), p. 213.

[58]Gundry, *Matthew*, p. 104, emphasis added. Matthew uses the verb *oida* to speak of God's knowledge as opposed to *ginōskō*. Yet, as Heinrich Seesemann notes, *oida* "can be synonymous with *ginōskō*; . . . in the *Koine*, it is hard to establish any distinction in meaning" ("οἶδα," *Theological Dictionary of the New Testament*, ed. Gerhard Kittel and Gerhard Friedrich, trans. Geoffrey Bromiley [Grand Rapids: Eerdmans, 1979], 5:116).

daily bread").[59] But this does not eliminate the importance of praying about our future needs. These too are to be entrusted to God in prayer in obedience to Jesus' command not to worry about tomorrow (Mt 6:34). Thus the needs the Father knows we have (Mt 6:32) even before we ask him (Mt 6:8) include our future needs. This means that the Father's knowledge of our needs does indeed include his foreknowledge.

But for our discussion the question still needs to be asked, Does this foreknowledge of the Father include free human decisions? A moment's reflection will indicate that our future needs are shaped and determined by a whole host of free human decisions or potential free decisions. Take, for example, the issue of whether I will have enough food to eat at some point in the future. The answer to that is in part determined by what appear at first glance to be nonhuman factors like the weather (e.g., will there be a drought or not?). Yet even here, there certainly exists the possibility that freely chosen human actions might influence the weather (e.g., the use of fossil fuels that contribute to global warming). And there are a myriad of other human decisions that will enter into the equation as well. Will there be a war that will interfere with the supply of food? Will I decide to get and to keep a job to earn the income to buy food? Will an employer hire me? And on and on. Thus, if God knows in advance what all our needs will be, he must know all the free decisions (and potential free decisions) that will shape those needs. It is not enough to simply say that God knows our general human needs (e.g., food), without knowing each disciple's individual and specific needs. For if Jesus intends for our prayers to be the antidote to worry and anxiety, and if our confidence in these prayers is to be grounded in God's knowledge of our needs, then this divine knowledge must be as individual and specific as our potential anxieties. The logic of Jesus' argument seems to demand that God knows our needs in individual specificity and detail, including all the free decisions that are involved in shaping and determining those needs. And if, as this passage clearly seems to imply, God also knows in advance what will best meet those needs, there are a whole host of other free decisions he must know. Therefore, I believe that the kind of divine foreknowledge that Jesus is appealing to here in the Sermon on the Mount does include God's foreknowledge of free human decisions.

But this is the very kind of divine foreknowledge that open theists argue makes petitionary prayer superfluous and irrelevant. This is a serious charge,

---

[59]The meaning of the phrase "daily bread" is much debated. Keener concludes helpfully, "Whether one asks for 'today's' bread or 'tomorrow's,' the prayer stresses that the requester needs it 'today' " (*Gospel of Matthew*, p. 221).

one we will examine in great detail in chapter six. But for now the crucial point is that in the Sermon on the Mount, Jesus specifically appeals to the Father's foreknowledge, including his foreknowledge of free human decisions, to encourage and motivate his disciples to a life of prayer.

THE FOREKNOWLEDGE OF JESUS

Jesus' predictions of his Passion. Each of the four Gospels describes Jesus' foreknowledge of his upcoming death and resurrection.[60] Perhaps the most explicit statement from Jesus recorded in the Gospel of John comes in John 2:19-22, where Jesus predicts the tearing down and the raising up of his body in three days. But Jesus' predictions of his own Passion are more explicit in the Synoptic Gospels, and thus we will devote our attention to them.

In each of the Synoptic Gospels, we find Jesus uttering three major, explicit predictions of his Passion and resurrection. They serve as landmarks in the unfolding narrative, relentlessly pointing ahead to Jesus' inescapable mission in Jerusalem that he would accomplish in obedience to the Father's will. In addition, they serve as "preparatory interpretations of the event of the passion."[61] There are significant contextual similarities: the first prediction in each Synoptic Gospel follows Peter's confession of Jesus as the Messiah; the second follows Jesus' transfiguration and subsequent exorcism; and the third prediction follows the discourse with the rich young man.[62] And with the exception of Luke 18:35-43, these predictions are followed by a discussion of discipleship, stressing the

---

[60]The foreknowledge of Jesus is relevant to our discussion of divine foreknowledge because of the nature of Jesus Christ as fully divine and fully human. Assumed throughout this volume is a Chalcedonian Christology in which the divine and human natures of Christ are united in one person "without confusion, without change, without division, without separation." Chalcedon also affirmed that in the one person of Christ "the characteristics of each nature [are] preserved" (*Documents of the Christian Church,* ed. Henry Bettenson, 2nd ed. [New York: Oxford University Press, 1980], p. 51). This means that when Jesus was speaking from his divine nature, any foreknowledge he displayed is truly divine foreknowledge. But the possibility exists that Jesus, in making his various predictions, was speaking from his human nature. Yet in such case, he was doing so as a prophet of God, indeed as *the* prophet "like Moses" who was promised in Deut 18:15 (cf. Acts 3:22; 7:37). This corresponds to Jesus' own statements that his teaching comes from the Father and that he speaks only what the Father commands him to speak (e.g., Jn 7:16; 8:28; 12:49-50; 14:24). Thus the foreknowledge Jesus evidences in his predictions is divine foreknowledge as well.

[61]H. E. Tödt, *The Son of Man in the Synoptic Tradition,* trans. Dorothea M. Barton (Philadelphia: Westminster, 1965), p. 145. Yet as Tödt notes, in none of the passion predictions in Mark is the soteriological significance of the death of Christ mentioned (ibid., p. 201). This comes to the fore in the ransom saying of Jesus in Mk 10:45.

[62]Matthew inserts the parable of the workers in the vineyard (Mt 20:1-16) between the dialogue with the rich young man (Mt 19:16-30) and Jesus' third passion prediction (Mt 20:17-19).

reality of future rejection and vindication for the disciples as well as for Jesus.[63] For reasons of space, I will quote only the Markan predictions.

[Jesus] then began to teach them that the Son of Man must[64] suffer many things and be rejected by the elders, chief priests and teachers of the law, and that he must be killed and after three days rise again. (Mk 8:31; par. Mt 16:21; Lk 9:22)

The Son of Man is going to be betrayed into the hands of men. They will kill him, and after three days he will rise. (Mk 9:31; par. Mt 17:22-23; Lk 9:44)

We are going up to Jerusalem, . . . and the Son of Man will be betrayed to the chief priests and teachers of the law. They will condemn him to death and will hand him over to the Gentiles, who will mock him and spit on him, flog him and kill him. Three days later, he will rise. (Mk 10:33-34; par. Mt 20:17-19; Lk 18:31-33)

While the first prediction is more specific than the second in that it identifies those who would reject the Son of Man, the third is clearly the most specific of all.[65] Not only does Jesus mention the officials who will reject him, he also states that they will condemn him and hand him over to the Gentiles to be mocked, spit on and flogged prior to being killed. And the Matthean form of the third prediction specifies crucifixion as the method of execution (Mt 20:19).[66]

The key question for our purposes is whether these Passion predictions evidence Jesus' foreknowledge of the freely chosen actions of those who would betray him, condemn him, mock him and ultimately kill him.

Those who argue against such a conclusion note that the initial predictions found in Mark (8:31; 9:31) are quite vague, and the more specific details come only in the third prediction (Mk 10:33-34). This has led to the argument that the

---

[63]Hans F. Bayer, "Predictions of Jesus' Passion and Resurrection," in *Dictionary of Jesus and the Gospels,* ed. Joel B. Green and Scot McKnight (Downers Grove, Ill.: InterVarsity Press, 1992), p. 631.

[64] Tödt interprets the "must" *(dei)* of Mark 8:31 as a divine must that comes "by way of Scriptural prophecy" *(The Son of Man,* p. 191). The *dei* should also be seen in terms of what John Murray calls the "consequent absolute necessity" of the death of Christ *(Redemption: Accomplished and Applied* [Grand Rapids: Eerdmans, 1955, 1977], p. 12). The death of Jesus became necessary only after God's free decision to redeem sinners. But once that decision was freely made, the cross of Christ became absolutely necessary, for there was no other way for God to justly and righteously save sinners. Thus the *dei* of Mark 8:31 comes not only from the necessity that Scriptural prophecy be fulfilled, but also from God the Father's eternal redemptive purpose and God the Son's whole-hearted commitment to be obedient to that will.

[65]Robert Gundry writes that in Mk 10:33-34 "the power of Jesus to predict even the details of his passion comes to full flower" *(Mark* [Grand Rapids: Eerdmans, 1993], p. 572).

[66]William Lane argues that the crucifixion would be presupposed by Mark since Gentiles were specifically identified as those who carried out the execution. Given the circumstances of the Roman occupation, this seems reasonable *(The Gospel of Mark,* New International Commentary on the New Testament [Grand Rapids: Eerdmans, 1974], p. 376).

current canonical form of the third Passion prediction (and to some extent the first two as well) is the result of a post-Easter redaction of an earlier, much more vague prediction of Jesus of an impending crisis event. Ferdinand Hahn, for example, regards the third Passion prediction as "a sheer redactional development," "invented by the evangelist" as "an expansion on Mark 9:31."[67] Vincent Taylor says, "In its precision the third [prediction] is a *vaticinium ex eventu* (a prediction coming out of the event)."[68] And Raymond Brown has noted:

> The disciples who are supposed to have heard these predictions do not seem to have foreseen the crucifixion even when it was imminent nor to have expected the resurrection (Luke 24:19-26 is typical of the attitude found in all the Gospels). One may attribute this failure to the slowness of the disciples, but one may also wonder if the original predictions were as exact as they have now come to us.[69]

Several arguments have been given, however, against this understanding. (1) The precise details of Mark 10:34 are not in the same order as they are recorded as fulfilled in Mark 15:15-20. In fact, they are just the reverse. In the prediction the order of events is mocking, spitting and flogging before death and resurrection. In the fulfillment, the order is flogging, spitting and mocking before death and resurrection.[70] (2) The vocabulary of the prediction does not conform to that of the fulfillment. One would think that an attempt after the fact to craft a "prediction" statement to fit Mark's version of the actual events would result in greater conformity of order and vocabulary. But such is not the case.[71] (3) The more precise details of Mark 10:34 are paralleled in Isaiah 50:6 and Psalm 22:7.[72] (4) None of the details of the predictions were utterly foreign to Jesus or his contemporaries. Jeremias argues that Mark 10:33-34 "contains no feature which

---

[67]Ferdinand Hahn, *The Titles of Jesus in Christology* (London: Lutterworth, 1969), p. 37.

[68]Vincent Taylor, *The Gospel According to St. Mark* (New York: St. Martin's Press, 1959), p. 437.

[69]Raymond E. Brown, "How Much Did Jesus Know?—A Survey of the Biblical Evidence," *Catholic Biblical Quarterly* 29, no. 3 (1967): 14. Sanders cites Brown's statement in support of his own conclusion that Jesus' rather vague predictions do not require exhaustive divine foreknowledge (*God Who Risks*, pp. 134-35).

[70]See Lane, *Gospel of Mark*, p. 375; and C. E. B. Cranfield, *The Gospel According to St. Mark* (Cambridge: Cambridge University Press), p. 335.

[71]Tödt gives an extensive analysis of what he calls the "train of terms" in the three passion predictions in Mark. From his analysis he concludes that none of the three predictions came ultimately from the Markan passion narrative (*Son of Man*, pp. 201-2). Note also Bayer's conclusion, "Detailed comparisons between the third Markan passion and resurrection prediction (Mk 10:33b-34) and the Markan passion narrative (see esp. Mk 14:43-44; 14:64; 15:1; 15:20, 31; 14:65; 15:19; 15:15; 15:24; 16:6) shows that both in terms of the sequence of events and in word usage the third passion prediction precedes the very old Markan passion narrative" ("Predictions of Jesus' Passion," p. 632).

[72]Cranfield, *Gospel According to St. Mark*, p. 335; and Lane, *Gospel of Mark*, p. 375.

could not normally be expected in capital proceedings against Jesus when we take into account the state of the law and execution customs."[73]

While these considerations do argue against the necessity of viewing these Passion predictions as post-Easter redactions, the last two in particular could also be seen as arguing against these predictions being examples of divine foreknowledge. The eighteenth-century Methodist theologian L. D. McCabe, for example, argued that these prophecies made by Christ about his own death "do not at all conflict with the denial of the foreknowledge of the free choices of accountable beings." He argues that the necessity of Jesus being crucified results from God's willingness to modify his own plan concerning the death of his Son to allow for the contingent choices of free moral agents as to the method of execution.[74] More recently, Sanders has argued for the same conclusion, citing Jeremias's arguments.[75]

Robert Gundry's responses to this kind of argument are very helpful. He argues that while Jesus' words may well show that he meditated on Isaiah 53:6 and Psalm 22:7, and applied these passages to himself, "such self-application does not necessarily follow from meditation, and, more importantly, the supernatural element remains if the prediction came true in detail—unless we are to think of a fulfillment purely by chance."[76] And Gundry argues that there is good reason to dispute the suggestion of Jeremias that the details of the predictions were readily foreseeable.

> The progression from Jewish to Gentile hands, from a capital sentence at the hands of the Sanhedrin through mockery, including spitting as well as flogging, to execution at the hands of the Gentiles is not so usual and therefore not quite so easy to foresee as this estimate makes it out to be.[77]

But even if the details and sequence of events articulated in the predictions were foreseeable, the fact the events occurred just as predicted requires an explanation.[78] Unless we are willing to affirm that the fulfillment occurred by

---

[73]This reality, argues Jeremias, "constitutes a warning to be cautious with a judgment of *'ex eventu'*" (Walter Zimmerli and Joachim Jeremias, *The Servant of God*, trans. Harold Knight [Naperville, Ill.: Alec R. Allenson, 1957], p. 100, n. 459). Cranfield also argues similarly. "There is no feature which could not readily have been foreseen as likely to happen in the carrying out of a death sentence under the circumstances of the times" (*Gospel According to St. Mark*, pp. 334-35).

[74]McCabe, *Foreknowledge of God*, pp. 106-9.

[75]Sanders, *God Who Risks*, p. 134.

[76]Gundry, *Mark*, p. 575.

[77]Ibid.

[78]The difference in order of events recorded in the prediction and events recorded in the fulfillment does not negate the remarkable agreement in what was predicted and what actually happened. It still is the case that what Jesus predicted did come to pass.

pure chance, three other options are open to us. The first is that this was in
fact a prediction arising out of divine foreknowledge of what would happen
to Jesus, as of all other free human decisions. The second option is that this
is a prediction arising out divine foreknowledge of this particular event because the individuals involved in bringing this about have already been so
shaped by prior free decisions that their actions are in fact determined. And
the third option is that Jesus proved to be an excellent prognosticator, whose
ability to anticipate the probabilities of future events is quite remarkable. The
second of these options will be discussed in more detail below with regard to
Peter's denial of Christ. The third option seems more unlikely in light of the
specificity of the predictions, and the additional evidence of other predictions
made by Jesus that we will consider presently. The conclusion that our present
discussion leads us to is that the most likely option is the one that is consistent
with our discoveries about the extent of the foreknowledge of God from the
Old Testament. The God of Scripture does indeed foreknow free human decisions, and such divine foreknowledge is the foundation of Jesus' predictions
of his upcoming death.

Jesus' predictions of the behavior of his disciples. The Gospels record
Jesus' predictions of certain key actions of his disciples. How are these predictions to be understood? Do they and their subsequent fulfillment demonstrate divine foreknowledge of free human actions? To answer these questions, we will concentrate on Jesus' predictions of Peter's denial and Judas'
betrayal.[79]

Jesus' prediction of Peter's denial. In each of the four Gospels Jesus predicts
Peter's denial of Christ.[80] Each prediction occurs in the context of Peter's rash
statement of (over)confidence that he would never deny Christ. Mark records
two such pronouncements by Peter, with Jesus' prediction of his denial sandwiched in between. After Jesus had predicted that all of his disciples would fall
away in accordance with Zechariah 13:7:

Peter declared, "Even if all fall away, I will not."

---

[79] In addition to Jesus' prediction of Peter's denial and Judas' betrayal, Jesus also predicted that
all of his disciples would forsake him (Mt 26:31; Mk 14:27). These predictions were fulfilled
in Mt 26:51 and Mark 14:50.

[80] Peter's denial of Christ is predicted in Mt 26:33-35; Mk 14:29-31; Lk 22:31-34; Jn 13:36-38.
These predictions are fulfilled in Mt 26:69-74; Mk 14:66-72; Lk 22:54-62; Jn 18:17-27. For a
helpful comparison of the four accounts of Jesus' prediction and the minor variations in them,
see Raymond E. Brown, *John XIII-XXI*, Anchor Bible 29a (Garden City, N.Y.: Doubleday,
1970), pp. 615-16. Brown concludes, "This was probably a saying of Jesus [that] has been
passed in slightly variant forms" (ibid., p. 616).

"I tell you the truth," Jesus answered, "today—yes, tonight—before the rooster crows twice,[81] you yourself will disown me three times."

But Peter insisted emphatically, "Even if I have to die with you, I will never disown you." (Mk 14:29-31)

It is important to see that this prediction (and the parallels in the other Gospels) includes details of when Peter would deny Christ (this very night before the cock crows [twice]) and how many times he would deny Christ (three times). Yet do these specific details and their subsequent fulfillment just as Jesus said mean that Mark and the other Gospel writers composed their predictions after the fact? Cranfield cautions against such a conclusion, arguing that the prediction of Mark 14:30 "cannot be explained as a *vaticinium ex eventu:* the early Church would hardly have created a prediction which aggravated the baseness of Peter's denial, even for the sake of showing that Jesus was not surprised."[82]

Luke adds one other detail to the prediction. Just prior to his prediction of Peter's threefold denial, Jesus described the spiritual attack Peter would undergo:

"Simon, Simon, Satan has asked to sift you as wheat. But I have prayed for you, Simon, that your faith may not fail. And when you have turned back, strengthen your brothers."

But [Peter] replied, "Lord I am ready to go with you to prison and to death."

---

[81]Each of the three other versions of Jesus' prediction envisions only one crowing. Cranfield notes that the "two" *(dis)* of Mk 14:30 is omitted by "a good many authorities" (e.g., ℵ , C*, D , W). Yet the corresponding phrase "the second time" *(ek deuterou)* in 14:72 is only omitted by a few authorities. Thus Cranfield argues that the omission of *hois* in 14:30 in some manuscripts "is probably assimilation to Matthew or Luke" (*Gospel According to St. Mark*, p. 439). See also Lane, *Gospel of Mark*, p. 510, n. 64. J. D. M. Derrett argues that the omission of the references to the two cock crowings in some manuscripts is owing to the efforts of the early church to "whitewash" the account, for it would not have Peter ignoring the warning of the first cock crowing to continue with his denials. ("The Reason for the Cock-Crowings," *New Testament Studies* 29, no. 1 [1983]: 142-44). David Brady agrees, arguing that this constitutes strong internal evidence for the originality of Mark's double cock crowing. "What therefore was compressed into one final cock-crow by the other evangelists was remembered by Peter as a more protracted and awesome event involving an early warning (in the first cock-crow), a hardening of conscience, and a persistence in denial engendering the greater guilt. What perhaps had been softened by the other evangelists on Peter's account, is told by Peter himself in all its horrific fullness as a testimony to his own weakness and ultimately as a testimony to the depths of Christ's mercy in his restoration" ("The Alarm to Peter in Mark's Gospel," *Journal for the Study of the New Testament* 4 [1979]: 53-54). For a contrary argument, asserting that the shorter form found in Matthew and Luke is most likely original, see John W. Wenham, "How Many Cock-Crowings? The Problem of Harmonistic Text-Variants," *New Testament Studies* 25, no. 4 (1979): 524.

[82]Cranfield, *Gospel According to St. Mark*, p. 429.

Jesus answered, "I tell you, Peter, before the rooster crows today, you will deny three times that you know me." (Lk 22:31-32)[83]

Thus immediately prior to Jesus' specific prediction of Peter's denials that would result from this Satanic sifting, Jesus also predicted Peter's ultimate repentance from his sin ("when you have turned back") and the nature of his future ministry ("strengthen your brothers").[84] John Piper describes Jesus as having "absolute knowledge *that* Peter would sin, *how often* he would sin, *when* he would sin, and *that he would repent.*"[85]

But this "absolute" foreknowledge did not remove Peter's moral responsibility for his actions. That he was morally guilty is shown by the Gospel writers when, after his denials, Peter is recorded to have wept bitterly as he remembered the words of Jesus' prediction (Mk 14:72, par. Mt 26:75; Lk 22:62).[86] But moral responsibility before God comes only through actions that one undertakes freely.[87] Thus if Peter was morally guilty for denying his Lord, it was because he chose to deny Christ freely. And therefore Christ's foreknowledge of Peter's denials, reflected in his very specific predictions, is in fact divine foreknowledge of free human actions.

But open theists do not agree with my analysis. They argue that Jesus' prediction of Peter's denial is not the result of exhaustive divine foreknowledge.

---

[83]Luke's text shifts from a second person plural pronoun ("Satan has asked to sift you *[hymas]*") to a second person singular pronoun ("But I have prayed for you *[sou]*"). While all the disciples are the intended objects of Satan's attack, Peter himself is the object of Jesus' intercession. But in light of Christ's command to Peter ("strengthen your brothers"), the ultimate purpose of Christ's prayer includes the strengthening of all the disciples. Obviously Peter's faith did fail temporarily during his denials. But the goal of Jesus' prayer is that this failure would not be permanent and final, or in the words of I. Howard Marshall, that "Satan would not be able to totally destroy Peter's faith [and] the process of sifting would not lead to its intended [by Satan] end" (*The Gospel of Luke,* New Internation Greek Testament Commentary [Grand Rapids: Eerdmans, 1978], p. 821).

[84]Luke's verb here is *epistrephō.* Joel Green notes that this is a commonly used verb in Luke-Acts for repentance; cf. Lk 17:4; Acts 3:19; 9:35; 11:21; 14:15; 15:19; 26:18, 20 (*The Gospel of Luke,* New International Commentary on the New Testament [Grand Rapids: Eerdmans, 1997], p. 773, n. 113.)

The reference to Peter's future ministry of strengthening his brothers is an imperative, but in context it is clearly prophetic as well. Luke's linking of Peter's future ministry with his denials calls to mind John's linkage between the risen Christ's threefold commissioning of Peter to ministry (Jn 21:15-17) and his threefold denial (Jn 18:15-18, 25-27).

[85]John Piper, "Why the Glory of God Is at Stake in the 'Foreknowledge' Debate," *Modern Reformation* 8, no. 5 [1999]: 41-42.

[86]Piper notes, "Peter did not say, 'Well, you [Jesus] predicted this sin, and so it had to take place, and so it can't have been part of my free willing, and so I am not responsible for it.' He wept bitterly. He was guilty and he knew it" (ibid., p. 42).

[87]All sides in the current debate agree on this, though they differ widely as to the nature of this freedom (libertarian or compatibilist).

Rather, Peter's denials were predictable behavior that could be inferred by Jesus from his exhaustive knowledge of the present and the past. Sanders points to three crucial factors that led Jesus to his prediction: (1) Jesus knew that Judas had already left to hand Jesus over to the authorities; thus he knew the kind of evil things that will soon begin to happen.[88] (2) Just prior to this, Luke records the disciples disputing among themselves as to who was the greatest (Lk 22:24). This meant that they were not in the best spiritual condition to respond success-fully to coming events. (3) Jesus told Peter of the impending spiritual attack from Satan on him and the other disciples (Lk 22:31). Following this comes Jesus' pre-diction of Peter's denial. Thus, Sanders argues, the prediction does not come out of the blue, but "it is on the basis of Jesus' knowledge of the situation that he makes his prediction regarding Peter's denial."[89]

Sanders also notes that in Matthew and Mark, Peter responds to Jesus' pre-diction with a strong protest.[90] He infers from this that Peter did not believe that Jesus' predictions were infallibly predestined to occur. And immediately after the prediction, Jesus urges his disciples to pray so that they might be able to resist temptation (Mt 26:40-41). Yet they fell asleep, thus making themselves even more vulnerable to a sinful lack of trust in God in the midst of the coming crisis. Sanders concludes:

> In light of these factors, I understand Jesus' prediction of Peter's denial to be a con-ditional one based on his knowledge of Peter's spiritual state and the situation at hand. In this case the "prediction" serves as a warning to Peter: Unless he takes some important steps he will fail. Jesus knows both the forces arrayed against him and his disciples as well as the disciples' spiritual unpreparedness for the forthcom-ing crisis. If Peter and his fellow disciples had followed Jesus' instructions to pray, they would have been prepared for temptation and the prediction might not have come about. However, Peter failed to pray and did succumb, so the conditional prediction was fulfilled.[91]

Boyd also understands Jesus' prediction to come from his divine knowledge of Peter's character and of the specific circumstances he was in.

---

[88]In Lk 22:3-6 (par. Mt 26:14-16; Mk 14:10-11), Satan had entered the heart of Judas (cf. Jn 13:2), and he had negotiated an agreement with the Jewish authorities to hand Jesus over to them. Jesus had predicted Judas's betrayal prior to his prediction of Peter's denial (Mt 26:21-25; Mk 14:18-21; Lk 22:21-22; Jn 13:21-27).

[89]Sanders, *God Who Risks*, p. 135.

[90]Mt 26:35 and Mk 14:31. Jesus' prediction in Matthew and Mark is sandwiched between two statements of Peter's brash (over)confidence. In Lk 22:33, Peter's statement of confidence comes between Jesus' statement of the upcoming spiritual attack and his prediction of Peter's denials, and in Jn 13:37, it comes before Jesus' prediction.

[91]Sanders, *God Who Risks*, p. 135.

Sometimes we may understand the Lord's foreknowledge of a person's behavior simply by supposing that the person's character, combined with the Lord's perfect knowledge of all future variables, makes the person's future behavior certain. . . . We do not need to believe that the future is exhaustively settled to explain this prediction. We only need to believe that God the Father knew and revealed to Jesus one very predictable aspect of Peter's character. Anyone who knew Peter's character perfectly could have predicted that under certain highly pressured circumstances (that God could easily orchestrate), he would act just the way he did.[92]

Several questions need to be asked, however, of this openness analysis. First, consider Boyd's statement "the person's character, combined with the Lord's perfect knowledge of all future variables, makes the person's future behavior certain." How, we may ask, is this "certainty" of future behavior consistent with libertarian freedom? One of the hallmarks of such freedom is that under any given set of internal and external circumstances, a choice between competing options is still possible. It is not necessary for anything to be different for a moral agent with libertarian freedom to choose differently. But if, according to Boyd, Peter's decision to deny Christ was "certain," given his character and the circumstances he was in, then his was not a free decision in the libertarian sense. And if the presence of libertarian freedom is the necessary prerequisite for genuine moral responsibility, Peter's "non-free" decision was one he was not morally responsible for. Does Boyd really want to affirm that Peter was not morally guilty for denying Christ?

Second, many if not most of the "highly pressured circumstances" surrounding Peter's denial, which Boyd claims God could "easily orchestrate," involved free human decisions (e.g., the betrayal of Judas, the fleeing of the other disciples so that Peter was alone, the three questions asked of Peter). For God to "orchestrate" all these factors, he would have to overrule human freedom on many, many occasions. This surely seems to be a different scenario than the very rare occasions of such divine overruling usually posited by open theists.[93]

Third, if God could (and evidently did) "orchestrate" all these circumstances as to make it certain that Peter would deny Christ, then it seems that God was actively entrapping Peter into sin—three distinct times. If so, one of the major

---

[92]Boyd, *God of the Possible,* p. 35. In *Satan and the Problem of Evil* Boyd presents an openness construction of Jesus' foreknowledge of Peter's denial utilizing God's middle knowledge of what he calls "might-counterfactuals" (pp. 130-32).

[93]Boyd seems to back away from these implications: "We do not know how much, if any, supernatural intervention was employed in God's orchestration of the events of that evening. But the outcome was just as he anticipated" (ibid., p. 36). But regardless of the amount of supernatural intervention that might or might not have been involved, it is the certain outcome guaranteed by God's orchestration that is inconsistent with libertarian freedom.

benefits claimed for open theism (i.e., its ability to handle the problem of evil) evaporates in this case. For if the divine orchestration of the surrounding circumstances that would make Peter's denials certain involves God's use of nonconstraining causes on Peter and the other human agents involved, the situation Boyd envisions is identical to what compatibilists affirm (that human freedom is compatible with divine determinism, so long as the causal factors God uses are nonconstraining). And Boyd would be in exactly the same position as compatibilists are in dealing with the problem of evil in this case. But if the causal forces God uses to orchestrate these circumstances were constraining (which no compatibilist would affirm), then Boyd would have even more significant difficulties with respect to the problem of evil, and he would have no way of accounting for Peter's moral guilt. This in no way minimizes the significant difficulties that compatibilists have in grappling with the implications of divine determinism and human sin. But Boyd and other open theists who agree with him here are in every bit as difficult a situation.[94]

Fourth, neither the analysis of Boyd or Sanders adequately deals with the specificity of Jesus predictions. The specific details include when Peter would deny Christ (this very night, before the cock crows), how many times he would deny him (three times), and that Peter would later repent of his denials. This makes it very implausible to understand Jesus' prediction as merely a probabilistic forecast based on his (or God the Father's) knowledge of Peter's character and the circumstances or a conditional prophecy that may or may not come true. The latter option seems especially unlikely when considered in light of the use Jesus makes of his predictions of Peter's denial and Judas's betrayal in John 13:19.

Jesus' prediction of Judas's betrayal. All four Gospels record the betrayal of Jesus by Judas Iscariot, one of the Twelve.[95] The three Synoptic Gospels tell how Judas plotted with the Jewish leaders to have Jesus arrested. They were concerned to arrest Jesus without a riot (Mt 26:5; Mk 14:2; Lk 22:2). At his own initiative Judas offered to solve their problem by leading them to the Garden of Gethsemane, where he knew they could find Jesus (Jn 18:1-2). Judas's arrangement with the Jewish leaders is recorded in Matthew 26:14-16,

---

[94]Refer to chap. 6 for more discussion on this difficult issue.

[95]A helpful survey of the biblical data concerning Judas is found in David John Williams, "Judas Iscariot," *Dictionary of Jesus and the Gospels,* ed. Joel B. Green and Scot McKnight (Downers Grove, Ill.: InterVarsity Press, 1992), pp. 406-8. On Judas, see Roman B. Halas, *Judas Iscariot* (Washington, D.C.: Catholic University of America Press, 1946); Albert Nicole, *Judas the Betrayer* (Grand Rapids: Baker, 1957); and William Klassen, *Judas* (Minneapolis: Fortress, 1996).

Mark 14:10-11 and Luke 22:3-6. Both Matthew and Mark describe Judas's arrangement immediately after the anointing of Jesus. Gundry understands Matthew to be showing how Jesus' own interpretation of his anointing ("When she poured this perfume on my body, she did it to prepare me for my burial" [Mt 26:12]) is starting to be fulfilled.[96] All three Synoptic accounts record that Judas was promised (or given) money, which reflects Judas's character as a thief (Jn 12:6). Matthew alone specifies the amount of money exchanged, thirty pieces of silver. The specific amount calls to mind the Old Testament context of Zechariah 11, in which thirty pieces of silver is viewed as a paltry amount. Carson comments, "That Jesus is lightly esteemed is reflected not only in the betrayal but in the low sum agreed on by Judas and the chief priests."[97] The actual betrayal of Jesus by Judas—his leading the Jewish authorities to Gethsemane and identifying Jesus with a kiss, resulting in his arrest—is recorded in Matthew 26:47-50, Mark 14:43-45, Luke 22:47-48 and John 18:2-4.[98]

---

[96]Gundry, *Matthew,* p. 522. He comments further, "Matthew stresses the fulfillment of Jesus' prediction, not Judas' motives, which remain obscure. Disappointment in Jesus' failure to satisfy political expectations of the Messiah, jealousy, avarice, and loss of face (cf. John 12:4-8) are possible motives" (ibid.).

[97]Carson, *Matthew,* p. 528.

[98]The primary New Testament verb used in the Judas accounts is *paradidōmi*. William Klassen understands the verb to mean "to hand over," without any necessary negative connotations of betrayal (*Judas,* pp. 47-58). This leads him to understand Judas as a friendly informer who "hands Jesus over" to the Jewish authorities in an effort to bring about reconciliation (ibid., pp. 62-76). Klassen argues, "It is certainly possible that Judas became convinced, after discussion with Jesus himself, that an opportunity to meet with the high priest and those in authority in the Temple needed to be arranged." This is due to Jesus' own teaching that when a fellow Jew sinned, he should be confronted directly (Mt 18:15-20; Lk 17:3). Jesus had followed this approach with Peter (Mt 16:23) and with James and John (Lk 9:56). Perhaps Judas thought he could serve as a mediator to enable such a meeting to take place. "He may have thought that, by meeting Temple authorities, Jesus could become better disposed toward the traditional way in which changes were made in the Temple and that Caiaphas could get a better understanding of the reform program Jesus had in mind for the renewal of Israel" (ibid., p. 69). Judas felt that Jesus had sanctioned his mission ("What you are about to do, do quickly" [Jn 13:27]). Klassen concludes, "Neither Judas nor Jesus was prepared for God's new way of achieving victory, but each of them carried out their part, and God's purpose was achieved through them. It is unfair to blame Judas for the role he played, just as it would be to blame Jesus for his. Each played his part with an uncertain script and with no assurance of how the drama would come out. Just as Jesus in the last analysis obeyed his Father, so Judas also obeyed his master. Their integrity and the integrity of their actions is not for us to judge, since we are beneficiaries of their actions" (ibid., p73). Sanders quotes approvingly Klassen's understanding of Judas and his actions, saying that "Klassen's exegetical study of the Judas narratives demonstrates that Judas was not 'betraying' Jesus" (*God Who Risks,* pp. 98-99). My own treatment of the biblical portrayal of Judas will show significant differences from the views of Klassen and Sanders.

But the Gospels testify that this act of betrayal was foreknown by Jesus. Judas is introduced from the beginning as one of the Twelve, chosen by Jesus (Mt 10:4; Mk 3:19; Lk 6:16). Yet in each passage Judas is identified as the one who would betray Christ.[99] Jesus also knew when he would be betrayed. In Matthew 26:2 he says, "As you know, the Passover is two days away—and the Son of Man will be handed over to be crucified." Each of the Synoptics records Jesus' prediction that Judas would betray him (Mt 26:20-25; Mk 14:18-21; Lk 22:21-23). In each case the prediction occurred at the Last Supper, as Jesus was eating the Passover meal with his disciples. Matthew's version reflects this Synoptic tradition.

> When evening came, Jesus was reclining at the table with the Twelve. And while they were eating, he said, "I tell you the truth, one of you will betray me."
>
> They were very sad and began to say to him one after the other, "Surely not I, Lord?"
>
> Jesus replied, "The one who has dipped his hand into the bowl with me will betray me. The Son of Man will go just as it is written about him. But woe to that man who betrays the Son of Man! It would be better for him if he had not been born.
>
> Then Judas, the one who would betray him, said, "Surely not I, Rabbi?"
>
> Jesus answered, "Yes, it is you." (Mt 26:20-25)

There are several elements of this passage that are worthy of comment. (1) Jesus' prediction moves from general to specific. To the Twelve, Jesus says first of all, "One of you will betray me." At this point, it could be any of them, as evidenced by their questions to Jesus in verse 22. Jesus' second statement, "The one who has dipped his hand into the bowl with me will betray me," is no less general. For all who were eating with Jesus would have dipped their hands into the bowl with him. Jesus' point here seems not to specify the one particular individual who would betray him, but to highlight the fact that the betrayer "is a friend, someone close, someone sharing the common dish, thus heightening the enormity of the betrayal."[100] The specific identification comes in Matthew 26:25, in which Judas asks specifically if it is he, and Jesus re-

---

[99]In each Synoptic account, Judas's name is listed last among the Twelve. Rice notes, rightly, the tendency to look at a person's life in light of the single most dramatic or memorable event that happened, especially if it occurred at the end. "The Gospel references to Judas seem to reflect this tendency. When he is listed with the disciples, his name always appears last, along with a reference to his future treachery. For the other disciples, Judas was always 'the one who would betray Jesus,' from the very beginning of his ministry. This was the single most impressive thing about the man, and it colored every recollection of him" (*God's Foreknowledge and Man's Free Will,* p. 97). Whether this explains Jesus' predictions of Judas's treachery is another question.
[100]Carson, *Matthew,* p. 534.

sponds, "Yes, it is you."[101] (2) The interaction between Jesus and Judas in Matthew 26:25 likely took place quietly, as is suggested by John 13:27-28. Blomberg notes that if verse 25 was a private conversation, it would mean that Judas was sitting next to Jesus, in one of the two most-favored positions, either on his right or his left. This would speak to the love Jesus had for the one he knew would betray him, and his efforts to try to dissuade Judas from his course of betrayal.[102] (3) Jesus' words in verse 24 affirm both the definite certainty of Judas's betrayal and the grave moral guilt incurred by the one who betrayed his Master. The certainty of the betrayal is owing both to the necessity of the fulfillment of Scripture ("The Son of Man will go *just as it is written about him*") and to the sovereign, redemptive decree of God ("The Son of Man will go *as it has been decreed*" [Lk 22:22]).[103] Yet this divine necessity does not invalidate the freedom and moral responsibility of Judas, for Jesus pronounces a woe on him.[104] Carson writes:

---

[101]Judas's question and Jesus' response are unique to the Matthean account. Jesus' response, *su eipas* (translated by the NIV as "Yes, it is you") is the same response Jesus will give to the high priest in Mt 26:64. Carson says that this answer is basically affirmative, "but it depends somewhat on spoken intonation for its full force." He argues that spoken by Jesus, "it is enough of an affirmation to give Judas a jolt without removing all ambiguity from the ears of the other disciples" (ibid., p. 535). Blomberg notes that this "ambiguous affirmative" also gives an opportunity for Judas to withdraw from his course of treachery before it was too late (*Matthew*, p. 389, n. 17). He also says that the form of the statement, "You said [it]," may well hint that Judas has indicted himself (ibid., p. 389). Gundry agrees, saying that by this "qualified affirmative," Jesus "heightens the guilt of Judas by implying that he already knows the affirmative answer to his question, which therefore lacks sincerity. Woe to the hypocrite!" (*Matthew*, p. 527).

[102]We will see this same phenomenon again in John 13:26. The tension between Jesus' foreknowledge of Judas's certain betrayal (expressed repeatedly in this text) and his efforts to persuade Judas to change directions clearly exists here. In Mt 26:24 we see another similar, though not identical, tension between the certainty of Judas's betrayal to fulfill Scripture and the woe Jesus pronounces on the betrayer. Clearly there is an awesome complexity in Jesus' relationship to the Judas that the Gospel writers record without explanatory comment.

[103]Neither Matthew nor Mark cites any specific Old Testament quotation to explain "as it is written about him." Blomberg argues that Jesus is probably alluding to the various suffering servant texts of Is 42—53. (*Matthew*, p. 389). Carson also sees the possibility of a reference to a text like Dan 9:26 or to an entire prophetic typology such as the Passover lamb (*Matthew*, p. 534).

"As it has been decreed" clearly reflects the predetermined character of the death of Jesus. Marshall notes that *horizō* ("decreed") is a characteristic term of Luke (cf. Acts 2:23; 10:42; 11:29; 17:26, 31), which in the passive is "a circumlocution for divine activity" (*Gospel of Luke*, p. 809). Green comments that "Jesus' affirmation [in Lk 22:22] of the underlying aim of God provides reassurance that the tragic events unfolding would come as no surprise to God, but were actually foreseen by God and factored into his redemptive calculus" (*Gospel of Luke*, p. 765).

[104]Klassen argues that the "woe" is not equivalent to a divine curse but rather an expression of sorrow (with a meaning equivalent to "alas for that man"). He understands Jesus' woe to be a prophetic lament that is meant to bring the other person to repentance. He sees the statement "It would have been better for that man not to have been born" to be a later addition

The divine necessity for the sacrifice of the Son of Man, grounded in the Word of God, does not excuse or mitigate the crime of betrayal (cf. Acts 1:6-18; 4:17-18). Nor is this an instance of divine "overruling" after the fact. Instead divine sovereignty and human responsibility are both involved in Judas' treason, the one effecting salvation and bringing redemption history to his fulfillment, the other answering the promptings of an evil heart. The one results in salvation from sin for Messiah's people (1:21), the other in personal and eternal ruin.[105]

For our purposes it is important to note that the moral guilt that is communicated by Jesus' woe implies that Judas's action was free. Thus Jesus' foreknowledge of his betrayal was an example of divine foreknowledge of free human decisions and actions.

We find additional material about Judas in the Gospel of John. John specifically speaks of Jesus' foreknowledge of Judas's future act when he chose him. John 6:64 records Jesus as saying, "Yet there are some of you who do not believe." John adds the interpretive comment, "For Jesus had known from the beginning which of them did not believe and who would betray him."[106] The one who would later betray Jesus is identified in John 6:70-71. " 'Have I not chosen you, the Twelve? Yet one of you is a devil!' (He meant Judas, the

---

in Matthew and Mark (Luke doesn't have it), adding a note of despair that doesn't fit the woe itself (*Judas,* pp. 81-84; Sanders cites Klassen's conclusion about the "woe" in *God Who Risks,* p. 300, n. 30). Klassen's evidence for the later addition is not convincing, nor does his interpretation of the woe fit the context, the subsequent statement that it would have been better if Judas had not been born, and other biblical statements about Judas (e.g., Jn 17:12).

[105]Carson, *Matthew,* p. 534. See the similar conclusion of Joel Green (*Gospel of Luke,* p. 765). The dual realities of divine sovereignty and human responsibility affirmed in Mt 26:24; Mk 14:21; Lk 22:22 are similar to what we have seen in Acts 2:23; 4:27-28.

[106]The phrase "from the beginning" *(ex archēs)* could mean "from the beginning of Jesus' ministry" (Carson, *John,* p. 302) or "from the beginning of the calling of the disciples" (Raymond E. Brown, *The Gospel According to John, I-XII,* Anchor Bible 29 [Garden City, N.Y.: Doubleday, 1979], p. 297). Morris acknowledges that "in view of the strongly predestinarian strain in this Gospel, it is not impossible that there is the thought of a knowledge going back to before the incarnation" (*The Gospel of John,* New International Commentary on the New Testament [Grand Rapids: Eerdmans, 1971], p. 386, n. 149). Boyd strongly disagrees with this latter possibility. He argues that *archē* "does not imply that Jesus knew who would betray him from a time before the person decided in his heart to betray him (let alone from all eternity). As in Phil 4:15, the word can mean 'early on.' This verse suggests that Jesus knew who would betray him from the moment this person resolved to betray him, or from the time Jesus chose him to be a disciple" (*God of the Possible,* p. 37). Boyd's former suggestion is just what we might expect from an open theist. His latter suggestion, while more in keeping with the context of Jn 6 (esp. 6:70-71), causes problems for Boyd's view of divine foreknowledge—unless we are prepared to believe that Judas had *already* purposed in his heart to betray Jesus when Jesus chose him. That seems very improbable.

son of Simon Iscariot, who, though one of the Twelve, was later to betray
him.)"[107]

Judas is referred to in the narrative of Jesus being anointed by Mary at Bethany, being identified as "one of [Jesus'] disciples . . . who was later to betray
him" (Jn 12:4). He complained about the exorbitant cost of the perfume used
by Mary, suggesting that it could be sold and the proceeds given to the poor
(though John identifies greed as Judas's true motive [v. 6]).

It is in John 13 that we find the most written about Judas. John 13:2 states
that as the evening meal was being served, "the devil had already prompted Judas Iscariot, son of Simon, to betray Jesus."[108] From here, the devil and Judas
are a conspiracy of evil against Jesus. But Jesus knew of Judas's evil intentions.
As he washed the feet of his disciples (including Judas), he said to Peter, "A person who has had a bath needs only to wash his feet; his whole body is clean.
And you are clean, though not every one of you."[109] John adds, "For [Jesus]
knew who was going to betray him, and that was why he said not every one
was clean" (Jn 13:10-11).

Jesus begins to zero in on the identity of his betrayer in John 13:18, saying,
"I am not referring to all of you; I know those I have chosen. But this is to fulfill
the scripture, 'He who shares my bread has lifted up his heel against me.' "[110]

---

[107]George R. Beasley-Murray argues that John "has almost certainly transferred to this point an
element of the Last Supper narrative (cf. 13:2, 21-30) to highlight the ultimate end of the apos-
tasy described in 6:66." Thus he is warning those in the Johannine community who might be
tempted to turn back not to join the company of Judas (*John*, Word Biblical Commentary 36
[Waco, Tex.: Word, 1987], p. 97).

[108]The Greek is awkward. Literally it reads that the devil had already put it into the heart that
Judas should betray Jesus. Whose heart? One might first think the heart of Judas. And some
manuscripts support this with the genitive form of Judas's name *(Iouda)*. But the nominative
Ioudas is better supported and, as the more difficult reading, probably should be preferred.
Morris thus takes the meaning to be "the devil had already made up his mind (= put it into his
own mind)," saying that "here John is rather discussing the devil's thoughts than those of Judas"
(*Gospel of John*, p. 614). On the other hand, Carson argues that it is doubtful that "to put into
one's own heart" ever means "to decide." Rather he thinks that "the nominative is original, but
was such an awkward way of saying that the devil put the thought into Judas' heart that some
later copyists made the point clear by 'correcting' to the genitive" (*John*, p. 462).

[109]Washing Judas's feet is yet another expression of love toward one Jesus knew would soon
betray him.

[110]We might take the statement "I am not referring to all of you; I know those I have chosen"
to be excluding Judas from those whom Jesus has chosen. Yet in light of Jn 6:70 ("Have I not
chosen you, the Twelve? Yet one of you is a devil"), Judas is here to be considered one of
the Twelve whom Jesus has chosen. Jesus' repeated inclusion of Judas among the chosen
Twelve is meant to assure the disciples "that the impending betrayal, far from being outside
the sphere of God's purposes, was planned and executed under his own control" (D. A. Carson, *Divine Sovereignty and Human Responsibility* [Grand Rapids: Baker, 1994], p. 191).

And then the specific identification of Judas Iscariot as the betrayer comes in John 13:21-30.

> After he had said this, Jesus was troubled in spirit and testified, "I tell you the truth, one of you is going to betray me."
>
> His disciples stared at one another, at a loss to know which of them he meant. One of them, the disciple whom Jesus loved, was reclining next to him. Simon Peter motioned to this disciple and said, "Ask him which one he means."
>
> Leaning back against Jesus, he asked him, "Lord, who is it?"
>
> Jesus answered, "It is the one to whom I will give this piece of bread when I have dipped it in the dish." Then, dipping the piece of bread, he gave it to Judas Iscariot, son of Simon. As soon as Judas took the bread, Satan entered into him.
>
> "What you are about to do, do quickly," Jesus told him. . . . As soon as Judas had taken the bread, he went out. And it was night.

This account is similar to those in the Synoptics in that it starts out with a general prediction ("one of you is going to betray me").[111] And once again this general prediction is followed by uncertainty among the disciples as to whom Jesus is referring to. John alone points to the piece of bread that Jesus dipped into the dish and gave to Judas as the signal that specifically identified the betrayer. Jesus, as host of the feast, gave it to Judas as a special sign of friendship and honor.[112] The fact that Jesus could give the bread to Judas quietly and unobtrusively (Jn 13:27-29) indicates that Judas was reclining close to Jesus, perhaps on his left, a place of honor. Clearly at this point Jesus was offering Judas a final gesture of his love (cf. Jn 13:1). Here was one final appeal to Judas to turn away from his planned sin. But rather than touching his heart and moving him toward repentance, this gesture served to harden Judas in his decision to betray Jesus.[113] And at that moment Satan entered Judas. He had already planted the thought and desire for betrayal in Judas's mind and heart (Jn 13:2), but now, with Judas's hardened resistance to the love of Jesus, Satan entered him more

---

Jesus cites Ps 41:9 to give the reason why he chose one who would betray him. The text refers to the pain of opposition and mocking by a close friend. Jesus' point is that his betrayal by one chosen to be an intimate friend is similar to that which David suffered. Thus Jesus' betrayal by Judas serves as a piece of an overall Davidic typology. See Carson, *John,* pp. 470-71.

[111]Halas identifies three distinct phases in the identification of the traitor: (1) a general allusion to the approaching crime (Jn 13:10, 18), (2) the designation of the traitor as one of the Twelve (Jn 13:21b; par. Mt 26:21; Mk 14:18; Lk 22:21), and (3) the positive identification of Judas as the betrayer (Jn 13:26). Yet in the context of the Last Supper, category 1 seems to collapse into category 2 (*Judas Iscariot,* p. 100).

[112]Brown calls this "a basic gesture of Oriental hospitality" and cites Ruth 2:14 as an Old Testament example (*John XIII-XXI,* p. 578).

[113]"Judas received the sop but not the love. Instead of breaking him and urging him to contrition, it hardened his resolve" (Carson, *John,* p. 475). See also Morris, *Gosopel of John,* pp. 626-27.

fully.[114] As in John 13:2, the role of Satan in Judas's betrayal does not diminish or eliminate Judas's responsibility. Rather it emphasizes and highlights the depth of the evil of the act.[115] But even after Judas was possessed by Satan, he still remained a free and morally responsible person. This is indicated in John 13:27, for Jesus addresses Judas, not Satan, as the one who will take action. " 'What you are about to do, do quickly,' Jesus told *him*."[116]

John 13:30 says that after Judas received the bread, he immediately went out. "And it was night."[117] Following this, we do not see Judas again in the text of John's Gospel until he arrives at Gethsemane, leading the Jewish authorities and soldiers to Jesus and identifying him as the one they are to arrest (Jn 18:2-5).[118]

There is one more statement made by Jesus about Judas in the Gospel of John. It is found in John 17:12, a part of Jesus' high priestly prayer. Jesus says to the Father, "While I was with them [the disciples], I protected them and kept them safe by that name you gave me. None has been lost except the one

---

[114]Carson says that "the expression probably signifies complete control" (*John*, p. 475). The terminology of Jn 13:27 is similar to that of Lk 22:3: both passages identify Satan by name and both use the aorist verb *eisēlthen* ("entered"). But chronologically, Luke places the entrance of Satan into Judas at the beginning of the Last Supper, a place corresponding more closely to Jn 13:2 than to Jn 13:27.

[115]Carson writes, "The idea, then, is not that Judas was not responsible, for a heart incited by Satan actually wills what the devil wills; rather, the plot against Jesus, however mediated by wicked human beings was nonetheless satanic" (ibid., p. 462.)

[116]Carson, *Divine Sovereignty and Human Responsibility*, p. 131. Klassen asserts that this command from Jesus (and the one in Mt 26:50) argues against an understanding of Judas's actions as sinful and eternally damning. "Can we really say that Jesus allowed his fellow Jew to write a passage ticket to hell? This becomes, then, an additional reason to reject the notion of betrayal. It would have violated a fundamental rule of Judaism if Jesus had told Judas to go out and deliberately commit a sin. Instead, it is more plausible to assume that he sent Judas forth on a mission and that Judas faithfully carried out that mission for his master" (*Judas*, p. 107). Sanders quotes this passage from Klassen also (*God Who Risks*, p. 99). Yet this fails to understand the decisiveness of Judas's rejection of the sop and of the entrance of Satan into him. Once Judas had decisively closed himself off to the love of Jesus and to any hope of repentance, Jesus told him to do what he had so decisively purposed to do, knowing the redemptive fruit that would come from his death.

[117]The term *night (nux)* serves not so much as a chronological marker but as a marker of the fulfillment of the prediction of Jn 9:4 and the arrival of the hour of darkness (cf. Lk 22:53). Even more significantly, it serves as a profound theological indicator of the darkness of Judas's own soul and the act he was about to perform (see Brown, *John XIII-XXI*, p. 579).

[118]Note in passing the remarkable statement of Jesus' foreknowledge in Jn 18:4. As Judas approached Jesus in Gethsemane, leading the chief priests and Pharisees, along with the soldiers, we read, "Jesus, *knowing all that was going to happen to him*, went out and asked them, 'Who is it you want?' " (emphasis added). Considering the fact that so much of what was gong to happen to Jesus—not only in his arrest but also in his trial, sufferings, death and subsequent resurrection—was the result of freely chosen human decisions, this statement is a strong affirmation of his foreknowledge of free human decisions.

doomed to destruction so that the Scripture would be fulfilled." Judas is clearly referred to in this verse as "the one doomed to destruction" (lit., "the son of perdition"—*ho huios tēs apōleias*). But what does this phrase mean?

There is much scholarly debate about whether the phrase refers to Judas's character or to his final destiny, to the "lostness" of his character or to the destruction that was his final destiny.[119] In my opinion the eschatological character of the noun *apōleia* and the word play of John 17:12 ("none of them was lost *[apōleto]* except the son of perdition *[apōleias]*") make it more likely that Judas's final destiny is in view here. Also supporting this view is the use of the entire phrase "the son of perdition," in 2 Thessalonians 2:3, where it occurs in apposition to the eschatological "man of sin." Carson writes: "Probably John 17:12 portrays Judas Iscariot as a horrible precursor belonging to the same genus as the eschatological 'son of perdition,' just as in 1 John 2:18, 22; 4:3, John portrays the heretical teachers he there confronts as of a piece with the antichrist."[120]

Boyd calls attention to the important issue of the timing of Jesus' statement relative to Judas's decision to betray Jesus. He notes that John 17:12 does not specify the time when Judas became a son of perdition. "We only know that by the time Jesus said this, Judas had, of his own free will, made himself into a

---

[119]With respect to the character option, Carson cites Is 57:4, in which the Masoretic Text's "children of rebellion" becomes in the LXX "children of perdition." And with respect to the final destiny option, he cites Is 35:4, in which the Masoretic Text's "people I have destroyed" becomes in the LXX "the people of perdition." In the end Carson views the latter option as "probably dominant in this context," citing the fact that in the New Testament *apōleia* commonly refers to eschatological damnation (cf. Mt 7:13; Acts 8:20; Rom 9:22; Phil 1:28; 3:19; 1 Tim 6:9; Heb 10:39; 2 Pet 2:1; 3:7; Rev 17:8, 11) (Carson, *John*, p. 563). Halas sees the phrase as a Hebraism with a meaning equivalent to "son of hell" in Mt 23:15 (*Judas Iscariot*, p. 183). Morris disagrees, saying that the expression points to character, not destiny. "The expression means that [Judas] was characterized by 'lostness,' not that he was predestined to be lost" (*Gospel of John*, p. 728). Brown seems to incorporate both understandings: "In the New Testament, 'perdition' frequently means damnation (Mt 7:13; Rev 17:8); and so 'the son of perdition' refers to one who belongs to the realm of damnation and is destined to final destruction" (*John XIII-XXI*, p. 760).

[120]Carson, *John*, p. 563. Klassen argues that the link with 2 Thess 2:3 points to "the son of perdition" as an eschatological, apocalyptic figure more than a historical person. This, linked with the role that Satan plays in Judas's act in John, leads Klassen to agree with W. Sproston that Judas is described in the Fourth Gospel as a symbol of evil—not a man acting, but Satan himself" (*Judas*, p. 153). Yet this assessment goes against two features in the Fourth Gospel that point to Judas as a free moral agent rather than an automaton whose strings are pulled by Satan or as merely as symbol of evil: (1) Jesus reaches out repeatedly in love to Judas—choosing him as one of the Twelve, washing his feet, giving him the sop, seating him in a place of honor at the Last Supper; and (2) Jesus addresses him as the one who will do the action (13:27). The Synoptic woe that Jesus pronounces against Judas also mitigates against Klassen's view.

person fit for destruction."[121] Boyd's point is well taken about the lack of chronological specificity of Jesus' prayer in John 17 relative to Judas's decisive rejection of Jesus in John 13. But the question of whether Jesus knew of Judas's betrayal in advance must be answered by looking at Jesus' earlier statements in John 6:64, 70-71; 13:10-11, 18, 21-26. And specifically the question of whether Jesus' statement in John 17:12 and his description of Judas as the "son of perdition" involves a predetermined certainty of the betrayal of Judas must be addressed by looking at the second half of the verse. Jesus said that only the son of perdition has been lost "so that the Scripture would be fulfilled."

Which Scripture text(s) does Jesus have in mind here? Most commentators believe that Jesus was thinking about Psalm 41:9, which he applied to Judas in John 13:18.[122] In addition, Brown believes that Jesus' reference might also be to Psalm 69:25 and Psalm 109:8 (quoted in Acts 1:16-20) and to Zechariah 11:12-13 (alluded to in Mt 27:3-10).[123]

But it is important to note that Jesus does not specify the precise text(s) he is thinking about. His focus is not on any single text or combination of texts. Rather Jesus cites the necessity of the fulfillment of Scripture to account for the loss of Judas in a way that is reminiscent of Matthew 26:23 and Mark 14:21 ("The Son of Man will go just as it is written about him"). God's purpose, as seen in his inspired Scriptures, is emphasized here, including even the defection and betrayal of Judas.[124] God knew about it in advance, as evidenced in the fulfillment of previously written Scripture, even as it is in the earlier predictions of Jesus. It is of great assurance to Jesus' disciples and to subsequent readers of the Fourth Gospel that God remains in control and that the betrayal of Jesus by

---

[121]Boyd, *God of the Possible*, p. 37. Boyd also argues that Jesus' foreknowledge of Judas's betrayal does not contradict the open view "as long as Judas was not *in particular* chosen to carry out this deed before Judas had *made himself* into the kind of person who *would* carry out this deed. After Judas had unfortunately hardened himself into this kind of person, God wove his character into a providential plan. Jesus could therefore foreknow that Judas would be the one to betray him. But nothing suggests that it was God's plan *from eternity* that Judas would play this role" (*Satan and the Problem of Evil*, p. 122).

[122]Carson, *John*, p. 564; Morris, *Gospel of John*, p. 729; Halas, *Judas Iscariot*, p. 185.

[123]Brown, *John XIII-XXI*, p. 760. Note the necessity of the fulfillment of Scripture that Peter cites with respect to the betrayal of Judas: "Brothers, the Scripture had to be *(edei)* fulfilled which the Holy Spirit spoke long ago through the mouth of David concerning Judas" (Acts 1:16). Peter then proceeds to quote Ps 69:25 and Ps 109:8.

[124]Morris writes, "The reference to the fulfilling of Scripture brings out the thought of divine purpose. This does not mean that Judas was an automaton. He was a responsible person and acted freely. But God used his evil act to bring about His purpose. There is a combination of the human and the divine, but in this passage it is the divine side rather than the human which receives stress. God's will in the end was done in the handing over of Christ to be crucified" (*Gospel of John*, p. 728).

one of his inner circle is not an evidence of failure on Jesus' part.[125]

And for the purposes of this study, it is important to note the similarity in thought between Jesus' assertion that the loss of Judas fulfills Scripture and reflects God's foreknowledge and determining redemptive purpose, and Peter's statement in Acts 2:23 that Jesus Christ was handed over to the Jews "by God's set purpose and foreknowledge."

The purpose of Jesus' predictions. The importance that Jesus places on his foreknowledge of and his predictions of the behavior of Judas and Peter can be seen in John 13:19. This crucial saying is sandwiched between Jesus' affirmation of his complete knowledge of his chosen Twelve and his quotation of Psalm 41:9 (Jn 13:18), and his prediction of Judas's betrayal (Jn 13:21-27) and Peter's denial (Jn 13:38). Jesus says in John 13:19, "I am telling you now before it happens, so that when it does happen you will believe that I am He *(egō eimi)*."

Here Jesus is telling his disciples the reason for his predictions of Judas's betrayal and Peter's denial. It is to prepare his disciples for what is to come, with the goal of preserving and strengthening their faith. He knew that their faith might well be shattered by the events that would soon transpire. But, as Morris writes:

> The prediction altered all that. It ensured that, on reflection, they would continue to see His mastery of the situation. When He was betrayed into the hands of His enemies it was just what He had foretold. He was not the deceived and helpless Victim of unsuspected treachery, but One sent by God to effect God's purposes going forward, calmly and unafraid, to do what God had planned for him to do.[126]

But Jesus was not only concerned to sustain and strengthen the faith of his disciples. He was also concerned with the content of their faith. His goal was that, after the unfolding events would prove his predictions to be accurate and true, his disciples would believe that *egō eimi* ("I am he"). Jesus had previously claimed this title for himself in John 8:24, 28 and especially in John 8:58. This expression has massive theological significance in the LXX. It is used to translate the name God gave to himself in Exodus 3:14 ("I am who I am" = *egō eimi ho ōn*). And the LXX uses *egō eimi* to translate the equivalent Hebrew phrase *'ănî hû'* in Deuteronomy 32:39; Isaiah 4:4; 43:10; 46:4; Ezekiel 24:24 and others. All of these passages involve Yahweh's claim to be the one true and living God.

---

[125]Note the words of Carson, "The reference to the fulfillment of Scripture also assures the reader that the defection of Judas is foreseen by Scripture, and therefore no evidence of failure on Jesus' part" (*John*, pp. 563-64).

[126]Morris, *Gospel of John*, p. 623.

The point in John 13 is clear. What Jesus is seeking to sustain and to strengthen through his predictions is precisely his disciples' faith in his own deity.[127] This concern of Jesus is strengthened by the very high christological claim that Jesus makes in the very next verse. "Whoever accepts me accepts the one who sent me" (Jn 13:20).[128]

The parallels of John 13:19 with the LXX's rendering of Isaiah 41:4 ("Who has done this and carried it through, / calling forth the generations from the beginning? / I, the LORD—with the first of them / and with the last—I am he *[egō eimi]*") and Isaiah 43:10 ("You are my witnesses, declares the LORD, / and my servant whom I have chosen, / so that you may know and believe me / and understand that I am he *[egō eimi]*") are especially important, for they come in contexts where Yahweh cites his foreknowledge as the evidence of his unique and unrivaled deity. Thus, in the same way that Yahweh appeals to his foreknowledge and his ability to predict the future in Isaiah 40—48 to demonstrate his deity, so here in John 13 Jesus appeals to his foreknowledge of Judas's betrayal and Peter's denial, and to his ability to tell his disciples of these events before they happened as supreme evidence of his deity. Just as Yahweh stakes his claim to deity on his foreknowledge of the free actions of Cyrus, so here Jesus stakes his claim to deity on his ability to foreknow and to predict the free actions of Judas and Peter.

It is exceedingly hard to see why Jesus would do this if all he possessed were a probabilistic forecast based on his insight into the character of Judas and Peter. This is the view of Rice. He claims that "with His astute insight into human behavior, or with divine aid, Jesus could have detected Judas' plan and perceived his disciple's weakness."[129] But no matter how astute Jesus was as a forecaster, if his predictions were not made with infallible foreknowledge, it was a risky undertaking. How much more likely that Jesus would ground something as crucial as his disciples ongoing faith in his deity in a knowledge of the future that is certain and infallible. Indeed it is Jesus' certain knowledge of Judas's future betrayal and Peter's future denial that is a crucial part of his glory as the divine *egō eimi*. Thus it is no small thing to deny that Jesus has divine foreknowledge of free human choices.[130]

---

[127]Brown, *John XII-XXI*, p. 571.

[128]On the christological link between vv. 19 and 20 of Jn 13, see Carson, *John*, p. 471.

[129]Rice, *God's Foreknowledge and Man's Free Will*, p. 96. Rice also suggests the possibility that by the time of the Last Supper, Judas had so hardened his heart that his betrayal was inevitable (ibid). But if his ultimate behavior was truly inevitable, then at the precise moment of betrayal, Judas did not possess libertarian freedom. Thus according to openness theology, he would not have been morally accountable.

[130]See Piper, "Why the Glory of God Is at Stake," p. 41.

Conclusion. Jesus' predictions of his own Passion and of Peter's denial and Judas's betrayal are not the only examples we find in Scripture of his foreknowledge or his supernatural knowledge in general.[131] Morris concludes, "Plainly the knowledge John attributes to Jesus is part of the way in which he shows us the divine Christ."[132]

This conclusion matches what we have seen, especially from John 13:19. Jesus points to his divine foreknowledge, especially in his predictions of Judas's betrayal and Peter's denial as crucial evidence for his deity and as warrant for his disciples' ongoing faith in him as the divine Son of God and Messiah. Just as in Isaiah 40—48, it is not only the frequency of Jesus' predictive prophecies, not only their specificity, but especially the use that Jesus makes of them that points to the crucial importance of affirming his foreknowledge of free human decisions.

---

[131]Jesus' foreknowledge is also evidenced in Jn 2:4 (he knew that his time had not yet come); Jn 11:4 (Jesus knew that the ultimate outcome of Lazarus's sickness would be the glorification of God's Son through it); Jn 18:4 (Jesus knew all that would befall him after his arrest); Mt 17:27 (Jesus knew that the first fish Peter would catch would have a coin in its mouth). More significantly, Jesus also predicted the destruction of the Temple in Jerusalem (Mt 24:2; Mk 13:2; Lk 21:6; cf. Lk 19:44) and his own parousia (e.g., Mt 10:23; 16:28; 24:29-51; Mk 8:38; 9:1; 13:24-36; Lk 9:27; 18:8; 21:25-36). With respect to Jesus' foreknowledge of his parousia, see Brown, "How Much Did Jesus Know?" pp. 20-25; and Carson, *Matthew*, pp. 250-53, 380-82, 488-95. With respect to the destruction of the Temple, Brown argues that Mk 13:2 and par. ("Not one stone will be left on another; every one will be thrown down") constitute evidence that Jesus did not possess exhaustive foreknowledge. "If anyone would propose that this represented an exact foreknowledge of what would happen in 70, he need simply be reminded that the gigantic blocks of the Temple foundation are still standing firmly one upon the other in Jerusalem" ("How Much Did Jesus Know?" p. 19). Sanders cites this quotation approvingly (*God Who Risks*, p. 135), yet also allows that Jesus could have been using hyperbole. Green understands Jesus' phrase in Lk 21:6 (leaving not "stone upon stone") to be "an emphatic prediction of total annihilation," couched in the language of Old Testament prophetic oracles of judgment" (*Gospel of Luke*, p. 733, cf. p. 691). Lane cites Josephus's account of the fulfillment of this prophecy: "Caesar [Titus] ordered the whole city and the Temple to be razed to the ground" (*Jewish Wars* 7.1.1 §1; cited in Lane, *Gospel of Mark*, p. 452, n. 25). Gundry notes, "We might have expected a *vaticinium ex eventu* to mention the burning of the Temple. That it is not mentioned argues in favor of a genuine prediction by Jesus. Such a prediction is favored also by the absence of other striking features of the first Jewish revolt—viz. cannibalism, pestilence, and internecine conflict" (*Matthew*, p. 475).

Regarding Jesus' supernatural knowledge in general, see Jn 1:47 (Jesus seeing Nathanael while he was under the fig tree and knowing his character); Jn 4:17-18 (Jesus knowing the marital history of the Samaritan woman at the well and the current status of her live-in boyfriend); Jn 9:3 (Jesus knowing why the blindness of the man born blind did and did not happen—not because of his own or his parents' sin but so that the work of God might be displayed in his life); Jn 10:14, 27 (Jesus knowing his sheep); Jn 11:11, 14 (Jesus knowing that Lazarus was dead); Jn 13:3 (Jesus knowing the full extent of the Father's gift to him); Jn 7:29; 8:55; 10:15; 17:25 (Jesus having a knowledge of the Father that no one else could). On Jesus' supernatural knowledge, see Carson, *John*, p. 161, and Morris, *Gospel of John* p. 265, n. 44.

[132]Morris, *Gospel of John* p. 265, n. 44.

Divine Foreknowledge of the Fall

Jonathan Edwards argued that a significant proof of God's foreknowledge of free human volitions comes from his foreknowledge of the Fall of humanity through the sin of our first parents and from his divine plan, prior to the creation of the world, to redeem his people through Christ. Edwards argued:

> If God does not know the volitions of moral agents, then he did not foreknow the fall of man, nor of angels, and so could not foreknow the great things which are consequent on these events; such as his sending his Son into the world to die for sinners, and all things pertaining to the great work of redemption; all things which were done for four thousand years before Christ came, to prepare the way for it; and the incarnation, life, death, resurrection, and ascension of Christ.[133]

Edwards says that if God were ignorant in this way, there are many biblical texts that would be "without meaning, or contrary to truth."[134] We will conclude our examination of New Testament evidence for God's foreknowledge of free human decisions by looking at several of these texts.

At issue in this discussion is not the question of whether the people God has foreknown and given grace to before the creation of the world are conceived by God as individuals or as a corporate group. Rather the question is why anyone (individually or corporately) would be foreknown to be saved by God's grace in Christ before creation if God had not foreknown the Fall. Each of these texts that speaks of God's advance planning of his redeeming work comes in a context of his overcoming of sin. Thus God's foreknowledge of the plan of redemption presupposes his foreknowledge of the human decisions involved in the fall of Adam and Eve (and of Lucifer before them). Let me illustrate.

Romans 8:29-30 says that all those foreknown by God have been predestined to be conformed to the likeness of Christ and that this will be accomplished as those foreknown people are called, justified and eventually glorified. The connection of God's foreknowing his people with his justifying them points to the existence of sin that must be forgiven through Christ. So if God has foreknown his people from before creation (which is not explicitly said in Rom 8:29, but which can be most reasonably inferred from the Pauline parallels in Eph 1:4 and 2 Tim 1:9), then he must have foreknown the Fall.

In 1 Peter 1:2, God's foreknowledge of his elect is expressly linked with the sanctifying work of the Spirit and with the elect being sprinkled by the blood

---

[133]Jonathan Edwards, *On the Freedom of the Will,* in The Works of Jonathan Edwards (Carlisle, Penn.: Banner of Truth Trust, 1974), p. 34.
[134]Ibid. Edwards specifically cites Rom 8:29; Eph 1:4; 3:11; 2 Tim 1:9; Tit 1:2; 1 Pet 1:2, 20. To this list I would add Mt 25:34; 1 Cor 2:7; Rev 3:8; 17:8.

of Christ. Once again we find presupposed the reality of sin from which God's people need to be forgiven through the blood of Christ and sanctified through the work of the Spirit. So if God's foreknowing of his people is from all eternity, then he must have foreknown the fall of humanity into sin as well. In 1 Peter 1:20, however, there is an explicit temporal indicator relating to God's foreknowledge. The verse speaks of Jesus Christ as being foreknown "before the creation of the world" *(pro kataboles kosmou)*.[135] But the context of 1 Peter 1:18-19 makes it clear that Christ was foreknown not merely as the incarnate Son of God, but as the Lamb of God whose precious blood redeems his people from sin and futility of life.[136] Thus the sin from which Christ redeems his people was also foreknown by God before the creation of the world.

In Ephesians 1, Paul speaks of God choosing us in Christ before the creation of the world *(pro kataboles kosmou)* to be holy and blameless (v. 4), and of God predestining us to be adopted as his children through Christ (v. 5). And all of this is "to the praise of the glory of his grace" (v. 6). Then Ephesians 1:7 gives the mechanism through which the purpose for which God chose and predestined his people is carried out. It is the cross of Christ. "In him we have redemption through his blood, the forgiveness of sins." This requires us to understand God's choosing of his people prior to creation in a redemptive context. He chose us and predestined us precisely to transform us into what we were not—

---

[135]The relationship of God to time is an extremely complex one that cannot be fully explored in this volume. My own position favors divine atemporality such that in his own essential being God does not experience events in sequence. But we humans are temporal beings who do experience such sequence. Thus issues of "before" and "after" are significant to us, and this is why Scripture uses such temporal language. Relative to our own experience of time, the question can be asked, What did God know even before we came to exist?

[136]Sanders argues, "First Peter 1:20 says that God foreknew Christ and thus can be understood as affirming that the cross was foreknown from eternity. But this verse does not necessitate such an interpretation, and so there is no problem for the relational model. All that is required is that the incarnation of the Son was decided on from the beginning as part of the divine project" (*God Who Risks,* p. 101). Sanders affirms the view of medieval theologians Albert the Great and John Duns Scotus, and more recently argued for by Colin Gunton, that even if the Fall had never happened, God would still have sent Christ into the world as the incarnate Son of God to perfect his people and be the climax of God's presence with them. "My own view is that the incarnation was always planned, for God intended to bring us joy and glory shared among the triune Godhead" (ibid., p. 103). Thus for Sanders the incarnation of Christ was theologically necessary and not contingent on free human decisions (such as the decision to sin). Therefore it could be foreknown before the creation of the world. The atonement, however, is contingent and could only be planned for after the free (and unforeseen) human decision to sin. In my opinion what God would have decided to do if humanity had never fallen is an interesting hypothetical question to contemplate, but the context of 1 Pet 1:18-19 makes it clear that Christ was foreknown as the Lamb of God whose blood would redeem his fallen people. This argues decisively against Sanders's interpretation.

holy and blameless children who have been forgiven through the death of Christ and adopted as children of God through him. And if these precreation actions of God are ultimately to abound to the praise of the glory of his grace, understood in Ephesians 1:3-14 to be redeeming grace, then God must have foreknown the fall of humanity into the sin from which he saved us by his grace through Christ (cf. Eph 2:5, 8).[137]

Similarly, Ephesians 3:11 speaks of God's manifold wisdom being made known to heavenly rulers and authorities, according to his eternal purpose *(kata prothesin tōn aiōnōn),* which he accomplished in Christ. God's purpose in Christ throughout Ephesians 1—3 is clearly redemptive, seeking to forgive the sins of those he has chosen (Eph 1:7), to bring them out of spiritual death due to sin to new life in Christ (Eph 2:1-5), and to reconcile them to himself and to one another through Christ (Eph 2:11-22). And this divine purpose, Paul argues, was conceived in eternity and accomplished in space and time through Jesus Christ. Clearly, then, this eternal purpose must also have involved God's foreknowledge of the sin from which his people need to be redeemed.

In 1 Corinthians 2:7, Paul writes of God's secret wisdom that has been hidden and "that God destined *[proōrisen]* for our glory before time began (lit., "before the ages" *[pro tōn aiōnōn]*)." Thus the eschatological glory of believers who have been redeemed by Christ crucified (1 Cor 2:2) and called to be God's own (1 Cor 1:2, 24, 26) had been destined by God before the ages.[138] Gordon Fee comments:

> What God determined "*before* the ages" has been worked out in the *present* age, which is being brought to its conclusion as the *final* glorious age has dawned and is awaiting its consummation—"for our glory." What has been predestined technically is God's wisdom; the larger context indicates that Paul has in view God's gracious activity in Christ, whereby though the crucifixion he had determined eternal salvation for his people.[139]

Once again we find Paul speaking of the precreation origins of the redemptive plan of God. Clearly the redemption of his people through Christ crucified

---

[137]Piper comments on Eph 1:4-6: "Before the foundation of the world—before the sinful choice of Adam—God chose us in Christ and predestined us for sonship through Christ so that the free and sovereign grace of God would be seen as glorious: 'unto the praise of the glory of his grace.' But if God did not foreknow the fall, and (as some argue) was surprised by it, then Paul's argument for the glory of God's grace manifest in his eternal plan to rescue us from it is not valid" ("Why the Glory of God Is at Stake," p. 42).

[138]On eschatological glory see Gordon Fee, *The First Epistle to the Corinthians,* New International Commentary on the New Testament (Grand Rapids: Eerdmans, 1987), p. 106. On "destined," the emphasis of the verb *proorizō* is on "deciding beforehand" (BAGD); hence, according to Fee, "predestining" (ibid., p. 105.)

[139]Ibid.

implies the existence of sin from which Christ's death atoned and from which his people need to be saved. Thus this text too implies a precreation divine foreknowledge of the Fall, which leads God to his precreation destining of salvation for his people through Christ crucified.

2 Timothy 1:9-10 also speaks of the eternal origin of God's saving grace.

> [God] who saved us and called us to a holy life—not because of anything we have done but because of his own purpose and grace. This grace was given us in Christ Jesus before the beginning of time (lit., "before times eternal" *[pro chronōn aiōniōn]*), but it now has been revealed through the appearing of our Savior, Christ Jesus, who has destroyed death and has brought life and immortality to light through the gospel.[140]

In this passage we find Paul linking God's saving grace to us in Christ with his own redemptive purpose ("his own purpose and grace").[141] And both God's redemptive purpose and his grace to his people in Christ are set in eternity *(pro chronōn aiōniōn)* in contrast with the historical appearing of "our Savior, Christ Jesus." The phrase *pro chronōn aiōniōn* is also used by Paul in Titus 1:2, speaking of the hope of eternal life which the God who cannot lie promised *pro chronōn aiōniōn.*[142] Paul's goal here seems to be to trace the source of Timothy's salvation back to the eternal gracious purpose of God rather than to his own works, thus giving him confidence and peace in the midst of his suffering for the sake of the gospel (2 Tim 1:8).[143] But if the grace of God that is given to us in Christ *pro chronōn aiōniōn* is truly saving grace, as the beginning of 2 Timothy 1:9 indicates, then God must have also known even before creation the sin from which we must be saved. Piper explains:

---

[140]Boyd views this text corporately. He writes, "Indeed, as a group we were given this grace 'in Christ Jesus before the ages began' [2 Tim 1:9]" (*God of the Possible,* p. 47).

[141]George W. Knight III cites Rom 8—9 and Eph 1—3 as other places where Paul "links these two elements, God's purpose or will and his gracious intention, elsewhere as the basis for human salvation" (*The Pastoral Epistles,* New International Greek Testament Commentary [Grand Rapids: Eerdmans, 1992], p. 374).

[142]Gordon D. Fee, *1 and 2 Timothy, Titus,* New Interpreter's Bible Commentary (Peabody, Mass.: Hendrickson, 1988), p. 230. J. N. D. Kelly also links 2 Tim 1:9 to Eph 1:4. He writes, "Both passages presuppose the idea of Christ's pre-existence and also imply that he is the unique mediator through union with whom men have the grace of God imparted to them" (*A Commentary on the Pastoral Epistles* [Grand Rapids: Baker, 1963], p. 163).

[143]Knight asserts that there is a "consensus" among commentators and translators. He argues that "the phrase, literally 'before times eternal,' is best understood here as 'from all eternity' (NASB, NEB) or 'before the beginning of time' (NIV, TEV). This is in accord with Paul's perspective which speaks of God's decision before time and the world began (cf. 1 Cor 2:7; Eph 1:4)" (*Pastoral Epistles,* p. 375). John Stott writes, "If we would trace the river of salvation back to its source, we must look right back beyond time to a past eternity" (*Guard the Gospel* [Downers Grove, Ill.: InterVarsity Press, 1973], p. 35).

God must have foreknown the fall of Adam with all its disastrous moral effects because . . . Paul says that *from all eternity* God has planned to give us saving grace
in Christ Jesus as our Savior [2 Tim 1:9]. In other words, God not only foreknew in
eternity the sinful choice that Adam would make (and Lucifer before him), but he
also planned to give us grace through Jesus Christ in response to the misery and
destruction and condemnation resulting from the fall that he foreknew.[144]

We turn our attention, finally, to the book of Revelation. We read in Revelation 13:8 that those who worship the beast are those whose "names have not
been written in the book of life belonging to the Lamb that was slain from the
creation of the world *(apo kataboles kosmou)*." The phrase "book of life" appears
five other times in Revelation (3:5; 17:8; 20:12, 15; 21:27). In each case the book
refers to a divine register in which the names of saints whose salvation has been
determined are recorded.[145] The book of life speaks of the destiny of those
whose names are written in it—eternal life in the New Jerusalem with God.[146]
In Revelation 13:8 (and 21:27), the book of life is explicitly said to belong to
"the Lamb that was slain." It was his death that redeemed for God an innumerable multitude from every tribe and language and people and nation (Rev 5:9-
10). Through Christ's sacrificial death on the cross God grants and preserves life
for all whose names are written in the book of life.[147]

Revelation 21:27 explicitly speaks of the saints whose names have been written in the book of life. Revelation 13:8 and 17:8, on the other hand, speak of
the opposite situation—those whose names have not been so written. The reason why those who inhabit the earth will worship the beast in 13:8 is precisely

---

[144]Piper, "Why the Glory of God Is at Stake," p. 42.
[145]Gregory K. Beale, *The Book of Revelation,* New International Greek Testament Commentary
(Grand Rapids: Eerdmans, 1999), pp. 701-2. Note that the singular "book" stands in contrast
to the "books" that record the sins of the ungodly (Rev 20:12-13). George Ladd notes that the
metaphor of a book in the presence of God in which the names of the saints are written also
occurs in Ex 32:32; Ps 69:28; Lk 10:20; Phil 4:3; Heb 12:23 (*A Commentary on the Revelation
of John* [Grand Rapids: Eerdmans, 1972], p. 57).
[146]Beale calls the book of life "the census book of the eternal new Jerusalem" (*Book of Revelation,* p. 702).
[147]Grant Osborne says, "The cross made the book of life possible, for it was the slain Lamb that
became the sacrifice for sin and enabled the people of God to have 'life.' Thus the final victory does not belong to Armageddon or the final battle of 20:7-10. . . . No, the final victory
was achieved on the cross by the Lamb of God" (*Revelation,* Baker Exegetical Commentary
on the New Testament [Grand Rapids: Baker, 2002], p. 503). Beale writes of the divine protection of the life of believers. "Genuine believers have assurance that their souls can weather
any Satanic storm because of the safety accorded by the Lamb's book. This safety is the precreation identification of God's people with the Lamb's death, which means that they also
identify with his resurrection life, which protects them from spiritual death and ultimate deception. No one can take this life from them" (*Book of Revelation,* p. 703).

because their names have not been written in the Lamb's book of life. They have not been given life by the Lamb, they are not protected by him, and thus they are deceived into worshiping the beast (Rev 13:14; cf. Rev 12:9; 18:23; 19:20).

The most highly debated interpretive question with respect to Revelation 13:8 involves the referent to the phrase "from the creation of the world." Does it refer to the writing of names in the book of life *apo kataboles kosmou* [as per NASB and NRSV]? Or is it a reference to the death of the Lamb, indicating that it was foreknown and planned *apo kataboles kosmou* [as per KJV and NIV]? Revelation 17:8 ("The inhabitants of the earth whose names have not been written in the book of life from the creation of the world will be astonished when they see the beast, because he once was, now is not, and yet will come") explicitly says that the names of these condemned people have not been written in the book *apo kataboles kosmou*. This parallel is the strongest argument for understanding Revelation 13:8 as speaking of God's precreation recording of the names of his saints in the Lamb's book of life, a precreation election similar to that affirmed by Paul in Ephesians 1:4.[148] The word order, on the other hand, is the primary argument for those who would understand that it is the Lamb who was slain before the creation of the world. Robert Mounce observes that the pretemporal phrase is separated from the verb *written* by twelve words. Thus he argues that the Greek syntax most naturally leads us to conclude that John is referring to "the death of Christ [which] was a redemptive sacrifice decreed in the counsels of eternity."[149] Thus we find here a conceptual parallel with 1 Peter 1:18-20.

The syntactical question is a difficult one. The strength of the argument from word order inclines me to lean in the direction of viewing the precreation reference as referring to the death of Christ. But for our purposes, the key question is whether Revelation 13:8 presupposes an understanding of divine foreknowledge that includes free human decision such as the fall of humanity.

Sanders argues that either understanding can be consistent with his view of

---

[148]This view is advocated by Ladd, *Commentary on the Revelation,* p. 181, and David E. Aune, *Revelation 6-16,* Word Biblical Commentary 52B (Nashville: Thomas Nelson, 1998), pp. 746-47. In addition to the argument from the parallel with Rev 17:8, Aune argues that his interpretation "is preferable since it is logically and theologically impossible to make sense of the statement that the Lamb 'was slaughtered *before* the foundation of the world.' . . . While it is possible to think of Christ as *destined* to die for the sins of the world, it is quite another thing to say that he was *slain* before the creation of the world" (Aune, *Revelation 6-16,* p. 747).

[149]Robert Mounce, *The Book of Revelation,* rev. ed. New International Commentary on the New Testament (Grand Rapids: Eerdmans, 1998), p. 252. This view is also held by Osborne, who says that the verse points to "God's redemptive plan that has been established 'from the foundation of the world' "(*Revelation,* pp. 503-4). See also Beale, *Book of Revelation,* p. 742 ("the death of Christ was decreed before time began").

divine foreknowledge as involving possibilities and not certainties where human decisions are involved.

> Perhaps God knew the possible outcomes (what might happen if sin did come about or did not come about) and planned a different course in each case. Each one included the incarnation, but it took a different course depending on which case came about. Hence it could be said that God planned before the foundation of the world that the Son would become incarnate. But God did not know which of the rationales for the incarnation would be actualized until after sin came on the scene.[150]

I believe, on the contrary, that whichever way the syntactical question is answered, John is still implying that *apo katabolēs kosmou* God foreknew the Fall, which led to his redemptive plan. Clearly, if Christ's death as the sacrificial Lamb of God was foreknown and decreed from the creation of the world, then God must have foreknown that sin would definitely, not just possibly, come, which made the redeeming death of Christ necessary.[151] But if the other interpretation is taken and the pretemporal phrase is taken to modify the verb *written,* such divine foreknowledge is still presupposed. Under this scenario, we are to understand the phrase "belonging to the Lamb who was slain" to be further describing the book of life—both the fact that the book rightfully belongs to the Lamb who was slain and that the life associated with the book is given and sustained by the slain Lamb.[152] But if the life of those whose names are written is given to them by the Lamb who was slain (redemptively, cf. Rev 5:9-10), then God must have foreknown that these people would need to be redeemed. And so he must have foreknown the reality of the sin they would need to be redeemed from. In addition, the fact that there are some whose names are not written in the Lamb's book of life (Rev 13:8; 17:8) indicates a knowledge of future sin on God's part. For if God was not anticipating sin when he wrote names into the book before the creation of the world, he would have written everyone's name in the book. Thus, however we exegete Revelation 13:8, the text points to the reality that God foreknew the fall of humanity and the free human decisions involved.

When contemplating God's writing of the names of his people in the Lamb's

---

[150]Sanders, *God Who Risks,* p. 102.

[151]Grant Osborne argues that understanding Rev 13:8 to refer to the Lamb that was slain from the creation of the world does not necessitate a supralapsarian view of divine history (in which God decreed the Fall because he had already predestined his Son to die on the cross). Rather, "'the Lamb slain from the foundation of the world' is based on *God's knowledge of the fall* rather than his predestining of the fall" (*Revelation,* pp. 503-4, emphasis added).

[152]Beale, *Book of Revelation,* p. 702.

book of life, Boyd argues that this writing is not final and unchangeable. He points to Revelation 3:5, in which the risen Christ promises the overcomer in the church of Sardis, "I will never blot out his name from the book of life" and Revelation 22:19, which he asserts its parallel, even though it uses the metaphor of the tree of life rather than the book of life: "And if anyone takes words away from this book of prophecy, God will take away from him his share in the tree of life and in the holy city."[153] Boyd argues:

> If God foreknew from all eternity that certain names would be "blotted out" of his book, why did he bother to put them there? . . . If we take these verses at face value, doesn't this "blotting out" and "taking away" describe a genuine change in God's attitude toward these people? And doesn't this change entail that the eternal destiny of these people was not fixed in God's mind from the start? . . . From an open view, God creates the people he creates because he sees the possibility (not the certainty) that they will become citizens of his eternal kingdom. He genuinely strives to win everyone because he hopes that they will surrender to him. When they do meet the condition of salvation by exercising faith in him, he writes them in his book. When the condition is lost, so are they.[154]

I disagree with Boyd's interpretation for two reasons. First, Boyd ignores the clear meaning of Revelatioin 17:8. There John speaks of those "whose names had not been written [by God] in the book of life from the creation of the world." The impression is clear. John is not describing a situation of people whose names were written in the book of life initially only to have them erased at some later point in time. No, their names were never written at all. Contrary to Boyd, God clearly does not wait to write until the individuals involved "meet the condition of salvation by exercising faith." God's writing or not, according to Revelation 17:8, is "before the creation of the world."[155]

Second, there are good exegetical reasons to understand Revelation 3:5 as not referring to the possible loss of eternal life. In addition to the testimony of Revelation 17:8, Beale argues that (1) none of the other promises to the "overcomer" in Revelation 2—3 contains an implicit threat of losing a salvation once

---

[153]Boyd, *God of the Possible*, p. 74. Boyd also cites Ex 32:33 to argue for the same point.
[154]Ibid. Boyd is following the interpretation of Rev 3:5 of G. B. Caird: "The predestination in which John believes is a conditional predestination. A man cannot earn the right to have his name on the citizen roll, but he can forfeit it. Christ may 'strike his name from the book of life.' The decrees of God are not irreversible but wait on the acceptance or rejection of man" (*A Commentary on the Revelation of St. John the Divine* [New York: Harper, 1966], pp. 49-50).
[155]Thus Beale writes that Rev 3:5 could not be referring to the possibility of an *actual* removal of certain names from the book of life that was already there, for "their names were never written there in the first place (as 13:8 and 17:8 clearly show)" (*Book of Revelation*, p. 280).

gained. Rather, all are framed in purely positive terms. Thus Beale argues the positive guarantee of a salvific inheritance is expressed negatively for emphasis ("I will not erase his name").[156] (2) The book of life is a symbol in Revelation 13:8; 17:8 and 21:27 for the security of the believer due to the sovereign redemptive purpose of God. Thus "it would be contradictory to view the book in 3:5 as a metaphor of insecurity."[157] (3) The word *onoma* ("name") is used four times in the letter of the risen Christ to the church in Sardis (Rev 3:1, 4, 5 [2x]). Throughout this letter there is a running contrast between the genuine Christian and the false believer (one who is a Christian in "name" only [v. 1]). Christ's point is that those who claim the name of being a Christian but are not will be exposed on the last day as having no Christian name at all. But on the other hand, those who remain faithful to their professed Christian name will be recognized as having that genuine identity. Their names will not be erased from the book of life, but they will be confessed as genuine by Jesus on the last day.[158]

In the end Beale rightly sees the promise of Revelation 3:5b as both an assurance to those who are persevering in faith and obedience (i.e., "overcomers") and as a warning to professing believers who are wavering. Christ is seeking to draw them back to repentance and to ongoing faith and obedience, lest they end up finding that their names are not at all in the book of life (which means, according to Rev 13:8 and 17:8, that they were never written there at all).[159]

The point I have been trying to make throughout this section is that the texts we have examined point to the existence of a redemptive plan of God that existed in his mind and heart before the beginning of creation and time. And I have argued that the existence of this precreation redemptive plan presupposes

---

[156]Beale writes, "The emphasis of this expression in 3:5b is that those who persevere and prove themselves genuine will surely receive the promise they deserve. If they are genuine believers, then their names, indeed, have already been written down in 'the book of life,' they are destined for a salvific inheritance, and nothing will prevent them from possessing it. In somewhat unusual fashion the positive guarantee of this inheritance is expressed negatively: 'I will not erase his name" (*Book of Revelation*, pp. 279-80). See the conclusion of Ladd, "The form of the promise is an assurance of salvation in the consummated Kingdom of God" (*Commentary on the Revelation*, p. 58).

[157]Beale, *Book of Revelation*, p. 281.

[158]Ibid., p. 280. J. William Fuller argues that the *onoma* of Rev 3:1; 5b means primarily "reputation." It is the untrue reputation of being a Christian (v. 1) that will be erased from heaven. Thus Fuller sees no potential loss of salvation once possessed. ("'I will Not Erase His Name From the Book of Life' [Rev 3:5]," *Journal of the Evangelical Theological Society* 26, no. 3 [1983]: 297-306).

[159]Beale, *Book of Revelation*, pp. 280-82.

God's foreknowledge of the fall of humanity into sin, which makes such a redemptive plan needed.[160]

Richard Rice seeks to blunt the force of this argument by saying:

> The existence of a plan for human salvation as early as Creation does not necessarily indicate God definitely knew that man would sin before He created him. It may indicate only that God was aware that sin was a distinct possibility with man's creation, rather than a future actuality, and that He was fully prepared to meet the situation should it arise.[161]

However, I believe that the texts examined above do not speak of the precreation redemptive plan of God as a mere contingency, ready to go into effect should the need arise due to unforeseen human sin. Rather Christ has already been foreknown as the Lamb of God (1 Pet 1:19-20) who was slain before the creation of the world (Rev 13:8). And we have already been chosen in Christ before the creation of the world (Eph 1:4) and have actually been given grace in him before the beginning of time (2 Tim 1:9). My point is that these texts envision a definite redemptive plan of God, and thus they argue for his definite, certain foreknowledge both of his redemptive work in Christ and of the sin that made it necessary.

CONCLUSION

In this chapter we have examined evidence from the New Testament for exhaustive divine foreknowledge of free human decisions. We have looked at the specific New Testament language for foreknowledge *(proginōskō* and *prognōsis)*; Jesus' teaching on prayer; Jesus' predictions of his own death and resurrection, Peter's denial and Judas's betrayal; and the teaching of the New Testament on the precreation redemptive plan of God that presupposes his foreknowledge of the Fall. In all theses cases, we have seen that the view that God can and does foreknow free decisions of human beings best accords with the data of the New Testament.

However, there are other biblical texts that have been understood to teach that God does not have this exhaustive foreknowledge. And examination of these texts will be our subject in chapter four.

---

[160]See Paul Helm, *The Providence of God* (Downers Grove, Ill.: InterVarsity Press, 1994), p. 100. Helm argues that "the fall has a critical place in the divine purposes, for it is pivotal in the biblical message of salvation through Christ. Without the fall being presupposed, salvation is unnecessary and the announcement of salvation is unintelligible. For if there is no fall into sin, from what would we need to be saved? What would Christ's work have accomplished? Why would any incarnation have been necessary?"

[161]Rice, *God's Foreknowledge and Man's Free Will,* pp. 84-85.

4

A DIFFERENT VIEW OF DIVINE FOREKNOWLEDGE

In spite of the kind and amount of biblical evidence cited in chapters two and three, open theists do not affirm that God infallibly foreknows free human decisions. In addition to philosophical arguments offered in support of their position, they also appeal to biblical texts to support their nonexhaustive view of divine foreknowledge.[1] In this chapter we will examine these texts to see

---

[1]A helpful overview of Old Testament arguments for a nonexhaustive understanding of God's foreknowledge is found in Terence Fretheim, *The Suffering of God* (Philadelphia: Fortress, 1984), pp. 45-59. He points to four lines of Old Testament evidence:
- "The Divine Perhaps," especially found when God is speaking of the anticipated response of his people (e.g., Jer 26:2-3). God's lack of certain foreknowledge of the responses of his people leads to genuine surprises for him (cf. Jer 3:7, 19).
- "The Divine If." These are truly conditional statements addressed by God to his people (e.g., Jer 7:5). For Fretheim the integrity of such conditions depends on the open possibility of the people's actions and the divine response.
- "The Divine Consultation." Here Fretheim cites Abraham's dialogue with God over his planned destruction of Sodom (Gen 18:17-22), Moses' intercession for the Israelites after their sin with the golden calf (Ex 32:7-14), and Samuel's ultimately unsuccessful intercession for Saul (1 Sam 15:35; 16:1). Such consultation, Fretheim argues, means that the future is not unalterably fixed in such a way that God can know it with certainty.
- "The Divine Question." These more-than-merely-rhetorical questions fall into two categories: questions that reflect God's decision-making process with regard to the future of Israel (Jer 5:7, 9, 29; 9:7, 9; Hos 6:4; 11:8), and questions about the present faithlessness of his people, implying that God is at a genuine loss to explain this inexplicable response (Is 5:4; 50:2; Jer 2:32; 8:5, 19; 30:6).

Fretheim concludes that from these considerations "any talk about divine omniscience in the Old Testament must be limited when it comes to talk about the future. It is limited in such a way as to include a genuine divine openness to the future—an openness, which, however, is constantly informed by the divine will to save. . . . God knows everything there is to be known. As new things happen and come to be knowable for the first time, God knows them as actualities, not only as possibilities. This, of course, implies that God's knowledge is thereby increased, which entails change for God; new knowledge means real change" (ibid., pp. 57-58).

Sanders reproduces Fretheim's fourfold argument in *God Who Risks* (pp. 73-74), and in his chapter on Old Testament support for his position, he has 30 different endnotes referring to the works of Fretheim.

whether they do support an open view of the extent of divine foreknowledge. We will begin with perhaps the most frequently cited group of texts—those that affirm the repentance of God.[2]

THE REPENTANCE OF GOD

John Sanders follows Terence Fretheim in calling divine repentance a "controlling metaphor" for our understanding of the nature of God, arguing that it "signifies God's ability to remain faithful to his project while altering his plans to accommodate the changing circumstances brought about by the creatures."[3] Pinnock also affirms the crucial importance of divine repentance as a biblical theme. His conclusion bears quoting.

> How history will go is not a foregone conclusion, even to God, because he is free to strike in new directions as may be appropriate. If we take divine repentance language seriously, it suggests that God does not work with a plan fixed in every detail but with general goals that can be fulfilled in different ways. God is faithful to these goals but flexible as to how to fulfill them. Although repentance is a metaphor, which should not be pressed too far, it is revelatory of the way God exercises his sovereignty. It depicts God as free to adjust plans in response to changing situations. It does not imply that God is fickle or untrustworthy but that he is flexible in faithfulness. He can take things into account when acting and be creative in pursuing his plans. We should not regard the metaphor as a mere accommodation but as indicative of how God works. God is able to remain faithful to his purposes even while altering plans to fit in with changing circumstances.[4]

This divine "flexibility" affirmed by Pinnock necessarily implies a limitation on the extent of his foreknowledge. If the way history will go "is not a foregone conclusion, even to God," then his foreknowledge is clearly not exhaustive and infallible at every point.

While I do not interpret divine repentance texts in the same way that open theists do, I am grateful to the openness movement for focusing attention on

---

[2]Richard Rice affirms that divine repentance is one of two biblical metaphors that have been underemphasized in classical theism (the other being divine suffering). Rice says that more weight will have to be given to these metaphors to achieve a biblically faithful understanding of God ("Biblical Support for a New Perspective," in *Openness of God* [Downers Grove, Ill.: InterVarsity Press, 1994], p. 17). Critics of open theism also understand the centrality of divine repentance to the biblical case presented by open theists. For example, Ware cites divine repentance as one of the two primary categories of biblical texts appealed to by open theists (the other being what Ware calls "divine growth-in-knowledge" texts) (Bruce A. Ware, *God's Lesser Glory* [Wheaton, Ill.: Crossway, 2000], pp. 86-98).
[3]John Sanders, *God Who Risks* (Downers Grove, Ill.: InterVarsity Press, 1998), p. 72.
[4]Clark H. Pinnock, *Most Moved Mover* (Grand Rapids: Baker, 2001), pp. 43-44.

them. I agree that the biblical theme of divine repentance has been underemphasized and underappreciated in many strands of classical theism. This must be rectified. Thus these texts are worthy of an extended investigation.

Lexical considerations. The repentance of God is primarily expressed in the Old Testament through the Hebrew verb *niham*.[5] For our purposes, the most important uses of the verb come in the niphal and hithpael stems, where an element of change is denoted by the verb. Hans Walter Wolff sees a crucial emotional component in the meaning of *niham* and connects this with a change of mind or direction. He argues that *niham* means "a change of mind prompted by the emotions, a turning away from an earlier decision on the part of someone deeply moved."[6] In the thirty-five Old Testament instances where God is the subject of the verb, Robert Chisholm argues that *niham* refers both to God's relenting from a course of action already underway and to God's decision to relent or change his mind about a stated course of action.[7]

Space limitations prevent a thorough discussion of all thirty-five passages in which God is the subject of *niham* and of other passages that deal with the theme of divine repentance but do not use the word. But in what follows I will discuss the major passages cited in the contemporary discussion about the relationship of God's repentance to his foreknowledge. The crucial question we will be considering throughout is whether God's emotional, mental or directional change indicated by *niham* demands a nonexhaustive view of his foreknowledge. I will begin with a survey of key passages that affirm God's repentance

---

[5]In a very thorough investigation of this Hebrew verb, H. Van Dyke Parunak concludes that "the basic meaning . . . attested both etymologically and in every form of the Hebrew, is 'comfort, console' " ("A Semantic Survey of *NHM*," *Biblica* 56 [1975]: 532).

[6]Hans Walter Wolff, *Joel and Amos,* trans. Waldemar Janzen, S. Dean McBride Jr. and Charles A. Muenchow (Philadelphia: Fortress, 1977), p. 298. Norman H. Snaith argues against the emotional component in the verb on the basis of Arabic usage and concludes, "When the word is translated 'repent,' as frequently of God, it means 'change of mind or intention,' and has no necessary connection with sorrow or regret" ("The Language of the Old Testament," in *The Interpreter's Bible* [New York: Abingdon, 1952], 1:225). James Barr opposes Snaith on methodological grounds. (*The Semantics of Biblical Language* [Oxford: Oxford University Press, 1961], p. 117).

[7]Of the thirty-five uses of the verb, there are twenty-seven that affirm that God may or does *niham* and eight cases where it is said that God does not or cannot *niham*. In the first category (God's turning away from a course of action already underway), Chisholm cites Deut 32:36 (= Ps 135:14); Judg 2:18; 2 Sam 24:16 (= 1 Chron 21:15); Ps 90:13; 106:45. In the second category (God changing his mind about a stated course of action), he cites two categories of texts: those that say God did, does or will not retract a statement or turn from a stated course of action (Num 23:19; 1 Sam 15:29; Ps 110:4; Jer 4:28; Ezek 24:14; Zech 8:14) and those which say that God does, will or might change his mind (Ex 32:12, 14; Is 57:6; Jer 15:6; 18:8, 10; 26:3, 13, 19; Joel 2:13-14; Amos 7:3, 6; Jon 3:9-10; 4:2) (Robert B. Chisholm Jr., "Does God Change His Mind?" *Bibliotheca Sacra* 152, no. 3 [1995]: 388).

before turning to a discussion of texts that affirm that God does not repent.[8]

God repents in response to human sin. *Genesis 6:6-7.* The early chapters of Genesis record the degeneration of the human race into sin. Following Cain's murder of his brother Abel (Gen 4:8), the polygamy of Lamech (Gen 4:19) and his thirst for excessive revenge (Gen 4:23-24), and the enigmatic marriage of the "sons of God" to the "daughters of men" (Gen 6:1-3), we read of God's assessment of how deep and pervasive is the reality of human sin. "The LORD saw how great man's wickedness on the earth had become, and that every inclination of the thoughts of his heart was only evil all the time" (Gen 6:5).

Clearly this was not God's intention in creating human beings as his image-bearers. In the words of Sanders, "creation has miscarried."[9] And this horrendous deviation from God's revealed will for his image-bearers pained him deeply.

> The LORD was grieved *[niham]* that he had made man on the earth, and his heart was filled with pain. So the LORD said, "I will wipe mankind, whom I have created, from the face of the earth—men and animals, and creatures that move along the ground, and birds of the air—for I am grieved *[niham]* that I have made them." (Gen 6:6-7)[10]

The depth of emotional pain experienced by Yahweh is shown by the parallel expression, translated by the NIV "his heart was filled with pain." The verb used here (ʿāṣab) expresses "the most intense form of human emotion, a mixture of rage and bitter anguish."[11] The same verbal root is used two times in Genesis 3:16-17 to describe the painful punishment imposed on Adam and Eve. But the pain of Adam and Eve was because of their own sin and its consequences. The emotional pain experienced by Yahweh in Genesis 6, on the other hand, is because of the sin of his image-bearers and because he must judge such

---

[8]In this discussion I will be utilizing categories of passages found in Marvin S. Davis, "An Investigation of the Concept of the Repentance of God in the Old Testament" (Th.D. diss., New Orleans Baptist Seminary, 1983).

[9]Sanders, *God Who Risks,* p. 49. Walter Brueggemann says that "the creation has refused to be God's creation" and that "this essential fracture between creator and creation is the premise and agenda of the [upcoming] flood narrative" (*Genesis,* Interpretation [Atlanta: John Knox Press, 1982], p. 74).

[10]The connection between Gen 6:5 (God's assessment of the depth of human sin) and Gen 6:6-7 (God's grief over this sin and his resolution to take action in judgment) demonstrates that the evil, sin and guilt that occasioned the flood is entirely the responsibility of humanity. Animals share in humanity's judgment only because of their close association with humans. See Francis I. Andersen and David Noel Freedman, "When God Repents," in *Amos,* Anchor Bible 24 (New York: Doubleday, 1989), p. 646.

[11]Gordon J. Wenham, *Genesis 1-15,* Word Biblical Commentary 1 (Waco, Tex.: Word, 1987), p. 144.

wickedness.[12] Sanders emphasizes the intensity of God's emotional pain:

> God regrets his decision to go ahead with the creation in light of these tragic developments. He is extremely disappointed at how things are turning out. Despite all the blessings God has provided, humanity turns away from the divine love. This pains God in his very heart. The narrator says that human hearts are continuously evil, and the divine heart suffers the pain of rejection. God is open to and affected by what he has made. . . . The cost to God is great in terms of personal suffering. God cares, and caring leads to pain when it sees the beloved destroying itself.[13]

But God's emotional pain leads him to action—in this case to a change in action. It leads him to act in judgment toward humanity through the flood. And it is precisely his change in action that demonstrates the reality of God's emotional pain. Boyd says, "The genuineness of God's regret is evidenced by the fact that the Lord immediately took measures to destroy humanity and start over."[14]

The Genesis flood narrative also records a second time that God changes his mind. Genesis 8:21 records God's decision to never again destroy humanity with a flood. Rather he promises Noah, the surviving head of the human race, "Never again will I curse the ground because of man, even though [lit. "for"] every inclination of his heart is evil from childhood. And never will I destroy all living creatures, as I have done." And God reiterates this covenant promise to Noah in Genesis 9:9-11. Francis Andersen and David Freedman note that this divine covenant oath represents God's commitment to sustain human life

> not only irrespective of human behavior but in full recognition of humans' evil tendencies and proclivities. . . . The first statement [of human sin and guilt, Gen 6:5] provides support for the decision to wipe out humanity, while the second [Gen 8:21] modifies the commitment never to do so again. We can speak therefore of a new decision based essentially on the same data, in which God promises not to do what was done before; thus, although the term is not used again in connection with the second statement, we can speak of a second repentance or change of mind (= heart).[15]

---

[12]Victor P. Hamilton, *The Book of Genesis: Chapter 1-17,* New International Commentary on the Old Testament (Grand Rapids: Eerdmans, 1990), p. 274. See also Claus Westermann, *Genesis 1-11,* trans. John J. Scullion (Minneapolis: Augsburg, 1984), pp. 410-11.

[13]Sanders, *God Who Risks,* p. 49.

[14]Gregory A. Boyd, *God of the Possible* (Grand Rapids: Baker, 2000), p. 55.

[15]Andersen and Freedman, *Amos,* Anchor Bible 24 (New York: Doubleday, 1989), pp. 646-47. Sanders agrees. "YWHW actually changes his mind twice in this story, once to destroy and then to never again destroy (6:5-7; 8:21). Both reversals are based on the *same* data: humans are sinful" (*God Who Risks,* p. 292, n. 46).

Of this second divine change, Sanders says, "It may be the case that although human evil caused God great pain, the destruction of what he had made caused him even greater suffering. Although his judgment was righteous, God decides to try different courses of action in the future."[16] While Sanders makes this suggestion somewhat tentative ("It *may* be the case"), his proposal is indeed striking. Sanders suggests that God's second change of mind came as a result of his reassessment of his prior decision to judge humanity through the flood. That action had caused him so much pain that he vows to never do it again. The implication seems inescapable. On further reflection, God determines that his first decision was a mistake; its unforeseen consequences were too great. Now Sanders is clear that God's first decision to judge was a righteous one, but his subsequent change leads us to believe that God concluded it was not a wise one.[17] The staggering implications of this portrayal of God's decision-making for our ongoing ability to trust God to lead and guide us will be examined further in chapter six.

1 Samuel 15:11, 35. In 1 Samuel 15 we find that Yahweh is grieved *(niham)* by his prior decision to make Saul king of Israel. This comes in response to Saul's disobedience to God in (1) offering sacrifices at Gilgal, even though he was not a priest (1 Sam 13:8-10), (2) his foolish curse on his army (1 Sam 14:24) that ultimately led to his condemnation of his son Jonathan (1 Sam 14:44)—a decision that was overturned by the people, resulting in the alienation of Saul from his army and his son, and (3) Saul's failure to obey God's explicit command to destroy the Amalekites and all their plunder (15:3, 9, 18-19, 22-24).[18] As a result Yahweh said, "I am grieved *[niham]* that I have made Saul king, because he has turned away from me and has not carried out my instructions" (1 Sam 15:11).

That Yahweh is grieved *(niham)* is also highlighted at the end of the chapter: "Until the day Samuel died, he did not go to see Saul again, though Samuel mourned for him. And the LORD was grieved *[niham]* that he had made Saul king

---

[16]Sanders, *God Who Risks,* p. 50.

[17]David Basinger agrees with Sanders that decisions God believes to be best may in the end turn out to be ones he regrets having made. "Since God does not necessarily know exactly what will happen in the future, it is always possible that even that which God in his unparalleled wisdom believes to be the best course of action at any given time may not produce the anticipated results in the long run" ("Practical Implications," in *The Openness of God* [Downers Grove, Ill.: InterVarsity Press, 1994], p. 165).

[18]The first act of disobedience resulted in God's rejection of Saul's dynastic succession (1 Sam 13:13-14). It is not until 1 Sam 15:28 that Yahweh rejects Saul himself as king. See Ralph W. Klein, *1 Samuel,* Word Biblical Commentary 10 (Waco, Tex.: Word, 1983), p. 127, and V. Philips Long, *The Reign and Rejection of King Saul,* Society of Biblical Literature Dissertation Series 118 (Atlanta: Scholars Press, 1989), p. 167.

over Israel" (1 Sam 15:35). Once again the verb *niham* describes God's experience of emotional pain as he grieved over his decision to make Saul king. As with Genesis 6:6-7, what arouses this emotional pain in Yahweh's heart is human sin—now not of humanity in general but of one individual, Saul. And once again God's grieving *(niham)* moves him to action—to reject Saul as king and to replace him with David.

Sanders also notes that because Yahweh was grieved *(niham)*, "Samuel was troubled, and he cried out to the LORD all that night" (1 Sam 15:11). He interprets Samuel's crying out to the Lord as intercessory prayer, specifically that he was "praying all night long for God to repent of his repentance."[19] Now in this case God in his sovereign freedom refuses to do that (1 Sam 15:29).[20] But to Sanders the fact that Samuel prayed is evidence that he did not believe God's pronouncements concerning the future were fixed and unchangeable.[21]

God repents in response to human repentance. *Jonah 3:9-10.* In the book of Jonah we find Yahweh commanding Jonah to go to Nineveh with a message of judgment. "Forty more days and Nineveh will be overturned" (Jon 3:4). As subsequent events would show, there was an implicit, unstated condition contained in this statement of impending divine wrath (i.e., "Forty more days and Nineveh will be destroyed *unless you repent*").[22] This is pointed to by God's announcement itself. Why would God bother to announce his judgment in advance if not to seek to move the Ninevites to repentance?

---

[19]Sanders, *God Who Risks*, pp. 69-70. See also Andersen and Freedman, *Amos*, pp. 654-55.

[20]Andersen and Freedman contrast Samuel's intercessory prayers with those of Moses (Ex 32:11-14) and Amos (Amos 7:1-6). The difference is the sovereign freedom of God. "The lesson to be learned is that Yahweh's judgments are his own, as is his repentance. The prophet may intercede, as in fact Moses and Samuel do, but Yahweh is free to respond positively (as in the case of Moses and the people) or negatively (as in the case of Samuel and Saul). . . . The outcome remains in doubt until Yahweh seals the decision by his action" (*Amos*, p. 656).

[21]There are other alternative explanations of 1 Sam 15:11. Joyce Baldwin, for example, suggests three sources of Samuel's anger: (1) Samuel's theology was being put into question, as now God, who will not lie or repent (1 Sam 15:29) does change his mind about the kingship of Saul. What does this reversal mean about God? (2) Samuel was also concerned about the ongoing leadership of Israel. And (3) "Samuel was torn within himself by the divine word" (*1 and 2 Samuel,* Tyndale Old Testament Commentary, Downers Grove, Ill.: InterVarsity Press, 1988], pp. 114-15.)

[22]This implicit condition is acknowledged by openness scholars (e.g., Clark Pinnock, "God Limits His Knowledge," in *Predestination and Free Will*, ed. David Basinger and Randall Basinger [Downers Grove, Ill.: InterVarsity Press, 1986]; p. 158; William Hasker, *God, Time, and Knowledge* [Ithaca, N.Y.: Cornell University Press, 1989], pp. 194-95; Sanders, *God Who Risks*, pp. 70, 131; and Boyd, *Satan and the Problem of Evil* [Downers Grove, Ill.: InterVarsity Press, 2001], p. 94) and by nonopenness scholars (e.g., William Lane Craig, *The Only Wise God* [Grand Rapids: Baker, 1987], pp. 41-44, and Wayne Grudem, *Systematic Theology* [Grand Rapids: Zondervan, 1994], pp. 164-65).

On hearing this message the entire city of Nineveh, "from the greatest to the least," responded with faith and repentance (Jon 3:5-9). Their repentance is all the more remarkable since Jonah had neither named the God whose wrath he was proclaiming nor stated the condition of repentance.[23] Yet the king of Nineveh covered himself with sackcloth and proclaimed a fast for the entire city, saying, "Who knows? God may yet relent and with compassion *[niham]* turn from his fierce anger so that we will not perish" (Jon 3:9).

Fretheim notes the emphasis on the sovereign freedom of God in the statement of the king. It is similar, he argues, to that expressed by the captain of the ship ("How can you [Jonah] sleep? Get up and call on your god! *Maybe* he will take notice of us, and we will not perish" [Jon 1:6, emphasis added]) and by the sailors ("O LORD . . . Do not hold us accountable for killing an innocent man, for you, O LORD, have done as you pleased" [Jon 1:14]). Surely the irony is intentional that it is a pagan ship captain (Jon 1:6), pagan sailors (Jon 1:14) and a pagan king (Jon 3:9) who show greater respect for the sovereign freedom of God in showing mercy than did the Hebrew prophet Jonah.[24] But they did. John Watts argues that the Ninevites "have no assurance of God's response. But on the bare possibility that God will honour their change of heart and alter his determined will, they launch their fast, their grief, and their petition."[25] And the hopes of the Ninevites were not disappointed, for God did respond with his decision to show compassion: "When God saw what they did and how they turned from their evil ways, he had compassion *[niham]* and did not bring upon them the destruction he had threatened" (Jon 3:10).

As in Genesis 6:6-7, Yahweh's decision to *niham* is once again based on what he saw. But in this case he did not see human sin but the repentance of the

---

[23]Jon 3:5 says, "The Ninevites believed God" (Elohim, as opposed to Yahweh). The generic Elohim is also used in the king's decree in Jon 3:7-9. See John D. Watts, *The Books of Joel, Obadiah, Jonah, Nahum, Habakkuk, and Zephaniah*, Cambridge Bible Commentary (New York: Cambridge University Press, 1975), p. 90.

[24]Fretheim is worth quoting at length here. "The heathen thus ironically understand clearly that their repentance is not something magical which would *automatically* result in God's grace being extended to them and judgment removed. While God's saving action is normally contingent upon some kind of human response, God does not *have* to act mercifully if humans so respond. There is no mechanical relationship between human acts of piety or worship and God's saving plan. Repentance does not *entitle* one to salvation. While God is indeed motivated to save because of human prayer and repentance, God remains ultimately free to decide for himself what he will do. For no human act, however repentant or pious or worthy of condemnation, is finally sufficient to make God's saving action *necessary*, or the only possible action on his part. His action is finally grounded totally in himself. And thus, if he chooses to deliver, this is an act of pure grace" (*The Message of Jonah* [Minneapolis: Augsburg, 1977], p. 113).

[25]Watts, *Books of Joel, Obadiah, Jonah*, pp. 89-90.

Ninevites. And in response God "changed his mind" and did not bring his threatened judgment on the city.[26] In God's great mercy he changed his course of action.

Jeremiah 18:7-10. In Jeremiah 18 we find a twofold example of divine repentance. Yahweh proclaims to Jeremiah both that he will repent of his announced judgment in response to human repentance and that he will repent of his announced blessing in the face of human sin.

> If at any time I announce that a nation or kingdom is to be uprooted, torn down and destroyed, and if that nation I warned repents of its evil, then I will relent *[niham]* and not inflict on it the disaster I had planned. And if at another time I announce that a nation or kingdom is to be built up and planted, and if it does evil in my sight and does not obey me, then I will reconsider *[niham]* the good that I had intended to do for it. (Jer 18:7-10)

Because this passage announces divine repentance that operates in both directions (from judgment to blessing and vice versa) and because it is applied impartially to all nations, Andersen and Freedman say that Jeremiah 18 provides "a general theory of divine repentance." As such, it gives us "a working definition of divine repentance in the world."[27]

Yahweh's oracle in Jeremiah 18:7-10 occurs while Jeremiah is visiting the potter's house. Jeremiah is instructed to watch the potter at work. He noticed that when the vessel turned out poorly, the potter would reshape the clay into another vessel, as seemed best to him (Jer 18:4). Yahweh then identifies himself as the potter and the "house of Israel" as the clay in his hands (Jer 18:6). Then comes our passage in which Yahweh lays out the options that Israel, as any other nation, would face. And he concludes by instructing Jeremiah to tell the people of Judah of the destruction he is preparing to unleash against them (Jer 18:11). Fretheim understands this to be a statement of divine intention that is not finalized until verse 17. This can be seen by Yahweh's exhortation, "So turn from your evil ways, each one of you, and reform your ways and your actions" (18:11). Thus there is an openness inherent in Israel's future. Yawheh's an-

---

[26]At this point in our discussion of the repentance of God, I am using the phrase "God changed his mind" in a very general way. The goal of our discussion in this chapter is to discern the nature of God's change of mind. Does God, in response to new and unanticipated developments, change his mind in ways that even he did not anticipate or foreknow? Or does God change his mind and revise his previously announced course of action in keeping with his ultimate purpose and plan? This question will be answered as a result of our investigation into divine repentance. Please understand the phrase *changed his mind* in general terms until that point.

[27]Andersen and Freedman, *Amos,* pp. 659, 661.

nounced judgment awaits a response from the people before it is executed.[28]

The analogy of the potter and the clay serves two purposes. It affirms both the potter's complete control of the clay and his freedom to shape it as he will, and second, it affirms a flexible response on the part of the potter. Walter Brueggemann captures this dual emphasis well. He observes that

> the potter completely controls the clay, can reshape it, and is not committed to any particular form of the clay (v. 4). The potter will completely reshape the clay until the potter has it the way he wants it. . . . Israel is not autonomous or independent, but is completely in the control of Yahweh. The oracle asserts Yahweh's complete sovereignty and Israel's complete subservience.[29]

Yet in light of the argument of Jeremiah 18:7-10, Brueggemann suggests that Yahweh's "complete sovereignty" operates in a way that truly responds to the actions of the people. His is in fact a "responsive sovereignty."[30]

All indications are that the potter is highly skilled, that he wants to make the best vessel possible out of the clay and that he will work patiently toward that objective. Thus we must affirm that the problem with the inferior pottery does not come from the potter. No, it is the clay (the people) that is responsible for any problem that exists.[31] This creates "a dynamic situation" in which, according to Fretheim:

> God is faced with the task of working with existing negative and positive factors in order to shape Israel into the best vessel possible. The focus is not on God's power and control but on God's initiative, creativity, patience, and responsiveness in relation to the possibilities inherent in the situation.[32]

---

[28]Fretheim sees this as an example of the "common distinction between God's plans and their execution" ("The Repentance of God: A Study of Jeremiah 18:7-10," in *Hebrew Annual Review*, ed. Reuben Ahroni [Columbus, Ohio: Department of Judaic and Near Eastern Languages and Literatures, 1987], 11:86-87).

[29]Walter Brueggemann, *To Pluck Up, To Tear Down* (Grand Rapids: Eerdmans, 1988), p. 160. This emphasis on the absolute sovereignty of the divine potter over his people corresponds to Paul's usage of the potter-clay imagery in Rom 9:20-21.

[30]Ibid., p. 161. Of course, the question of whether God's "responsive sovereignty" entails the possibility of God acting in ways that he himself did not foreknow is the very issue we are discussing in this chapter.

[31]Fretheim, "Repentance of God," p. 85. See also William Holladay, *Jeremiah* (Philadelphia: Fortress, 1986), 1:515, and John T. Willis, "The 'Repentance' of God in the Books of Samuel, Jeremiah, and Jonah," *Horizons in Biblical Theology* 16, no. 2 (1994): 164-65. Davis argues that this identification is made all the more sure in light of Jeremiah's statements of Israel's sin in the preceding chapter (Jer 17:1, 9) ("Investigation of the Concept of the Repentance of God," p. 72).

[32]Fretheim, "The Repentance of God," p. 86. Fretheim cites v. 12, where Yahweh predicts the response of the people to his appeal of v. 11, "But they will reply, 'It's no use. We will continue with our own plans; each of us will follow the stubbornness of his evil heart.'" Thus he argues, "God's future activity with respect to people is not predetermined; by their response the people have the God-given capacity to shape God's own response, but only in a limited way" (ibid.).

This view is shared by open theists. Pinnock sees this passage as proof of the fact that "the future is not something fixed in God's mind in meticulous detail, [but rather] some things can go one way or another." Thus God's "creation project has an unquestionably dynamic character."[33] Rice agrees:

> This important passage indicates that God is not unilaterally directive in his dealings with human beings. Instead, his relation to us is one of dynamic interaction. God expresses certain intentions and waits to see how people will react. What he finally decides to do depends on their response. As a result, the general course of events is not something for which God is exclusively responsible. To a significant extent it depends on the actions and decisions of human beings.[34]

Boyd sees in Jeremiah 18 a God who is "willing to revise his initial plan when circumstances call for it. He is not a unilaterally controlling God; he is a graciously flexible God."[35]

The flexibility and responsiveness of God's relationship is indicated by the two conditional scenarios presented in Jeremiah 18:7-10.[36] The point once again is that Yahweh is free and willing to revise his originally stated intention based on what the people choose to do. And this revision can go in either direction—from blessing to judgment in response to human sin (as in Gen 6:6-7; 1 Sam 15:11, 35) and from judgment to blessing in response to human repentance (as in Jon 3:6-10; Joel 2:12-13).

Fretheim notes that unlike verses 6 and 11, Jeremiah 18:7-10 speaks not of Israel specifically but more generally of "a nation or kingdom." As in Genesis 6, Yahweh's repentance here occurs in the context of his dealings with the whole of humanity and not with his covenant people exclusively. Here there is what Fretheim calls "a creation-wide ethical consistency" on the part of God, the creator and judge of all the world.[37] God's actions toward Israel (e.g., his call for it to repent of its sins that he in turn might repent and be gracious to it [Jer 18:11]) are not unique. Rather, Yahweh treats Israel in the same way he treats every nation.

---

[33]Pinnock, *Most Moved Mover*, p. 48.

[34]Rice, "Biblical Support for a New Perspective," p. 32.

[35]Boyd, *God of the Possible*, pp. 76-77. Note, however, that God's "flexibility" does not always result in the granting of more grace. In Jer 18:10, God's flexible repentance results in judgment for his disobedient people.

[36]Jer 18:7-8 is balanced exactly by vv. 9-10. In each case, an identical three-part pattern is followed: (1) a statement of God's initial decree, (2) a statement of the people's response to God and to his decree, and (3) a final "then" clause that refers to God's readiness to change his mind and act in new ways in response to freely chosen human behavior. On this threefold pattern, see Brueggemann, *To Pluck Up*, p. 161.

[37]Fretheim, "The Repentance of God," p. 89.

God repents in response to intercessory prayer. *Exodus 32:11-14.*
While Moses was receiving the law from Yahweh on Mt. Sinai, the Israelites suc-
cumbed to the sin of idolatry.[38] Yahweh told Moses that

> your people, whom you brought up out of Egypt, have become corrupt. They have
> been quick to turn away from what I commanded them and have made themselves an
> idol cast in the shape of a calf. They have bowed down to it and sacrificed to it and
> have said, "These are your gods, O Israel, who brought you up out of Egypt." (Ex 32:7-8)

In response to this sin, Yahweh said to Moses in verse 10, "Now leave me
alone so that my anger may burn against them and that I may destroy them.
Then I will make you into a great nation."

As in Genesis 6, God confronted the reality of the grievous sin of his people
and decided to send judgment. While the verb *niham* is not used here, this decision of Yahweh could legitimately be called one of divine repentance, for here
God "changed his mind" about his prior act of grace in the exodus and his
promise to bring the Israelites into the Promised Land.[39] Yet he says to Moses,
"*Leave me alone* so that my anger may burn against them." Andersen and Freedman note that this phrase "makes it appear that Yahweh is asking Moses to re-
lease or allow him to go ahead with this plan."[40] Brevard Childs notes perceptively that here God is implicitly giving Moses room to intercede for his people.
"God vows the severest punishment imaginable, but then suddenly he conditions it, as it were, on Moses' agreement. 'Let me alone that I may consume

---

[38]In addition to Ex 32:11-14 and 2 Kings 20:1-6 that will be discussed more fully in this section,
Amos 7—8 also portrays God as relenting from threatened judgment in response to the intercession of his prophet. In Amos 7:1-3, God sends a vision of a locust plague that he will send
on his people in judgment for their sins. Amos prays for mercy and forgiveness for Israel,
appealing to God's compassion on his people who are so small. And God relents *(niham)*
(v. 3). A second vision is portrayed in Amos 7:4-6. Again judgment is threatened by Yahweh,
this time by fire. Again Amos intercedes and Yahweh relents *(niham)* (v. 6). However there is
a second pair of visions that Amos receives in Amos 7:7-9; 8:1-3. This time there is no divine
repentance, for there has been no lasting change in the people. Thus we can learn from Amos
7—8 that Yahweh is willing at times to change his mind in response to the intercession of his
prophet. But not always. He alone decides when he will repent of his decision to judge and
when he will allow his prior decision to stand irreversibly. In addition to Ex 32, 2 Kings 20
and Amos 7—8, Davis cites three additional texts in this category: Judg 2:18; Ps 90:13; 106:44-
45 ("Investigation of the Concept of the Repentance of God," pp. 76-78, 82, 86).

[39]Andersen and Freedman comment on the similarity between Yahweh's decision to destroy in
Ex 32:10 and in Gen 6:6-7 (both decisions based on the reality of human sin): "In that situation
[Genesis 6] the decision to destroy was denoted as an act of repentance, Yahweh's change of
mind. Clearly a similar change of mind about his act of grace, in bringing Israel out of Egypt,
has taken place, and he will now punish the people who abandoned him for an idol. That
decision, however, is not the one connected with divine repentance, though it clearly could
have been. In this case, it is the next reversal that is called repentance" *(Amos,* p. 648).

[40]Ibid., p. 647.

them.' The effect is that God himself leaves the door open for intercession. He allows himself to be persuaded. That is what a mediator is for!"[41]

The implication is that Yahweh's decision to judge his people has not yet been finalized. So Fretheim argues that for the phrase "Leave me alone" to make sense

> one must assume that, while God has decided to execute wrath (v. 14, "the evil which he thought to do"), the decision had not yet reached an irretrievable point. Moses could conceivably contribute something to the divine deliberation that might occasion a future for Israel other than wrath. The devastation of Israel by the divine wrath is thus conditional upon Moses' leaving God alone.[42]

Confronted with this threatened judgment, Moses interceded for the Israelites.

> O LORD . . . why should your anger burn against your people, whom you brought out of Egypt with great power and a mighty hand? Why should the Egyptians say, "It was with evil intent that he brought them out, to kill them in the mountains and to wipe them off the face of the earth?" Turn from your fierce anger; relent *[niham]* and do not bring disaster on your people. Remember your servants Abraham, Isaac, and Israel, to whom you swore by your own self: "I will make your descendants as numerous as the stars in the sky and I will give your descendants all this land I promised them, and it will be their inheritance forever." (Ex 32:11-13)[43]

Moses appeals to Yahweh to change his emotional state and to turn from his previously announced course of action on three primary grounds: (1) Israel is

---

[41]Brevard S. Childs, *The Book of Exodus* (Philadelphia: Westminster, 1974), p. 567. Terrence Fretheim contends that Yahweh's willingness to allow Moses to dialogue with him about Israel's future was based on the relationship he had with Moses. "What Moses has to contribute counts with God. *God has so entered into relationship with him that God is not the only one who has something important to say*" ("Suffering God and Sovereign God in Exodus: A Collision of Images," *Horizons in Biblical Theology* 11, no. 2 [1989]: 41). Sanders argues similarly, "Apparently Moses has a relationship with God such that God values what Moses desires. . . . The real basis for the change in God's decision comes from a forceful presentation by one who is in a special relationship with God. Being in relationship to Moses, God is willing to allow him to influence the path he will take. God permits human input into the divine future. One of the most remarkable features in the Old Testament is that people can argue with God" (*God Who Risks*, p. 64.)

[42]Fretheim, *Suffering of God*, p. 50.

[43]The imperative form of *niham* that Moses uses in prayer is very rare. Its force is increased with the parallel imperative "turn" *[sûb]*. The only other occurrence of *niham* in the imperative used in addressing God is found in Ps 90:13—and it is also accompanied by the imperative *sûb*: "Relent *[sûb]*, O LORD! How long will it be? / Have compassion *[niham]* on your servants." Psalm 90 is also attributed to Moses. Andersen and Freedman comment, "Apparently only Moses in the Bible expresses this idea quite so forcefully, commanding God to repent. . . . To instruct God to repent (using this verb with its connotations and overtones) is a privilege claimed by Moses and restricted to him" (*Amos*, p. 649).

God's people, whom he had powerfully redeemed from slavery in Egypt, (2) the Egyptians would mock Yahweh if he had destroyed his recently redeemed people, and (3) Yahweh had sworn his covenant oath to the patriarchs of Israel.[44]

And in response to the intercession of Moses, "the LORD relented *[niham]* and did not bring on his people the disaster he had threatened" (Ex 32:14). Yahweh's relenting here involves both emotion and action. He turns from his fierce anger to a stance of mercy toward his sinful people, and he decides not to destroy them. He relents.

2 Kings 20:1-6 (par. Is 38:1-6; 2 Chron 32:24). While the verb *niham* is not used in these narratives in which God decides to extend the life of Hezekiah, king of Judah, they deserve to be mentioned here, for here too God "changes his mind" in response to the prayer of his servant.[45]

In a time of illness, God comes to King Hezekiah and says to him through the prophet Isaiah: "This is what the LORD says: Put your house in order, because you are going to die; you will not recover" (2 Kings 20:1; cf. Is 38:1). This is a strong statement from Yahweh, intensified by the dual affirmation ("you are going to die; you will not recover").[46]

While it is often the case that an announcement of impending death reflects the judgment of God (e.g., 1 Sam 2:31-34; 1 Kings 14:10; 2 Kings 1:2-4), in this case there is no hint of Hezekiah being punished for any misdeeds. But as with God's declaration of impending judgment against Nineveh in the book of Jonah, so here too God's declaration comes with an implicit condition.[47] Hezekiah un-

---

[44]Note that on the second reason Moses is following God's own expressed concern for his reputation among the Egyptians (Ex 9:13-19, 29-30). On this threefold rationale for Moses' request, see Davis, "Investigation of the Concept of the Repentance of God," p. 96, and Fretheim, *Suffering of God,* p. 50.

[45]Boyd argues that *niham* is used in Jeremiah's reflection on the experience of Hezekiah in Jer 26:19 ("Did not Hezekiah fear the LORD and seek his favor? And did not the LORD relent *[niham]* so that he did not bring the disaster he pronounced against them?"). Boyd sees this verse to be Jeremiah's reflection on God's decision to extend Hezekiah's life (*God of the Possible,* p. 82). But Andersen and Freedman argue persuasively that Jeremiah 26 is referring to another incident in the life of Hezekiah. They see Jer 26:19 referring to the fact that Hezekiah and the people of Judah did not kill Micah when he came with a prediction of God's judgment (the elders quote Mic 3:12 in Jer 26:18); rather, they repented and sought God's favor. And God changed his mind and spared the city (2 Kings 18—19). In the same way, Jeremiah argues, the people of Jerusalem should not attack him when he brings a word of judgment from Yahweh. Rather they should repent and pray, with confidence that God will relent in response (Jer 2:14) (see Andersen and Freedman, *Amos,* p. 661).

[46]Thus the rendering of E. J. Young: "You are going to die and there is no hope of escape" (*The Book of Isaiah* [Grand Rapids: Eerdmans, 1972], 2:509).

[47]Thus Pinnock says of God's statement to Hezekiah, "Evidently the initial prediction had been conditional without the point being stated" (*Most Moved Mover,* p. 48).

derstood that God's announcement of his impending death brought with it the opportunity for prayer. Evidently he had learned from the example of Moses that God is a God who can be entreated. He is a God who is free to repent of his declared intention if he so desires.[48] In this case, Hezekiah responded to this implicit condition by turning to the Lord with weeping and with heartfelt prayer. He prayed, "Remember, O LORD, how I have walked before you faithfully and with wholehearted devotion and have done what is good in your eyes" (2 Kings 20:3).[49] And in response, God changes his declared course of action.

> This is what the LORD, the God of your father David, says: I have heard your prayer and seen your tears; I will heal you. On the third day from now you will go up to the temple of the LORD. I will add fifteen years to your life. And I will deliver you and this city from the hand of the king of Assyria. I will defend this city for my sake and for the sake of my servant David. (2 Kings 20:5-6, cf. Is 38:5-6)

Because he has heard Hezekiah's prayer and seen his tears, Yahweh promises to bring healing to Hezekiah and to extend his life for an additional fifteen years.[50] But the additional promise of deliverance for Hezekiah and the city of Jerusalem from the king of Assyria is not made because of Hezekiah but on the basis of Yahweh's zeal for his own glory and for the sake of David.[51]

The repentance of God in creedal statements. The repentance of God is listed, along with four other divine attributes, in the Old Testament creedal statements of Joel 2:21 and Jonah 4:2. These two identical statements reflect a significant creed in Israel, for, minus the reference of God's repentance, it is found five other times in the Old Testament (Ex 34:6-7; Neh 9:17; Ps 86:15; 103:8; 145:8). Fragments of this creed are also found in Exodus 20:5-6 (cf. Deut 5:9-10;

---

[48]Sanders writes, "Yahweh is free to change his mind in response to human beings. Not even the authoritative 'thus says the Lord' can prevent Yahweh from repenting if he so decides. God, using his wisdom in conjunction with input from the human relationships, freely decides when he will carry out the prediction and when he will alter it" (*God Who Risks,* p. 71).

[49]Hezekiah's prayer concentrates on his own piety (in contrast to his earlier prayer in 2 Kings 19:15-16 which focused on the greatness and majesty of Yahweh). Jones argues that this emphasizes how exceptional is the deliverance of Hezekiah, "an exceptional act due to an exceptional life" (Gwilym H. Jones, *1 and 2 Kings,* New Century Bible Commentary [Grand Rapids: Eerdmans, 1984], p. 586). Yet Watts notes that in Yahweh's response, "God takes account of the prayer and the tears. But he makes no reference to Hezekiah's claim to piety. Humility counts more than piety" (John D. W. Watts, *Isaiah 34—66,* Word Biblical Commentary [Waco, Tex.: Word, 1987], p. 51).

[50]Watts argues that this declaration is only a reprieve. "The original judgment stands, but is delayed" (ibid.). Yet even so, the delay does constitute a real change of mind on God's part.

[51]Oswalt notes the impact of the faithfulness of David on his descendant. As promised in Ex 34:6-7, the results of a person's faithfulness (in this case, David's) will reach to a thousand generations (John N. Oswalt, *The Book of Isaiah: Chapters 40-66,* New International Commentary on the Old Testament [Grand Rapids: Eerdmans, 1998], p. 677).

7:9; Num 14:18; 2 Chron 30:9; Ps 111:4; 112:4; Jer 32:18 and Nahum 1:3). The parallels of thought and vocabulary in these passages seem to indicate a literary dependence on a common original. The most frequently suggested original, due to the fullness of its expression and its strategic location in the Sinai narrative, is Exodus 34:6-7. Therefore, a brief look at this passage is in order before we turn our attention to the creedal statements in Joel and Jonah that specifically speak of God's willingness to *niham*.

Exodus 34:6-7. We have seen that after Israel's sin with the golden calf, Moses' intercession for the people led to Yahweh's relenting from his threatened destruction. When Moses came down from the mountain, he confronted the sin of the people himself. In anger, he shattered the tablets upon which the Ten Commandments had been written, burned the golden calf and ground it into powder, which he made the Israelites drink (Ex 32:19-20). He called forth judgment against the leaders of the rebellion, which was to be executed by the Levites (Ex 32:25-29). Once again, Moses interceded for the people, seeking to make atonement for them by offering to have his own name blotted out of God's book on their behalf (Ex 32:30-32). However, Moses' request was refused by Yahweh, who struck the people with a plague (Ex 32:35).[52] Yahweh once again commissioned Moses to lead the people up to the Promised Land. But he promised to send his angel before Moses and the people, rather than going with them himself (Ex 33:1-3). Moses again prayed, asking Yahweh to come with them himself. This time Yahweh did change his promised course of action (though the verb *niham* is not used here), promising first that his Presence would go with Moses (Ex 33:14) and ultimately that he himself would go with Moses (Ex 33:16-17). Then Moses asked Yahweh, "Show me your glory" (Ex 33:18). Yahweh mercifully responds and shows Moses his glory by declaring his name to him two times.

The first explanation Yahweh gives of his name stresses his sovereign divine freedom in dispensing mercy according to his good pleasure. He said, "I will cause all my goodness to pass in front of you, and I will proclaim my name, the LORD, in your presence. I will have mercy on whom I will have mercy, and I will have compassion on whom I will have compassion" (Ex 33:19). In chapter 34 we find the second declaration of Yahweh's name. And this declaration stresses his moral character.

---

[52]Peter Enns argues eloquently that God's refusal to accept the substitution of Moses to make atonement for the sins of Israel pointed ahead to the ultimate mediator, Jesus Christ, who would successfully make atonement for God's people through dying on the cross in their place (*Exodus,* The NIV Application Commentary [Grand Rapids: Zondervan, 2000], pp. 577, 594).

Then the LORD came down in the cloud and stood there with him and proclaimed his name, the LORD. And he passed in front of Moses, proclaiming, "The LORD, the LORD, the compassionate and gracious God, slow to anger, abounding in love and faithfulness, maintaining love to thousands, and forgiving wickedness, rebellion and sin. Yet he does not leave the guilty unpunished; he punishes the children and their children for the sin of the fathers to the third and fourth generation. (Ex 34:5-7)

There is no explicit mention of God's turning from judgment in this proclamation of God's name, although as we have seen God did in fact repent two times in the previous chapters of Exodus. But later prophetic usages of this creedal statement explicitly include the repentance of God.

Joel 2:12-14. After Joel's description of the disaster caused by locust plagues in chapter 1 and in 2:1-11, the prophet now calls the people of Judah to repentance and holds out to them an offer of grace and the promise that Yahweh will relent from sending calamity if they will in fact repent.[53] He says in Joel 2:12-14:

> "Even now," declares the LORD,
>> "return to me with all your heart,
>> with fasting and weeping and mourning.
> Rend your heart
>> and not your garments.
> Return to the LORD your God
>> for he is gracious and compassionate,
>> slow to anger and abounding in love,
>> and he relents *[niham]* from sending calamity.
> Who knows? He may turn and have pity *[niham]*
>> and leave behind a blessing—
>> grain offerings and drink offerings
> for the LORD your God.

Joel's call to repentance is urgent and insistent ("even now"). Since their sin is the cause of Yahweh's judgment, the people must respond before it is too late.[54] While Joel calls for traditional outward expressions of repentance ("fast-

---

[53]Because of the prominence of this call of God to the people to repent and return to him, this passage could well have been treated under the previous category, "God Repents in Response to Human Repentance." The same is true of Jon 4:2, coming as it does after the repentance of the Ninevites. But because of the creedal form of these statements and their importance for the ongoing faith of Israel, they are being considered here. On Joel's linkage of the repentance of the people and the repentance of God, see Raymond Dillard, "Joel," in *The Minor Prophets*, ed. Thomas E. McComiskey (Grand Rapids: Baker, 1992), p. 280.

[54]Leslie C. Allen, *The Books of Joel, Obadiah, Jonah, and Micah*, New International Commentary on the Old Testament (Grand Rapids: Eerdmans, 1976), p. 78.

ing and weeping and mourning"), his emphasis is radically internal. "Rend your hearts and not your garments."[55] He is not advocating a radical antithesis between internal heart repentance and its external, ritual expression. Rather he is calling for the necessity and primacy of the internal so as to avoid a hollow ritualism. Douglas Stuart compares this call with that of Hosea 14:2 and Amos 5:4, 21-24. "In each of these instances, the fuller context shows no prophetic disdain for the sacrificial system *per se*. They call for more than *mere* ritual or *mere* outward piety. Formal mourning was easy. True conversion to a godly life was not."[56]

Joel grounds his call for repentance and for returning to Yahweh on the basis of the covenant relationship that exists between Yahweh and his people ("return to Yahweh *your* God") and on the basis of the moral character of Yahweh.[57] The moral character of Yahweh is described by a creedal formula in Joel 2:13 that is based on, but not identical to, Exodus 34:6-7. The first two terms ("gracious and compassionate") are in reverse order as compared to Exodus 34:6. But more significantly, the phrase "and faithfulness" of Exodus 34:6 has been replaced by a description of God as one who "relents *[niham]* from sending calamity." This precise wording is found elsewhere in the Old Testament only in Jonah 4:2. In addition, the phrase "Who knows, he may turn and have pity *[niham]*" is found in both contexts (Joel 2:14; Jon 3:9). And thematically it is clear that in both Joel 2:14 and Jonah 4:2 the repentance of God follows the repentance of the people in response to the prophetic word. These similarities argue for what Wolff calls an "inescapable relationship" between these two creedal statements.[58]

"Who knows" at the beginning of Joel 2:14 (also found in Jon 3:9) introduces a note of contingency and expresses respect for the sovereign freedom of God in showing his mercy to whomever he wills (cf. Ex 33:19). Stuart notes the implications of this acknowledgment of the sovereign freedom of God: "Human repentance does not control God. People cannot force God to show them his forgiveness. They can only appeal to him for mercy in not meting out against them what they very well deserve. They may hope for his compassion but they

---

[55]This is the only place in the Old Testament where the command to rend one's heart is found. Dillard sees the thrust of this command to be similar to the command for the people to circumcise their hearts, found in Deut 10:16; 30:6 and Jer 9:25 ("Joel," p. 280).

[56]Douglas Stuart, *Hosea-Jonah*, Word Biblical Commentary (Waco, Tex.: Word, 1987), p. 252.

[57]Allen calls the phrase *return to Yahweh your God* "one side of the traditional formula of the covenant" (e.g., "I will be your God and you will be my people," Lev 26:12; cf. Gen 17:8; Jer 7:23; Hos 5:4). This points to the fact that Yahweh is "the God of the covenant, who both claims his people's allegiance and cares for them with a forbearing love" (*Joel*, p. 80).

[58]Wolff, *Joel and Amos*, p. 49.

cannot command it."[59] And the contingency expressed in this phrase is designed to humble those who boasted of Jerusalem's election with far too much self-assurance.[60]

But contingency does not rule out hope, which Joel is trying to engender.[61] He is calling the people to repentance, faith and renewed obedience to Yahweh, who can truly be described as a God "who relents from sending calamity."

Jonah 4:2. After Yahweh had repented and did not destroy repentant Nineveh, Jonah spoke to him out of frustration and anger at the mercy of Yahweh to the Ninevites. He said that the very reason he did not want to come to Nineveh at all was his confidence that Yahweh is a God who turns from his threatened judgment.

> O LORD, is this not what I said when I was still at home? That is why I was so quick
> to flee to Tarshish. I knew that you are a gracious and compassionate God, slow
> to anger and abounding in love, a God who relents *[niham]* from sending calamity.
> (Jon 4:2)

What was declared by Joel in prophetic oracle is now fleshed out in the story of Jonah and the Ninevites. We have already noted the verbal and thematic parallels with Joel 2:12-14. One distinctive element of Jonah 4:2 is that the list of divine attributes is introduced by the general title El (God) rather than the covenant name Yahweh. Allen argues that this is owing to the author's desire to stress that God's heart is universal in its concern.[62] And it was precisely the fact that this kind of relationship with this kind of God, a hallmark of Yahweh's covenant with Israel since his repentance following their sin with the golden calf, could be extended to pagan Nineveh that made Jonah so angry. Thus Davis argues that while the creedal statements in Jonah 4 and Joel 2 are identical in form, they are very different in intent.

---

[59]Stuart, *Hosea-Jonah*, p. 252. Dillard agrees that the phrase is very important: "Even in the face of [human] repentance, God remains sovereign. Repentance no more controls him than do the magic incantations of pagan priests. Neither the rite nor sincere contrition automatically guarantees the result" ("Joel," p. 280). Richard Rice notes the freedom of God to exercise his repentance even when human repentance does not exist. He cites Ex 32:14 where God repents in response to the intercession of Moses and does not bring judgment, even though the people have not repented ("Biblical Support for a New Perspective," p. 28).

[60]Wolff says, "The 'perhaps' of hope is appropriate to the humility of one who prays" (*Joel and Amos*, p. 50).

[61]Andersen and Freedman argue that the expression "Who knows?" does not have a negative expectation. "It is a polite way of expressing a positive hope for an affirmative response without being overbearing" (*Amos*, p. 664).

[62]Allen, *Joel*, p. 228. This universal emphasis of Jonah is in line with the pattern we saw earlier in Jer 18:7-10. While Jonah records the fulfillment of Jer 18:7-8 in the experience of a pagan nation, Joel 2:12-14 is a prophetic call for it to happen among the people of Jerusalem.

Joel 2:13 stressed God's repentance to the Jewish people in a book that stressed Jewish exclusivism, but Jonah 4:2 indicates that God's repentance (and other virtues) is not Israel's exclusive property but is universal in nature.[63]

Conclusion. We have surveyed several key biblical passages in which God is said to repent. They include times when God repents in response to human sin (Gen 6:6-7; 1 Sam 15:11, 35), times when God repents in response to human repentance (Jon 3:9-10; Jer 18:7-10), times when God repents in response to intercessory prayer (Ex 32:11-15; 2 Kings 20:1-6 and parallels), and creedal statements that include the repentance of God (Joel 2:12-14; Jon 4:2). It must be said that the number and breadth and diversity of these passages is impressive. Fretheim argues that the pervasiveness of the theme of divine repentance throughout Scripture, the diversity of Old Testament traditions in which it is affirmed and the variety of literary genres in which the theme occurs combine to make the repentance of God a "controlling metaphor" that must shape our understanding of God as a whole.[64] He writes:

> Divine repentance thus becomes one of the controlling metaphors for understanding the God of Israel, providing a hermeneutical key for interpreting Old Testament texts which speak of God. It must be a prominent theme at the center of all efforts to bring coherence to a wide range of Old Testament reflection about God.[65]

But the crucial question before us in this chapter is how this widespread biblical evidence of divine repentance affects our understanding of the extent of God's foreknowledge. Does the fact that God repents mean that his is a less-than-exhaustive foreknowledge? Open theists are uniformly insistent that it does. They stress that the reality and genuineness of God's repentance demands a less-than-exhaustive understanding of the extent of his foreknowledge. This

---

[63]Davis, "Investigation of the Concept of the Repentance of God," p. 120.

[64]In addition to the thirty-five uses of *niham* with God as subject, there are also verses that use the related verb *šûb* to speak of God turning away from his wrath (e.g., Deut 13:17; Josh 7:26; 2 Kings 23:16; Is 5:25; Jer 4:8; Ezek 10:22; cf. Ps 78:38). There are also other texts that speak of the crucial role of human intercessors who mediated between Yahweh and humanity (e.g., Num 25:11; Ps 106:23; Jer 18:20) (see Terence Fretheim, "The Repentance of God," pp. 53-54). Especially important literary genres in which the theme of divine repentance occurs are direct divine speech (e.g., Jer 18:7-10; 26:3) where God himself claims to repent; psalmody (e.g., Ps 106:45), in which the community of faith incorporates this theme into its praise to God; and creedal statements (Joel 2:12-14; Jon 4:2), in which God's repentance is affirmed and praised on an equal level with his other moral attributes such as grace, compassion, slowness of anger and abundance of love. These all point to the crucial importance of the repentance of God in Israelite thought and worship (ibid., pp. 57-58).

[65]Ibid., p. 59. Fretheim discusses the concept of a "controlling metaphor" on p. 52 of this article. Sanders appropriates this term and Fretheim's understanding as a whole (*God Who Risks*, pp. 72-73).

case is made most consistently and insistently by Gregory Boyd. Consider the following statements from him.

Concerning Gen 6:6-7, Boyd writes that if God had in fact foreknown with absolute certainty exactly what humans would do before he created them, "how, then, could [God] authentically regret having made humankind? Doesn't the fact that God regretted the way things turned out—to the point of starting over—suggest that it *wasn't* a foregone conclusion at the time God created human beings that they would fall into this state of wickedness?"[66]

Boyd also argues that the authenticity of God's regret in 1 Samuel 15 is dependent on his not knowing the sin of Saul in advance.

> We must wonder how the Lord could truly experience regret for making Saul king if he was absolutely certain that Saul would act the way he did. Could God genuinely confess, "I regret that I made Saul king" if he could in the same breath also proclaim, "I was certain of what Saul would do when I made him king?" I do not see how. . . . Common sense tells us that we can only regret a decision we made if the decision resulted in an outcome other than what we expected or hoped for when the decision was made.[67]

Regarding Jeremiah 18:7-10, Boyd once again insists that Yahweh's promise to repent *(niham)* requires a nonexhaustive view of divine foreknowledge for its authenticity. He argues that

---

[66]Boyd, *God of the Possible,* p. 55. See also Boyd, *Satan and the Problem of Evil,* p. 102. And if exhaustive divine foreknowledge is tied to God's specific sovereignty and determination (as many, though not all, proponents of exhaustive divine foreknowledge would affirm), the situation is deemed to be even more problematic. Sanders says, "If God always gets precisely what he desires in each and every situation, then it is incoherent to speak of God's being grieved about or responding to the human situation. How can God be grieved if precisely what God wanted to happen did happen?" (*God Who Risks,* p. 213).

[67]Boyd, *God of the Possible,* p. 56. Yet this does not mean that God's decision was unwise. "Once we understand that the future is partly open and that humans are genuinely free, the paradox of how God could experience genuine regret over a decision he made disappears. God made a wise decision because it had the greatest *possibility* of yielding the best results. God's decision wasn't the only variable in this matter, however; there was also the variable of Saul's will. Saul freely strayed from God's plan, but that is not God's fault, nor does it make God's decision unwise" (ibid., p. 57). Boyd is not alone in his view. Terence Fretheim makes a similar argument with respect to 1 Sam 15. He states that God decided to replace Saul with David because he "learned something new from the experience (and experiment) with Saul." This means that the ultimate outcome of Saul's kingship must have been known by God only as a possibility and not as a certainty. Fretheim writes, "If the alternatives offered [to Saul] in 1 Sam 12:14-15 are indeed genuine possibilities, then the future is open. If the negative possibility is known in advance, then to hold out the positive possibility is a deception of Saul and the people. For each of these options to have integrity, they must both be understood to be possibilities, and only possibilities" ("Divine Foreknowledge, Divine Consistency, and the Rejection of Saul's Kingship," *Catholic Biblical Quarterly* 47 [1986]: 599-600).

we must take very seriously the Lord's word in Jeremiah 18 that he will "change [his] mind about the disaster that [he] intended to bring" on one nation (v. 8) and/ or "change [his] mind about the good [he] intended to do to" another nation, if these nations change (v. 10). If the future were exhaustively fixed, could the Lord genuinely intend to bring something about and then genuinely *change his mind* and not bring it about? How can someone sincerely intend to do something they are certain they will never do? And how can they truly change their mind if their mind is eternally made up?[68]

And finally, with regard to Yahweh's repentance in response to Hezekiah's prayers, Boyd argues that this kind of divine change, reflected in the statements God made both before and after his reversal, is incompatible with the traditional view of exhaustive divine foreknowledge.

> Now, if we accept the classical view of foreknowledge and suppose that the Lord was certain that he would *not* let Hezekiah die, wasn't he being duplicitous when he initially told Hezekiah that he would not recover? And if we suppose that the Lord was certain all along that Hezekiah would, in fact, live fifteen years after this episode, wasn't it misleading for God to tell him that he was *adding* fifteen years to his life?[69]

A brief comment is called for at this point to clarify the precise issue under debate. The real issue is not divine duplicity in this instance, for in reality that same charge could also be brought against Boyd's understanding. For both openness and nonopenness interpreters alike understand that there is an implicit, unexpressed condition in God's statement to Hezekiah—something like "You are going to die; you will not recover, unless you repent and pray." Well, if it would have been deceptive for God to say to Hezekiah that he will die if,

---

[68]Boyd, *God of the Possible*, p. 77.

[69]Ibid., p. 82. See also Boyd, *Satan and the Problem of Evil*, p. 95. Ware notes perceptively that the certainty and specificity of God's promise to Hezekiah—that he would add fifteen years to his life, no more and no less—demands a vast amount of foreknowledge on the part of God. He asks, "On openness grounds, how could God know [this]? Over a fifteen-year span, the contingencies are staggering! The number of future freewill choices, made by Hezekiah and by innumerable others, that relate directly to Hezekiah's life and well-being, none of which God knows (in the openness view) is *enormous*. . . . Because in the openness view, there are so many variables, so much of which God is absolutely ignorant, so few things God can know for sure of human lives and situations the further one projects into the future, it is inconceivable that God could know and predict *exactly* this fifteen-year extension of life to Hezekiah—inconceivable, that is, so long as God keeps the libertarian freedom of Hezekiah and innumerable others with whom he relates intact over the span of these years. . . . [Yet] with absolute confidence and assurance, God promises and predicts. Does not this expression of God's certain knowledge of the future cause one to question whether the openness interpretation of the added fifteen years is correct?" (*God's Lesser Glory,* pp. 95-96).

in fact, God knew that he would repent and pray and thus not die, God would be no less deceptive if he said, "You will surely die" while really meaning "You might die, but you won't if you repent and pray." Again, both views assume the reality of an implicit, unspoken condition, similar to that found in Jonah 3:4. And in neither case is divine truthfulness negated by such an implicit condition. Thus at issue is not divine truthfulness but rather whether God knew in advance that Hezekiah would meet this unspoken condition.

The point, I trust, is clear. Boyd, and other open theists with him, insist that the reality and genuineness of God's repentance demands a less-than-exhaustive foreknowledge on his part.[70] Thus the widespread biblical evidence of God's repentance provides a strong biblical argument for their revised understanding of the extent of divine foreknowledge. This is indeed a significant argument. But before we can fully evaluate this openness claim, we must look at certain Old Testament texts which affirm that God does *not* repent.

SELECT PASSAGES AFFIRMING THAT GOD DOES NOT REPENT

Davis cites eight Old Testament passages that speak of the nonrepentance of God (Num 23:19; 1 Sam 15:29; Ps 110:4; Jer 4:28; 20:16; Ezek 24:14; Hos 13:14; Zech 8:14).[71] Space constraints limit us to a brief comment on Psalm 110:4 and more significant discussion of the two most explicit of these passages, Numbers 23:19 and 1 Samuel 15:29.

Psalm 110:4. Psalm 110 is a royal psalm, seen as strongly messianic in its widespread New Testament usage.[72] It can be divided into two strophes (vv. 1-3 and 4-7). Each is structured around a divine oracle (vv. 1, 4), which is then amplified and explained. In each strophe the divine oracle comes in the form of a promise that Yahweh makes to his king, and in each strophe the implica-

---

[70]For the view of other open theists on divine repentance, see Rice, "Biblical Support for a New Perspective," pp. 26-34; Sanders, *God Who Risks,* pp. 66-75; and Pinnock, *Most Moved Mover,* pp. 43-44.

[71]Davis, "Investigation of the Concept of the Repentance of God," p. 48.

[72]Perhaps the most popular suggestion is that Ps 110 is celebrating a royal enthronement or coronation at the temple in Jerusalem (see Leslie C. Allen, *Psalms 101-150,* Word Biblical Commentary 21 [Waco, Tex: Word, 1983], pp. 83-84). Mitchell Dahood offers an alternative view, viewing it as being composed to celebrate a military victory (*Psalms III: 101-150,* Anchor Bible 17A [Garden City, N.Y.: Doubleday, 1970], p. 112). New Testament quotations of or allusions to Psalm 110 are exemplified by Mt 22:44; 26:64; Mk 12:36; 14:62; 16:19; Lk 20:42-44; 22:69; Acts 2:34-35; Rom 8:34; 1 Cor 15:25; Eph 1:20; Col 3:1; Heb 1:3, 13; 5:6; 7:17, 21; 8:1; 10:12-13; 12:2. (This list is taken from Willem A. VanGemeren, *Psalms, Expositor's Bible Commentary* 5 [Grand Rapids: Zondervan, 1991], p. 696). On the history of Christian interpretation of Psalm 110, see David M. Hay, *Glory at the Right Hand,* Society of Biblical Literature Monograph 18 (Nashville: Abingdon, 1973).

tions that follow the divine oracle involve great victory that God promises to give to his king.[73]

Psalm 110:4 introduces the second strophe with a promise from Yahweh to the king, given in terms of a divine oath. And this oath is one from which Yahweh promises never to deviate.

> The LORD has sworn
> and will not change his mind [niham]:
> "You are a priest forever,
> in the order of Melchizedek."

For our purposes, it is important to note that the verb *niham* (which Yahweh promises he will not do with respect to this promise) is parallel to the Hebrew verb *šābaʿ* ("to swear"). It is because Yahweh swears this oath to his Davidic king that he promises that he will never *niham* from it.

Victor Hamilton notes the significance of swearing an oath in the Old Testament: "To swear in the Old Testament was to give one's sacred unbreakable word in testimony that the one swearing would faithfully perform some promised deed, or that he would faithfully refrain from some evil act."[74] Great stress is placed in Scripture on the fact that Yahweh swore ("by myself") to Abraham to bless him, his seed and indeed all nations through his seed (Gen 22:16, 18; cf. Gal 3:8, 16). We also see God swearing by his holiness (Ps 89:35), by his right hand (Is 62:8) and by his great name (Jer 44:26). This is done "in order that [Yahweh] might stress the absolute certainty and immutability of his performing that which he swore to Abraham, to Israel, and to David."[75]

Robert Chisholm sees a strong connection between the oath sworn by Yahweh and his promise of nonrepentance. He divides biblical statements of God's intentions into two categories: declarations or oaths, which are unconditional and binding, and announcements, which retain a conditional elements and may be modified in the future.

> A divine decree (or oath) is an unconditional declaration. Because it is certain to come to pass, the response of the recipient cannot alter it, though . . . the exact timing of its timing can be conditional. An announcement is a conditional statement of divine intention, which may or may not be realized, depending on the response of the recipient or someone else whose interests it affects.[76]

---

[73]VanGemeren, *Psalms,* p. 697.
[74]Victor P. Hamilton, *"šābaʿ,"* in *Theological Wordbook of the Old Testament,* ed. R. Laird Harris, Gleason L. Archer Jr., and Bruce K. Waltke (Chicago: Moody Press, 1980), 2:900.
[75]Ibid.
[76]Chisholm, "Does God 'Change His Mind'?" p. 389.

To put this in terms of our current discussion, divine announcements can be repented of by God, while God will not repent of his decrees/oaths.

But how can we as readers of Scripture discern which of God's statements are divine decrees (nonrepentable) and which are divine announcements (repentable)? Chisholm says that usually the text itself gives us the indication. "Divine decrees are usually clearly marked out as such. Something in the statement itself or in the immediate context indicates its unconditional status."[77] The contextual markers indicating that Psalm 110:4 is in fact an unconditional divine decree are twofold: Yahweh's use of the verb *šāba‘*, indicating that this is his sworn oath, and second, his explicit promise not to *niham* of his oath.[78] Yet Chisholm understands God's promise to not repent in Psalm 110:4a to apply to the specific promise that follows in Ps 110:4b. Thus, he argues, we should not interpret this particular divine promise as a generalized statement that applies to all of God's decisions and actions.[79]

Numbers 23:19. Numbers 23:19 is found within the story of Balaam—in a portion of the narrative known as the oracles of Balaam. Seven oracles are attributed to Balaam (Num 23:7-10, 18-24; 24:3-9, 15-19, 20, 21-22, 23-25). Our passage is found within the second of these oracles.

After having conquered Arad, Sihon and Og (Num 21), the Israelites were encamped on the plains of Moab. As a result the Moabites were filled with fear (Num 23:3).[80] Then Balak, the Moabite king, summoned Balaam, a famous diviner from Mesopotamia to curse Israel so that Moab could defeat Israel.[81] But as the story unfolded, Balaam would only bless Israel, for he would only speak

---

[77] Ibid.

[78] Chisholm says, "The declaration that God will not change his mind, or retract his statement, clearly pertains to the specific pronouncement that follows and, together with the reference to an oath, marks the statement as a decree" (ibid., p. 395).

[79] Ibid. Davis agrees with Chisholm on this point ("Investigation of the Concept of the Repentance of God," p. 51).

[80] Ronald Allen points out that the Moabites' fear was ultimately unnecessary because Yahweh had specifically prohibited Israel from taking even the smallest part of Moabite land (Deut 2:5). He had told his people not to harass or provoke them, "for I will not give you any part of their land" (Deut 2:9). But the Moabites could scarcely have known of this command, and their fear can also be explained as a fulfillment of the prophecy of Deut 2:25, "This very day I will begin to put terror and fear of you on all the nations under heaven. They will hear reports of you and will tremble and be in anguish because of you." [Note: this is another example of a prophecy based on divine knowledge of future free decisions.] See Ronald B. Allen, "The Theology of the Balaam Oracles," in *Tradition and Testament,* ed. John S. Feinberg and Paul D. Feinberg (Chicago: Moody Press, 1981), p. 80.

[81] Allen calls Balaam "the pagan counterpart to Moses, the man of God." He notes that the discovery of the prophetic texts of Balaam in Aramaic from the sixth century at Deir-'Allah "shows how very famous this man was in the ancient Near East, even centuries after his death" (*Numbers,* Expositor's Bible Commentary 2 [Grand Rapids: Zondervan, 1990], p. 887).

what Yahweh had declared. Thus in his first oracle Balaam declares:

> How can I curse
> > those whom God has not cursed?
> How can I denounce
> > those whom the LORD has not denounced? (Num 23:8)

Having failed in his first attempt to get Balaam to curse Israel, Balak took him to another place (the field of Zophim, at the top of Pisgah [v. 14]) in a second attempt to secure the curse. Evidently he thought that a change of scenery would help in bringing about an oracle that was favorable from his perspective. But while the location was different, the preparations were the same—seven altars were built and a bull and a ram were offered on each. Once again, Yahweh met Balaam and put his words into his mouth. And within this second oracle, we read:

> Arise, Balak, and listen;
> > hear me, son of Zippor.
> God is not a man that he should lie,
> > nor a son of man, that he should change his mind [niham].
> Does he speak and then not act?
> Does he promise and not fulfill?
> I have received a command to bless;
> > he has blessed, and I cannot change it. (23:18-20)

The oracle then goes on to speak of the presence of Yahweh with his people (v. 21) and their invincibility through his power (vv. 22-24).

Central to this passage is the huge difference that is proclaimed between Yahweh and human beings. "God is not a man . . . / nor a son of man."[82] The specific area of contrast focused on in Numbers 23:19 is that of steadfastness and unchangeability. Whereas human beings are changing and changeable, God does not lie.[83] He will not change his mind [niham].[84] No, he remains unchanging, and his word of promise remains sure.

---

[82]Most likely the phrase "son of man" is used to denote an inherently mortal human being, given the idiomatic usage of the phrase in Ps 8:4 (see Philip J. Budd, *Numbers,* Word Biblical Commentary 5 [Waco, Tex.: Word, 1984], p. 267; and George Buchanan Gray, *A Critical and Exegetical Commentary on Numbers,* International Critical Commentary [Edinburgh: T & T Clark, 1903], pp. 351-52).

[83]The changeableness of human beings is exemplified by "the shifting, equivocating Balaam," seen by Allen in this text as "a foil for God . . . the prime example of the distinction between God and man" (*Numbers,* p. 901).

[84]The Hebrew word order of Num 23:19, beginning with the negative particle *lô,* places the emphasis on the negation (see Allen, "Theology of the Balaam Oracles," p. 116, n. 33).

The verb *niḥam* in Numbers 23:19 is used in parallel with the verb *kāzab* (to lie). John Oswalt argues that the basic meaning of *kāzab* is "to speak that which is untrue and therefore false to reality."[85] A fundamental truth of the Old Testament, affirmed here and in 1 Samuel 15:29 and Psalm 89:35, is that the God of Israel does not lie. However, because of their alienation from this God, lying is endemic to human beings (e.g., Ps 4:2).[86] Thus the contrast of Numbers 23:19, "God is not a man that he should lie."

Chisholm cites several contextual features that point to this oracle as a divine decree and thus as being unchangeable. (1) The oracle is designated as a divine blessing and thus cannot be altered. Balaam himself acknowledges his inability to change God's blessing through sorcery or divination. "I have received a command to bless; / he has blessed, and I cannot change it" (Num 23:20). (2) The blessing is a prediction of Israel's success in the Promised Land, an extension of Yahweh's unconditional promise to give Abraham's descendants the land of Canaan (Gen 15:16; 17:8; 22:17). Thus Balaam's oracle shares the binding nature of those earlier promises. (3) Psalm 89:35 uses the verb *kāzab* in a similar manner to mean the retraction of an unconditional promise ("Once for all, I have sworn by my holiness— / and I will not lie *[kāzab]* to David"). (4) Most important, the introduction to the oracle, in which Balaam explicitly affirms that God will not lie or change his mind (Num 23:19), marks this out as a divine decree. Chisholm argues that *niḥam* and *kāzab* are synonymous in this verse, both meaning "to retract (an unconditional promise)."[87]

The meaning of Numbers 23:19 is clear. God has decreed a blessing for his people Israel. The pagan seer Balaam cannot change it because God will not lie or change his mind concerning it. But is Numbers 23:19 a statement of a universal principle governing all of God's actions, or does it relate to this specific oracle only? Before we address this question, we must turn to examine a parallel passage.

1 Samuel 15:29. Earlier in this chapter we examined the passage that speaks of God's grieving *(niḥam)* over the fact that he had made Saul to be king in Israel (1 Sam 15:11, 35). Imbedded in this passage, however, is a statement that God does not *niḥam*. After Samuel had rebuked Saul for his disobedience in not totally destroying the Amelekites and declared that God had rejected him as king (1 Sam

---

[85] John N. Oswalt, "*kāzab*," *Theological Wordbook of the Old Testament,* ed. R. Laird Harris, Gleason L. Archer Jr. and Bruce K. Waltke (Chicago: Moody Press, 1980), 1:435.

[86] Ibid., 1:436.

[87] Chisholm, "Does God 'Change His Mind'?" p. 392. Andersen and Freedman agree. "When does changing your mind become *kazab* (or *shaqar,* as in 1 Sam 15:29)? Answer, when you swear an oath, which is what *dabar* means in Num 23:19" (*Amos,* pp. 669-70).

15:23), Saul pled for forgiveness (vv. 24-25). But Samuel repeated the Lord's decision (v. 26) and said to Saul in verses 28-29, "The LORD has torn the kingdom
of Israel from you today and has given it to one of your neighbors—to one who
is better than you. He who is the Glory of Israel does not lie or change his mind
[niḥam]; for he is not a man that he should change his mind [niḥam]."

The statement is very similar to that of Numbers 23:19. Once again the contrast is between Yahweh, "the glory of Israel," and human beings, with the point
of contrast being the unchangeability of God as opposed to human changeableness.[88] And once again, this truth is expressed through parallel verbs, saying that
God does not lie or change his mind.[89] Here, though, the verb for lying is different. Rather than kāzab used in Numbers 23:19, the author of 1 Samuel uses
the verb šāqar. Andersen and Freedman argue that šāqar is in fact a stronger
verb than kāzab, meaning "to be a traitor."[90] Hermann Austel says that the verb
refers to "the breaking of a promise, being false to a treaty or commitment,
hence an empty promise." But he regards the verb as a "close synonym" with
kāzab, citing Psalm 89:33-36 as a context in which both verbs are used in parallel
with God violating his covenant to David and his royal descendants.[91]

> I will not take my love from him,
> nor will I ever betray [šāqar] my faithfulness.
> I will not violate my covenant
> or alter what my lips have uttered.
> Once for all, I have sworn by my holiness—
> and I will not lie [kāzab] to David—
> that his line will continue forever
> and his throne endure before me like the sun.

As with Numbers 23:19, Chisholm understands 1 Samuel 15:28-29 to be an
unalterable divine decree (as opposed to Samuel's first rebuke of Saul in
1 Sam 13:13-14). He cites the following contextual markers: (1) The fact that
Samuel rejected Saul's plea for forgiveness shows that this second rebuke is
a decree that cannot be changed. (2) The temporal marker "today" in verse

---

[88]The Hebrew for "the glory of Israel," is quite obscure. Ralph Klein translates it, "the Faithful
One of Israel" (1 Samuel, p. 154). P. Kyle McCarter renders the title "Israel's Everlasting One"
(1 Samuel, Anchor Bible 8 [Garden City, N.Y.: Doubleday, 1980], pp. 264, 268).

[89]The force of the negation is intensified by the double use of the Hebrew negative particle lô
(see Davis, "Investigation of the Concept of the Repentance of God," p. 59, n. 5).

[90]Andersen and Freedman, Amos, p. 669. Davis translates šāqar as "deceive," while he translates
kāzab as "lie" ("Investigation of the Concept of the Repentance of God," pp. 54, 59).

[91]Hermann J. Austel, "shāqar," in Theological Wordbook of the Old Testament, ed. R. Laird Harris, Gleason L. Archer Jr., and Bruce K. Waltke (Chicago: Moody Press, 1980), 2:955.

28 emphasizes the final nature of God's decision here as opposed to the provisional nature of Samuel's first rebuke. (3) The explicit statement that God will not lie or change his mind concerning his decision in verse 29 marks it out as a divine decree.[92]

The major interpretive difficulty in 1 Samuel 15 comes from the fact that this chapter, which so strongly affirms that God does not change his mind (v. 29), also contains two other statements that God did in fact change his mind with regard to Saul's kingship (vv. 11, 35). How can these seemingly contradictory statements be reconciled?

The difficulty has led some to conclude that 1 Samuel 15:29 is a gloss, added by a later redactor who was uncomfortable with the concept of divine repentance.[93] Other interpreters, however, are hesitant to affirm this because several other alternative explanations have been offered to reconcile 1 Samuel 15:29 (and Num 23:19) with 1 Samuel 15:11, 35 (and other texts which speak of the repentance of God).[94]

One such explanation involves the meaning of *niham*. Chisholm looks at the semantic diversity of the verb and argues:

> The statement in verse 11 (also verse 35) does not contradict verse 29, for the verb *naham* is used in different semantic senses with different referents in this chapter. In verses 11, 35 it means "to experience emotional pain" and refers to God's response to Saul's disobedience which in turn moved Him to decree Saul's fate. In verse 29, the word is negated and used in the sense of "to retract." Here it refers to God's decree that Saul will be replaced by another. In the one case it pertains to a past action (God's making Saul king); in the other it concerns a future course of action (the rejection of Saul as king).[95]

---

[92]Chisholm, "Does God 'Change His Mind'?" p. 393. Chisholm argues for the specificity of the referent of the promise of 1 Sam 15:29, suggesting that the verbs *lie* and *change his mind* have a specific future, as opposed to a habitual nuance.

[93]For example, McCarter says, "The contradiction of vs. 11 that this statement [15:29] contains is so blatant that we must question its originality. It may be a later addition to the text (derived from Num 23:19?), penned by a redactor to whom the suggestion of a divine change of mind was unacceptable" (*1 Samuel,* p. 268). This solution is also adopted by Davis, "Investigation of the Concept of the Repentance of God," pp. 60-61 and is suggested as a possibility by William Kane, *I and II Samuel,* Torch Bible Commentaries (London: SCM Press, 1963), p. 103.

[94]For example, Long argues that "the assumption of logical or theological contradiction is not sufficient to decide the issue [of whether v. 29 is a gloss]" (*Reign and Rejection,* p. 163). Long does acknowledge the possibility that v. 29 is a gloss for other reasons and cites F. Foresti, *The Rejection of Saul in the Perspective of the Deuteronomistic School,* Studia Theologica-Teresianum 5 (Rome: Edizione del Teresianum, 1984), pp. 28-29, n. 8.

[95]Chisholm, "Does God 'Change His Mind'?" p. 394, n. 19.

Recognizing this semantic variation, Chisholm argues, makes any need to posit a later redaction in the text of 1 Samuel 15 unnecessary.[96] Richard Rice also appeals to the semantic diversity of *niham* and argues that the key to recognizing it is the fact that in both 1 Samuel 15:29 and Numbers 13:19, the verb *niham* is used synonymously with verbs that mean "to lie." "The point is not that God never changes but that God never says one thing while fully intending to do something else. Only in this limited sense of the word does God not 'repent.'"[97]

A more frequent argument is that 1 Samuel 15:29 and Numbers 23:19 do not teach a universal principle that covers all of God's ways but rather are promises relating to specific situations. We have seen that Chisholm interprets these statements of divine nonrepentance as unalterable divine decrees contextually marked as such, but statements that have a specific rather than a general referent. Fretheim has argued this case extensively with respect to 1 Samuel 15:29. He understands this verse to be referring not to God's rejection of Saul as king but rather to his appointment of David as the next king, appealing primarily to the Davidic focus of verse 28, which sets the stage for the pronouncement of verse 29.[98] Fretheim concludes:

> With regard to the giving of the kingdom to David, this is a matter concerning which God will not repent, come what may. . . . Unlike the fickleness so characteristic of human action, God has made a decision with respect to David, and with respect to that decision, he will not repent. This statement, therefore, does not have general reference to God as one who never repents with regard to anything. Rather, it has reference to God's decision to give the kingdom to David. That decision is irrevocable. God has chosen to limit his options in this regard. The point is not that God's repentance is a divine action which is not to be repeated ever again in any situation; the point is that God's repentance regarding the promise to *David* is foreclosed.[99]

---

[96]Ibid. Long also makes a similar argument about the broad range of semantic meaning of the verb *niham* (*Reign and Rejection,* p. 164).

[97]Rice, "Biblical Support for a New Perspective," p. 33. Chisholm also sees *niham* as being parallel to and synonymous with *šāqar* in 1 Sam 15:29, both verbs meaning "to retract" ("Does God 'Change His Mind'?" p. 393).

[98]Terence E. Fretheim, "Divine Foreknowledge, Divine Constancy, and the Rejection of Saul's Kingship," *Catholic Biblical Quarterly* 47 (1986): 598. In addition, Fretheim argues that the other two primary passages that speak of divine nonrepentance (Ps 110:4; Num 23:19) also pertain to the Davidic kingship. McCarter, on the other hand, argues that the primary referent of 1 Sam 15:29 is God's rejection of Saul as king. He sees the goal of Samuel's statement as that of discouraging further pleading by Saul. It could thus be paraphrased, "Yahweh has rejected you [Saul] and since Yahweh does not change his mind, there is no reason for discussion" (*1 Samuel,* p. 268).

[99]Fretheim, "Divine Foreknowledge," pp. 597-98. He argues, "If this statement referred to Saul, it would be a general reference regarding divine repentance and would thus stand in contradiction to vs. 11 and 35. If, however, it has specific reference to God's decision to give the

Sanders does not follow Fretheim in restricting 1 Samuel 15:29 to a Davidic referent. But he does agree that both this verse and Numbers 23:19 are specific rather than general.[100] Specifically with respect to 1 Samuel 15, Sanders says:

> This chapter says both that God changes his mind and that God will not change his mind. In its context the teaching is clear: God reserves the right to alter his plans in response to human initiative, and it is also the divine right not to alter an alteration. . . . God had originally planned to establish Saul's household as a perpetual kingship in Israel (1 Sam 13:13-14) but then changed his mind. Despite Samuel's intercession, God proclaims that he will not change his mind about this change of mind that he has had. Taken in their literary and historical contexts, these "I will not change my mind" texts are not abstract propositions about divine immutability. Rather, they speak of God's steadfastness in certain concrete situations.[101]

In addition, open theists also argue that the meaningfulness and integrity of these nonrepentance statements demand the possibility of God's repentance in other situations. Listen, for example, to the following statements of Boyd and Rice.

> Note carefully that these exceptions [1 Sam 15:29 and Num 23:19] prove the rule. It is only meaningful for God to say he *will not* change his mind if it is true that he *could* change his mind if he wanted to, and it is true that many times he does want to (see Jer 18:7-10; Jonah 4:2; Joel 2:12-13).[102]
>
> The assurance that God will *not* repent presupposes the general possibility that God *can* repent when he chooses. God does not repent in certain cases, not because it is impossible or inconceivable for him to do so, nor because he never does so; he does not repent simply because he chooses not to do so.[103]

Bruce Ware, on the other hand, disagrees with this "specific, not general" argument. Speaking of Numbers 23:19, Ware affirms the specific historical context of this statement and its clear purpose to reinforce the certainty with which God

---

kingdom to David, it can have a future reference with respect to this particular matter" (ibid., p. 597, n. 11). Chisholm argues, however, that Fretheim's distinction (the promise of divine nonrepentance relates only to David and not to Saul) is "overly fine," for "Saul's rejection and David's election are two sides of the same coin" ("Does God 'Change His Mind'?" pp. 393-94, n. 16). Nevertheless, he shares Fretheim's conclusion that 1 Sam 15:29 has a specific rather than a general referent.

[100]"The two texts asserting that God will not repent refer to specific situations in which God refuses to reverse a particular decision. In one case, God refuses to allow Balaam to change the divine mind and curse Israel (Num 23:19). In the other case, God rejects Saul's plea to keep the kingship in his family (1 Sam 15:29)" (Sanders, *God Who Risks,* p. 69).

[101]Ibid., p. 70.

[102]Boyd, *God of the Possible,* p. 80.

[103]Rice, "Biblical Support for a New Perspective," p. 33.

pledges to accomplish the blessing on Israel that Balaam had declared in his first oracle. Yet Ware argues that "it simply will not do to turn this declaration *merely* into a statement concerning God's pledge in this particular, concrete, historical situation *alone*."[104] He gives two reasons for his argument.

The first involves the parallelism between God's promise not to repent and his promise not to lie. If we take a "specific, not general" approach to God's nonrepentance, then the parallelism would argue that we should take a similar "specific, not general" approach to the possibility of God's lying. "If, as open theists understand [Num 23:19], it is taken as *generally* true that God *can* repent, but that in this *particular* case he chooses not to, then does it not follow from this text that, while it is *generally* true that God *can* lie, in this *particular* case he chooses not to?"[105] But can God ever lie? Ware argues that texts like 2 Timothy 2:13, Titus 1:2 and Hebrews 6:18 explicitly teach not only that God does not lie but that he *cannot* lie. So he concludes:

> It appears, then, that the parallel relation of God's repentance with lying would lead one to conclude that this passage is teaching more than simply that in this particular historical situation God chooses not to lie or repent. Rather, just as God *can never* lie, so He *can never* repent.[106]

Ware's second argument involves the contrast made in both Numbers 23:19 and 1 Samuel 15:29 between God and humans. Both texts explicitly affirm that God is not like a human being, who presumably both lies and repents. Ware questions whether the force of this contrast can hold given the "specific, not general" interpretation.

> Does not the force of this clam [that God is not like human beings] evaporate the instant one reads it to say, *in this particular situation* God is not like a man and so does not repent? Do men (i.e., human beings) *always* repent of what they say they will do? If so, the contrast can be maintained. But if human beings *sometimes* carry out what they say and *sometimes* repent and do otherwise, and if God, likewise *sometimes* carries out what he says and *sometimes* repents and does otherwise, then how is God different than humans. The only way the contrast works is if God, unlike men, *never* repents. It is generally true, not merely situationally true, that God does not repent.[107]

Sanders, however, would dispute the conclusions Ware draws from the divine-human contrast in these verses. Interacting with Ware's earlier discussion

---

[104]Ware, *God's Lesser Glory*, p. 87.
[105]Ibid.
[106]Ibid.
[107]Ibid., p. 88.

of divine repentance, Sanders appeals to Hosea 11:8-9.[108] In that passage Yahweh says to Israel:

> How can I give you up, Ephraim?
>> How can I hand you over, Israel?
> How can I treat you like Admah?
>> How can I make you like Zeboiim?
> My heart is changed within me;
>> all my compassion is aroused.
> I will not carry out my fierce anger
>> nor will I turn and devastate Ephraim.
> For I am God, and not man—
>> the Holy One among you.
> I will not come in wrath.

This passage, Sanders argues, teaches that God repents precisely because he is not human. His heart can be changed within him, his compassion is aroused, precisely because he is not like human beings who stubbornly refuse to show mercy to those who reject them. This then creates a problem for Ware's interpretation, for, as Sanders writes, "the Bible teaches both (1) that God cannot change his mind because he is not human and (2) that God literally does change his mind because he is not human."[109]

Three brief comments about Hosea 11:8-9 are in order at this point. First, the passage does speak of a change within God, specifically an emotional change. The noun translated "my compassion" is derived from the verbal root *niham*. The translation of compassion is right in line with what Parunak discerned to be the primary lexical meaning of the root. But the warmness of Yahweh's compassion for Israel is placed in stark contrast with the judgment he has unleashed against his people (Hos 11:5-6). The picture is one of emotional turmoil within God, what Hans Walter Wolff memorably calls "God in conflict with himself over Israel."[110] This leads to his change of heart.

Second, the divine-human contrast which we have seen in both Numbers 23:19 and 1 Samuel 15:29 is also very prominent here in Hosea 11. Yahweh says "I am God, and not man— / the Holy One among you." Yahweh's identification of himself as "The Holy One among you" intensifies this contrast, for throughout

---

[108]Bruce Ware, "An Evangelical Reformulation of the Doctrine of the Immutability of God," *Journal of the Evangelical Theological Society* 29 no. 4 (1986): 441-45.
[109]Sanders, *God Who Risks,* pp. 68-69.
[110]Hans Walter Wolff, *Hosea*, ed. Paul D. Hanson, trans. Gary Stansell (Philadelphia: Fortress, 1974), p. 201. In support of this description, Wolff cites Hos 6:4 and other divine repentance texts such as Amos 7:3, 6 and Jer 26:3, 13, 19.

Scripture, the holiness of God refers to his separateness, his differentness, his uniqueness. God's holiness is a comprehensive term denoting everything that sets him out as separate from and superior to everything he has made—including human beings.[111] Thus, although God is "among you" (i.e., in the midst of his people actively intervening on their behalf), he remains fundamentally different from his people. "I am God and not man— / the Holy One among you."

Third, Yahweh's stated contrast between himself and human beings is *not* used in this passage to ground his change in heart (as Sanders argues) but rather to ground his decision to remain true and faithful to his covenant promises to Israel and not destroy them completely. Before his statement of this contrast, Yahweh says, "I will not carry out my fierce anger / nor will I turn and devastate Ephraim" (11:9).[112] And following the statement of contrast, he says, "I will not come in wrath" (11:9). Though God has judged his people (vv. 5-6), he will not unleash the fierceness of his anger so as to destroy his people finally and completely as was the case with Admah and Zeboiim.[113] To be sure, this decision comes as his compassion rises in his heart and "displaces" his wrath.[114] But this is not the way that God is so radically different from humans. Human beings often experience changes of heart. The point of the contrast between God and humans in Hosea 11:8-9 is that God will remain absolutely faithful to his covenant promises to his people. To God, quoting James Luther Mays, "his election of Israel is stronger than their sin."[115] And so in his absolute faithfulness to his covenant, he will not utterly destroy his people, though under the covenant he had every right to eliminate them from the face of the earth. McComiskey argues that in this passage

> the emphasis is on the fact that God will not destroy his people a second time. Yahweh's refusal to execute his wrath must mean that he will not execute it to its fullest intensity. . . . Such an action would vitiate the ancient promise given to Abraham (Gen

---

[111]On the absolute uniqueness of the holy God, see also 1 Sam 2:2; Is 40:25 and Rev 15:4.

[112]Thomas McComiskey argues for the translation of the NASB—"I will not destroy Ephraim again" (see also the NRSV and ESV). He notes that when the Hebrew verb *šûb* (translated "turn" by the NIV) is followed by another verb, it frequently functions as an auxiliary verb with the sense of "again" ("Hosea," in *The Minor Prophets,* ed. Thomas E. McComiskey [Grand Rapids: Baker, 1992], p. 192).

[113]The decisiveness of Yahweh's decision is emphasized by the fourfold repetition of the Hebrew negative particle *lō* in v. 11. The cities of Admah and Zeboiim were obliterated along with Sodom and Gomorrah in God's fierce wrath (Gen 10:19; 14:2-8). The covenant curses of Deut 29:23 mentions these four cities as paradigms of what would happen to Israel if it disobeyed the covenant (see Stuart, *Hosea-Jonah,* p. 181).

[114]The phrase comes from James Luther Mays, *Hosea* (Philadelphia: Westminster Press, 1969), p. 157.

[115]Ibid.

12:1-7; cf Lev 26:44). . . . The reason that Yahweh will not give up his people is that he is God, not man. This contrast between the divine and human is not one of power, but of moral purity. This verse describes Yahweh as the Holy One; it is thus similar to Num 23:19, which states that God is not a man in that God does not lie.[116]

In the end, I would argue that the teaching of Hosea 11:8-9 does not contradict that of Numbers 23:19 and 1 Samuel 15:29. Rather, the point of the divine-human contrast is the same in all three passages. This is a crucial point.

Ultimately I am persuaded by Ware's arguments that the "merely specific and not at all general" interpretation is not the most faithful reading of 1 Samuel 15:11 and Numbers 23:19. On the basis of both the parallelism of divine repentance with lying and the contrast between God and humans, we must affirm that the divine nonrepentance taught in these passages is God's universal rather than his situationally specific pattern of operating. Universally God does not repent *in the human sense of the word implied in Numbers 23:19 and 1 Samuel 15:29.* But if we allow this point, we must ask: What of the other twenty-eight passages that teach that God does or may repent? How are we to interpret them? The answer must await a discussion of metaphors, models and anthropomorphisms.

METAPHORS, MODELS AND ANTHROPOMORPHISMS

George B. Caird says that "all, or almost all, of the language used by the Bible to refer to God is metaphor."[117] No doubt this is true because of the infinite qualitative difference that exists between the Creator and his creation.[118] But this is also true because of what Vincent Brümmer calls "the fundamentally metaphorical nature of all human thought and experience."[119] Sallie McFague says, "Far from being an esoteric or ornamental rhetorical device super-imposed *on* ordi-

---

[116]McComiskey, "Hosea," pp. 191-92. Ware concurs, arguing that the passage "affirms that God, unlike humans, is absolutely faithful to his covenant promises. . . . The point is that, unlike humans, God will faithfully do what he previously pledged to Israel. He will not ultimately destroy them ('come in wrath'); he will be merciful (see Mal 3:6 for a similar pledge based on God's immutable promise). So, contrary to Sanders' interpretation, Hos 11:8-9 does not teach that 'God repents because he is not human,' but rather that God will not judge them utterly because, unlike humans, he always keeps his promises" (*God's Lesser Glory,* pp. 89-90).

[117]George B. Caird, *The Language and Imagery of the Bible* (Grand Rapids: Eerdmans, 1997), p. 18. He says that one possible exception is the word *holy.* Terence Fretheim offers a similar conclusion, though with a different exception: "Virtually all the language used in the Bible to refer to God is metaphorical; the word 'God' would be an exception" (*Suffering of God,* p. 5).

[118]See, for example, Ps 145:3; 147:5; 139:6, 17-18; Is 55:8-9; Rom 11:33-34 which speak of the vast superiority and ultimate incomprehensibility of God's goodness, understanding, knowledge, thoughts, wisdom and ways.

[119]Vincent Brümmer, *The Model of Love* (Cambridge: Cambridge University Press, 1993), p. 8.

nary language, metaphor *is* ordinary language. It is the *way* we think."[120]
McFague defines a metaphor as follows:

> Most simply, a metaphor is seeing one thing *as* something else, pretending "this"
> is "that" because we do not know how to think or talk about "this," so we use "that"
> as a way of saying something about it. Thinking metaphorically means spotting a
> thread of similarity between two dissimilar objects, events, or whatever, one of
> which is better known than the other, and using the better-known one as a way of
> speaking about the lesser known.[121]

Thus through metaphorical language, something that is well known becomes a
window through which we can gain insight into something that is less well known.[122]

But since no one thing is exactly identical to another thing, every metaphor
expresses both similarities and differences between the two objects. McFague says
that metaphorical statements "always contain the whisper, 'it is *and it is not.*'" She
continues, "The only way we have of dealing with the unfamiliar and new is in
terms of the familiar and the old, thinking of 'this' as 'that' *although we know the
new thing is both like and unlike the old.*"[123] Fretheim says that insight into the
meaning of metaphors comes "through observing what is similar between the two
terms, but also through that which is different. Crucial to a proper understanding
of a metaphor is the recognition of both similarity and difference."[124]

The similarity side is crucial. While neither one metaphor nor the entire variety of biblical metaphors taken together can completely and exhaustively describe God, they do nonetheless have real meaning. They are, in the words of
Sanders, "reality depicting." Sanders describes such metaphors:

---

[120]Sallie McFague, *Metaphorical Theology* (Philadelphia: Fortress, 1982), p. 16.

[121]Ibid., p. 15. McFague also cites the definition of I. A. Richards, "In the simplest formulation,
when we use a metaphor, we have two thoughts of different things active together and supported by a single word, or phrase, whose meaning is a resultant of their interaction" (*The
Philosophy of Rhetoric* [New York: Oxford University Press, 1956], p. 89, quoted in McFague,
Metaphorical Theology, p. 37).

[122]Fretheim, *Suffering of God,* p. 5. Note the emphasis on new insight and understanding in
James B. Torrance's definition: "A metaphor is a word (noun) with a dictionary meaning,
boldly transferred to something or someone else to show significance and provide new understanding" (*Worship, Community, and the Triune God of Grace* [Downers Grove, Ill.: InterVarsity Press, 1996], p. 121).

[123]McFague, *Metaphorical Theology,* p. 13. Thus, metaphors must always be interpreted, for "im-
agistic language does not just tolerate interpretation but *demands* it" (ibid., p. 22).

[124]Fretheim, *Suffering of God,* p. 5. Recognizing this, Sanders calls us to avoid two extremes in
interpreting biblical metaphors about God: (1) saying that there is no essential relationship
between the metaphor and God, and (2) saying that there is a literal correspondence in all
aspects ("God as Personal," in *The Grace of God, the Will of Man* [Grand Rapids: Zondervan,
1989], p. 169). Another way of saying this would be that metaphorical statements must be
understood analogically rather than univocally.

Metaphors (even those about God) are reality depicting in that they tell us of a real relationship between God and the world. If we claim that our language about God depicts nothing about God or portrays no divine-human relationship, then our discourse about God will be severely restricted.[125]

Fretheim agrees, saying that while there isn't an exact one-to-one correspondence between the metaphor and reality, there is some significant correlation.

The metaphor does say some things about God that correspond to the reality which is God. . . . The metaphor does in fact describe God, though it is not fully descriptive. . . . The metaphor does not stand over against the literal. Though the *use* of the metaphor is not literal, there is literalness intended in the relationship to which the metaphor has reference.[126]

But a failure to recognize the differences is equally damaging. Brümmer speaks of the "ever-present danger" in metaphorical thinking and speaking "that we shall fail to hear this whisper [i.e., McFague's whisper, 'it is and it is not']. We become so used to looking on A as B that we fail to notice the difference between them."[127] Because of this inherent limitation of metaphorical language, an exclusive focus on one metaphor can become dangerous. With metaphorical language about God, a very real danger can come with the presumption that any one metaphor is the one and only way to understand God and his relationship to humanity. Thus we need many metaphors, "a piling up on images," to guard ourselves from this danger and to begin to grasp the richness of the divine-human relationship.[128]

Not all metaphors are used in the same way, however. As in science, so in theology, "some metaphors are developed in a sustained and systematic way as conceptual models."[129] Yet these models remain metaphors, and as such they require the kind of interpretation that recognizes both similarities

---

[125]Sanders, *God Who Risks*, pp. 15-16.

[126]Fretheim, *Suffering of God*, p. 7.

[127]Brümmer, *Model of Love*, p. 8.

[128]McFague, *Metaphorical Theology*, p. 20.

[129]Brümmer, *Model of Love*, p. 14. Brümmer illustrates by contrasting two biblical metaphors used to describe God. At times, God is referred to as a rock (e.g., Ps 18:2; 19:14) to express his eternal dependability and trustworthiness. Thus the metaphor is reality-depicting. But the differences between God and a rock are so great that the application of this metaphor is limited. And so it does not lend itself to the kind of sustained development needed for a theological model. But by contrast, God is also called a person. Brümmer says, "The analogy between God and human persons is so rich that it has been developed as the most fundamental and characteristic conceptual model in theistic god-talk" (ibid.). Caird notes that the five most common biblical metaphors to describe God's relationship with his people are all personal ones: king-subject; judge-litigant; husband-wife; father-child; master-servant (*Language and Imagery*, p. 177). This points to the appropriate dominance of the conceptual model of God as person.

and differences. Brümmer describes the interpretive caution that must remain, even with a model as fundamental and fruitful as describing God as a person.

> Like all conceptual models, those in theology remain metaphors and therefore what they assert is always accompanied by the whisper "and it is not." The fruitfulness of personalist models for talking about God should therefore never make us deaf to the whisper that God is not like other people.[130]

McFague also speaks of both the necessity and the dangers of theological models.

> Models are necessary . . . for they give us something to think about when we do not know what to think, a way of talking when we do not know how to talk. But they are also dangerous, for they exclude other ways of thinking and talking, and in so doing they can become literalized, that is identified as *the* one and only way of understanding a subject. This danger is more prevalent with models than with metaphors because models have a wider range and are more permanent; they also tend to object to competition in ways that metaphors do not.[131]

This danger is especially relevant when certain metaphors rise to the level of what McFague calls a "root metaphor." This is a metaphor, the content of which forms a paradigm that specifies the limits of acceptable models.[132] Thus these root metaphors exercise a controlling function, serving as a grid or a lens through which to view, evaluate and organize the data of the rest of Scripture. Fretheim uses the terminology of "controlling metaphors," which, he argues, "function to delimit metaphorical possibilities." In addition, they serve "as metaphors among metaphors, not unlike a 'canon' within the canon. Thus they are able to bring coherence to a range of biblical thinking about God; they provide a hermeneutical key for interpreting the whole."[133]

Brümmer argues that the more comprehensive the key model (his term), the

---

[130]Brümmer, *Model of Love*, p. 14.

[131]McFague, *Metaphorical Theology*, p. 24, italics original.

[132]Ibid., pp. 108-9. Sanders prefers the term "key model" (*God Who Risks*, p. 16), while Brümmer prefers an expanded term "comprehensive key model" (*Model of Love*, p. 21).

[133]Fretheim, *Suffering of God*, p. 11. Sanders emphasizes this controlling function with the phrase "control beliefs." He argues that they "are used as paradigms and ultimate presuppositions to interpret our experiences, recognize problems, and organize information. . . . Often our control beliefs revolve around or hinge on a few metaphors from the Bible that serve as keys to unlock the doors of interpretation to all other passages" ("God as Personal," p. 168). Pinnock also uses the term "control belief," understanding such a belief to be "a large scale conviction that affects many smaller issues" (*A Wideness in God's Mercy* [Grand Rapids: Zondervan, 1992], p. 18).

greater the danger of one-sidedness.[134] Therefore, he says that the theologian must remember the words of R. B. Braithwaite, spoken originally about scientific models, but which are equally true for theological models: "The price of the employment of models is eternal vigilance."[135]

But what must we be vigilant in looking for? First we must remind ourselves of our earlier discussion in chapter one of what makes a good theological model. In that chapter, I built on the work of Sanders and proposed that a theological model must be evaluated in terms of biblical fidelity (both quantitatively [does it deal with all the relevant biblical data?] and qualitatively [does it deal with the biblical data fairly and accurately?]), in terms of rational consistency and coherence (is the model logically consistent within itself and do all of its meanings cohere with each other and with the rest of Scripture?), and in terms of adequacy to meet the demands of life and ministry. These too are the standards of evaluation we must use when we consider the anthropomorphic metaphors used in Scripture to describe God and the theological models that may be derived from them.

Anthropomorphisms, representations of God in terms of human physical or emotional experience, abound in Scripture.[136] Old Testament theologian Ludwig Köhler claims that "The language which ascribes to God the attributes of man is neither restrained nor incidental; indeed, anthropomorphism is to be found on every page of the Old Testament in a wealth of detail, unashamed and even drastic."[137]

Köhler divides Old Testament anthropomorphisms into three broad categories: (1) Texts that represent God as possessing parts of the human body, or functions thereof, (2) texts that depict God with the feelings and emotions of

---

[134]"The danger of one-sidedness which is inherent in the use of metaphors and models increases as models are comprehensively developed" (Brümmer, *Model of Love*, p. 21).

[135] R. B. Braithwaite, quoted in ibid., pp. 12, 22.

[136]In a restricted sense the term *anthropomorphism* refers to representations of deity with the physical forms and functions of humanity. Thus it could be distinguished from an "anthropopathism," which is a representation of deity with the feelings of humanity, and from what Edwin M. Yamauchi calls an "anthropopraxism," a representation of deity with the activities of humanity ("Anthropomorphism in Ancient Religions," *Bibliotheca Sacra* 125, no. 497 [1968]: 29). But in a broader sense the term *anthropomorphism* can include all three of these aspects. In the discussion that follows, I will be employing this broader, more general sense of the word.

[137]Ludwig Köhler, *Old Testament Theology,* trans. A. S. Todd (1935; reprint, Philadelphia: Westminster Press, 1957), p. 22. Similarly, Caird says, "We have no other language besides metaphor with which to speak about God. . . . The only choice open to us, therefore, is whether we derive our metaphors from the human realm or from the non-human. . . . By far the greater proportion of the biblical language that refers to God is anthropomorphic" (*Language and Imagery*, p. 174).

human beings, and (3) texts that describe God's works and ways anthropomor-
phically.[138] While the pagan religions of the ancient world were replete with anthropomorphisms (and theriomorphisms, i.e., God represented in the form of
animals), Edwin Yamauchi argues that Old Testament anthropomorphisms stand
in sharp contrast to their counterparts in other ancient religions.[139] There is, he
concludes, a qualitative difference between the two. The God of the Old Testament is vastly different than the pagan gods, just as he is vastly different from
his human creatures. "The God of Israel, described as He is in anthropomorphic
terms as were the pagan deities, is quite distinct from the latter as He is from
mankind. . . . He remains absolutely unique."[140]

Anthropomorphisms are not found only in the Old Testament. The New Testament is also filled with anthropomorphisms, both in its quotations from the
Old Testament and in its own expressions. These New Testament anthropomorphisms also speak in terms of God's form, his feelings, and his actions.[141]

In spite of the fact that there has often been a remarkably negative view of
biblical anthropomorphisms in the history of the church, it must be affirmed
that the anthropomorphic metaphors of Scripture are truly reality depicting
and thus are very valuable.[142] David Clines argues that "Anthropomorphic lan-

---

[138]For examples of each of these three categories, see Köhler, *Old Testament Theology,* p. 23.

[139]Yamauchi asserts that theriomorphism "occurs occasionally in Greek religion, frequently in
Canaanite religion, and most frequently in Egyptian religion" ("Anthropomorphism in Ancient Religions," p. 30). While there is in the Old Testament the occasional use of animal imagery to describe Yahweh (e.g., as a moth [Hos 5:2] and as a lion [Hos 5:14; 11:10]), Yamauchi
argues that "The God of the Old Testament is depicted not in theriomorphic, but in consistently anthropomorphic fashion" (ibid., p. 31).

Yamauchi cites seven distinctions between the Old Testament and other religions: pagan
anthropomorphisms (1) could be exchanged with theriomorphisms, (2) described a multi-
plicity of deities with distinctive spheres of influence, (3) did not conceive of a sovereign
God, (4) conceived of gods with an origin similar to that of humans, (5) depicted gods who
were subject to the same passions as men, (6) described gods who were subject to human
needs of sustenance, and (7) depicted gods who were selfish, fickle and murderous in their
relationship to humanity. The fact that Old Testament anthromoprphisms do not fit any of
these seven categories shows their qualitative difference from their counterparts in other ancient religions (ibid., pp. 32-44).

[140]Ibid., p. 44.

[141]See examples in each of these three categories cited in Adrio König, *Here Am I!* (Grand Rapids: Eerdmans, 1982]), p. 61.

[142]König traces this negative view of anthropomorphism to the reaction of Greek philosophy
against the anthropomorphisms of the Homeric gods, stemming from their often unworthy
behavior (dishonesty, deceit, theft, violence, immorality) and from the rise of a philosophical
conception of an independent, self-sufficient, unchangeable deity under the influence of
Plato and Aristotle (ibid., p. 62; see also Edwin M. Yamauchi, "Anthropomorphism in Hellenism and Judaism," *Bibliotheca Sacra* 127, no. 507 [1970]: 213-14). There is considerable debate over how much the Hellenistic anti-anthropomorphic bias affected the translators of

guage is . . . part of the Biblical apprehension of God. It is to be evaluated, not negatively as accommodation to human language or divine condescension to human understanding, but positively, as a vital element of our knowledge of God."[143] Köhler argues that anthropomorphisms reveal the personal nature of God.

> To describe God in terms of human characteristics is not to humanize Him. . . . Rather the purpose of anthropomorphisms is to make God accessible to man. They hold open the door for encounter and controversy between God's will and man's will. They represent God as person. They avoid the error of presenting God as a careless and soulless abstract Idea or fixed Principle standing over against man like a strong silent battlement. God is personal . . . Through the anthropomorphisms God stands before man as the personal and living God.[144]

And Wilhelm Vischer emphasizes the relational goal of this personal God in his use of anthropomorphisms in his Word.

> It is the wonder of grace that in spite of [human sin], the Holy One enters into the most personal relationship with the sinner. . . . For this reason God comes near to us in human form. . . . In whatever measure we remove the human features from his revelation, in that measure we remove ourselves from God.[145]

Thus any attempt to "spiritualize" these anthropomorphic descriptions of God

---

the LXX (see Yamauchi, "Anthropomorphism in Hellenism and Judaism," pp. 215-16; and Aubrey W. Argyle, "God's 'Repentance' and the LXX," *Expository Times* 75 [1964]: 367 for contrasting views). The evidence is much more clear in the case of Philo, who served as the bridge through which anti-anthropomorphic Hellenistic thought entered the theology of the early church. König summarizes Philo's thought, "It is clear that God is not like a man. The other principle is too vulnerable to misunderstanding, is inappropriate and is therefore dangerous. . . . [But] because we would not be able to grasp it if God were to reveal himself to us as he really is, he revealed himself in human terms. But the spiritual person must move beyond this phase as quickly as possible. God is, after all, not only non-human, he is even without attributes!" Philo's exegesis of Gen 6:6-7 is a striking example. He followed the LXX, which sought to remove any trace of anthropomorphism ("The LORD *took to heart* the fact that he made man on earth and he *reflected* on this"). König says, "Philo accepted this translation as correct because God could not feel sorry, or repent. . . . This would indeed mean that God had changed, and what greater godlessness could there be than to suggest such a thing?" (*Here I Am!*, pp. 64-65).

[143]David Clines, "Yahweh and the God of Christian Theology," *Theology* 83, no. 695 (1980): 326. Clines is likely contrasting his view with that of Calvin. Calvin spoke of God's accommodation to reveal himself to us in human language as God "lisping" to us as nurses commonly do with infants. He goes on, "Such forms of speaking do not so much express what God is like as accommodate the knowledge of him to our slight capacity" (*Institutes* 1.13.1, Library of Christian Classics, ed. John T. McNeill (Philadelphia: Westminster, 1960).

[144]Köhler, *Old Testament Theology*, pp. 24-25.

[145]Wilhelm Vischer, "Words and the Word: The Anthropomorphisms of the Biblical Revelation," trans. John Bright, *Interpretation* 3 (1949): 7.

ends up depersonalizing him and impoverishing us. Vischer argues that even when we engage in such spiritualizing efforts, our descriptions "remain anthropomorphisms, for our abstract conceptions are no less anthropomorphic than the concrete portrayals. The only thing we achieve with such 'spiritualizing' is that all expressions become more abstract, and that is to say paler, weaker, and more impersonal."[146]

Sanders gives two reasons for the appropriateness of biblical anthropomorphisms. First is the reality of the "shared context" that exists between God and humans. God has created human beings in his own image (Gen 1:26-27) and has been pleased to communicate to us in human language. If God has truly created human beings to be his unique image-bearers, then metaphors drawn from the realm of human experience can tell us more about the nature of the one whose image we bear than can metaphors from any other realm of experience.[147] And if God chooses to reveal himself to us in the human language of Scripture, then of necessity his revelation must to one extent or another be anthropomorphic. Sanders says, "All the language we employ to speak of God is human language and thus is tinged with anthropomorphism."[148]

The second and even more important reason for the appropriateness of anthropomorphic descriptions of God is the incarnation of God the Son. Sanders describes Jesus Christ as the "consummate anthropomorphism" and argues, "If Jesus is God incarnate, then it does not seem that God is especially concerned about having human characteristics predicated of him."[149]

But while affirming the tremendous value of biblical anthropomorphisms, we must still recognize that they are metaphors. And as metaphors, they retain the whisper "it is and it is not." Thus anthropomorphic metaphors retain both sim-

---

[146]Ibid., p. 4.

[147]Sanders, *God Who Risks,* pp. 23-24. Because God has indeed created human beings in his image, Sanders refers to men and women as "theomorphisms" and argues that much of what we think of as anthropomorphisms in describing God are actually theomorphisms in describing humans. For example, "God's concern for justice and love is not anthropomorphism; rather, our concern for justice and love is theomorphism" (ibid., p. 21).

[148]Ibid., 19. The Dutch Reformed theologian Herman Bavinck agrees: "God uses human language to reveal himself and manifests himself in human forms. It follows that Scripture does not merely contain a few anthropomorphisms; on the contrary *all* Scripture is anthropomorphic. . . . Even the most abstract names; e.g., essence, substance, the absolute, the one, spirit, reason, etc. are and ever remain anthropomorphisms. For man there are only two alternatives: absolute silence with reference to God, or speaking about him in a human way; either agnosticism, i.e., theoretical atheism, or anthropomorphism" (*The Doctrine of God,* trans. William Hendricksen [Grand Rapids: Baker, 1951], pp. 86, 91).

[149]Sanders, *God Who Risks,* p. 21.

ilarities with and differences from the divine reality they depict.[150] Both the similarities and the differences are crucial to come to grips with if we want to truly
understand biblical anthropomorphisms.

The similarities are crucial to remember. There must be an element in the nature and experience of God and his relationship with humans to which the anthropomorphic metaphor corresponds. Sanders calls this the "univocal or hard
literal core." He says:

> There must be some properties that are used of God in the same sense that they
> are used of things in the created order. Otherwise we will be back in the cave of
> agnosticism. Anthropomorphic language does not preclude literal predication to
> God. . . . What I mean by the word *literal* is that our language about God is reality
> depicting (truthful) such that there is a referent, an other, with whom we are in
> relationship and of whom we have genuine knowledge. Even though God may not
> be exhaustively known by us, we can have actual knowledge of God, since God
> enters into relationship with us.[151]

Yet the differences are also real and significant, and they must be kept in mind
as well. Vischer notes, "If we observe that the relationship of God and man in
the biblical revelation is not reversible, then we will also recognize that the biblical anthropomorphisms do not remove the distinction between God and man,
and in no sense permit us to exchange God and man."[152] And Fretheim observes
that while failing to see the similarities between the metaphorical description and
the divine reality it points to ends up viewing God "as so wholly other than no
relationship and therefore no knowledge is possible," failing to see the differences is no less dangerous, for it "reduce[s] God to human frailty." Rather:

> the discontinuities inherent in the metaphor need to be lifted up. Anthropomorphic
> metaphors ought not be conceived in terms of pictures, replicas, scale models, copies,
> or the like. . . . There is always that which is discontinuous with the reality of God.
> God outdistances all our images; God cannot finally be captured by any of them.[153]

One final observation. Metaphors (including anthropomorphic metaphors) are
not all equal in terms of how similar and how different they are in relation to the
divine reality they depict. There are varying "degrees of correspondence" or vary-

---

[150]Richard Swinburne speaks of the similarities and differences of these metaphors as the "old
and new senses" of the words of theology (*The Coherence of Theism,* rev. ed. [Oxford: Clarendon Press, 1993], pp. 51-87).
[151]Sanders, *God Who Risks,* pp. 25-26.
[152]Vischer, "Words and the Word," p. 6.
[153]Fretheim, *Suffering of God,* p. 8. Fretheim argues that both approaches end up leading to
idolatry.

ing "degrees of revelatory capacity" in the metaphors. Not all biblical metaphors are equally reality-depicting.[154] Fretheim gives examples, citing biblical metaphors that have a low degree of revelatory capacity (God as dry rot [Hos 5:12]; God as lion [Hos 5:14]; God as whistler [Is 7:18]) and other metaphors with a moderate capacity (God as rock [Ps 31:2-3]; God's arm [Is 53:1]) and finally other biblical metaphors with a very high degree of revelatory capacity (God as parent [Hos 11:1]).[155] The point is that in the interpretation of any particular metaphor, we must seek to determine the degree of correspondence. This must be done through the application of the criteria for the evaluation of a metaphor or model cited above (see p. 163), particularly looking at the degree of correspondence of this particular metaphor with the biblical revelation as a whole.

ANTHROPOMORPHISM AND THE REPENTANCE OF GOD

How does this discussion of metaphors, models and anthropomorphisms relate to our preceding discussion of the repentance of God? And how does it relate to the larger issue under discussion throughout this book—the extent of the foreknowledge of God?

Since all Scripture is to some extent anthropomorphic and since all biblical descriptions of God are metaphorical to one degree or another, we must hold that the repentance of God is an anthropomorphic metaphor. The same is true of the foreknowledge of God. As such, in each case there are both similarities and differences between the human experience from which the metaphor is drawn and the divine experience. Thus, for example, I believe that God's foreknowledge is similar to its human counterpart in God's experience of cognition and relationship, but it is very different in that it is infinitely more vast, is uniformly certain and true, and has an entirely different relationship to time.[156]

With respect to the metaphor of divine repentance, we must note first of all the genuine similarities that exist between divine and human repentance. The divine repentance texts surveyed in this chapter do point to a real change in the emotions or actions of God. And while a full discussion of the impassibility and immutability of God is outside the scope of this book, we must affirm that biblical teaching on

---

[154]Caird, *Language and Imagery,* p. 153; and Fretheim, *Suffering of God,* p. 10.

[155]Fretheim, *Suffering of God,* p. 10.

[156]Obviously open theists differ from classical theists in their denial of God's certain foreknowledge of free human decisions. But they also affirm that God's knowledge of the past and present and of nonfreedom-dependent elements of the future is infinitely more vast than the most knowledgeable of human beings.

  While open theists affirm that God's probabilistic predictions of the future can at times be mistaken, they too are in agreement that in the areas in which God has genuine foreknowledge, this foreknowledge is uniformly true.

the repentance of God argues against an extreme understanding of either divine impassibility (which affirms no emotions at all in God) or divine immutability (affirming no change of any kind in God).[157] A real change in emotion or action is clearly a central point of similarity in the metaphor of divine repentance. And Fretheim's argument from the pervasiveness of this metaphor in the Hebrew Scriptures and the diversity of textual traditions and genres in which it is found gives strong evidence that divine repentance is a significant biblical metaphor about God that cannot be dismissed or taken lightly. But the issue of difference must also be faced. So we must ask what ways divine repentance is different from human repentance.

Bruce Ware cites the biblically stated contrast between God and humanity in Numbers 23:19 and 1 Samuel 15:29 to emphasize the fact that God does not repent as humans do. This is an illustration of his larger criterion that should be used to determine when a particular biblical statement may rightly be understood as anthropomorphic (or more accurately, as "more strongly anthropomorphic," i.e., with a greater difference-similarity ratio). Ware says, "A given ascription to God may rightly be understood as anthropomorphic when Scripture clearly presents God as transcending the very human or finite features it elsewhere attributes to him."[158] He argues that the divine-human contrast in

---

A detailed examination of the relationship of God's knowledge to time is outside the scope of this discussion. I affirm that in his essential being God exists outside of time and thus his knowledge could truthfully be called atemporal. Yet I do not believe that atemporal divine knowledge solves the foreknowledge-freedom problem in the way affirmed by Boethius. But even if we affirm that God is temporal in his essential being, there is still a profound difference in God's experience of time (though not of the same magnitude). For a helpful introduction to various views of God's relationship to time, see *God and Time: Four Views,* ed. Gregory E. Ganssle (Downers Grove, Ill.: InterVarsity Press, 2001).

[157]Most evangelical theologians today do not affirm such a strict view of either divine impassibility or immutability. For example, see Ware, "Immutability of God," and Richard Creel, *Divine Impassibility* (Cambridge: Cambridge University Press, 1986). See also Wayne Grudem, *Systematic Theology,* pp. 163-68, and Millard Erickson, *Christian Theology,* 2nd ed. (Grand Rapids: Baker, 1998), pp. 305, 728, 753, and Millard Erickson, *God the Father Almighty* (Grand Rapids: Baker, 1998), pp. 95-113, 141-64.

[158]Ware, "Immutability of God," p. 442. Ware cites what he believes to be the clearest example in Scripture—the ascription to God of bodily parts. "It seems clear that the fundamental reason why one may feel confident in understanding these physical ascriptions in a non-literal way is that elsewhere God's self-revelation discloses that God is not confined physically (1 Kings 8:27), nor can he be seen (1 John 4:2), but he is in fact spirit (John 4:24). That is, Scripture clearly presents God (*qua* Spirit) as transcending the finite physical features it elsewhere attributes to him. It seems justifiable, then, to take these physical descriptions as anthropomorphic" (ibid., pp. 442-43). (For a contrary view which argues that taking biblical anthropomorphisms seriously should make us open to understanding God as being in some way embodied, see Pinnock, *Most Moved Mover,* pp. 33-35.) Boyd proposes two criteria for recognizing more strongly anthropomorphic metaphors: "There are certainly passages in the Bible that are figurative and portray God in human terms. You can recognize them because

1 Samuel 15:29 and Numbers 23:19 is just such a clear portrayal of God transcending the human elements attributed to him in the divine repentance passages. Thus whatever is meant by God's repentance (especially in 1 Sam 15:11, 35, coming in the same chapter as the statement of divine nonrepentance in 15:29), it cannot be understood to be exactly the same as human repentance. The divine-human contrast is a deliberate textual indicator of the fact that the differences between divine and human repentance are especially significant and crucial.

This fact has been noted by other commentators as well. William McKane says that in 1 Samuel 15:29 "the writer of vs. 11 and 35 is telling us that he is perfectly aware that his anthropopathism should not be pushed too far."[159] Walther Eichrodt agrees, noting the danger of bringing God down to the level of humans if these metaphors are pressed too far.

> When certain anthropopathisms are endangering the purity of the idea of God, their voice is heard in clear condemnation. "God is not a man that he should lie; neither the son of man that he should repent;" the purpose of both Num 23:19 and 1 Sam 15:29 in making this declaration is to combat the erroneous idea that it is easy to talk God round, and that his threats and promises need not be taken seriously.[160]

This is clearly the way of wisdom with respect to 1 Samuel 15. The author of 1 Samuel does affirm a very real regret on God's part. Saul's disobedience truly makes God regret that he has made him king over Israel. The twofold repetition of this reality (vv. 11, 35) emphasizes this point. But lest we get the wrong idea of the nature of God's repentance, the writer tells us in the very same chapter that God's repentance is not at all like that of a human being.

---

what is said about God is either ridiculous if taken literally (e.g., God has an 'outstretched arm,' Deut 4:34; God as 'our husband,' Hos 2:2), or because the genre of the passage is poetic (e.g., God has 'protective wings,' Ps 17:8)" (*God of the Possible*, p. 118). However, Boyd does not explain exactly what his criteria mean. I take it that by describing certain anthropomorphic passages as "figurative" as opposed to literal, Boyd means that in these cases the differences between the human description and its corresponding divine referent vastly outweigh the similarities. I also assume that we can identify the "ridiculous" nature of a literal understanding of these metaphors through comparison with the clear teaching of Scripture elsewhere. Thus there end up being significant similarities between Boyd's first criterion and Ware's.

[159]William McKane, *I and II Samuel,* Torch Bible Commentaries (London: SCM Press, 1963), p. 103.

[160]Walther Eichrodt, *Theology of the Old Testament,* trans. J. A. Baker (Philadelphia: Westminster, 1961), 1:216. V. Philips Long cites Eichrodt's comment to counter those who argue that 1 Sam 15:29 must be a gloss, and says, "Given this understanding, v. 29 makes very good sense in its present context" (*Reign and Rejection,* pp. 163-64).

"God is not a man that he should change his mind."[161]

Eichrodt immediately follows his statement on the meaning and purpose of Numbers 23:19 and 1 Samuel 15:29 by affirming a very similar understanding of Hosea 11:9.

> Again, Hosea protests against the reproach that his God allows himself to be carried away into executing punitive judgment by caprice or passion: "I will not execute the fierceness of mine anger . . . for I am God and not man; the Holy One in the midst of thee, and I do not come to carry off (the prey) like a roaring lion." (11:9).[162]

This is in accord with what we have have already seen in our analysis of Hosea 11:8-9. After Yahweh speaks of a very real change of heart with respect to his people (v. 8), he quickly qualifies that by affirming that "I will not carry out my fierce anger, / nor will I turn and devastate Ephraim. / For I am God, and not man— / the Holy One among you. / I will not come in wrath" (v. 9). Thus Yahweh wants to insure that we do not misunderstand the implications of his change of heart. Yes, it is real. The statement is reality depicting. But his is not a human change of heart. The comments of James Luther Mays are appropriate and to the point.

> The apparent inconsistency [between the emotional change of 11:8 and the resolute intention of Yahweh in 11:9 not to come in wrath, grounded in his utter difference from man] is a warning that Hosea's many anthropomorphisms are meant as interpretive analogies, not as essential definitions. The metaphors are incarnations in language. The actions and feelings of Yahweh can be translated into representations of human, and even animal, life. In the dramatic metaphor the personal reality of Yahweh's incursion into human life and history is present and comprehensible. But he transcends the metaphor, is different from that to which he is compared, and free of all its limitations. He is wrathful and loving *like* man, but *as* God.[163]

---

[161]John Piper comments, "We should say that there is a sense in which God does repent and there is a sense in which he does not. The strong declaration that God cannot repent (1 Sam 15:29; Num 23:19) is intended to keep us from seeing the repentance of God in a way that would put him in the limited category of a man. God's repentance is not like ours. I take that to mean that God is not taken off guard by unexpected turns of events as we are. He knows all the future. . . . Nor does God ever sin. So his repentance does not spring from a lack of foresight nor [from] folly." Piper defines the repentance of God as "his expression of a different attitude and action about something past or future, not because events have taken him off guard, but because the turn of events (which he himself has ordered—Eph 1:11) makes a different attitude more fitting now than would have been the case earlier. God's mind 'changes,' not because it responds to unforeseen circumstances, but because he has ordained that his mind accord with the way he himself orders the changing events of the world" ("The Repentance of God: Meditation on the Mind of God," in *A Godward Life* [Sisters, Ore.: Multnomah Publishers, 1997], p. 191).

[162]Eichrodt, *Theology of the Old Testament,* 1:216.

[163]Mays, *Hosea,* p. 157.

Thus, far from affirming with Sanders that the divine-human contrast functions differently in Hosea 11:9 than it does in Numbers 23:19 and 1 Samuel 15:11 (to ground God's repentance in the former case while it grounds God's nonrepentance in the latter two cases), I contend that the contrast functions in *exactly the same way* in all three cases. In Hosea 11:8, as in 1 Samuel 15:11, there is an explicit affirmation of the repentance of God. But in both cases, the statement is then qualified by the divine-human contrast (Hos 11:9; 1 Sam 15:29) to show that God's repentance is not at all like human repentance.[164] Rather the emphasis in both passages (and also in Num 23:19) is on God's dependability, reliability and faithfulness to his covenant promises. From these he will not turn away.

If this is true, then we must ask, In what ways could God's repentance be different from human repentance? John Calvin is helpful here. He seeks to understand how humans might come to change their minds and then asks whether any or all of those factors might be present in God. Calvin proposes that a change of mind can come in a human being when one is "ignorant of what is going to happen, or cannot escape it, or hastily and rashly rushes into a decision of which he immediately needs to repent."[165] In other words, human beings might repent if they learn something new that they had been previously ignorant of, or if they realize they do not have the power to do what was originally planned, or if they develop a new perspective in which what was originally thought to be a good plan is now understood to be not so good.[166] Calvin, then, argues that none of these conditions (lack of power, lack of knowledge, lack of a proper perspective) apply to God. "Concerning repentance, we ought so to hold that it is no more chargeable to God than is ignorance, or error, or powerlessness."[167]

---

[164]Vischer agrees that Hos 11:9 is designed to keep us from understanding God's repentance in a human way. He links this with his understanding of Gen 6:6. "To be sure, the expressions of emotional excitement are highly inadequate for that they bear witness to, insofar as no human heart is capable of this feeling, but the heart of God alone in the transcendence of his Godhead. It must be clear to us that it means something quite other when it is said of God, 'It repented the Lᴏʀᴅ and it grieved him at his heart' (Gen 6:6), than when the same is said of man. . . . If, therefore, in the above-named passages [including Hos 11] the wonder of grace is attested by the most shocking anthropopathisms, that does not mean that the image of God is distorted into a human, all-too-human, one; 'I am God, and not man.' 'Mine heart is turned within me, my repentings are kindled together. I will not execute the fierceness of mine anger . . . for I am God, and not man, the Holy One in the midst of thee' (Hos 11:8-9)" ("Words and the Word," p. 10).

[165]Calvin *Institutes* 1.17.12.

[166]Ware summarizes Calvin's criteria as follows: "Essentially, then [Calvin is saying that] a true change of mind can occur when one learns something of which one was ignorant, or when one lacks the power to do as first planned, or when one gains a fresh insight or a new perspective on a situation leading to a reconsideration of one's former intent" ("Immutability of God," p. 442).

[167]Calvin *Institutes* 1.17.12.

While a full treatment of these other divine attributes is also outside the bounds of this volume, I believe that the Bible portrays God as always having sufficient power to do all that he wills to do. And the Bible portrays God to be utterly and completely and consistently holy, so there would never be a change of perspective on his part that would involve changing moral judgments.[168] Whether God's repentance is or could be the result of his ignorance or lack of wisdom, however, goes to the very heart of this book.

With regard to divine repentance and the knowledge of God, it must be noted that in none of the divine repentance texts is God's ignorance of future free human decisions specifically affirmed. John Piper perceptively notes, "These [divine repentance] texts do not say or teach that God does not foreknow the future in question. . . . That is always an inference based on what someone thinks is possible for God to do or say."[169]

One example will have to suffice to show Piper's point. Regarding 1 Samuel 15:11, Boyd argues:

> We must wonder how the Lord could truly experience regret for making Saul king if he was absolutely certain that Saul would act the way he did. Could God genuinely confess, "I regret that I made Saul king" if he could in the same breath also proclaim, "I was certain of what Saul would do when I made him king?" I do not see how. . . . *Common sense tells us* that we can only regret a decision we made if the decision resulted in an outcome other than what we expected or hoped for when the decision was made.[170]

Boyd's appeal to "common sense" seems to imply that he is beginning with an analysis of what repentance looks like when it is experienced by humans and then assumes that God's repentance must be the same at every point. Specifically with respect to knowledge, Boyd is assuming (I use this word because Boyd gives no argument at this point) that the relationship of repentance to knowledge is one of the *similarities* between God's repentance and its human counterpart rather than one of the *differences* between the two realities. But why? Why the assumption of similarity rather than difference, especially in light of the explicit statements of the divine-human contrast in Numbers 23:19,

---

[168]Neither God's unimpeachable moral holiness nor his omnipotent power are under debate between openness and nonopenness theologians. While there is significant differences as to what these different positions hold that God wills to do, there is agreement that God has sufficient power to do whatever he wills. For an excellent treatment of these and other divine attributes, see John Feinberg, *No One Like Him* (Wheaton, Ill.: Crossway, 2001).

[169]John Piper, "Why the Glory of God Is at Stake in the 'Foreknowledge' Debate," *Modern Reformation* 8, no. 5 [1999]: 43.

[170]Boyd, *God of the Possible*, p. 56, emphasis added.

1 Samuel 15:29 and Hosea 11:9? At this point, the words of Vischer must be taken seriously.

> The proper understanding of the biblical revelation hangs on the recognition that the sentence, "God created man in his image" is *irreversible*. As soon as it is turned around, revelation is inverted into human speculation, the truth into a lie, and human thoughts about God will take the place of the Word that imparts God's thoughts. God, who has said, "Let us make man in our image, after our likeness," asks passionately: "To whom will ye liken God? Or what likeness will ye compare unto him? . . . To whom will ye liken me, or shall I be equal? Saith the Holy One" (Is 40:12-15). The LORD is a jealous God, whether this anthropomorphism pleases us or not. He does not tolerate the reversal of it, that man, instead of being the image of God, should conceive for himself God after the likeness of man.[171]

A far preferable approach then is to take the whole of biblical revelation into account in trying to determine what is similar and what is different between divine and human repentance. This certainly includes the vast amount of Scripture that teaches or illustrates God's foreknowledge of free human decisions (such as has been presented in chaps. 2 and 3). And it also includes the incredibly significant use made of such foreknowledge by Yahweh in Isaiah 40—48 and by Jesus in John 13:19. Yes, the repentance of God is a significant biblical metaphor, as Fretheim and others have helpfully argued. But its frequency of usage is dwarfed by the 2,323 predictive prophecies in Scripture that concern free human decisions or events that have such decisions as a causal component. Thus we must be careful not to interpret the metaphor of divine repentance in such as way that it diminishes the far more frequent metaphor of divine foreknowledge. Both metaphors must be understood to be reality depicting, but the extent and intensity of the biblical portrayal of divine foreknowledge must in no way be diminished.[172] The witness of Scripture as a whole lends considerable weight to understanding the relationship of divine knowledge to divine repentance as fundamentally different than that of its human counterpart.

So how should we understand the repentance of God if we affirm his foreknowledge of free human decisions? I suggest that divine repentance denotes God's awareness of a change in the human situation and his resulting change

---

[171]Vischer, "Words and the Word," p. 13.

[172]Paul Helm argues that this is true not only for statements of God's knowledge but also for statements about God's power and goodness. "The statements about the extent and intensity of God's knowledge, power, and goodness must control the anthropomorphic and weaker statements, and not vice versa. The alternative approach would appear to be quite unacceptable, for it would result in a theological reductionism in which God is distilled to human proportions" (*The Providence of God* [Downers Grove, Ill.: InterVarsity Press, 1994], p. 52).

of emotions or actions in light of this changed situation. This change in the human situation could involve human sin (e.g., Gen 6:6; 1 Sam 15:11, 35; Jer 18:9-10) or human repentance (e.g., Jer 18:7-8; Jon 3:9) or human intercession (e.g., Ex 32:14; 2 Kings 20:1-6; Amos 7:1-6). And in his repentance, God changes his emotions or actions as is appropriate and fitting in light of these changed circumstances. But this does not necessarily imply that the changed human circumstances were unforeseen by God and that God has learned something new as a result of these free human decisions. As Ware comments:

> In no cases of divine repentance is it necessary to go further than this and say that God *learned* something new *by* this changed situation. Rather, these expressions of repentance may indicate more narrowly that God was aware of what had changed and chose to act in accordance with this new situation. His awareness and choice to act accordingly *may have been from eternity,* yet he interacted in the temporal and existential flow of developing and changing human situations. . . . Just because God knows in advance that some event will occur, this does not preclude God from experiencing appropriate emotions and expressing appropriate reactions when it actually happens. So, although God may have known that the world would become morally corrupt (Gen 6:5-6), that Nineveh would repent (Jonah 3:5-10), that Moses would plead for his people (Exod 32:11-14), and that Saul would fail as king (1 Sam 13:8-14; 15:1-9), nonetheless God may *experience internally* and *express outwardly* appropriate moral responses to these situations *when they occur in history.*[173]

Clearly this is very different than the kind of repentance we experience as humans. We cannot conceive of ourselves responding with genuine grief and regret over sin that we infallibly foreknew would happen and responding with a genuine change of action in response to a situation we infallibly foreknew. "Common sense" would dictate differently, as Boyd has in fact argued. But that is precisely the point. God's repentance is not like human repentance, certainly not in its relationship to the foreknowledge of God. Piper's words about Genesis 6:6 and 1 Samuel 15:11 are very much to the point.

> God foreknows the grievous and sorrowful effects of some of his own choices—for example to create Adam and Eve or to make Saul king. These effects are genuinely grievous to God as he sees them in themselves. Yet he does not regard his choices as mistakes that he would do differently if only he foreknew what was coming. Rather, he wills to do some things which he then genuinely grieves over in part when the grievous effect comes to pass. Now, if someone should say, This does not sound like what we ordinarily mean by "regret" or "repentance," I would

---

[173]Ware, *God's Lesser Glory,* pp. 90-92.

respond that this is exactly what Samuel said: God "will not lie or repent, for he is not a man that he should repent" (1 Sam 15:29). In other words, Samuel means something like this: when I say "[God] repented that he made Saul king" (or when Moses said that God repented that he created Adam and Eve), I do not mean that God experiences "repentance" this way. He experiences it *his* way—the way one experiences "repentance" when one is all-wise and foreknows the entire future perfectly. The experience is real, but it is not like finite man experiences it.[174]

Conclusion. We have seen that the repentance of God in Scripture is a widespread anthropomorphic metaphor that is indeed reality-depicting (as opposed to being dismissively minimized as a mere anthropomorphism).[175] But the metaphor also points to significant differences that exist between divine repentance and its human counterpart. Absolutely crucial for our purposes in this study is the fact that God's repentance does not necessarily imply a lack of foreknowledge on his part. Nor does it imply any admission of mistake on the part of God (e.g., God saying "If I knew then what I know now, I would have done things differently"). Admittedly, it is difficult from our human perspective to conceive of genuine repentance coexisting with exhaustive foreknowledge. But the extent and intensity of biblical teaching on God's foreknowledge of free human actions is even greater than it is on divine repentance. Therefore we must not understand the repentance of God in any way that diminishes or minimizes his foreknowledge of free human decisions. Strange as it may seem from our human vantage point, this is precisely one way that "God is not a man that he should repent."

---

[174]Piper, "Why the Glory of God Is at Stake," p. 43. In another context, Piper argues that the question of whether God could genuinely be sorry for a past act if he knew when he did it exactly what the consequences would be ultimately boils down to the question of whether God is capable of feeling genuine sorrow and genuine joy at the same time about an act he will perform. This must be the case if God infallibly knew that humanity would commit sin in such a way as would genuinely grieve his heart and yet went ahead and created humanity nonetheless. Piper argues from the parallel with the cross of Christ that this is in fact possible. Acts 2:23 teaches that God foreknew the fact and the circumstances of the death of Christ. He knew in advance that in sending his Son into the world he was sending Jesus to his death. And God was certainly grieved over the sin that led to the undeserved suffering of his one and only Son. Yet Acts 2:23 and Is 53:10 explicitly tell us that God not only knew that his Son would die, but planned it. Thus with respect to the cross of Christ, we must affirm that God both approved of it in some sense and grieved over it in another sense. Piper argues that God experienced the same complex of emotions in Gen 6. Thus the authenticity of God's grief over the sin of humanity is not compromised by his foreknowing what humans would do. Clearly it is a different kind of grief, but it is real, nonetheless (see Piper, *Godward Life*, pp. 220-22).

[175]One of the great benefits of open theism is its insistence that we take seriously the widespread metaphor of divine repentance and incorporate into our theology the reality it depicts.

OTHER OPENNESS TEXTS

Of necessity, we will not be able to deal with other openness texts in much detail. I will mention four categories and will look at the first more fully. Then we will look very briefly at the final three categories, focusing on only one example from each category.

God's testing of his people. Boyd claims that "God frequently tests his covenant partners to see if they will choose to follow him or not." He says:

> This testing isn't a game for God. It lies at the heart of God's call to keep covenant with him. He creates us free, for his goal is love, and love must be chosen. It cannot be pre-programmed. And so from the very beginning (Genesis 3), God's call to covenantal faithfulness has involved testing. God is seeking to *find out* whether or not the people he calls will lovingly choose him above all else. However, if the future is exhaustively settled, and if God foreknows the future only in terms of certainties, never possibilities, then there is nothing for God to "find out."[176]

These Scriptural testings can be corporate, as for example when God tested his people in the wilderness (cf. Deut 8:2: "Remember how the LORD your God led you all the way in the desert these forty years, to humble you and to test you in order to know what was in your heart, whether or not you would keep his commands").[177] On other occasions God tests his people individually. For example, we read in 2 Chronicles 32:31: "But when envoys were sent by the rulers of Babylon to ask [Hezekiah] about the miraculous sign that had occurred in the land, God left him to test him and to know everything that was in his heart."[178]

The most well-known and widely discussed occurrence of such divine testing comes in Genesis 22, when God tested Abraham by commanding him to offer his son Isaac. In the first verse of this chapter we are introduced to the true nature of what is going on: "Some time later God tested *[nāsâ]* Abraham."[179] The content of the test is given in God's command to Abraham in

---

[176]Boyd, *God of the Possible,* pp. 63-64.

[177]Other examples of corporate testing of Israel by God include Ex 16:4; Deut 13:1-3; Judg 2:21-22; 3:4.

[178]Concerning 2 Chron 32:31, Boyd says, "if God eternally knew how Hezekiah would respond to him, God couldn't have *really* been testing him in order to gain this knowledge. Unfortunately for the classical view, however, *this is exactly what the text says*" ("The Open-Theism View," in *Divine Foreknowledge: Four Views,* ed. James K. Bielby and Paul R. Eddy [Downers Grove, Ill.: InterVarsity Press, 2001], p. 32).

[179]Victor Hamilton argues that the closest parallel to this divine test comes in Ex 20:20, where Moses tells the people that in giving the Decalogue "God is coming to test *[nāsâ]* you, so that the fear of God will be with you to keep you from sinning." Hamilton notes that in each case Elohim is the subject of the verb *nāsâ* and that the aim of the testing in each case is to evidence the fear of God. The major difference is that in Ex 20:20 the people know, through Moses, that through his giving of his law, God is testing his people. On the other hand, it is

verse 2, "Take your son, your only son, Isaac, whom you love, and go to the region of Moriah. Sacrifice him there as a burnt offering on one of the mountains I will tell you about."[180] This testing goes beyond the unbelievably wrenching emotions Abraham must have felt in being asked to sacrifice his beloved son Isaac. The testing was primarily theological. God had promised Abraham a son through Sarah (Gen 17:6) and had miraculously brought about his birth (Gen 21:1-5). God had promised that Abraham's offspring, through whom the whole world would be blessed (Gen 12:3), would come through Isaac, not Ishmael (Gen 21:12). And now God was asking Abraham to sacrifice to him that very child of promise.

> The test for Abraham is not primarily whether to sacrifice a beloved son, though that is no doubt involved emotionally. The real test is whether Abraham will sacrifice the one person who can perpetuate the promises of God, and particularly those promises that his posterity should thrive.[181]

In faith, Abraham obeyed (cf. Heb 11:17-19), traveling three days to Mt. Moriah. When the moment of truth came Abraham continued in the course of obedience. He took the knife, fully prepared to kill his son. At the last moment, the angel of the Lord told Abraham to stop. " 'Do not lay a hand on the boy,' he said. 'Do not do anything to him. Now I know that you fear God, because you have not withheld from me your son, your only son'" (Gen 22:12).

Our chief concern in this section is with the meaning and implications of the angel's statement, who clearly spoke for God: "Now I know that you fear God, because you have not withheld from me your son, your only son." Does this mean that God did not know whether Abraham truly feared him before the test was complete?

Boyd argues that this is exactly the case. He cites the importance of the word *because* in verse 12. He says, "The verse clearly says that it was *because* Abraham did what he did that the Lord *now* knew that he was a faithful covenant partner. The verse has no clear meaning if God was certain that Abra-

---

the reader, not Abraham, who knows that what is to follow is a divine test (*The Book of Genesis: Chapters 18-50*, New International Commentary on the Old Testament [Grand Rapids: Eerdmans, 1995], p. 101). This fact is deemed very important by Terence Fretheim. "If Abraham had known in advance that it was a test, it would have been no real test" (*The Book of Genesis*, The New Interpreters Bible 1 [Nashville: Abingdon, 1994], p. 497). Yet Ex 20:20 seems to argue, against Fretheim, that it is possible to know in advance that you are going to be tested and have it nonetheless be a genuine test.

[180]Fretheim says, "The offering language places this entire episode within the context of the sacrificial system. The deed will be a specifically religious act, an act of faith, a giving to God of what Abraham loves (only then would it be a true sacrifice)" (*Book of Genesis*, p. 495).

[181]Hamilton, *Book of Genesis, Chapters 18-50*, p. 104.

ham would fear him before he offered up his son."[182]

Walter Brueggemann agrees about God's prior ignorance of Abraham's response and his desire to learn through this test. He cites the linkage between verse 1 and verse 12 of the text.

> Verse 1 sets the test, suggesting that God wants to know something. . . . It is not a game with God. God genuinely does not know. And that is settled in verse 12, "Now I know." There is real development in the plot. The flow of the narrative accomplishes something in the awareness of God. He did not know. Now he knows.[183]

Sanders cites this statement from Brueggemann approvingly, arguing that God's movement from ignorance to knowledge is proof that "the test is genuine, not fake." He opposes those who suggest that the test is for Abraham's benefit, not for God's.

> It should be noted, however, that the only one in the text said to learn anything from the test is *God*. Abraham probably learned something in his relationship with God, but that is not the point of the text. If one presupposes that God already "knew" the results of the test beforehand, then the text is at least worded poorly and at the most simply false.[184]

Thus for Sanders not only is the genuineness of the test contingent on God's prior ignorance of Abraham's response; his truthfulness is also at stake. Sanders continues:

> If the test is genuine for both God and Abraham, then what is the reason for it? The answer is to be found in God's desire to bless all the nations of the earth (Gen 12:3). God needs to know if Abraham is the sort of person on whom God can count for collaboration toward the fulfillment of the divine project. Will he be faithful? Or must God find someone else through whom to achieve his purpose? God has been faithful; will Abraham be faithful? In 15:8 Abraham asked God for assurance. Now it is God seeking assurance from Abraham. . . . There is risk involved for both God and Abraham. God takes the risk that Abraham will exercise trust. Abraham takes

---

[182]Boyd, *God of the Possible*, p. 64. Boyd argues that God's experience of learning in Gen 22 is not unusual or unique. Rather this is God's normal experience. "Except in cases in which a solidified character or God's predestining plan makes people predictable, Scripture teaches us that God literally finds out *how* people will choose *when* they choose" (ibid., p. 65).

[183]Brueggemann, *Genesis*, p. 187.

[184]Sanders, *God Who Risks*, p. 52. Pinnock sees the learning that comes from the test of Gen 22 as being two-sided: "It was a wrenching experience and both partners, God and Abraham, learned from it: Abraham learned to trust God more deeply and God learned what Abraham would do under these circumstances" (*Most Moved Mover*, p. 42). But Pinnock is in agreement with Sanders on the key point: God really learns something new through this test.

the risk that God will provide a way into the future. In the dialogical relationship God finds reason to have confidence in Abraham, and Abraham's confidence in God proves to be well placed. God does provide an offering.[185]

But does the genuineness and truthfulness of Genesis 22:12 really require God to be ignorant of the outcome of the test prior to Abraham's actions? It is important to note that the text does not explicitly teach God's prior ignorance. All it says is that because of Abraham's obedience God now knows that he fears him. It is an inference drawn by open theists that prior to Abraham's obedience God was ignorant. But could there be other ways to explain Genesis 22:12?

Norman Geisler speaks of the difference between cognition and demonstration.

> There is nothing here [in Gen 22] about God's desire to *learn* anything. Rather, God wanted to *prove* something (cf. 2 Chr 32:31). What God knew by *cognition*, he desired to show by *demonstration*. By passing the test, Abraham demonstrated what God already knew: namely that he feared God.[186]

Geisler gives an illustration of a math teacher who might say to her class, "Let's see if we can find the square root of 49." Then, after demonstrating to her class what the square root of 49 is, she declares, "Now we know that the square root of 49 is 7." And she could legitimately say this even though she knew the correct answer all along. Geisler comments, "Even so, God, who knows all things cognitively from the beginning, could appropriately say after Abraham had proved his faith, "Now I know [demonstratively] that you fear God."[187]

---

[185]Sanders, *God Who Risks,* pp. 52-53. A question must be asked, however, about how "risky" this test of Abraham really is for God in light of his explicit promise to Abraham in Gen 12:3 (the very passage referenced by Sanders) that "all peoples on earth will be blessed *through you.*" Given this promise, is God genuinely worried that he might have to find someone else to work through if Abraham failed the test? Sanders replies that "God had unilaterally made promises to Abraham, yet there was a conditional element, for God wanted Abraham's obedience in order to bring about the promise (18:19)" (ibid., p. 53). Yet in Gen 18:19, Abraham's obedience which is indeed a necessary condition to the fulfillment of God's promises to and through Abraham is seen to be the result of God's choice of Abraham. "For I have chosen [lit. known—*yāda'*] him *so that* he will direct his children and his household after him to keep the way of the LORD by doing what is right and just, so that the LORD will bring about for Abraham what he has promised." Even if the verb *yāda'* is taken to refer to God's cognition rather than to his electing choice, God knows Abraham will fulfill the necessary conditions so that his promise will be fulfilled. Thus the "risk" taken by God cannot be viewed as great.
[186]Norman Geisler, *Creating God in the Image of Man?* (Minneapolis: Bethany House, 1997), p. 88.
[187]Ibid. In addition to arguing that the openness interpretation of Gen 22:12 is not necessary in its context, Geisler also argues that it is contrary to the teaching of the rest of Scripture. He affirms that Scripture teaches that God cognitively knows all things from the beginning, citing Ps 147:5; Is 46:10 and Rom 8:29-30. He concludes: "So, in his omniscience God knew exactly what Abraham would do before he tested him, since he knows all things (cf. Ps 139:2-4; Jer 17:10; Acts 1:24; Heb 4:13)."

John Piper proposes another understanding of the nature of God's knowledge in Genesis 22:12. He sees a difference between what God knows in his eternal foreknowledge and what God knows in terms of observation and experience as his plan is actualized in history.

> If God knows what will come to pass, does that mean that all testings *in history* are pointless? I don't think so. God has not created the world just to be known in terms of what would be if tests were given. He created the world to be actualized in history. That is, he wills not just to foreknow, but to know by observation and experience. That is the point of creating a real world, rather than just knowing one that might be. Therefore, may not God truly know what Abraham is going to do, and yet want to externalize that in a test that enables him to know it by observation, not just prognostication?[188]

Ware agrees, stating rightly that the "Now I know" of Geneis 22:12 cannot be taken to simply mean "I have eternally known." He argues that "there is something that takes place *in relation to God* when Abraham lifts his knife." What is it? Ware agrees with Piper that it is God experiencing in the present moment what he has foreknown all along.[189]

> When God observes Abraham bind his son to the altar he has crafted and raise his knife to plunge it into his body, God literally sees and experiences in this moment what he has known from eternity. When the angel of the Lord utters the statement, "for now I know that you fear God," this expresses the idea that *"in the experience of this action, I (God) am witnessing Abraham demonstrate dramatically and afresh that he fears me, and I find this both pleasing and acceptable in my sight."* Through Abraham's action of faith and fear of God, God sees and enters into the experience of this action of obedience, which action and heart of faith he has previously known fully and perfectly. What this kind of interpretation offers is a way to understand the text as communicating a *present and experiential reality that is true of God* at the moment of Abraham's faith, while it also safeguards what Scripture elsewhere demands, the *previous full and perfect knowledge God had of Abraham's fear of him.*[190]

Each of these explanations provides a plausible understanding of the nature of God's knowledge in Genesis 22:12 that is consistent with his exhaustive foreknowledge of Abraham and his actions.

---

[188]John Piper, "Answering Greg Boyd's Openness of God Texts," www.ondoctrine.com/2pip1201.htm.

[189]Even those who hold to divine atemporality recognize that God does relate to beings who are in time. Thus an atemporal God can know in the present, as experienced by human beings, what he has foreknown all along.

[190]Ware, *God's Lesser Glory,* pp. 73-74.

A significant problem for the openness understanding of Genesis 22:12 is the content of the knowledge that God gained through this text. Open theists regularly appeal to the need to take biblical texts "at face value" and interpret them "straightforwardly."[191] But when taking Genesis 22:12 at face value, we notice an interesting fact. The text does not say that God learned which action Abraham would decide to take. What it speaks of is God's knowledge of the state of Abraham's heart. "Now I know that you fear me." This is what God was ignorant of, according to the openness exegesis—not a future action but the present state of Abraham's heart. Millard Erickson comments:

> Apparently, taking this passage straightforwardly, until the moment of Abraham's action, God did not know the present state of his heart, whether he truly loved God. God's present knowledge was incomplete. Scripture does not say that now God knew what Abraham would do, but rather that he now knew that Abraham loved him. God was ignorant, not just of Abraham's future action, but of his present condition.[192]

This is problematic for the open view of presentism—that in his omniscience God exhaustively knows the past and the present but knows future free decisions only as possibilities.[193]

Similar problems come when we try to apply this "straightforward hermeneutic" to other passages of Scripture. Consider, for example, Genesis 3:9-13, which records God's actions after the fall of Adam and Eve. After their sin, Adam and Eve tried to hide from God among the trees of the garden. Then we read, "But the LORD God called to the man, 'Where are you?' " (v. 9). Following openness suggestions to "simply accept the plain meaning of Scripture," this text seems to

---

[191]Boyd, for example, speaks of taking biblical texts at face value (*God of the Possible,* pp. 60, 71-72) and of interpreting them straightforwardly (ibid., p. 67).

[192]Millard J. Erickson, *What Does God Know and When Does He Know It?* (Grand Rapids: Zondervan, 2003), pp. 63-64. Erickson's observation is not a new one, as reflected in an interchange recorded by the seventeenth-century Puritan theologian John Owen. He quotes the comments of a Socinian named John Biddle, who shares a view of Gen 22 similar to that of open theists: "God knew not that which he inquired after, and therefore tempted Abraham that he might so do, and upon the issue of that trial says, 'Now I know.' " But Owen drew another conclusion from these words: "But what was it that God affirms that now he knew? Not any thing future, not any free action that was not as yet done, but something of the present condition and frame of his heart towards God—namely, his fear of God; not whether he would fear him, but whether he did fear him then. If this, then, be properly spoken of God, and really as to the nature of the thing itself, then is he ignorant no less of things present than of those that are far to come. He knows not who fears him nor who hates him, unless he have opportunity to try them in some such way as he did Abraham" (*Vindiciae Evangelicae or The Mystery of the Gospel Vindicated and Socinianism Examined,* Works of John Owen 12, ed. William H. Goold [Carlisle, Penn: Banner of Truth, 1966], p. 120).

[193]Sanders, *God Who Risks,* pp. 194-200.

imply that God does not know the present location of Adam and Eve. And as the narrative of Genesis 3 proceeds, another problem emerges. In verse 11, God asks Adam, "Who told you that you were naked? Have you eaten from the tree that I commanded you not to eat from?" Does not a straightforward reading of this verse lead to the conclusion that in this case God was ignorant of what Adam had done in the past? And God's similar question to Eve in verse 13 ("What is this you have done?") seems to imply a similar divine ignorance of the past as far as Eve's actions were concerned. Thus reading Genesis 3:9-13 in the same manner that open theists encourage us to read Genesis 22:12 seems to result in a denial of God's exhaustive knowledge of both the present and the past (contra presentism).[194]

Boyd, however, does not want to read Genesis 3 in this way. He specifically identifies God's questions about location in Genesis as "rhetorical" and thus to be understood in a nonliteral, nonstraightforward way.[195] Boyd gives no argument for his position, but we may try to discover what his reasons for this affirmation are by applying his two stated criteria for identifying anthropomorphisms that should be interpreted nonliterally. Boyd argues that this should be done if the passage would be "ridiculous if taken literally" or if "the genre of the passage is poetic."[196] Clearly Genesis 3 is not poetic in literary genre but rather a historical narrative, so Boyd's second criterion does not apply. That leaves us with the first. The reason Boyd understands these questions asked by God in Genesis 3 to be rhetorical must be that he understands that the implications of taking them literally would be "ridiculous." But how could he come to that conclusion? Presumably because the fullness of Scripture clearly teaches that God knows the past and the present exhaustively. This would be a very proper attempt to understand the metaphor of God's questioning within the context of the whole of Scripture. But we must ask a similar question of God's knowledge

---

[194]Another example comes from Gen 18. In this chapter three men visit Abraham. After eating together, they walk along with Abraham toward Sodom. Evidently at least one of them is a theophany, for vv. 17, 20 specifically indicate that Yahweh is speaking. In vv. 20-21 Yahweh says, "The outcry against Sodom and Gomorrah is so great and their sin so grievous that I will go down and see if what they have done is as bad as the outcry that has reached me. If not, I will know." Reading this text according to the openness "straightforward" hermeneutic leads us to conclude that (1) God does not fully know the past sin of Sodom and Gomorrah since he must investigate to see if "what they *have done* is as bad as the outcry that has reached me;" and (2) God is not omnipresent, since he has to go to Sodom and Gomorrah to be able to "see" what they have in fact done; and only after that, "then" he will know. Again we see the difficulties that would come with the consistent application of this openness hermeneutic.

[195]Boyd, *God of the Possible*, p. 59.

[196]Ibid., p. 118. See n. 158 of this chap.

in Genesis 22:12. Is an understanding of the text that posits a movement from divine ignorance to divine knowledge of Abraham's fear of God consistent with the teaching of the rest of Scripture? Or does Scripture teach, with sufficient clarity and fullness, that God does in fact foreknow free human decisions? If so, then we must consider an alternative understanding of the nature of God's knowledge in Genesis 22:12. The evidence cited in chapters 2 and 3 leads me to conclude that this is in fact the case. God does foreknow future free decisions, including whether Abraham would pass the test by sacrificing his son. What he affirms in Genesis 22:12 is not, therefore, that God now has cognitive knowledge of something that he was previously ignorant of but rather that he now knows in experience and by demonstration what he has previously foreknown certainly and infallibly.

There is a third problem with the openness interpretation of Geneis 22:12 that is perhaps the most serious of all. Given the theological commitments of open theism, God cannot be sure of the truth of his statement that he now knows that Abraham fears God. The "now" of God's knowledge clearly relates to the moment when the angel of the Lord commanded Abraham to stop and not proceed with his plan to kill his son. At that point, there was, obviously, still time for him to stop. But this means that had the Lord not intervened and changed his command, there was still time for Abraham to change his mind and stop out of rebellion against God. And if there was still time for Abraham to change his mind, we must say that the final volition of obedience had not yet been formed in the mind and heart of Abraham. Thus, given an openness understanding, God could not know Abraham's ultimate fear of God and his ultimate volition of obedience. All God could say is, "Now I believe with a very high probability that you fear God." But open theists argue as well, as we will see from Jeremiah 3, that sometimes God's beliefs about the future can be mistaken. Perhaps that would be the case here as well.

In addition, we must remember that Abraham's future responses to God remain free and thus, for open theists, unknowable to God. So even if Abraham had killed his son, God could not know with certainty that in the very next moment Abraham would not rebel against the God who had asked him to do this. So the very most that God could know is that at that instant, Abraham feared God. This means that God could not know with certainty what Sanders asserts was the whole purpose of the test: to find out whether or not "Abraham is the sort of person on whom God can count for collaboration toward the fulfillment of his divine project."[197] Yet, in Genesis 22:16-18, God explicitly links Abraham's

---

[197]Sanders, *God Who Risks*, p. 53.

obedience, which he knows in Genesis 22:12, to the future, tying it by divine oath to the future fulfillment of his promises to and through Abraham.

> I swear by myself, declares the LORD, that because you have done this and have not withheld your son, your only son, I will surely bless you and make your descendants as numerous as the stars in the sky. . . . And through your offspring all nations on earth will be blessed, because you obeyed me.

For these three reasons—the inability of open theism to account for the kind of knowledge claimed by God in Genesis 22:12, the difficulties arising from a consistent application of the "straightforward" openness hermeneutic, and the plausibility of other ways of understanding God's claim "Now I know . . ." that do not involve his movement from ignorance to cognitive knowledge—I would argue that the interpretation of Genesis 22:12 that is most faithful to the immediate context and to the whole of Scripture is one that affirms God's exhaustive foreknowledge of free human actions.

When God says "perhaps." In the Old Testament, there are five passages in which the word *perhaps* (*ʾûlay*) is used in divine speech (Is 47:12; Jer 26:2-3; 36:3, 7; 51:8; Ezek 12:1-3). When the term is used in human speech, it indicates uncertainty about the future, often tinged with hope. But when *ʾûlay* is used in divine speech, does it indicate the same level of uncertainty? Specifically, does it indicate God's uncertainty as to how his people will respond to the word of his prophets?[198] In this section we will consider one of the most prominent of these "divine perhaps" passages, Jeremiah 26:2-3. This passage is of special interest to us, for it connects the divine *ʾûlay* with the possibility of God's repentance. In Jeremiah 26:2-3, Yahweh says to Jeremiah:

> Stand in the courtyard of the LORD's house and speak to all the people of the towns of Judah who come to worship in the house of the LORD. Tell them everything I command you; do not omit a word. Perhaps [*ʾûlay*] they will listen and each will turn from his evil way. Then I will relent [*niham*] and not bring on them the disaster I was planning because of the evil they have done.

The uncertainty expressed in this text is not over whether God will repent (Jon 3:9; Joel 2:14). Rather the uncertainty is over whether or not the Israelites will repent. Yet, by saying "perhaps," God offers the people the opportunity to repent and save themselves from disaster.[199]

---

[198]This is the claim of Terence Fretheim (*Suffering of God*, p. 45).

[199]Brueggemann comments that as in Jer 18:7-8, the choice offered to the people here "places in human hands the destiny of Jerusalem to be received from God" (*To Build, To Plant* [Grand Rapids: Eerdmans, 1991], p. 6).

Fretheim understands this text to teach that God did not have certain fore-knowledge of the response of the people of Judah. He argues that this lack of certainty is essential to the integrity of what God commanded Jeremiah to tell the people.[200] Boyd agrees, linking the uncertainty of God's foreknowledge with the possibility of his repenting.

> If God was certain that the Judeans would not repent, was he not lying when he led Jeremiah to believe that they *might* repent? Indeed, if God never really changes his mind, was he not misleading Jeremiah and all the people by encouraging them to think of him as one who *might* change his mind?[201]

But is God's usage of the word *perhaps* (*'ûlay*) necessarily inconsistent with his foreknowledge of the free responses of the people of Judah? Is it necessarily inauthentic or even deceptive for God to speak of the response of the Judeans using the word *perhaps,* even while knowing all along what their response would be? Or is it possible that God is choosing to speak to his people from a human vantage point? If so, then from the perspective of his people the direction of their future response is indeed uncertain. Piper argues that "The word 'perhaps' may be spoken here by God not to express that he is unsure what they will do, but to express that from a *human vantage point* the people may or may not listen to him. But if they do, he will have mercy and not bring calamity."[202]

In support of this idea that God is choosing to speak from a human vantage point is not only the obvious fact that God is accommodating himself to speak to his people in human language but also the fact that Jeremiah 26:2-3 is not, in and of itself, what God told the people but rather the record of what God instructed his human prophet, Jeremiah, to speak to the people.

Putting this in the terms of our previous discussion, we can say that God's use of the word *perhaps* is another anthropomorphic metaphor. It is reality depicting, evidencing similarities with the human experience of uncertainty. But there are differences as well.

The primary similarity involves the uncertainty about the direction of the future decision of the people of God that God, speaking from a human vantage point, communicates to Jeremiah. But this uncertainty does not necessarily mean that God himself has no certain knowledge of their future decision. Rather it is a way of speaking in which God recognizes that the people's decision to repent is a free one. All sides in the present debate would agree that this is the

---

[200]Fretheim, *Suffering of God,* pp. 46-74. Cf. Sanders, *God Who Risks,* p. 74.
[201]Boyd, *God of the Possible,* p. 70. See also Boyd, *Satan and the Problem of Evil,* p. 111.
[202]Piper, "Answering Greg Boyd's Openness of God Texts," p. 6.

case, although as we have seen there are different understandings of the nature of that freedom. But whether a person would affirm a libertarian or a compatibilist understanding of human freedom, the decision would still be made according to the desires of the human decision-makers. God would not be constraining the people of Jerusalem to act against their will.[203] Thus they *can* repent if they only want to. And should they choose to repent, God tells the people through Jeremiah that he will act in response to avert the destruction he had intended to bring upon *unrepentant* Jerusalem. This is surely not deceptive, for the choice really is before the people. And God's statement of what he would do *if* they chose to repent remains true, even though he knows with certainty that they will in fact choose not to repent. God's statement would be false or his promise insincere only if God would *not* relent if the people had repented or if he would have relented even if the people did not repent.

Furthermore, there can be reasons for God to speak in terms of "perhaps" other than to indicate his own personal uncertainty. I believe that God's statement of the possibility of the people's repentance (which they are free to do if only they would want to), coupled with his gracious promise to relent and avert his judgment if they would do so, serves to heighten the folly and the moral guilt of the people when they continue on in their unrepentant disobedience and experience God's judgment as a result. And God's promise of mercy if the people would repent also serves to highlight the justice of his judgment on his people who so stubbornly cling to their rebellion. These two motives would clearly warrant God speaking as he does in Jeremiah 26:2-3. And neither of these is based on a limitation in God's foreknowledge.

Thus we can conclude that God is not necessarily deceptive or inauthentic when he says "perhaps" to his people while at the same time possessing certain knowledge of what their future decisions will be. This enables us to see more clearly both the similarities and the differences between God's anthropomorphic usage of "perhaps" and what would be the case if human beings spoke in the same way.

Are God's questions more than rhetorical? We have seen in our previous discussion that open theists do understand some of the questions God asks to be rhetorical and thus to be interpreted in figurative ways (e.g., Gen 3:9, 11, 13). Fretheim argues, however, that there are other divine questions that are more than rhetorical. In fact, he says that there are two categories of such nonrhetor-

---

[203]For a helpful discussion of God's use of nonconstraining causes to determine free human decisions on a compatibilist model, see John Feinberg, "God Determines All Things," in *Predestination and Free Will,* ed. David Basinger and Randall Basinger (Downers Grove, Ill.: InterVarsity Press, 1986), pp. 24-29.

ical questions. There are, first of all, questions that reflect God's decision-making process with respect to the future of Israel. An example of this kind of question is Hosea 11:8, where God asks, "How can I give you up, Ephraim? / How
can I hand you over, Israel? / How can I treat you like Admah? / How can I
make you like Zeboiim?"[204] Fretheim suggests that questions like these are "reflective of the divine council deliberations between God and prophet," thus including his people in Yahweh's decision-making process. The divine question
"is a genuine question for God, and one from which God will learn, as God and
people move toward an answer together."[205]

    Second, there are also divine questions that speak of the present in relation-
ship to the past. One example of this kind of question is Isaiah 5:4, where Yahweh speaks of Israel as his vineyard and asks, "What more could have been
done for my vineyard / than I have done for it? / When I looked for good grapes,
/ why did it yield only bad?"[206] Fretheim says:

> These questions seem to imply a genuine loss on God's part as to what might ex-
> plain the faithlessness of the people. . . . The lament character of the passages sug-
> gests a genuine questioning with regard to the explanation of events. . . . Yet there
> might be another note here. God knows all there is to know about what has
> prompted the people to take this direction with their lives; it still makes no sense.
> Thus, it would appear that there simply is no explanation available, nor will there
> ever be, even for God.[207]

These divine questions, along with other Old Testament considerations such
as we have been surveying in this chapter, lead Fretheim to a conclusion about
the extent of God's foreknowledge that is remarkably similar to that found in
open theism.

> From these considerations regarding divine foreknowledge one may conclude that
> any talk about divine omniscience in the Old Testament must be limited when it
> comes to talk about the future. It is limited in such a way as to include a genuine
> divine openness to the future—an openness which, however, is constantly in-
> formed by the divine will to save. . . . As new things happen and come to be know-
> able for the first time, God knows them as actualities, not only as possibilities. This,
> of course, implies that God's knowledge is thereby increased, which entails change
> for God; new knowledge means real change.[208]

---

[204]In addition to Hos 11:8, Fretheim also cites Hos 6:4; Jer 5:7, 9, 29; 9:7, 9 as examples of more-
than-rhetorical divine questions. See Fretheim, *Suffering of God,* pp. 54-56.
[205]Ibid., p. 56.
[206]In addition, Fretheim cites Is 50:2; Jer 2:32; 8:5, 19; 30:6 in this category (ibid., p. 57).
[207]Ibid.
[208]Ibid., pp. 57-58.

But do these divine questions demand, in fact, that God's foreknowledge be less than exhaustive? I contend this is not necessarily the case. In his own discussion of these more-than-rhetorical divine questions, Fretheim gives two reasons why God would utter them. And neither of these reasons demands a nonexhaustive view of divine foreknowledge.

The first reason cited by Fretheim is that God asks these questions to move Israel to repentance. He says, "[God's] announcements of judgment are 'interrupted' with such divine questions in order to move Israel to repentance." God does this by revealing to his people his own heart as a risk-taking and suffering God.

> What is crucial for the discussion is the kind of God who is revealed in the sharing of the question. The very fact that God asks such questions reveals something about God; God opens himself up to risk; God becomes vulnerable. For the more one shares of oneself, the greater the possibility of being hurt. Finally, it is such a portrait of God, a suffering God, that, it is hoped, will prompt repentance.[209]

I agree with Fretheim that the questions God asks reveal who he is. But is the focus of God's self-revelation here necessarily his risk-taking, vulnerability and suffering? Mays rightly sees in Hosea 11:8 God's revelation of this "suffering agony" brought on by Israel's unfaithfulness. But he sees an even greater revelation of "his love [which] will not let them go."[210] McComiskey also does not see the emphasis on God's riskiness and vulnerability but on his grace.

> We feel [in Hos 11:8] Yahweh's deep emotions welling up within his heart. He looks at his erring child and is overwhelmed by love; he knows that what his rebellious son has done is worthy of expulsion from his house, but he cannot reject him forever. The punishment will not be ultimate. We see the grace of God here as we have not yet seen it in the whole prophecy. Yahweh will not give up his people.[211]

Does a divine motive of eliciting repentance necessarily involve the kind of risk-taking and vulnerability that Fretheim believes is inconsistent with exhaustive divine foreknowledge? I believe that this need not necessarily be the case as long as we realize that there are differences as well as similarities between God's efforts to elicit repentance and human efforts to bring about the same result. A genuine goal of eliciting repentance does not necessarily demand the kind of divine risk-taking, vulnerability and suffering that would be inconsistent with exhaustive divine foreknowledge. For example, it is possible to view God's

---

[209]Ibid.
[210]Mays, *Hosea*, p. 151.
[211]McComiskey, "Hosea," p. 191.

questions as the means that he uses to bring about repentance in his people.[212] If this is the case, the repentance God seeks to bring about is precisely the repentance he foresees will happen. Truly exhaustive divine foreknowledge will foreknow not only the end (the repentance of his people) but also the means (the questions God asks) to achieve that end.

Fretheim also suggests a second reason for these divine questions. He suggests that God is intending to highlight the rightness and justice of his judgment, should the repentance of his people not be forthcoming. By showing the people the divine agony that God feels in his judgment "they could have no uncertainty regarding the highly personal—nonlegal, nonhasty, nonvindictive, and noncapricious—way in which God has deliberated over the matter. Indeed, God has shared the decision-making process with those whose future is at stake."[213]

John Oswalt argues that this is precisely what is going on in Isaiah 5:1-7. Through Yahweh's "Song of the Vineyard," Isaiah leads his hearers to make their own judgment. "God has cared for them like a vineyard, yet the fruits of their lives are bitter and sour. Is not God more than justified if he decides to remove his protection from them?"[214] And through God's questions the depth and fullness of his loving care for his vineyard is communicated in a way that invites the readers to agree with the justice of his judgment.

> Everyone who heard Isaiah could empathize with the farmer's hard work and anxious expectation. Likewise, every one of them could feel the shock and disgust over the bitter fruit. When the singer asked what more he could have done to ensure good grapes, given the degree of audience participation common in that part of the world, it is likely that some shouted "nothing!" while others announced what they would do with such a disappointing investment.[215]

But clearly, this reason for God asking these questions would still hold even if God knew for certain that his people would not repent and would therefore experience his judgment.

The point of the preceding discussion is that, contra Fretheim, God's use of questions that truly reveal the depths of his heart to his people does not demand his inability to know with certainty the future responses of his people. If the rest of Scripture reveals God to be one who does foreknow free human decisions

---

[212]See the argument of John Piper, "Answering Greg Boyd's Openness of God Texts," p. 3.

[213]Fretheim, *Suffering of God*, p. 55.

[214]John Oswalt, *Isaiah: Chapters 1-39*, New International Commentary on the Old Testament (Grand Rapids: Eerdmans, 1986), pp. 151-52.

[215]Ibid., p. 154. J. A. Motyer agrees, arguing that the reader should conclude from the question of v. 4 that "no conceivable blame can attach to the owner; it must lie elsewhere" (*The Prophecy of Isaiah* [Downers Grove, Ill.: InterVarsity Press, 1993], p. 59).

(as I have argued in chaps. 2-3), these questions can fairly be interpreted in a manner consistent with that biblical witness.

Can God's expectations fail to come to pass? Open theists argue that God's predictions about future human behavior can at times be mistaken, and his expectations about the future may fail to come to pass. Perhaps the most significant illustration of this comes from the words of Yahweh in Jeremiah 3.

> Have you seen what faithless Israel has done? She has gone up on every high hill and under every spreading tree and has committed adultery there. I thought that after she had done all this she would return to me but she did not, and her unfaithful sister Judah saw it. (Jer 3:6-7)

> I myself said,
>   "How gladly would I treat you like sons
>   and give you a desirable land,
>   the most beautiful inheritance of any nation."
> I thought you would call me "Father"
>   and not turn away from following me.
> "But like a woman unfaithful to her husband,
>   so you have been unfaithful to me, O house of Israel,"
>   declares the LORD. (Jer 3:19-20).

Fretheim interprets these passages as indicating a clear limitation on God's foreknowledge. "Here, God is depicted as actually thinking that the people would respond positively to the initial election, or that they would return after a time of straying. But events proved that God's outlook on thé future was too optimistic. The people did not respond as God thought they would. God's knowledge of the future is thus clearly represented as limited."[216]

Sanders states his conclusion from these verses even more strongly. God is not only limited in his knowledge; he is in fact mistaken. "In these texts God is explicitly depicted as not knowing the specific future. God himself says that he was mistaken about what was going to happen."[217]

Boyd is perhaps the strongest yet in his assessment of these verses.

> We need to ask ourselves seriously, how could the Lord honestly say he *thought* Israel would return to him if he was always certain that they would never do so? If God tells us he thought something was going to occur while being eternally certain it would not occur, is he not lying to us? If God cannot lie (Heb 6:18) and yet tells us he thought something would occur that did not occur, doesn't that imply that

---

[216]Fretheim, *Suffering of God,* p. 46.
[217]Sanders, *God Who Risks,* p. 74.

the future contains possibilities as well as certainties?[218]

But are these conclusions warranted by Jeremiah 3:6-7, 19-20? Several factors must be cited that call them into question. First, it is not absolutely clear that these texts are speaking about God's own thoughts and beliefs about the future. The verb that the NIV translates as "I thought" in vv. 7, 19 is 'āmar ("to say"). Now it is certainly possible to take the verb in the sense of "I said to myself" (i.e., "I thought"). But the use of 'āmar does raise the possibility that these texts are not so much dealing with Yahweh's private thought life but with what he communicated to Jeremiah and to Judah. Boyd says that this suggestion is of no help at all to those who would affirm exhaustive divine foreknowledge because "it only transfers the problem of God *thinking* something was going to happen that didn't happen, to him *saying* he expected something to happen that he knew would not happen."[219] But Boyd's critique assumes that the purpose of God's statement would only be to communicate what he actually thought would happen. But what God said was what he *expected* would happen—and expectations can be real even if we know they will not be fulfilled. And if God had other purposes for what he said to Jeremiah and through him to the nation, such as the purposes of eliciting repentance and highlighting the justice of his judgment, then we need not necessarily assume that God was mistaken in his own beliefs about the future.

Another suggestion has been made by J. A. Thompson. He concludes that Jeremiah 3:19 should be rendered, "I said, 'You must call me, My Father, and not turn back from following me.' " He argues that rendering the verb 'āmar more literally as "I said" leads us to see an imperatival force in the second person plural verb (rendering it "you must call" rather than the future "you will call").[220] If this rendering is accurate, then what Yahweh is recounting is his command to his people that they have sadly disobeyed. But this would not require a nonexhaustive view of God's foreknowledge.

If, however, we follow the translation of the NIV and understand Jeremiah 3:7, 19 to be speaking of what Yahweh was actually thinking or saying to himself,

---

[218]Boyd, *God of the Possible*, p. 60. Boyd expands on this thought: "If God in truth never anticipates that something is going to happen that turns out not to happen, his telling us that he is sometimes surprised or disappointed (Jer 3:6-7, 19; Is 5:1-7) tells us nothing true; it is simply misleading" (ibid., p. 119).

[219]Boyd, *God of the Possible*, p. 60.

[220]J. A. Thompson, *The Book of Jeremiah*, New International Commentary on the Old Testament (Grand Rapids: Eerdmans, 1980), pp. 204, 206-7. This translation is also followed by John Bright, *Jeremiah*, Anchor Bible 21 (Garden City, N.Y.: Doubleday, 1965), pp. 20, 23, and by the NASB.

it still does not necessarily follow that he was mistaken. Piper suggests that there is an implicit qualification in these verses, that is, "I thought they would repent, given the ordinary expectations under these circumstances."[221] In other words, God was telling Judah that he had so ordered their circumstances that the normal human expectation was they would turn back to him. This was in fact a true statement. God was not being deceptive at all in saying that circumstances were such that if he were to think in terms of normal human responses, he would have expected Judah to repent. But that kind of expectation, which was in fact disappointed, does not necessarily mean that God did not know that they would not repent.

The consequences of affirming that God actually was mistaken about his beliefs and predictions about the future in Jeremiah 3 (and potentially other places as well) are indeed devastating—especially for the level of eschatological confidence that is affirmed by open theists. This crucial issue will be discussed in depth in chapter six, but it is appropriate to point out here that an interpretation of Jeremiah 3 that is not demanded by the context and which goes against the broad sweep of biblical teaching concerning God's certain foreknowledge of free human decisions has very serious consequences that affect the hope we can rightly have of the ultimate triumph of God and his kingdom.

CONCLUSION

The question I have been asking in this chapter is whether there are texts in Scripture that demand a view in which God does not foreknow free human decisions. The primary focus of our examination has been texts that speak of divine repentance, though we also looked more briefly at other texts claimed by open theists to support a nonexhaustive view of divine foreknowledge. Our conclusion was that none of these texts, nor all of them together, necessarily demand the open view of God's foreknowledge.

This is not to say that these texts are without meaning. I have concluded that the divine repentance texts (and divine foreknowledge texts as well) are reality-depicting anthropomorphic metaphors. As such, they speak to both similarities and differences between the divine reality and its human counterpart. The similarities are significant and real; thus these texts cannot be dismissed or minimized as mere anthropomorphisms. But the differences are significant and real as well. Specifically, we have seen that the relationship of these texts to God's foreknowledge (which is never specifically stated to be limited or restricted in any way) is one of the differences involved. This conclusion is warranted by an

---

[221]Piper, "Answering Greg Boyd's Openness of God Texts," p. 7.

effort to take seriously the whole teaching of Scripture on this issue—including the massive testimony to God's foreknowledge of free human decisions presented in chapters two and three of this book. Thus my final conclusion is that the "openness texts" examined in this chapter are best interpreted in a way that is consistent with this abundant wealth of biblical testimony.

5

TWO CRITICAL
INTERPRETIVE QUESTIONS

So far we have examined evidence from both the Old Testament and New Testament for an exhaustive view of the foreknowledge of God as well as biblical evidence put forward to argue for a nonexhaustive view. My conclusion is that the biblical evidence arguing positively for exhaustive divine foreknowledge is very strong, both quantitatively and qualitatively. And the proposed counterevidence does not demand a nonexhaustive understanding. Read fairly, in light of both the similarities and the differences between the divine reality and its human counterpart that exist in the anthropomorphic language of Scripture, these biblical texts are in fact consistent with the broader Scriptural witness to exhaustive divine foreknowledge.

But before we look to the practical implications of this understanding for Christian life and ministry, two additional hermeneutical questions need to be addressed. These questions have been raised by open theists, and if answered positively they would call into question the validity of the results of this study so far. These two questions are (1) Has our analysis of the biblical evidence been so shaped by the influence of Greek philosophy that we have not read these scriptural texts fairly? (2) Does the Bible teach a twofold understanding of the future and of God's knowledge of it? Specifically, does Scripture teach that a portion of the future is definite and fixed, and thus can be known by God with infallible certainty, while another portion of the future is indefinite and open and thus cannot be known by God infallibly? If so, then both texts that emphasize divine foreknowledge of free human decisions and texts that emphasize God's foreknowledge as being of possibilities rather than certainties are situationally specific and not universal. Let's examine these two questions.

THE ROLE OF GREEK PHILOSOPHY

When asked why the church, in all of its major eras and theological traditions, has so consistently held to an exhaustive view of divine foreknowledge, open theists consistently speak of the influence of Greek philosophy. For much of its history, they argue, Christian theology has been unduly influenced by Greek philosophy, so much so that its understanding of Scripture has been distorted. Open theists charge that classical theism as a whole, and its view of exhaustive divine foreknowledge in particular, is the product of the influence of Hellenistic philosophy on the early church's reflection on biblical revelation.[1] While there were undoubtedly important missiological reasons for the early church to make use of Greek thought, open theists charge that early in the church's history, Hellenistic philosophical categories got the upper hand and started to shape the contours of Christian thinking about God.[2] Thus the distinctive areas that make up classical theism in the end are more the product of Greek philosophy than they are of the teaching of Scripture itself.

For example, when Sanders asks why Christians do not usually read the Bible in the way suggested by the openness model, he says:

> The answer, in part, is found in the way Christian thinkers have used certain Greek philosophical ideas. . . . [It] lies in an understanding of the cultural framework within which the early church developed its view of God. The early church fathers lived in the intellectual atmosphere where Greek philosophy (especially middle Platonism) dominated.[3]

According to Sanders, this "Greek metaphysical system 'boxed up' the God described in the Bible." And the resulting view of God has come to so dominate

---

[1]John Feinberg gives a recent description of classical theism. He argues that the classical view of God includes the following twelve divine attributes: absoluteness, absolute perfection, pure actuality, necessity, immutability, impassibility, timelessness, simplicity, omniscience, omnipotence, creation ex nihilo and incorporeality (*No One Like Him* [Wheaton, Ill.: Crossway, 2001], p. 64). For other definitions of the classical view of God, see H. P. Owen, *Concepts of Deity* [New York: Herder & Herder, 1971], p. 1, and Ronald Nash, *The Concept of God* [Grand Rapids: Zondervan, 1983], p. 20. While authors may disagree on some specifics, there is broad agreement about the basic shape of the classical view of God.

John Sanders calls the result of this Hellenistic influence "the biblical-classical synthesis" ("Historical Considerations," in *The Openness of God* [Downers Grove, Ill.: InterVarsity Press, 1994], p. 60). See also *God Who Risks* (Downers Grove, Ill.: InterVarsity Press, 1998), p. 141. It is not only open theists who affirm this synthesis. H. P. Owen, himself a supporter of classical theism, says, "So far as the Western world is concerned, [classical] theism has a double origin: the Bible and Greek philosophy" (*Concepts of Deity*, p. 1). On the influence of Greek philosophy on Christian views of God, see Wolfhart Pannenberg, "The Appropriation of the Philosophical Concept of God as a Dogmatic Problem of Early Christian Theology," in *Basic Questions in Theology*, trans. George H. Kehm (Philadelphia: Fortress, 1971), 2:119-83.

[2]Sanders, "Historical Considerations," p. 72.

[3]Ibid., p. 59. While Sanders's statement on the surface suggests that the negative influence of Greek philosophy may be only partially responsible for the unbiblical views of classical theism, this is the overwhelming thesis of the entirety of Sanders's chapters and also the historical portions of *God Who Risks*, pp. 140-66.

Christian theology that it decisively filters out any alternative understanding of God and his relationship to the universe.[4]

Pinnock agrees, asserting that Hellenistic thinking has distorted the early church's understanding of God's transcendence and immutability.

> Traditional theology has been biased in the direction of transcendence as a result of undue philosophical influences. Greek thinking located the ultimate and the perfect in the realm of the immutable and absolutely transcendent. This led early theologians (given that the biblical God is also transcendent) to experiment with equating the God of revelation with the Greek ideal of deity. However a price had to be paid in terms of faithfulness to Scripture and relevance to human life.[5]

This position has also been argued forcefully by Gregory Boyd. In *God of the Possible,* he states: "My fundamental thesis is that the classical theological tradition became misguided when, under the influence of Hellenistic philosophy, it defined God's perfection in static, timeless terms."[6] When he acknowledges the fact that throughout its history, only a small minority of the church has held to his position, he gives the following explanation.

> In my estimation this is because almost from the start the church's theology was significantly influenced by Plato's notion that God's perfection must mean that he is in every respect unchanging—including in his knowledge and experience. . . .
>
> The problem, as I see it, is that since Plato, Western philosophy has been infatuated with the idea of an unchanging, timeless realm. . . . This infatuation with the "unchanging" unfortunately crept into the church early on and has colored the way Christians look at the world, read their Bibles, and develop their theology.[7]

This Platonic concept can blind us to the plain meaning of key biblical texts. For example, with respect to the divine repentance text Jeremiah 18:7-10, Boyd argues that "if this text isn't enough to convince us that God's mind is not eternally settled, then our philosophical presuppositions are controlling our exegesis to a degree that no text could ever teach us this."[8] So what are we to do? For Boyd, the task before us is clear.

---

[4]Sanders says, "The classical view is so taken for granted that it functions as a preunderstanding that rules out certain interpretations that do not 'fit' with the conception of what is 'appropriate' for God to be like, as derived from Greek metaphysics" (ibid., p. 60).

[5]Pinnock, "Systematic Theology," in *The Openness of God* (Downers Grove, Ill.: InterVarsity Press, 1994), p. 106. See also Pinnock's assessment of the negative influence of Hellenistic thinking on traditional understandings of God in "Between Classical and Process Theism," in *Process Theology,* ed. Ronald Nash (Grand Rapids: Baker, 1987), pp. 313, 315, 317.

[6]Gregory A. Boyd, *God of the Possible* (Grand Rapids: Baker, 2000), p. 17.

[7]Ibid., pp. 115, 130.

[8]Ibid., p. 78.

If we simply free ourselves from the Hellenistic philosophical assumptions that God must be unchanging *in every respect* and that time is an illusion, we will be able to embrace the plain meaning of these texts along with the glorious picture of divine sovereignty and openness that they engender. God is not only the God of future certainties; he's the God of future possibilities.[9]

This liberation of biblical interpretation from the shackles of Hellenistic philosophy so that we can embrace the plain meaning of the biblical text is the task to which Boyd and other open theists have set themselves.

This charge of the distorting influence of Greek philosophy is one that Boyd and other open theists would undoubtedly lodge against the argument of this book. What do I have to say in response to it? Without doubt, it is outside the bounds of this volume to address all the philosophical factors that have influenced both classical and open theism. But with respect to the extent of God's foreknowledge, I would like to offer six observations that, taken together, argue that this openness charge is not sufficient to invalidate the conclusions of our study.

Which Greek philosophy? Often the charge is made of the distorting influence of Greek philosophy as if there were a singular, unified Greek philosophy that spoke with one voice on the nature and extent of divine foreknowledge and its relationship to free human decisions. But in actuality there is a broad diversity of opinion on these questions within Hellenistic thought. Thus we must ask, Which Greek philosophy?

Under the rubric of Greek philosophy, we can find strains of thought that are echoed in both classical theism and open theism. For example, both Socrates and Plato affirmed the universal omniscience of the gods, which would presumably include an exhaustive divine foreknowledge.[10] Yet Aristotle offered a significantly different understanding. In the ninth chapter of *De Interpretatione*, Aristotle argued that if future singular propositions must be either true or false, then fatalism necessarily results.

> If it at all times were true to affirm that "it is" or "will be," how impossible that it should not be or not be about to be so! When a thing cannot not come to be, how

---

[9]Ibid., p. 85. For other instances of Boyd's argument that Hellenistic philosophical thinking has shaped and ultimately distorted classical theism, see *God of the Possible*, pp. 86-87, 109, 130-31.

[10]Xenophon reported that Socrates believed that the gods knew literally everything, including all that was said and done, even those things planned in silence. (See Anthony Kenny, *The God of the Philosophers* [Oxford: Clarendon Press, 1986], p. 6). And Plato provided for the death penalty, not only for those who denied the existence of the gods but also for those who believed that the gods existed yet denied that they took any notice of the affairs of human beings, thus affirming both God's knowledge of human affairs and his providential action on their behalf (Plato *Laws* 10.885b).

impossible that it should not! If, again, its not coming to be is impossible, as we assume, come to be then it certainly must. And in consequence future events, as we said, come about of necessity. Nothing is causal, contingent. For if a thing happened by chance, it would not come about of necessity. . . .

[If there is] a pair of contrary opposites, having universals for subjects and being themselves universal or having an individual subject, then "one must be true [and] the other false" [and in this case] contingency there can be none and that all things that are or take place come about in the world by necessity. No need would there be for mankind to be deliberate or to take pains.[11]

The most common understanding of Aristotle is that he is arguing a *reductio ad absurdum* here. Anthony Kenny explains this view: "If future-tensed propositions about singulars are already true, then fatalism follows: but fatalism is absurd, therefore, since many future events are not yet determined, statements about such events are not yet true or false, though they later will be."[12]

Aristotle himself did not apply this understanding to the issue of divine foreknowledge. Yet the implications are not hard to see. Aristotle's thought would lead to the view that if God infallibly knows future singular propositions (including those about human decisions), then they are no longer contingent and fatalism necessarily ensues. But if future-contingent propositions are not true, then not even God can know them, since only what is true can be known. Clearly this line of thinking is much closer to the thought of open theism than of classical theism.

Within Greek philosophy, we also find the theological determinism of the Stoics and the subsequent fixity of all future events. An early Stoic fragment gives clear voice to this argument for a law of universal causation.

Prior events are causes of those following them, and in this manner all things are bound together with one another, and thus nothing happens in the world such that something else is not entirely a consequence of it and attached to it as cause. . . . From everything that happens something else follows depending on it by necessity as cause.[13]

---

[11]Aristotle *De Interpretatione* 9, Loeb Classical Library, pp. 135, 137. For helpful discussions of Aristotle's thought in this crucial chapter, see William Lane Craig, *The Problem of Divine Foreknowledge and Future Contingents from Aristotle to Suarez* (New York: E. J. Brill, 1988), pp. 1-58; Anthony Kenny, *God of the Philosophers,* pp. 52-53; and Millard Erickson, *What Does God Know and When Does He Know It?* (Grand Rapids: Zondervan, 2003), pp. 148-49.

[12]Kenny, *God of the Philosophers,* p. 52. Other scholars, following G. E. M. Anscombe ("Aristotle and the Sea Battle," *Mind* 65 [1956]: 1-15), say that Aristotle is denying not the truth of future contingents but their necessity. For a concise survey of these and two other minority interpretive options, along with a helpful bibliography on recent interpretation of Aristotle's *De Interpretatione* 9; see Craig, *Problem of Divine Foreknowledge,* pp. 281-83.

[13]*Stoicum Veterum Fragmenta* 2, quoted in A. A. Long, *Hellenistic Philosophy* (New York: Charles Scribner's, 1974), p. 164.

In the Stoic worldview these causes are such that, given them, nothing else could happen. Chance for the Stoics was simply a name for undiscovered causes. And the ultimate cause of all things is God, as Seneca asserted: "We Stoics look for a primary and universal cause. This must be single because matter is single. We ask what that cause is? The answer is 'creative reason,' that is God."[14]

But also within Greek philosophy is an emphasis on flux and change that characterized the thought of Heraclitus. His convictions about the dynamic and everchanging nature of everything in the world are summed up in the well-known dictum that it is impossible to step into the same river twice.[15] And Heraclitus's follower Cratylus went even further, arguing that since all sensible things are continually changing and always in a state of flux, they are in principle inaccessible to knowledge.[16]

And if the Roman philosopher Cicero (106-43 B.C.) is added into the mix and considered as a part of the non-Christian philosophical environment in which the early church found itself, the situation is even more diverse. Cicero forcefully rejected Stoic understandings of fate and necessity and their accompanying determinism. While agreeing with the Stoics that all things take place by preceeding causes, Cicero argued that some of these causes involved human free will. Thus it is not the case that all things take place by necessity.[17]

> Those who say that things that are going to be are immutable and that a true future event cannot be changed into a false one, are not asserting the necessity of fate but explaining the meaning of terms; whereas those who bring in an everlasting series of causes rob the human mind of freewill and fetter it in the chains of a fated necessity.[18]

Cicero's belief in human freedom and the resulting openness of the world's future led him to deny that God has foreknowledge of future events. In his work *De Divinitione*, Cicero argued that if God foreknows all future events, then these events must occur as he foresees them. Otherwise God would not be an infallible knower. But if God does know everything that is going to happen, then

---

[14]Seneca, *Epistulae morales*, quoted in A. A. Long, *Hellenistic Philosophy* (New York: Charles Scribner's, 1974), p. 165. Sanders also understands the Stoic view of divine determination to be absolute, "amounting to absolute predestination" ("Historical Considerations," p. 67).

[15]See Michael C. Stokes, "Heraclitus of Ephesus," in *The Encyclopedia of Philosophy*, ed. Paul Edwards (New York: Macmillan, 1967), 3:477-80.

[16]G. B. Kerferd, "Cratylus," *The Encyclopedia of Philosophy*, ed. Paul Edwards (New York: Macmillan, 1967), 2:251-52.

[17]Cicero *De Fato* 10.21, Loeb Classical Library, p. 217.

[18]Ibid., 10.20, Loeb Classical Library, pp. 215, 217.

nothing can happen other than what he foresees. And this would violate human freedom and the reality of chance happenings in the world.

> It seems to me that it is not in the power even of God himself to know what event is going to happen accidentally and by chance. For if He knows, then the event is certain to happen; but if it is certain to happen, chance does not exist. And yet chance does exist, therefore there is no foreknowledge of things that happen by chance.[19]

Thus we find that a crucial lynchpin of the openness view—the incompatibility of divine foreknowledge and libertarian human free will—to be already existing in the Greco-Roman philosophical environment surrounding the early church.

One final person needs to be discussed at this point, the Jewish thinker Philo (c. 25 B.C.-A.D. 45). He self-consciously sought to reconcile biblical teaching with Greek philosophy and so perhaps became the preeminent bridge between Judaism and the Hellenistic world.[20] Philo agreed with Cicero that human free choices are not determined by any antecedent causes. And indeed this undetermined freedom is necessary for humans to be held morally accountable before God.

> Man, possessed of a spontaneous and self-determined will, whose activities for the most part rest on deliberate choice, is with reason blamed for what he does wrong with intent [and] praised when he acts rightly of his own will. . . . The soul of man alone has received from God the faculty of voluntary movement, and in his way especially is made like to Him, and thus being liberated, as far as might be, from that hard and ruthless mistress, necessity, may justly be charged with guilt, in that it does not honor its Liberator.[21]

But Philo disagreed with Cicero that this human freedom was incompatible with divine foreknowledge. He held strongly to the exhaustive foreknowledge of God, regarding it to be the basis of God's providential activity.

> A mere man cannot foresee the course of future events, or the judgments of others, but to God as in pure sunlight all things are manifest. For already He has pierced into the recesses of our soul, and what is invisible to others is clear as daylight to

---

[19]Cicero, *De Divinatione* 2.7, Loeb Classical Library, pp. 389, 391. For a helpful analysis of Cicero's argument at this point, see Benjamin Wirt Farley, *The Providence of God* (Grand Rapids: Baker, 1988), pp. 68-70. According to William Hasker, Cicero is the first philosopher to explicitly argue for the incompatibility of divine foreknowledge and human free will (*God, Time, and Knowledge,* [Ithaca, N.Y.: Cornell University Press, 1989], p. 1).

[20]Farley, *Providence of God,* p. 72. Sanders gives a similar assessment ("Historical Considerations," pp. 69-71).

[21]Philo, *Quod Deus Immutabilis Sit,* Loeb Classical Library 10, pp. 33, 35.

His eyes. He employs the forethought and foreknowledge which are virtues peculiarly His own and suffers nothing to escape His control or pass outside His comprehension. For not even about the future can uncertainty be found with Him, since nothing is uncertain or future to God.[22]

Philo does not explain exactly how God's foreknowledge is in fact compatible with human freedom, but his statement that "nothing is future to God" may point to the direction of his thinking. Philo understood God's eternity to be timeless.[23] And while not elaborating on the relationship between God's timeless eternity and his foreknowledge, as Boethius later would, Philo does seem to hint that this is what resolves the foreknowledge-freedom dilemma. And so we find yet more diversity in the potential impact of Hellenistic thinking on divine foreknowledge on the early church.

The main point of the preceding discussion is, I trust, abundantly clear. The Hellenistic philosophical world, in which the early church found itself, was itself very diverse and multifaceted on issues relating to divine foreknowledge and the fixity or openness of history that results. Thus when we seek to evaluate the openness charge of the distorting influence of Greek philosophy on the early church, we need to ask, Which Greek philosophy?

Do conceptual similarities necessarily indicate a causal influence?
Does the existence of similarities in thought between classical theism's view of exhaustive divine foreknowledge and certain strains of Greek philosophy necessarily mean that Hellenistic thinking had a causal influence on classical theism? I say no. Similarity of ideas does not always necessarily indicate a causal influence. Consider the following example offered by Millard Erickson.

Plato speaks in *The Republic* of the distinction between two realms of existence. There is the unseen realm of forms or ideas and the visible realm, in which are found actual instances of these forms or ideas. Thus a chair is a chair because it is an expression of the form or idea of "chairness." The form of "chairness" is not itself a chair, it is that reality which defines each and every individual chair. But for Plato, specific, visible chairs are less real than the unseen form or idea. Physical chairs are reflections or shadows cast by the form of "chairness."[24]

Erickson notes the conceptual similarity between this strand of Plato's

---

[22]Ibid., Loeb Classical Library 6, p. 25.

[23]Philo says, "God is the maker of time also. . . . And thus with God there is no future, since He has made the boundaries of the ages subject to Himself. For God's life is not a time, but eternity, which is the archetype and pattern of time; and in eternity there is no past nor future, but only present existence" (ibid., pp. 25-27).

[24]Plato *The Republic of Plato*, vols. 6-7, trans. Francis MacDonald Cornford (New York: Oxford University Press, 1966), see esp. 7:509d-511e, pp. 224-26.

thought and that of Paul in 2 Corinthians 4:18. "So we fix our eyes not on what is seen, but on what is unseen. For what is seen is temporary, but what is unseen is eternal." Clearly both Plato and Paul affirm the reality and the superiority of the unseen realm of existence.

But what accounts for this conceptual similarity? Is it the case that Paul was influenced by Plato at this point of his thinking? Were subsequent Christian interpreters, who read Paul as affirming the greater reality of the unseen, spiritual world, reading him only through Platonic spectacles? Were both Plato and Paul influenced by the same God in their writings, Plato by the truth of God's general revelation even as Paul was directed by God's special revelation? Or could it simply be the case that at this point Plato and Paul have similar (though not identical) ideas? Erickson argues that the latter option is the most likely.[25] I suggest that we also be open to the possibility that the source of this conceptual similarity is that it is the same God who is the source of both his general revelation (whose truth is available to all people, including non-Christian philosophers like Plato) and his special revelation given to and through Paul and other biblical authors. But whichever option we consider most likely, the point is that the similarity of ideas that we find in Plato and Paul is not necessarily indicative of a causal influence by Plato on Paul.

With regard to the later NeoPlatonic thought of Plotinus, which clearly has conceptual and vocabulary similarities with the theology of Origen and other Christian theologians who followed him, Gerald Bray has suggested a mutuality of influence. Noting that Plotinus himself was deeply influenced by Christianity in his youth (possibly even being a Christian himself at some stage), Bray argues, "In this reworking of the Platonic tradition, it is at least likely that [Plotinus] was as much influenced by Christianity as Origen had been influenced by Plato, so that to picture the interaction between the two schools of thought as a one-way street is basically wrong."[26]

Erickson suggests that underlying the oft-stated insistence that similarities of thought between Greek philosophy and classical theism must necessarily indicate a causal influence may well be a criterion of dissimilarity much like that used by form critics in assessing the authenticity of sayings attributed to Jesus. This criterion would affirm that a particular saying should be viewed as an authentic saying of Jesus only if no parallel to it can be found in Judaism or in the early church. In essence, it required that Jesus be absolutely original in all that he said. By analogy, this argument would say that a theological model could be

---

[25]Erickson, *What Does God Know?* p. 144.
[26]Gerald Bray, *The Doctrine of God,* Contours of Christian Theology (Downers Grove, Ill.: InterVarsity Press, 1993), p. 32.

considered biblical only if no parallel to it could be found in the surrounding
Greco-Roman culture. Erickson rejects this demand for conceptual originality for
theological constructs and helpfully suggests that in theology this criterion may
rightly be used positively but not negatively. He says:

> If the conception of God is markedly different from the background culture, that
> would be a positive indication of the fidelity of the idea to the Bible. . . . On the
> other hand, a similarity between a theologian's concept and that found in an extant
> philosophy should not necessarily be considered a mark of derivation or influence.[27]

Are causal influences from Greek philosophy uniformly negative? If a
causal influence from Greek philosophy on Christian theology could be determined, we must still ask two key questions: First, how important was that influence? And second, was that influence necessarily negative? Let's look at them.

First, how important was the causal influence of Greek philosophy? Was it
the only influence or the most important influence on the thinking of the church
on a particular issue, or were there multiple influences? Specifically, how does
the influence from Greek philosophy compare to the influence of the text of
Scripture itself? Thomas Oden believes that the importance of the causal influence of Greek philosophy has often been overstated, while the influence of biblical exegesis may well be understated.[28] At any rate, the issue of the relative
influence of multiple traditions must at least be considered.

The second question, however, is even more important. If such a causal influence of Greek philosophy does in fact exist, is it necessarily negative? Does
Hellenistic thought necessarily distort the church's understanding of the Scriptures? I would argue no.

If God's general revelation is indeed universal (e.g., Ps 19:1-6; Rom 1:19-21),
then as we noted above, its truth can be found at times in Greek philosophy.[29]

---

[27]Erickson, *What Does God Know?*, p. 145.

[28]For example, Thomas Oden speaks of the relationship of Aristotelian thought to the doctrine
of divine immutability. "Overestimating the stranglehold of Aristotle upon the ancient ecu-
menical Christian tradition, recent theologians may have *under*estimated the perduring
counter-Aristotelian influences of the tradition of exegesis of the psalms, Isaiah, Paul and
John" (*The Living God,* Systematic Theology 1 [San Francisco: Harper & Row, 1987], pp. 113).

[29]Consider, for example, Paul's willingness to quote the Greek poets Epimenides and Aratus in
Acts 17:28, Menander in 1 Cor 15:33 and Epimenides again in Tit 1:12. See John R. W. Stott,
The Spirit, the Church and the World (Downers Grove, Ill.: InterVarsity Press, 1990), p. 286.
The apprehension of truth from general revelation shows that the Holy Spirit is free and universal in his work of illumination. Romans 1 emphasizes the negative impact of human sin
on those humans who suppress the knowledge of God they rightly should embrace through
general revelation. Thus when the unregenerate do apprehend this truth, it is evidence of the
work of the Holy Spirit.

Thus the influence Greek philosophy might have on Christian theology could be positive or negative—or more likely mixed. The automatic assumption that its influence would necessarily be negative and distorting seems to come from the conviction, commonly held within the Biblical Theology movement of the early to mid-twentieth century, that there is a strong and enduring contrast between Greek thought and Hebraic thought. Each tradition of thought was held to be a distinct mentality, with Hebraic thinking being the distinctly biblical mindset.[30] Semantic variations within the Greek and Hebrew languages were taken to be reflective of differences in thought patterns. And these in turn were given a theological value judgment—with Hebraic thinking being considered essentially good while Greek thinking was considered to be bad. This hard and fast distinction has been thoroughly critiqued by James Barr in *The Semantics of Biblical Language* as being rooted in illegitimate semantic transfers and the failure to treat both Hebrew and Greek as true languages.[31] The success of Barr's critique has been noted by Brevard Childs:

> In reflecting on the effect of Barr's book, one cannot help being impressed with the success of his attack. Seldom has one book brought down so much superstructure with such effectiveness. Barr's arguments seemed to most English scholars and a majority of Americans to be fully convincing. . . . Even among those Biblical theologians who remained unconvinced, there was an agreement that the emphasis of the Biblical Theology Movement on a distinctive mentality could never be carried out without a major revision.[32]

Yet there seems to be little evidence of such a major revision among open theists, given their consistent affirmations that the impact of Greek philosophy on classical theism is overwhelmingly negative. A better and more nuanced approach to analyzing the impact of Hellenistic thinking on Christian theology can be found in Harold O. J. Brown. Reflecting on the church's resolution of the trinitarian and christological controversies of the fourth and fifth centuries, Brown writes:

> The adoption of the Nicene Creed in 325 and the Chalcedonian Creed in 451 sta-

---

[30]James Barr describes this proposed contrast in the following terms: static thought (Greek) versus dynamic thought (Hebraic); an emphasis on the abstract (Greek) versus an emphasis on the concrete (Hebraic); and a dualistic view of human beings (Greek) versus a holistic view (Hebraic) (*Semantics of Biblical Language* [Oxford: Oxford University Press, 1961], pp. 8-13). He concludes, "Finally, and to sum up, the contrast may be expressed as the contrast between the divisive, distinction-forming, analytic type of Greek thought and the totality type of Hebrew thought" (ibid., p. 13).

[31]This description of Barr's critique comes from Brevard S. Childs, *Biblical Theology in Crisis* (Philadelphia: Westminster Press, 1970), p. 72.

[32]Ibid.

bilized the doctrines of the Trinity and Christ for over one thousand years. They made use of Hellenistic categories and thinking to do so. The important question to ask is not whether orthodox theology betrays Hellenistic influence. Nothing else was possible in the cultural climate of the time. The important question is whether this orthodoxy represents a proper and correct interpretation of New Testament Christology or whether it seriously distorts it.[33]

This approach distinguishes between the possibility of a Hellenistic influence that is helpful to "a proper and correct understanding" of biblical truth and one that is harmful and distorting. The end result of this more nuanced approach is that it forces us to go back to the text of Scripture itself, interpreted in reliance on the Holy Spirit and in the context of the broader Christian community, to seek a fresh understanding of its teaching. While we must always acknowledge and grapple with the reality of philosophical preconceptions, including those of Greek philosophy, that shape the way we approach the text of Scripture, we must be open to discerning whether that influence could be either helpful or harmful.

A selective appropriation. Throughout its history Christian theology has indeed taken a selective approach to its appropriation of Hellenistic categories of thought, rather than a naive, uncritical, blind acceptance of Greek thought in its totality. Three brief examples of this selectivity can demonstrate the point.

During the Arian controversy the church confronted a theology distinctly influenced by Hellenistic philosophy. The theology of Arius was shaped in great measure by the Neo-Platonic contrast between the utterly transcendent God and the world of created things. This lead Arius to affirm that in order for God to create the universe, he first had to create the Logos to serve as a mediator between God and the world.[34] Thus Arius affirmed that the Logos was not coeternal and not *homoousios* with the Father. But at the Council of Ephesus in 325 and the Council of Constantinople in 381, the church ultimately sided with the theology of Athanasius against Arianism and affirmed the eternal existence of the divine Son who is *homoousios* with God the Father. Thus, in the final analysis the teaching of Scripture overwhelmed the Hellenistic ideas that drove Arius. While the creeds coming from these councils utilized Hellenistic words and categories in expressing their conclusions, they did so specifically to reject theological conclusions coming from one strand of Greek philosophy. The point is

---

[33]Harold O. J. Brown, *Heresies* (Peabody, Mass.: Hendrickson, 1998), p. 105.

[34]Ibid., p. 115. See also Erickson, *Christian Theology,* 2nd ed. (Grand Rapids: Baker, 1998), pp. 711-13, and Kevin Giles, *The Trinity and Subordinationism* (Downers Grove, Ill.: InterVarsity Press, 2002), p. 34.

that the church's appropriation of Greek philosophical categories was selective.

A second example comes from the individual who by all accounts is considered to be the highest example of the kind of classical theism that is rejected by open theism—Thomas Aquinas. Sanders describes Aquinas as "the apex of medieval theology, [who] sought to harmonize the biblical-classical synthesis he inherited from the Christian tradition with the newly discovered works of Aristotle."[35] But with regard to his view of divine foreknowledge, Aquinas differed conspicuously from his Greek mentor. Aristotle held to a view of foreknowledge and freedom that would deny God's infallible foreknowledge of future contingent events. Yet Thomas affirmed again and again that God's foreknowledge does in fact embrace all future contingents (including all free human decisions).

For example, in response to the question, "Has God knowledge of non-existent things?" Aquinas replies:

> God knows all things that are in anyway whatever. . . . Things that are not actually existent exist potentially either by God himself or by a creature: whether in active power or in passive potentiality. . . . Therefore whatever can be produced or thought or said by a creature, and also whatever God himself can produce, all is known by God, even if it is not actually existing. In this sense it can be said that he has knowledge of non-existent things.[36]

From this, "it follows that God knows contingent future events."[37] Thomas follows Boethius in affirming that God can know future contingent events because of his timeless eternity: "The reason [for God's knowledge of future contingent events] is that God's act of knowledge, which is his existence, is measured by eternity, which, itself without succession, takes in the whole of time, and to all that exists in time, as to what is present before him."[38]

> God does not, as we do, know [contingent events] in their actual existence successively, but all at once; because his knowledge is measured by eternity, as is also his existence; and eternity, which exists as a simultaneous whole, takes in the whole of time, as we have said above. Hence all that takes place in time is eternally present to God . . . because he eternally surveys all things as they are in their presence to him. It is clear, then, that contingent events are known infallibly by God because they are objects of the divine gaze in their presence to him;

---

[35]Sanders, "Historical Considerations," p. 86.
[36]Thomas Aquinas *Summa Theologicae* Ia.Q14.A9.reply, trans. Thomas J. Gornall (London: Blackfriars, 1964), 4:33.
[37]Ibid., Ia.Q14.A13.reply, p. 47.
[38]Ibid.

while on the other hand, they are future contingent events in relation to their proximate causes.[39]

It is clear that as much as Aquinas was influenced by Aristotle, he was also selective in the elements of Aristotelian thought that he appropriated. This raises the possibility that his view of the exhaustive extent of divine foreknowledge is not merely the result of Greek philosophical influences.[40]

Third, many contemporary evangelical theologians exhibit a critical nuancing when approaching the divine attributes generally considered to be characteristic of classical theism. Pinnock asserts that this classical view of God is such a unified package that one cannot pick and choose among these divine attributes. Affirming one inevitably leads to affirming the others as well. He writes:

> The conventional attributes rise and fall together. If God is personal and enters into relationships, God cannot be immutable in every respect, timelessly eternal, impassible, or meticulously sovereign. . . .
>
> The conventional package of attributes is tightly woven. You cannot deny one, such as impassibility, without casting doubt on others, like immutability. It's like pulling on a thread and unraveling a sweater.[41]

Yet when looking at several prominent contemporary evangelical theologians who affirm exhaustive divine foreknowledge (an understanding that would fit into the "package" of classical theism), the situation seems much more complex. For example, Wayne Grudem does not hold to the version of divine impassibility that is rejected by open theists. Rather he speaks of an emotional dimension that is crucial to God's experience.

> The idea that God has no passions or emotions *at all* clearly conflicts with much of the rest of Scripture, and for that reason I have not affirmed God's impassibility in this book. Instead, quite the opposite is true, for God, who is the origin of our emotions and who created our emotions, certainly does feel emotions.[42]

---

[39]Ibid., Ia.Q14.A13.reply, pp. 47, 49. Aquinas uses two significant illustrations to drive home his point: (1) Just as every point on the circumference of a circle is equally related to the center of that circle, so every point in time is equally related to God's eternity and to his eternal knowledge (*The Summa Contra Gentiles,* trans. Dominican Fathers [London: Burns, Oates & Washbourne, 1924], 1:141). (2) Just as a man looking down on a road from a high vantage point is able to see everything on the road at the same time, so the eternal God, being outside of time, is able to see all future events at the same time. This enables the future event eternally foreknown by God to be both certain as to its occurrence and contingent with respect to its secondary causes (*Summa Theologicae,* Ia.Q14.A13.reply obj.3, p. 51).
[40]Erickson, *What Does God Know?,* pp. 139-40.
[41]Clark Pinnock, *Most Moved Mover* (Grand Rapids: Baker, 2001), pp. 72, 77-78.
[42]Wayne Grudem, *Systematic Theology* (Grand Rapids: Zondervan, 1994), p. 166l.

Similar views on the nature of divine impassibility are held by John Feinberg, Millard Erickson, Thomas Oden, Bruce Ware and Ronald Nash.[43] Each of these theologians has also carefully nuanced his understanding of divine immutability to allow for a genuine relational and emotional mutability to coexist with God's ontological immutability.[44] In addition, Nash expresses uncertainty about the timeless nature of God's eternity, while John Feinberg is among those evangelicals who affirm a temporal understanding of God's relationship to time.[45] Yet each of these nonopenness theologians affirms God's foreknowledge of free human decisions.[46] Thus to the extent that Greek philosophy has influenced the understanding of divine attributes stressed by classical theism, these contemporary nonopenness evangelicals have intentionally been selective in their appropriation of the classical model with its Greek influences. This fact certainly argues against the impression often times given in the openness literature that the only two evangelical options available to us are a strict form of Thomistic classical theism (generally understood through the lens of Reformed theology) or open theism.[47] The reality is that there are many other evangelical options available for consideration.

What must a perfect God look like? One strand of Hellenistic thought that open theists have argued contributes mightily to the classical view of God has been called "perfect being theology." This is a way of arguing for a particular understanding of the nature of God based on what must be true of the absolutely perfect being we call God. Anything less than absolute perfection would be unworthy of God. But, in the final analysis, argues Sanders, it is an a priori

---

[43]Feinberg, *No One Like Him*, pp. 241-43, 277; Erickson, *Christian Theology*, p. 295, n. 14, and *God the Father Almighty*, pp. 141-64; Oden, *Living God*, pp. 128-29; Bruce Ware, "An Evangelical Reformulation of the Doctrine of the Immutability of God," *Journal of the Evangelical Theological Society* 29 no. 4 (1986): 444-46; and Nash, *Concept of God*, pp. 100, 114.

[44]Grudem, *Systematic Theology*, pp. 163-68; Feinberg, *No One Like Him*, pp. 264-76; Erickson, *Christian Theology*, pp. 304-8, and Erickson, *God the Father Almighty*, pp. 95-113; Oden, *Living God*, pp. 110-14; Ware, "Immutability of God," pp. 431-46; and Nash, *Concept of God*, pp. 95-105.

[45]Nash, *Concept of God*, pp. 73-83. Feinberg, *No One Like Him*, p. 428. See Feinberg's entire discussion of the issue of God, time and eternity on pp. 255-64, 375-436.

[46]Grudem, *Systematic Theology*, pp. 190-93; Feinberg, *No One Like Him*, pp. 299-320, 735-75; Erickson, *Christian Theology*, pp. 301-2; Millard Erickson, *God the Father Almighty* (Grand Rapids: Baker, 1998), pp. 184-209; and *What Does God Know?*, Oden, *Living God*, pp. 69-73; Bruce Ware, *God's Lesser Glory* (Wheaton, Ill.: Crossway, 2000); and Nash, *Concept of God*, pp. 51-72.

[47]This limited option, either-or approach can be seen especially in the multi-authored *Openness of God* and in Boyd, *God of the Possible*. Exceptions to this approach can be found in Sanders (*God Who Risks*, pp. 200-206) and David Basinger (*The Case For Freewill Theism: A Philosophical Assessment* [Downers Grove, Ill.: InterVarsity Press, 1996], pp. 123-34), who each discuss the kind of simple foreknowledge most commonly found in classical Arminianism.

conception of what perfection must look like that ultimately determines the classical view of divine attributes like eternity, immutability and foreknowledge, and the interpretation of specific texts (especially divine repentance texts). He asserts that perfect being theology has its origins in the thinking of Greek philosophy.[48] It strongly influenced Christian theology in the post-Nicea era when

> the focus on the eternal (timeless) relationship between the Father and the Son . . . takes precedence over God's relationship to us in incarnation and salvation history. . . . Arguing from what is "fitting" for God to be (theoprepēs), significant aspects of the biblical revelation (such as suffering and temporality) were revised to fit this understanding. Though they had good intentions in applying the ideas of immutability and impassibility, they used them in an absolute sense and so distorted the faithfulness and love of the biblical God. In the end the true understanding of the divine nature was derived from metaphysics and the biblical revelation was made to conform to it.[49]

This perfect being theology reached its zenith in the Middle Ages in the theology of John Scotus Erigena, Anselm of Canterbury and Thomas Aquinas.[50] But Sanders argues that it still exists today in classical theologians such as Thomas Morris and Norman Geisler.[51]

While the value of perfect being theology and the extent of its influence on classical views of God can be debated, I assert that the argument presented in this book has not been made on such a basis. Especially in chapter four, where I argued that the various openness texts do not necessitate a nonexhaustive view of the foreknowledge of God, this conclusion has not been made on the basis of a

---

[48]Sanders writes, "Greek philosophy did not reject religion, but it did seek to purify it by submitting it to the constraints of an abstract and impersonal notion of ultimate reality. Utilizing the methods of natural theology, philosophers deduced their understanding of deity from the concept of 'perfection' since nothing less than perfection would be appropriate for God (theoprepēs). In this way they critiqued the older mythology and sought to rid the conception of deity of anthropomorphism" ("Historical Considerations," p. 61).

[49]Ibid., pp. 79-80.

[50]Ibid., pp. 86-87.

[51]Thomas Morris argues that while "the method of perfect being theology needs a revelational control . . . it's also true that perfect being theology itself can act as an interpretive constraint on how we read the Bible" (Our Idea of God [Downers Grove, Ill.: InterVarsity Press, 1991], p. 43). He also says that we should not ascribe to God "any limitations which imply imperfection" (ibid., p. 85). Sanders's conclusion is Morris is representative of those for whom "the classical philosophical conception of God has far too often been allowed to overturn the biblical text in favor of what we deem it fitting for God to be (dignum Deo)" (God Who Risks, p. 291, n. 22). In discussing the issue of anthropomorphism and divine repentance, Sanders says that Geisler "uses philosophical reasoning to establish a priori what is appropriate for a deity to be like (dignum Deo). Since it is not 'proper' for a deity to change his mind, biblical assertions to that effect must be revised to say something else" (ibid., p. 68). Sanders references Geisler's work Creating God in the Image of Man? (Minneapolis: Bethany House, 1997).

prior philosophical conception about what a perfect God must be like. For example, in my treatment of the repentance of God, I sought to highlight the areas where this anthropomorphic metaphor is similar to its human counterpart and areas where it is different. I argued that the relationship of God's repentance to his foreknowledge was one of the differences. While all are agreed that genuine human repentance presupposes a lack of certain and infallible knowledge of the future in every detail, I argued that this is not the case for God's repentance. Why? Because of the massive biblical testimony to God's foreknowledge of free human decisions (see chaps. 2-3). If we seek to take into account all the biblical evidence, including both texts that speak of God's repentance and those that affirm his foreknowledge of free human decisions (which are numerically far greater and which emphasize and highlight the "God-ness" of Yahweh and of Jesus Christ), we must understand divine repentance as a genuinely real experience, yet one that is not based on a lack of certain foreknowledge of future free actions. My attempt has not been to advance a primarily philosophical argument; rather, it has been to put forth a biblical one. The argument has not been made on the basis of a philosophically derived perfect being theology.

Philosophical influences on open theism. Believers in God's foreknowledge of free human decisions are not alone in having philosophical influences that play a role in shaping their views. The views of open theists are similarly shaped. I have already mentioned the conceptual similarities between the open view of divine foreknowledge and the views of Aristotle and Cicero. While conceptual similarity does not necessarily mean causal influence, the possibility does exist that open theism has been influenced to some extent by this strand of Greco-Roman philosophy.

There are other significant philosophical influences that have even more clearly shaped the nonexhaustive openness view of divine foreknowledge. Take, for example, the openness commitment to a libertarian view of human freedom. While open theists do at times present biblical arguments for this understanding of the nature of human freedom, the majority of the arguments are philosophical (especially the necessity of libertarian freedom to ground human moral responsibility) and intuitive.[52] This libertarian understanding of human

---

[52]An example of a biblical argument for libertarian freedom comes from Pinnock: "According to the Bible, it was not only possible for God to create a world with significantly free finite agents. God actually did that. This is apparent from two central biblical assertions about human beings: (1) they are historical agents who can respond to God in love; and (2) they are sinners who have deliberately rejected God's plan for them. Neither assertion would make sense unless we posit the gift of freedom in the strong (i.e., libertarian) sense" ("God Limits His Knowledge," in *Predestination and Free Will,* ed. David Basinger and Randall Basinger [Downers Grove, Ill.: InterVarsity Press, 1986], p. 147).

freedom is central to open theism. And Pinnock gives testimony to the shaping influence that his commitment to libertarian freedom and its logical implications played in his emerging open view of divine foreknowledge. His questioning of exhaustive divine foreknowledge began with his sense that such foreknowledge would inevitably lead to determinism and thus a loss of human freedom (and moral responsibility).

> I found that I could not shake off the intuition that such a total omniscience would necessarily mean that everything we will ever choose in the future will have been already spelled out in the divine knowledge register, and consequently the belief that we have truly significant choices would seem to be mistaken.[53]

As a result, Pinnock says:

> I had to ask myself if it was biblically possible to hold that God knows everything that can be known, but that free choices would not be something that can be known even by God because they are not yet settled in reality. . . . When I went to Scripture with this question in mind, I found more support than I had expected.[54]

In the end, Pinnock changed his view of the extent of divine foreknowledge, one of several doctrinal shifts "that logic required and I believed Scripture permitted me to make."[55] Thus he asserts in *The Openness of God,* "Philosophically

---

Philosophically, Pinnock argues that "The idea of moral responsibility requires us to believe that actions are not determined either internally or externally. . . . The love God wants from us is a love we are not compelled to give. The sin God condemns us for is a sin we did not have to commit. They are actions for which there are no prior conditions which render them certain 'actions which result from the genuine choices of historical agents' " (ibid., p. 149). See also Bruce Reichenbach, "God Limits His Power," in *Predestination and Free Will* ed. David Basinger and Randall Basinger [Downers Grove, Ill.: InterVarsity Press, 1986], p. 104.

Pinnock also argues for the reality of libertarian free will on the basis of universal, fundamental, unarguable human self-perception. "One of the deepest of all human intuitions . . . is the sense of freedom to determine what they shall do and what they shall be. Universal man almost without exception talks and feels *as if* he were free. He perceives himself to be a person capable of rising above his situation, of shaping his life and destiny, and of making a significant impact on history. This fundamental self-perception is, I believe, an important clue as to the nature of reality" ("Responsible Freedom and the Flow of Biblical History," in *Grace Unlimited,* ed. Clark H. Pinnock [Minneapolis: Bethany Fellowship, 1975], p. 95).

[53]Clark Pinnock, "From Augustine to Arminius: A Pilgrimage in Theology," in *The Grace of God, the Will of Man,* ed. Clark H. Pinnock (Grand Rapids: Zondervan, 1989), p. 25.

[54]Ibid. Pinnock goes on to say, "Evidently the logic of Calvinism had worked effectively to silence some of the biblical data even for me" (ibid., pp. 25-26). Whatever influence Calvinistic logic had on his reading of biblical texts in the past, it seems clear that the logic of libertarian freedom has shaped Pinnock's current reading of the text. Why the influence of logical inferences is negative when it comes from Calvinism but positive when it comes from libertarian freedom is not explained by Pinnock.

[55]Ibid., pp. 18-19.

speaking, if choices are real and freedom significant, future decisions cannot be exhaustively foreknown."[56] It is clear, is it not, that Pinnock's commitment to libertarian freedom and its logical implications is a primary factor in shaping his reading of the biblical portrayal of the extent of the foreknowledge of God.

Another significant philosophical presupposition of open theists is their commitment to an A-theory of time. The A-theory of time (also called the *process* or *tensed* theory of time) is one in which objective becoming is essential to time. Future events do not yet exist in reality; rather, they become existent when the future becomes present. The A-theory of time is opposed to the B-theory of time (also called the *stasis* or *tenseless* theory), in which past, present and future events are all equally real. According to this theory, when future events become present, this does not mean that they have only now begun to exist; rather, it means that our minds have now become aware of them as present.[57] This A-theory of time, much debated among philosophers, is a crucial underpinning of the openness argument that future free decisions of human beings cannot be known by God because they do not yet exist.[58] Now, it is clearly outside the bounds of this volume to enter into a full debate over the nature of time. Yet the influence of this particular view can clearly be seen. And Erickson notes that Boyd especially assumes this theory, and one view of its implications without argument.[59]

Perhaps the most significant philosophical influence on open theism comes from process thought. While open theists clearly and correctly proclaim their differences from process theists, similarities do remain.[60] Autobiographical state-

---

[56]Pinnock, "Systematic Theology," p. 123. Pinnock is not alone in seeing philosophical problems in trying to reconcile exhaustive divine foreknowledge and libertarian human freedom. See William Hasker, "A Philosophical Perspective," in *Openness of God* (Downers Grove, Ill.: InterVarsity Press, 1994), p. 147. See also his extended and very helpful discussion in *God, Time, and Knowledge,* pp. 1-143.

[57]This description of the A and B theories of time comes from William Lane Craig, "Divine Knowledge and Future Contingencies," in *Process Theology,* ed. Ronald Nash (Grand Rapids: Baker, 1987), pp. 98-103. See also the helpful descriptions of Gregory E. Ganssle in the introduction to *God and Time: Four Views,* ed. Gregory E. Gannsle (Downers Grove, Ill.: InterVarsity Press), pp. 14-15. The entire volume edited by Gannsle is a good introduction to the issues.

[58]Not all advocates of the A-theory of time hold to an openness understanding of the extent of the foreknowledge of God. Craig, for example, holds to the A-theory and yet also affirms exhaustive divine foreknowledge. He bases his understanding on his view of God's middle knowledge ("Divine Knowledge and Future Contingencies," pp. 98-103).

[59]Erickson, *What Does God Know?* p. 160.

[60]The reality of these similarities and differences led Clark Pinnock to describe his own view as a "via media" between classical and process theism ("Between Classical and Process Theism," pp. 316-21).

ments from prominent open theists reveal the significant influence that process thought has had on their theological development.

Richard Rice writes that as a Ph.D. student at the University of Chicago:

> It was Hartshorne's philosophical theology that particularly attracted me. There were several reasons for this. On the most basic level, I was impressed that a powerful mind, determined to follow reason to the end in matters of religion, found abundant evidence for God and developed impressive arguments for God's existence. I also felt that Hartshorne's particular conception of natural theology could benefit theologians in a number of important ways. Most important, I found what growing numbers of conservative Christian thinkers have also discovered in recent years. If we accept a version of Hartshorne's dipolar theism, we can formulate a doctrine of God that is superior by every relevant criterion to the God of classical theism.[61]

Rice describes some of the ways in which he believes this Hartshorne-influenced view of God is superior.

> The notion that a perfect being can change is not only conceptually coherent—a point Hartshorne argues at great length—but it gives us an idea of God that is more faithful to the biblical portrait than is classical theism and more helpful to us on the level of personal religion as well. The idea that God's relation to the world is interactive, or dynamic, makes it possible for us to develop coherent concepts of divine love and creaturely freedom. In so doing it helps us to overcome some of the problems that have perplexed Christian thinkers for centuries, such as the relation of human freedom and divine foreknowledge.[62]

William Hasker is another open theist who acknowledges his debt to Hartshorne.

> On a personal note, let me state that I first became clearly convinced of [the fact that God's creatures really make a difference with him] through reading Charles Hartshorne's *Divine Relativity*. Prior to reading Hartshorne, I had puzzled over the

---

[61]Richard Rice, "Process Theism and the Open View of God," in *Searching for an Adequate God*, ed. John B. Cobb Jr. and Clark H. Pinnock (Grand Rapids: Eerdmans, 2000), p. 166. In an earlier work, Rice had described the similarities that his own view has with that of process theism. "The concept of God proposed here shares the process view that God's relation to the temporal world consists in a succession of concrete experiences, rather than a single timeless perception. It also shares with process theism the twofold analysis of God, or the 'dipolar theism,' described above. It conceives God as both absolute and relative, necessary and contingent, eternal and temporal, changeless and changing. It attributes one element in each pair of contrasts to the appropriate aspect of God's being—the essential divine nature or the concrete divine experience" (*God's Foreknowledge and Man's Free Will*, [Minneapolis: Bethany House, 1985], pp. 32-33).

[62]Rice, "Process Theism and the Open View of God," p. 166.

medieval doctrine that, while the creatures are really related to God, God has only a "relation of reason" to the creatures. That God is really related to the creatures is a genuine and important point of agreement between process theism and the open view of God.[63]

Hasker speaks of the contributions of process thinkers to his own development.

A second point of agreement [between open and process theists], which builds on the first, is that God is affected by the state of his creatures, and suffers when things go badly for them. Here again, I am indebted to process thinkers for nudging me out of my state of perplexed indecision about the medieval doctrine of divine impassibility. The decisive impetus in this case came from John Cobb and David Griffin's trenchant critique of the views of Anselm and Thomas Aquinas concerning divine compassion. Both of these worthies held, in essence, that God acts as we would expect a compassionate being to act, but that any feelings of sympathy or compassion is altogether alien to God. Once I saw clearly what the doctrine of impassibility amounted to, it seemed entirely evident to me that such a doctrine cannot possibly be true.[64]

Boyd also speaks of the influence of the process view of Hartshorne in the preface to his work *Trinity and Process.*

It is our conviction that the fundamental vision of the process worldview, especially as espoused by Charles Hartshorne, is correct. But it is our conviction as well that the scriptural and traditional understanding of God as triune and antecedently actual within Godself is true, and is, in fact, a foundational doctrine of the Christian faith. But, we contend, these two views, when properly understood within a proper framework, do not conflict. Indeed, it shall be our contention that Hartshorne's a priori process metaphysics, when corrected of certain misconstrued elements, actually *requires* something like a trinitarian understanding of God to make it consistent and complete! . . . My warmest appreciation must also be expressed to Charles Hartshorne. Though I disagree with him on a great many points, he has influenced my thinking more than any other single philosopher, living or dead.[65]

Boyd clearly and rightly points to the substantive differences that exist be-

---

[63]William Hasker, "An Adequate God," in *Searching for an Adequate God,* ed. John B. Cobb Jr. and Clark H. Pinnock (Grand Rapids: Eerdmans, 2000), pp. 216-17.

[64]Ibid. Hasker is referring to John B. Cobb Jr. and David Ray Griffin, *Process Theology* (Philadelphia: Westminster Press, 1976), pp. 44-46. Hasker also notes a third area that process and open theists share in common—their commitment to a libertarian view of freedom that rejects a view of God as all-controlling and the determiner of everything that takes place in the universe ("Adequate God," p. 217).

[65]Gregory A. Boyd, *Trinity and Process* (New York: Peter Lang, 1992), preface.

tween his thought and that of Hartshorne, but at the same time he does acknowledge the substantial influence of this significant process thinker on his own perspective.

One final example. Clark Pinnock is yet another open theist who acknowledges the influence of process thinkers like Hartshorne on his own thought.

> Now if we [open theists] are honest, we would have to admit that it has been process thinkers who have called our attention to some of these problems. I have to acknowledge the stimulus I have personally received from them, and how they have made me aware of the need to introduce changes into the received doctrine of God. Hartshorne, for example, has put a lot of effort into exposing the difficulties and suggesting alternatives. I have been helped by his ideas on various things. He has taught me that thinking of God as literally *all*-powerful divests the finite universe of a degree of power. He has pressed the point that God, though unchanging in his character, is certainly able to change in response to a changing creation. In my theology, at least, God has used process thinkers to compel me to change certain ideas which I had and bring them up to scriptural standards. Without being a process theologian myself, I am certainly indebted to such thinkers for many good insights.[66]

Statements like these make it abundantly clear that process thought in general and Hartshorne in particular have been significant influences to open theists and their views. Whether that influence is a positive or a negative thing is a question that volumes like this are trying to answer. But it cannot be denied that these philosophical influences have helped to shape open theism into the theological system that it is.

But equally so, we must also say that open theists are selective in their appropriation of process categories and insights. Pinnock argues that open theists "can adapt a [process] metaphysics but we should not adopt one. We can utilize process insights to help us communicate the Christian faith without accepting the total system."[67] None of these openness writers claims to be a process theologian. All of them clearly highlight differences they have with key elements of the process system. The primary differences include creation ex nihilo, God's ontological independence from the world, his eternal triune existence and its implications for his own self-sufficiency and his sovereign freedom with respect

---

[66]Clark Pinnock, "Between Classical and Process Theism," pp. 316-17.
[67]Clark Pinnock, "Introduction," in *Searching for an Adequate God,* ed. John B. Cobb Jr. and Clark H. Pinnock (Grand Rapids: Eerdmans, 2000), p. xi. In an earlier work Pinnock described open theism as arising from the process of "taking what is positive from [both] classical and process theism and abandoning what is not helpful" ("Between Classical and Process Theism," pp. 316-21).

to the world, God's omnipotence, and the multifaceted nature of his influence in the world.[68]

This consistently affirmed combination of similarities and differences argues that open theists do indeed selectively appropriate some concepts and categories from process thought while self-consciously rejecting others. But if this is the case with open theists, why can't it be affirmed that nonopenness theologians are equally selective in their appropriations of Greek concepts and categories and the contributions of historic forms of classical theism? And if this is possible, it surely raises the possibility that an exhaustive view of God's foreknowledge is not primarily the result of Hellenistic philosophical constructs or of an uncritical and nonselective adoption of that worldview in its entirety.

Conclusion. In the preceding discussion I have argued against the charge that the reading of biblical texts I have presented and the conclusions I have drawn in the earlier chapters of this book have been severely distorted by the shaping influence of Greek philosophy. Specifically, I have argued the following points:

1. Greek philosophy is indeed a multifaceted reality, especially concerning the relationship of God to this world. Thus questions of divine providence and foreknowledge and human freedom do not have a single answer in the Hellenistic (or more broadly Greco-Roman) philosophical world. As a result, any influence from these sources on New Testament writers and on the interpretation of Christian theologians is not uniform. Thus we must ask, Which Greek philosophy is supposed to be so influential?

2. Conceptual similarities between the classical view of exhaustive divine foreknowledge and certain strains of Greek philosophy do not necessarily mean that there is a causal influence. Other noncausal reasons for conceptual similarity are indeed possible, as is the possibility of a mutuality of influence. A criterion of dissimilarity between Christian theological constructs and their Hellenistic counterparts may rightly function positively, but not negatively so as to deny the validity of theological constructions with such conceptual similarity.

3. If a causal or shaping influence from Greek philosophy could indeed be determined, its influence would not necessarily be negative. The truth of God's general revelation, accessible to all people, including Greek philosophers, creates the possibility that a Hellenistic influence can help Christian thinkers come

---

[68]Among the many statements of these differences between open theism and process theology, see Rice, "Process Theism and the Open View of God," p. 185; Pinnock, "Systematic Theology," pp. 108-9, and "Introduction," pp. ix-xi; Boyd, *Trinity and Process*, pp. 332-33; and Hasker, "A Philosophical Persepective," in *Openness of God* (Downers Grove, Ill.: InterVarsity Press, 1994), p. 140, and "An Adequate God," pp. 218-45.

to a more accurate understanding of biblical truth. Both possibilities (either a distorting or a helpful influence) must be considered as biblical texts are examined and theological models are constructed and tested in the context of the community of interpreters in reliance on the Holy Spirit.

4. Classical theists have long engaged in a selective appropriation of categories and concepts arising from Hellenistic thought. This can be seen in the church's resolution of the Arian crisis in the Councils of Nicea and Constantinople, in Thomas Aquinas's break with Aristotle's view of divine foreknowledge and human freedom, and in the careful and critical nuancing of many contemporary nonopenness evangelical theologians when they deal with the divine attributes regularly associated with classical theism. While holding to positions on certain divine attributes that reflect classical theism, these contemporary theologians either reject altogether or substantially modify their views of other classical attributes. What must be said then is that these theologians are intentionally selective in their appropriation of the classical model of God with its (supposed) Hellenistic influences.

5. My attempt in this volume to argue for exhaustive divine foreknowledge has not come from the common classical theological approach called "perfect being theology" (arguing for an understanding of God and his attributes from an a priori understanding of what the perfection of God must be like). I have not been primarily considering what perfection must look like or what is appropriate for such a perfect being. Instead, I have argued from the broad stream of teaching of the Old Testament and the New Testament.

6. Classical theists and those associated with nonopenness evangelical theology are not the only ones who have been influenced at some level by philosophical ideas and influences. Substantial philosophical influences can be detected in the writings of open theists. These include the openness commitment to a libertarian view of human freedom (often argued for intuitively and philosophically) and to an A-theory of time. But the philosophical influence most often cited by open theists comes from process thought—especially that of Charles Hartshorne. Thus we saw several significant similarities between open and process theism. But we also saw the crucial fact that no open theist claims a complete commitment to process theism in all its forms. All of them clearly distinguish themselves from process theists at several crucial points. The point is that open theists are intentionally selective in their commitment to elements of the process understanding of God. But if this is true of open theists, it is equally the case with classically oriented nonopenness theologians. They are equally selective in their appropriations of Greek concepts and categories represented in the classical tradition. And surely this raises the possibility that the

primary influence on the exhaustive view of the extent of divine foreknowledge that they affirm is not an uncritical acceptance of Hellenistic thinking.

The point of all six considerations taken together is that the argument for exhaustive divine foreknowledge presented in this volume must be considered on its own merits. It would be naive, to be sure, to say that preconceptions based on philosophical influences have no part to play in the way I interpret biblical texts. But it would be equally naive to say that these philosophical influences are the dominant and necessarily distorting influence on these views.

IS THE FUTURE PARTIALLY FIXED AND PARTIALLY OPEN?

In his book *God of the Possible,* Gregory Boyd says that the open view embraces the idea that the future is "*partly* determined and foreknown by God, but also partly *open* and known by God as such."[69] In the teaching of Scripture, Boyd sees two complimentary motifs, a "motif of future determinism" and a "motif of future openness."[70] He rejects "the classical view of divine foreknowledge" in which the motif of future determinism is understood to describe God as he truly is, while the motif of future openness speaks about God only figuratively, as he appears to us.[71] Rather, Boyd regards both motifs to be

> equally descriptive of the way God and the future actually are. On this basis, I arrive at the conclusion that the future is to some degree *settled* and known by God as such, and to some degree *open* and known by God as such. To some extent, God knows the future as *definitely* this way and *definitely* not that way. To some extent, however, he knows it as *possibly* this way and *possibly* not that way.[72]

Thus neither passages that describe the future as fixed and determined (and thus infallibly foreknown by God) nor passages that describe the future as open and indeterminate (and hence incapable of being foreknown with infallible certainty) are universal in their extent. Rather each passage is situationally specific.[73]

Sanders agrees with Boyd and says that the open view

> can explain both scriptural passages in which the future is sometimes definite and passages in which it is indefinite, even for God. Texts indicating that a future event

---

[69]Boyd, *God of the Possible*, p. 11.
[70]Ibid., p. 13.
[71]Ibid., p. 14.
[72]Ibid., p. 15.
[73]"The motif of future determinism does not warrant the conclusion that God predestines and foreknows as settled *everything* about the future. . . . Balancing the determined aspects of the future is a realm composed of open possibilities that will be resolved only by the decisions of free agents" (ibid., pp. 53-54).

is definite suggest that either the event is determined by God to happen that way or God knows that the event will result from a chain of causal factors that are presently in place. Passages in which God does not know the future indicate that God has not decided what will be. The matter is open for both God and creatures. Both sets of texts have straightforward explanations.[74]

Thus, for example, we saw in chapter two that open theists interpret Isaiah 46:9-11, which predicts the future liberating ministry of Cyrus, as a reference to a specific situation that God was pleased to determine in advance, apart from the decisions of his creatures (see pp. 53, 64-65). This then is the reason God could foreknow and predict Cyrus and the liberation of the Jews from Babylon he would bring about. But we should not universalize Isaiah 46:9-11 and its claim about the extent of God's foreknowledge.

How should we evaluate this claim? Is it the best way to put together all the biblical data? Let me suggest five reasons why I do not believe this is the case.

A straightforward reading of omniscience texts. Many biblical texts speak of God's knowledge in very universal terms. For example, God's knowledge is described in Scripture as being perfect (Job 37:16), vast (Ps 139:17-18), limitless (Ps 147:5) and all-encompassing (1 Jn 3:20). These are the kind of texts that have led Christians from every tradition to understand God as being omniscient. Open theists are quick to agree and to affirm God's omniscience. But, employing a parallel with God's omnipotence, they affirm that God's omniscience means that he knows truly everything that is logically possible to know.[75] This, I believe, is a helpful definition and is also affirmed by nonopenness theologians such as Millard Erickson.[76] But open theists differ from their nonopenness counterparts by arguing that future free decisions are not logically possible to know, even by God, because they do not yet exist as definite certainties but only as possibilities. Thus, according to the open view, future free decisions and any future events that are causally dependent in any way on free decisions make up that portion of the future that is open and thus known by God only in terms of possibilities.

But biblical evidence put forward in support of the open portion of the future does not consist of clear, explicit statements of God's lack of certain and infallible foreknowledge. Rather this limitation on God's knowledge of the future is

---

[74]Sanders, *God Who Risks,* p. 75. Sanders credits this insight to Boyd (ibid., p. 297, n. 136).

[75]Pinnock, "Systematic Theology," pp. 121-23; Rice, *God's Foreknowledge and Man's Free Will,* p. 128; Sanders, *God Who Risks,* p. 199; Hasker, *God, Time, and Knowledge,* p. 73; Richard Swinburne, *Coherence of Theism,* rev. ed. (Oxford: Clarendon Press, 1993), p. 180.

[76]Erickson defines God's omniscience as his "ability to know all things that are proper objects of knowledge" (*God the Father Almighty,* p. 184).

inferred from biblical statements about God's repentance, his surprise, his disappointment and so forth. Inferential arguments are not necessarily wrong, and open theists are certainly not alone in using them (think of inferential arguments for the Trinity). But inferential evidence does differ from clear and explicit teaching. And in the absence of clear and explicit biblical teaching on the existence of a certain portion of the future that God does not know certainly and infallibly, the open interpretation is not the most natural, straightforward way to understand the omniscience texts.[77] Unless we are required by clear biblical teaching to believe the contrary, these texts most normally would lead us to believe that God's knowledge extends to all of the future and not only to the portion of the future which God decides to determine.[78]

The absence of clear, explicit biblical teaching of an open, unknowable future. I have argued that Scripture does not in fact provide us with clear and explicit teaching that a portion of the future is unknowable to God because he has decided to leave it open and undetermined. In chapter four I noted that the biblical texts most often claimed to teach an open view of the future do not in fact require God's foreknowledge to be restricted in its scope.

For example, none of the divine repentance texts explicitly teach God's ignorance of future free decisions. Rather that is an openness inference from the analogy that exists between divine and human repentance, based on understanding that the relationship of knowledge to repentance to be an area of similarity between these two kinds of repentance. But since divine repentance texts (along with divine knowledge texts and indeed to one extent or another all of Scripture) are anthropomorphic metaphors, the divine reality to which they refer has differences as well as similarities as compared with its human counterpart. Thus there cannot be an automatic assumption that if genuine human repentance is inconceivable with full foreknowledge, the same must necessarily be true of genuine divine repentance. Rather, we must look at the whole revelation of God in Scripture to determine where the similarities and where the differ-

---

[77]Remember, open theists regularly appeal to the natural, straightforward reading of biblical texts, as opposed to the reading of classical theists which, they argue, has been shaped and distorted by philosophical presuppositions. See, for example, Boyd's comments on Gen 22:12 (*God of the Possible*, pp. 86-97). But the goal of a natural, straightforward reading of the text must also operate with regard to these omniscience texts—especially in light of the absence of texts that clearly teach that there is a portion of the future which God does not and cannot know.

[78]Boyd makes it clear that ultimately it is God's decision that determines which part of the future is open and which is determined and fixed. "The open view concludes that the future is literally settled to whatever extent that God wants to settle it, and literally open to the extent that God desires to leave it open to be resolved by the decisions of his creatures" (*God of the Possible*, p. 54).

ences are. And I have argued that in light of the massive biblical testimony to God's foreknowledge of free human decisions (as described in chaps. 2-3), it is most consistent with all of Scripture to understand the relationship of God's repentance to his foreknowledge to be one of the areas of difference. If God truly does not repent as humans do (as Num 23:19, 1 Sam 15:29 and Hos 11:8-9 teach), then his repentance is not inconsistent with his full and exhaustive foreknowledge of free human decisions.

And I have argued that the same kind of reasoning holds for other openness texts as well. None of them demand a less-than-exhaustive view of God's foreknowledge.

But if this is true, then the clear teaching of Scripture does not require us to affirm Boyd's position of a partially definite, partially open future. Boyd's vision may be supported by inferential arguments from Scripture, but he cannot claim that it is explicitly taught by Scripture.

How can the open God know the definite portion of the future? If the openness claim is that a part of the future is definite and fixed and thus foreknown by God, we must ask how the God of open theism can know this portion of the future. We have seen that Sanders gives two possible ways. God can foreknow a particular event either because he has determined it independent of any creaturely decision or because God knows that the event will result from a chain of present and past causal factors.[79] Two questions must be asked to evaluate how coherent this proposal actually is.

First, how much of the future is fixed because of either of these two reasons? In other words, how much of the future does God foreknow? Both Boyd and Rice argue that these two categories of future events that God can and does foreknow may well include the vast majority of all that will happen in the future.[80] But on the contrary, I would argue that, given the central theological assumptions of open theism, God's foreknowledge does not embrace the vast majority of the future.

---

[79]Sanders writes, "Texts indicating that a future event is definite suggest that either the event is determined by God to happen in that way or God knows the event will result from a chain of causal factors that are presently in place" (*God Who Risks*, p. 75). Richard Rice had earlier expressed the view this way: "Possessing exhaustive knowledge of the past, God therefore knows all that will happen as the result of factors already in existence. In other words, God knows infallibly (or foreknows absolutely) all the future consequences of the past and the present. . . . [In addition, God infallibly foreknows] divine decisions that are not dependent upon circumstances in the creaturely world but arise solely from God's personal decision" (*God's Foreknowledge and Man's Free Will*, pp. 55-56).

[80]Rice, *God's Foreknowledge and Man's Free Will*, p. 55. Boyd made this claim in a lecture titled "Does God Know the Future?" given at Northwestern College, St. Paul, Minn., January 15, 1998.

For example, according to open theism God can have definite and infallible knowledge of future events that flow from causal factors currently in place. But this is true only if it is impossible for these future events to be interfered with by the free choices of human (or angelic) beings. Otherwise God's knowledge would necessarily have to be of probabilities only. Consider the following example: God could infallibly foreknow the temperature in front of the Sears Tower in downtown Chicago at 3:00 p.m. CDT on July 21, 2025, only if it is impossible for any free human decision(s) to affect the temperature. But if one or more free decisions could affect the temperature in Chicago on that day (e.g., decisions about how much to drive automobiles, decisions relating to the possible development of vehicles that do not burn fossil fuels, etc.), then God cannot infallibly know this aspect of the future. The God of open theism cannot infallibly know whether human beings will freely choose to do or to refrain from doing those activities that would impact the temperature in the future. The point is that as long as the *possibility* exists of a future free decision affecting a future event in any way, God cannot definitely and infallibly know that future event.

And when the reality of God and his free choices is brought into the picture, things get even more complicated. Richard Swinburne argues that because of the libertarian nature of God's own freedom, he cannot infallibly know what he himself will choose to do in the future.[81] His view is controversial, but even apart from the implications of God's freedom, openness convictions that God is genuinely responsive to human beings and that he can unilaterally intervene in human history, if necessary, are sufficient to cast doubt on the basis of God's knowledge of many, if not most, of these future events.[82]

Think once again about future events that God knows will flow out of present and past causal factors: Might not future circumstances, affected by freely chosen actions of human and angelic beings, be such that God would decide to intervene miraculously to change what otherwise would have happened? If the possibility of God's intervention to change climate conditions or any decision or action or event in human history exists, then God in principle cannot foreknow such events infallibly.

And the same question holds for future events that God himself will cause.

---

[81]Swinburne concludes "that it seems doubtful whether it is logically possible that there be both an omniscient person and also free men; but that it is definitely logically impossible that there be an omniscient person who is himself perfectly free" (*Coherence of Theism,* p. 177).

[82]The controversial nature of Swinburne's position is evidenced by the conviction of open theists like Rice, Sanders and Boyd that God can know at least some of what he will do in the future.

Is it not possible that future freely chosen actions would move God to change his mind and do something other than what he originally intended to do? If that possibility exists—and it is hard to see how it could not, given openness interpretations of God's repentance in response to human sin (as at the time of the flood [Gen 6:6]) or to human repentance (as in the case of Nineveh [Jon 3]) or to human intercession (as in the cases of Moses in Ex 32 and Hezekiah in Is 38)—then in principle it is impossible for God to know his own future actions definitely and infallibly. God's present intention to do something is not enough in and of itself to ground his certain knowledge of his own future actions. The possibility always exists that one or more future free actions (that by definition are unknowable in advance) could move a genuinely responsive God to change his mind. To argue that God cannot change his mind in these instances would require that he be locked into a particular course of action. That would undermine the freedom of God to change his mind and the genuinely responsive nature of his relationship to humans. In addition, it would also undermine the wisdom of God, for it would involve him making unchangeable decisions now, without taking into account the possibility of new and relevant information that, under openness assumptions, he could only learn in the future. This hardly seems to be a description of the all-wise God of Scripture.

In light of these realities, Greg Gannsle argues that the only kind of future events that the God of open theism could infallibly foreknow are those that are theologically necessary (sufficiently related to God's essential nature such that were he not to perform such an action, it would constitute a violation of his essential and necessary nature) or otherwise logically or metaphysically necessary.[83] This certainly confirms the conclusion that we must draw: Given the central theological tenants of open theism, God's foreknowledge does not embrace the vast majority of the future.

Second, we must ask, How is it possible for the God of open theism to

---

[83]Gannsle includes as theologically necessary those actions that God has specifically promised. Faithfulness to his promises is a necessary part of his divine character. Thus if God has specifically promised to carry out a particular action, that action, by virtue of his promise, becomes theologically necessary ("God's Knowledge of the Future," presented at the Evangelical Theological Society Annual Meeting, Danvers, Mass., November 18, 1999). Richard L. Pratt argues that these promises rise to this level of certainty only when they do not contain any expressed or unexpressed conditions. Specifically he sees predictions accompanied by a divine oath to be in this category. Particularly significant are divine oaths in the form "As Yahweh lives . . ." or "As I live . . ." Pratt argues that these promises, and these alone, rise "to the level of covenantal certainty" ("Historical Contingencies and Biblical Predictions," presidential inaugural address presented to the faculty of Reformed Theological Seminary, November 23, 1993, p. 17).

know the portions of the future (however large or small) that are definite and fixed? Specifically, how consistent are the two ways God can know particular events in the future with the central doctrinal beliefs of open theism? I believe that the larger the percentage of the future that is fixed for either of these two reasons (and thus able to be foreknown by God), the more problematic this is for the central openness doctrines of libertarian human freedom and the genuine responsiveness of God to his human creation. And the smaller the percentage of the future that is fixed and foreknown, the less this account fits the massive biblical testimony to God's foreknowledge that we find in Scripture.

Remember, according to Sanders and other open theists, if any portion of the future is fixed, it is so either because God has so determined those future events or because they are the certain result of present and past factors. In neither case does libertarian freedom function, because this kind of freedom demands the ability to choose differently in exactly the same circumstances. Anything that would render future human decisions certain, whether it is God himself or some nondivine but presently existing causal factor(s), is incompatible with libertarian freedom. But if human decision-makers remain free in the libertarian sense, their future decisions are not certain, and thus they cannot be a part of the fixed, determined future that is foreknown by God. Thus if God has decided to overrule libertarian freedom in a large number of cases so as to render a significant portion of the future determined and fixed, the centrality of God's respect for the gift of libertarian freedom that he has endowed his human image bearers with is compromised. Equally so, in this large number of cases human decision-makers, who lack libertarian freedom because God has chosen to override it, are no longer morally responsible for a large number of their decisions. And in addition, the more of the future that is fixed and definitely foreknown by God and therefore unchangeable, the less opportunity there is for God to be genuinely responsive to his people in an authentic give-and-take relationship, as open theists would understand such a relationship. For if God has fixed large portions of the future unchangeably, then there exists no possibility that the free actions of human beings could cause God to change his mind about these things. For openness advocates this is the very kind of thing that calls into question the authenticity of the relationship between God and his people.

Thus there are serious problems if we affirm that the God of open theism has in fact fixed a large portion of the future so that he could foreknow it with definite certainty. But if, on the other hand, only a very small portion of the future is considered fixed, how can we account for the reality of such vast biblical testimony to God's foreknowledge?

Predictive prophecies about free human decisions. Much of this biblical testimony to God's foreknowledge of free human actions involves predictive
prophecies. We have surveyed some of this testimony in chapters two and three
(e.g., the fourteen examples of the promise-fulfillment motif in 1-2 Kings that
specifically deal with free human decisions, the prophecies of Cyrus and more
generally the "things to come" in Is 40—48, messianic prophecies like Mic 5:2
and Ps 22:18, Jesus' predictions of his own suffering, death and resurrection, and
Jesus' predictions of Peter's denial and Judas' betrayal).

One of the striking things about these predictive prophecies is the wide
range of human activities that they predict. Some of the events predicted are
central to redemptive history (e.g., the exodus, Cyrus' decision to allow the Jews
to leave captivity and return to Jerusalem, the birth and death of Jesus Christ,
etc.). Because these events are so central and so crucial, it would not be surprising if God wanted to take special, extraordinary measures to render them fixed
and certain to occur. Yet even in these cases, specific details are predicted that
do not seem absolutely necessary to accomplish the purposes of these events
in redemptive history (e.g., the number of years of the Jews' slavery in Egypt
[Gen 15:13-14]; the exact name of Cyrus [Is 44:28, 45:1]; that the location of the
house where Jesus would celebrate the Last Supper with his disciples would be
identified by a man, who, contrary to prevailing social custom, would be carrying a jar of water [Lk 22:10-11]; that Peter would deny Christ three times and not
two or four [Mt 26:33-35, 69-74]).

But other events predicted in Scripture are far smaller and far more ordinary.
These include the precise name Josiah's parents would choose to give their son
(1 Kings 13:2); that Jereboam's wife, pretending to be someone else, would
come to Ahijah to inquire about her sick son (1 Kings 14:5); the exact price
charged for a seah of flour (2 Kings 7:1); and the specific locations of the deaths
of Ahab (1 Kings 21:19) and Jezebel (2 Kings 9:10). There would seem to be
little reason for God to overrule libertarian freedom in these relatively insignificant cases.

The implications of this vast quantity and diversity of predictive prophecies
are staggering. If all the human decisions foretold by these predictive prophecies are part of the fixed portion of the future, then the role of libertarian freedom in human life and decision making seems to be severely limited. Huge
numbers of human decisions would not be free in the libertarian sense, and this
would go against the crucial importance of such freedom in open theism. But
if these predicted events are indeed free, then we must affirm that in principle,
at least, it is possible for God to foreknow future free actions. If he can predict

them, he must foreknow them.[84] And if this is true, a major reason for wanting to posit a partially fixed, partially open future is eliminated. Human freedom would not necessarily be eliminated by God's foreknowledge of decisions made with that freedom. But this also would violate a central tenet of open theism, which is uniformly incompatibilistic when it comes to the relationship of exhaustive divine foreknowledge and libertarian human freedom. And finally, if we account for the freedom of these predicted actions by affirming that it is in fact a compatibilistic freedom, then we have no problems with God's foreknowledge. But once again, we are outside the bounds of open theism.

The point of this discussion is, I trust, very clear. The massive biblical phenomenon of predictive prophecy is very hard to account for given the openness commitment to libertarian human freedom and its perceived incompatibility with exhaustive divine foreknowledge.

The use Scripture makes of God's foreknowledge of free human decisions. Finally we must consider the use that Scripture makes of God's ability to know and predict future free actions. In Isaiah 40—48 Yahweh repeatedly appeals to his foreknowledge, especially his foreknowledge of Cyrus, to demonstrate his absolute and unique deity as compared to the pagan gods of the surrounding nations. Jesus makes a similar claim in John 13:19, where he appeals to his predictions of Peter's denial and Judas's betrayal to ground his disciples' belief that "I am he." Now if we adopt Boyd's partially fixed and partially open framework, we would have to affirm that Yahweh in Isaiah and Jesus in John 13 appealed to the divine foreknowledge of only the portion of the future that is fixed and therefore foreknowable. That is certainly possible. But it does seem highly unlikely that Yahweh and Jesus would stake so much (the proof of their "God-ness") on an ability that they would possess only a portion of the time. If God cannot foreknow future free events that are in any way dependent on free human actions or possible free human actions, then he can have certain foreknowledge of only a small amount of the future. Therefore his predictions could be counted on absolutely only very rarely. Yet it is this very ability that Yahweh in Isaiah 40—48 and Jesus in John 13 appeal to as the ultimate proof of their divine nature. How much more likely would it be that this ability that Yahweh and Jesus appeal to is one that they possess absolutely and exhaustively? Thus it is not only the quantity, diversity and the specificity of the predictive proph-

---

[84]Unless, of course, these "predictions" are merely probabilistic forecasts based on God's knowledge of the past and present—forecasts that could be mistaken (e.g., Jer 3:6-7, 19-20). But it is hard to see how probabilistic forecasts can function in the way that predictive prophecies do.

ecies of Scripture but also the use that Yahweh and Jesus make of them that poses serious problems for Boyd's partially fixed and partially open view of the future and of God's foreknowledge.

CONCLUSION

The preceding five reasons, when taken together, combine to argue that the partially fixed and partially open hypothesis is an inadequate way to account for the biblical data. The scriptural testimony, taken as a whole, does not require us to posit a portion of the future that has been left open by God and thus is unforeknowable by him. And there is abundant positive biblical evidence, particularly in the area of predictive prophecies, that argues for God's foreknowledge of free human decisions. And if God foreknows some free human decisions, why can't he know them all? In the absence of clear and explicit biblical teaching to the contrary, the view that God's foreknowledge is indeed exhaustive, including and embracing all free human decisions, is the best model to explain all the biblical data.

6

PRACTICAL IMPLICATIONS

Throughout this book I have been trying to make the case that a view of God's foreknowledge in which he foreknows free human decisions completely and with certainty is the theological model that best accords with the data of Scripture. But as we conclude, it is very appropriate to ask the "so what" question. What difference does it make to Christian life and ministry if God's foreknowledge is in fact exhaustive? In other words, we turn our attention now to the adequacy criterion for assessing a theological model. Is the model of exhaustive divine foreknowledge truly adequate to meet the demands of life and ministry?

It is in the realm of practical implications that open theists argue their model shines the brightest. Pinnock, for example, argues that "the open view of God possesses strong practical appeal and close existential fit." As such, it "describes our experience so admirably, whether or not we consent to it intellectually, that it commends itself on that basis."[1]

My contention, however, is just the opposite. In this chapter we will look at five areas of crucial importance in the Christian life: (1) worship (2) prayer, (3) God's guidance, (4) suffering and the problem of evil, and (5) hope in the ultimate and final triumph of God and his kingdom. In each of these areas, I will seek to show that an exhaustive understanding of God's foreknowledge leads to Christian experience that is more in accord with biblical teaching and biblical expectations than its nonexhaustive alternative. In short, exhaustive divine foreknowledge, not the openness view of presentism, passes the adequacy test most successfully.

It must be said that our comparison of the practical life impact of these two views of divine foreknowledge will necessarily involve other elements of their respective theological positions. In our examination, therefore, we will be looking at how the open position as a whole functions, as well as how various positions that embrace exhaustive divine foreknowledge function. The differences

---

[1]Clark H. Pinnock, *Most Moved Mover* (Grand Rapids: Baker, 2001), p. 154.

in these positions come from various explanations of how God knows the future exhaustively and from the impact of other theological factors (e.g., varying views of the function of divine sovereignty, divine omnipotence, etc.). While it is not the purpose of this chapter nor of this book as a whole to deal thoroughly with these differences, where they affect the practical functioning of exhaustive divine foreknowledge, they will be noted in the discussion that follows.

WORSHIP

We begin our discussion of the practical implications of the extent of divine foreknowledge by looking at our privilege and responsibility as Christians to worship God. This is an appropriate place to begin because I believe that worship is of supreme importance in the Christian life.[2] Whether we consider (1) what Jesus says to be the greatest commandment in all the law of God ("Love the Lord your God with all your heart and with all your soul and with all your mind" [Mt 22:37]); or (2) Paul's description of spiritual worship as involving the offering of our bodies as living sacrifices to God (Rom 12:1), which involves the commitment of all of ourselves and all of our lives to God; or (3) the reality that the eternal business of heaven is worship offered "to him who sits on the throne and to the Lamb" (Rev 5:13) and that in the Lord's Prayer, Jesus commands us to pray that God's will be done on earth as it is in heaven (Mt 6:10); or (4) that worship is understood to be the primary goal of God's gracious redemption in both the Old and the New Testaments—the point is clear.[3] Worship matters to God. It matters to him supremely. And so it must be equally important to us as his people.

---

[2]Worship in the broadest sense of the term embraces the whole of the life of God's people in loving him both individually and corporately. It is tied up with all our conscious efforts to love God, to honor him, to ascribe glory to him and praise him. Thus we must say that worship is of supreme importance to God. And so it should be to us.

[3]Regarding (2) David Peterson describes the worship of Rom 12:1 as "a whole-person commitment lived out in daily existence" (*Engaging with God* [Downers Grove, Ill.: InterVarsity Press, 1992], p. 177). Thomas Schreiner describes it as "the yielding of one's whole life to God in the concrete reality of everyday existence" (*Romans*, Baker Exegetical Commentary on the New Testament [Grand Rapids: Baker, 1998], p. 646).

Regarding (3) the most prominent New Testament verb for worship, *proskuneō*, is used more times in the book of Revelation (24) than in any other New Testament book. Whether it is the angelic worship of God as the three times holy Creator in Revelation 4 or the angelic worship of Jesus Christ, the Lion of the tribe of Judah who is at the same time the Lamb who was slain in Revelation 5; whether it is the priestly service or worship (the other key New Testament worship verb—*latreuō*) of the innumerable multitude, redeemed by Christ from every tribe and language and people and nation who day and night cry out "Salvation belongs to our God who sits on the throne, and to the Lamb" (Rev 7:10); or whether it is the eschatological vision of the redeemed in the New Jerusalem in which "the throne of God and of the Lamb will be in the city and his servants will serve *(latreuō)* him" (Rev 22:3)—the point is clear. The agenda of heaven is above all else the worship of God. And if we are commanded by Jesus to pray that

This means that anything that enhances our genuine worship of God must be embraced. And equally so, anything that diminishes our worship must be modified or rejected. We turn our attention now to two considerations, which will help us see which view of divine foreknowledge will in fact enhance our lives of worship as Christian people.

Worship and the greatness of God. The worship that God repeatedly commands of his people (e.g., 1 Chron 16:29; Ps 96:7; 100:2; Mt 4:10; Rev 19:10; 22:9) is a proper response to him because of the greatness and glory of his character. Often Scripture makes explicit links between the command to worship God and his greatness. For example, Psalm 29 calls on God's people to "ascribe to the LORD the glory due his name; / worship the LORD in the splendor of his holiness." (Ps 29:2). It is right for God's people to ascribe to him the "glory due his name," since God's glory is a reflection of all that he is and all that he does. When the text goes on to exhort the people of God to "worship the LORD in the splendor of his holi-

---

God's will would be done by us here on earth as it is done in heaven, there is an agenda set out for us. Worship needs to be the focus of our prayers and our lives here on earth, even as it will be forever and ever in heaven.

Regarding (4) when Yahweh called Moses to go to Pharaoh and bring the Israelites out of bondage in Egypt, he said, "This will be the sign to you that it is I who have sent you: When you have brought the people out of Egypt, you will worship God on this mountain" (Ex 3:12). In Ex 4:22-23, Yahweh specifically instructed Moses to say to Pharaoh, "This is what the LORD says: Israel is my firstborn son, . . . 'Let my son go, so he may worship me.' " And seven times in his ongoing interaction with Pharaoh, Moses confronted Pharaoh with Yahweh's demand: "Let my people go so that they may worship me" (Ex 7:16; 8:1, 20; 9:1, 13; 10:3, 25-26). In each case the Hebrew verb *ʿābad* is used, the verb translated in the LXX by *latreuō*. And after the Exodus, at Mt. Sinai, just prior to the giving of the ten commandments, Yahweh said to Israel, "You yourselves have seen what I did to Egypt, and how I carried you on eagles' wings and brought you to myself. Now if you obey me fully and keep my covenant, then out of all nations you will be my treasured possession. Although the whole earth is mine, you will be for me a kingdom of priests and a holy nation" (Ex 19:4-6). God's purpose was that the whole nation of Israel would honor and worship him as a kingdom of priests. Peterson says Israel's "engagement with God at Sinai was to inaugurate a total life-pattern of worship or service for the nation" (*Engaging with God,* p. 28). The point is clear: God redeemed his people that they might worship him.

And again we turn to the book of Revelation. The doxology in Rev 1:5-6 says, "To him who loves us and has freed us from our sins by his blood, and has made us to be a kingdom and priests to serve his God and Father—to him be glory and power for ever and ever! Amen." (The verb *latreuō* is not used in this verse; the NIV and NRSV insert the English verb *serve* to try make explicit what it means for Christians to be priests to our God because Christ has freed us from our sins by his blood. [Cf. the similar insertion in Rev 5:10].) But *latreuō* is used in Rev 7:15 and in Rev 22:3 to describe the ultimate and eternal vocation of those redeemed by Jesus Christ in the New Jerusalem. John's point is clear: the priestly service/worship of God is the goal of Christ's redeeming work. What was promised to Israel at Sinai has been fulfilled in the eschatological assembly of the people of God from every nation, tribe, people and language. As in the Old Testament, so in the New, redemption is for the purpose of worship or service to God. See Peterson, *Engaging with God,* pp. 267-68.

ness," the thought is that we who belong to God are to worship him in the radiant splendor of everything that makes him God. It is his absolutely unique "Godness," in other words his holiness, that makes God alone worthy of our worship. Or as Psalm 145 notes, it is because of God's unfathomable greatness, or "the glorious splendor of your majesty" that God is worthy to be praised (Ps 145:5).[4]

This is precisely the way God's knowledge is described in Scripture. God's matchless and limitless knowledge (including his exhaustive knowledge of the future) is an essential element of his greatness. "Great is the LORD and mighty in power; / his understanding has no limit" (Ps 147:5). Thus if God's greatness is to ground and to motivate our worship, the limitlessness of his knowledge and understanding should be part of our worship. Indeed the all-encompassing nature of God's knowledge is one of those realities that makes him greater than we are ("God is greater than our hearts, and he knows everything" [1 Jn 3:20]).

But it is at this very point that open theists propose a different understanding. Gregory Boyd in particular takes great pains to affirm that the openness model presents a God who is far greater and far more glorious than he is under a classical model. He argues that God's decision to limit his knowledge of the future by creating a world populated with creatures possessing the gift of libertarian freedom actually enhances the display of his wisdom and intelligence. A God who knows much of the future only in terms of possibilities and responds to it as such actually displays far more wisdom and far more intelligence than a God who possesses exhaustive foreknowledge.

> We might imagine God as something like an infinitely intelligent chess player. . . .
> God's perfect knowledge would allow him to anticipate *every* possible move and
> *every* possible combination of moves, together with *every* possible response he

---

[4]The greatness of God is regularly seen in his work of creation. As our creator, God is worthy of our worship. Because he made us, we rightly belong to him and ought to worship him. This can be seen in the Old Testament (e.g., Ps 95:6-7; 100:2-3) and in the New Testament (supremely in Rev 4:10-11, where the twenty-four elders worship him who lives forever, saying "You are worthy, our Lord and God, / to receive glory and honor and power, / for you created all things, / and by your will they were created / and have their being"). God's greatness is seen in even more radiant glory in his work as Redeemer. Thus the worship of God the Creator in Rev 4 gives way to the worship of Christ the Redeemer in Rev 5. Jesus Christ, who is simultaneously "the Lion of the tribe of Judah," the victorious messianic warrior, and the sacrificial Lamb of God who has been slain (Rev 5:5-6), is worshiped by the four living creatures and the twenty-four elders. "You are worthy to take the scroll / and to open its seals, / because you were slain / and with your blood you purchased men for God / from every tribe and language and people and nation. / You have made them to be a kingdom and priests to serve our God, / and they will reign on the earth" (Rev 5:9-10). On the link between worship and the greatness of God, see Carson, "Worship Under the Word," in *Worship by the Book*, ed. D. A. Carson (Grand Rapids: Zondervan, 2002), pp. 28-29.

might make to each of them, for *every* possible agent throughout history. And he would be able to do this from eternity past.

Isn't a God who is able to know perfectly these possibilities wiser than a God who simply foreknows or predetermines one story line that the future will follow? And isn't a God who perfectly anticipates and wisely responds to everything a free agent *might* do more intelligent than a God who simply knows what a free agent *will* do? . . . Why, then, should we regard a God who knows all that *will* happen to be wiser than a God who can perfectly anticipate and respond to all that *might* happen.[5]

Equally so, God's sovereignty over a future that is partly definite and partly open is in fact greater and more glorious than it would be had God decided to exercise total control over absolutely everything that happens.

> God is so confident in his sovereignty, we [open theists] hold, he does not need to micromanage everything. He could if he wanted to, but this would demean his sovereignty. So he chooses to leave some of the future open to possibilities, allowing them to be resolved by the decisions of free agents. It takes a greater God to steer a world populated with free agents than it does to steer a world of preprogrammed automatons.[6]
>
> God is *so* wise, resourceful, and sovereign over history that he doesn't need or want to have everything in the future settled ahead of time. He is *so* confident in his power and wisdom that he is willing to grant an appropriate degree of freedom to humans (and angels) to determine their own futures. . . . The true God is far wiser, far more powerful, and far more secure than we could ever imagine.[7]

I appreciate the spiritual instinct behind these statements from Boyd. I share with him the realization that the God we worship is indeed infinitely and incomparably great. And I agree that it is precisely that greatness that moves us to worship him. So if the open God of nonexhaustive foreknowledge really is greater and more glorious than the God who possesses exhaustive foreknowledge, then we ought to adopt the open view. For its enhanced understanding of the greatness of God would indeed be a strong argument for it as a preferable theological model.

---

[5]Gregory A. Boyd, *God of the Possible* (Grand Rapids: Baker, 2000), pp. 127-28.
[6]Ibid., p. 31.
[7]Ibid., p. 68. Consider as well one more statement from Boyd: "It takes a truly self-confident, sovereign God to make himself vulnerable. It takes a God who is truly in authority to give away some of his control, knowing that doing so might cause him incredible pain. By contrast, to simply control others so that you always get your way is the surest sign of insecurity and weakness. . . . How much more glorious is the portrait of a God who chooses to create a cosmos populated with free agents" (ibid., pp. 149-50).

But I suggest that our assessment of how these competing models of the extent of the foreknowledge of God enhance or diminish the greatness and glory of God cannot be determined by our own sense of what greatness might look like. Rather, it must be determined by biblical teaching about the extent of God's foreknowledge and how that foreknowledge relates to God's greatness and glory.

Throughout this volume I have argued that Scripture teaches the exhaustive foreknowledge of God widely and pervasively. And God explicitly connects his foreknowledge of free human decisions with his own unique divine glory. Throughout Isaiah 40—48 Yahweh repeatedly cites his ability to foreknow and predict the free actions of human beings (particularly those of Cyrus) as the distinguishing characteristic of his divine glory. To demonstrate that he alone is the true and living God, as opposed to the gods of the surrounding nations, Yahweh appeals to his exhaustive foreknowledge. And Jesus cites his ability to predict the free actions of both Judas and Peter before they happen in order to ground the faith of his disciples that "I am he" (Jn 13:19). It is these biblical teachings rather than our conceptions of what might or might not be greater that must rule our thinking. It is the truth of God's revealed Word that must shape our thinking about the nature of his greatness. I have argued that biblical teaching does indeed teach the truth of exhaustive divine foreknowledge and that this is an essential part of his greatness and glory. These biblical truths are essential for our worship because of a second consideration, to which we turn our attention now.

Worship and the truth of God. Central to biblical teaching on the issue of worship are the words Jesus spoke to the Samaritan woman at the well. After she had raised the issue of the religious controversy between Samaritans and Jews over the proper place of worship (Mt. Gerazim and the temple in Jerusalem, respectively), Jesus responds in John 4:21-24:

> Believe me, woman, a time is coming when you will worship the Father neither on this mountain nor in Jerusalem. You Samaritans worship what you do not know; we worship what we do know, for salvation is from the Jews. Yet a time is coming and has now come when the true worshipers will worship the Father in spirit and truth, for they are the kind of worshipers the Father seeks. God is spirit, and his worshipers must worship in spirit and in truth.

Jesus reinterprets the crucial importance in the law of a centralized worship location, saying that far more important than geography is worship in spirit and truth. And the time for this transition is coming "and has now come"—precisely because Jesus himself has come.[8] Jesus' coming and in particular his death, resurrection, exaltation and the giving of his Spirit is what enables the kind of true worship that the Father seeks, worship "in spirit and in truth."[9] Thus the true worship that the Father seeks is Christ-centered—worshiping in his Spirit and in his truth.[10] If we are truly to worship the Father, we must worship by means of Christ, who is the truth (Jn 14:6) and who pours out his Spirit upon his followers (Jn 1:33; 14:16; 16:7).[11]

A crucial point for our discussion comes from the relationship between worship and God's truth embodied and incarnated in Jesus Christ. If the worship the Father seeks must be in spirit and *truth,* then we cannot ignore issues of truth as we come to worship. Jesus says that the God we worship is indeed Spirit (Jn 4:24), invisible and unknowable unless he chooses to reveal himself.[12] And he has revealed himself through his prophets, his written Word and supremely through his incarnate Word, the Lord Jesus Christ (Jn 1:14, 18). Thus our worship of God must be built on the foundation of the truth he has revealed about him-

---

[8]Jesus' reference to the "time" (lit., "hour" *[hōra]*) is an eschatological marker. The term is most often associated in the Gospel of John with Jesus' glorification on the cross. Yet D. A. Carson notes that this era of true worship in spirit and truth is present proleptically before the cross in the person and ministry of Jesus (*The Gospel According to John* [Grand Rapids: Eerdmans, 1991], p. 224).

[9]The fact that there is only one preposition (*en*—"in") governing both "spirit" and "truth" in John 4:23-24 shows that the two terms are meant to be considered together.

[10]The entire passage has a christological focus. It is Christ's hour that has come, inaugurating the era of true worship in spirit and truth and he identifies himself to the Samaritan woman as the Messiah (Jn 4:25-26). This Christocentric focus is in line with the consistent identification throughout the Fourth Gospel of Jesus as the *true* vine, the *true* manna, the *true* Shepherd, the *true* temple, the *true* Son. See D. A. Carson, "Worship Under the Word," p. 37. That the Father seeks such Christ-centered worship is consistent with his stated intention "that all may honor the Son just as they honor the Father" (Jn 5:23). More broadly, this is in keeping with the whole tenor of New Testament teaching on worship under the new covenant; it is not only God-centered but Christ-centered (cf. Rev 5) and gospel-centered (see Peterson, *Engaging With God,* 98-100).

[11]John Frame argues that all Christian worship must be trinitarian: worshiping the Father in the name of Christ by the power of the Spirit (*Worship in Spirit and Truth* [Phillipsburg, N.J.: Presbyterian & Reformed, 1996], pp. 6-7). James Torrence says that Christian worship "is the gift of participating through the Spirit in the incarnate Son's communion with the Father" (*Worship, Community and the Triune God of Grace* [Downers Grove, Ill.: InterVarsity Press, 1996], p. 20). The book of Hebrews makes it clear that Christ's death enables us to draw near to the Father in worship. Christ has gone before us and opened the way into the holy of holies for us. Christ takes our worship and presents it to the Father.

[12]While Jesus' statement "God is spirit" is clearly meant to underscore the fact that God's being cannot be limited to a single physical location and so true worship of this God cannot be exclusively tied to one geographic location, the linkage of true worship of this God who is spirit to the truth he had revealed is inescapable (see Carson, *Gospel According to John,* p. 225).

self. Inadequate or diminished understandings of this truth lead to inadequate or diminished worship. Doctrinal truths matter for the issue of worship.[13]

These doctrinal truths that are crucial for truly God-honoring worship include the extent of his foreknowledge. To the extent that Jesus taught and exhibited this kind of divine foreknowledge (see the argument of chap. 3) and affirmed its crucial importance (see esp. Jn 13:19), and to the extent that this view is consistent with the teaching of the rest of Scripture (the thesis of this book), then affirming this truth, celebrating it, and honoring God for it is an important part of worshiping him in spirit and *truth*. If Scripture truly does affirm God's exhaustive and infallible foreknowledge as widely and as pervasively as I have tried to show, then we must worship God for this attribute of his as for all others. Christian people are to worship God for his greatness as revealed in the truth of his Word.

Conclusion. Worship is indeed crucial for the people of God. It is the reason we have been made by God, and it is the reason we have been redeemed in Christ. Worship will be our joyful delight throughout eternity in the new heavens and the new earth. And God desires that worship be our priority here on earth as well. Thus anything that diminishes our worship of God is a great danger to our spiritual lives, both individually and corporately. And any view of God that diminishes his infinite greatness as taught in Scripture will hinder our worship. The way we understand God is critically important.

J. I. Packer argues that while the first of the Ten Commandments prohibits the worship of false gods (Ex 20:3), the second commandment prohibits the worship of the true God by means of images (Ex 20:4-6). The reason for this prohibition, according to Packer, is that images inevitably obscure elements of God's glory, thus dishonoring him, and as a result they end up misleading people.[14] But the kind of images that in the end dishonor God and mislead his people are not only physical ones, such as the golden calf.[15] Mental images of God that are untrue to Scripture also do the same thing. They obscure the glory of God, and they end up misleading his people. A. W. Tozer speaks of this kind of idolatry:

The idolatrous heart assumes that God is other than he is—in itself a monstrous sin—

---

[13]See John Piper, *Desiring God* (Sisters, Ore.: Multnomah Publishers, 2003), pp. 81-82, 102-4.
[14]J. I. Packer, *Knowing God* (Downers Grove, Ill.: InterVarsity Press, 1973), pp. 44-47.
[15]A strong argument can be made for the fact that for Aaron, if not for all the people, the golden calf represented Yahweh (cf. Ex 32:4-5). No doubt the form of the image was chosen to represent Yahweh's great strength. But it could hardly represent omnipotence, infinite strength. And more seriously, the image of the golden calf obscured Yahweh's moral character altogether. And so it mislead the people into thinking that Yahweh was a God who could be worshiped acceptably by frenzied debauchery. And so the festival to Yahweh that Aaron proclaimed in front of the calf (Ex 32:5) became a shameful orgy (ibid., pp. 46-47).

and substitutes for the true God one made after its own likeness. . . . The essence of idolatry is the entertainment of thoughts about God that are unworthy of him. It begins in the mind and may be present where no overt act of worship has taken place.[16]

And he speaks of the great damage that comes from such a view.

Perverted notions about God soon rot the religion in which they appear. The long career of Israel demonstrates this clearly enough, and the history of the Church confirms it. So necessary to the Church is a lofty concept of God that when that concept in any measure declines, the Church with her worship and her moral standards declines along with it. The first step down for any church is taken when it surrenders its high opinion of God.[17]

The challenge, of course, is to make sure that this "lofty concept of God" is in fact biblically accurate. With respect to the lofty view of the exhaustive, definite foreknowledge of God, it has been the burden of this book to demonstrate that it is in fact biblically accurate. And therefore it will be helpful to God's people. First and foremost, it will enlarge their worship of the all-glorious God. It will contribute to their worship truly being in spirit and truth. God will be glorified, and God's people will be enriched.

PRAYER

One of the primary benefits claimed by openness proponents involves prayer, specifically petitionary prayer.[18] Indeed, they often argue that their model best accounts for the reality and efficacy of petitionary prayer. For example, Boyd says, "Because it holds that the future is *not* entirely settled and that God's plans *can* change, the open view is able to render the purpose and urgency of prayer intelligible in a way that neither classical Arminianism nor classical Calvinism can."[19]

And Pinnock argues:

In prayer the practicality of the open view of God shines. In prayer God treats us as subjects and not objects and real dialogue takes place. . . . He treats us as partners in a two-way conversation and wants our input—our gratitude, our concur-

---

[16]A. W. Tozer, *The Knowledge of the Holy* (San Francisco: Harper & Row, 1961), p. 3.

[17]Ibid., p. 4.

[18]Much of the material in this section was presented earlier in a paper I gave to the annual meeting of the Evangelical Theological Society in Colorado Springs, Colo. on Nov 16, 2001. The paper is titled "'Your Father Knows What You Need Before You Ask': The Implications of Matthew 6 for the Open View of Petitionary Prayer."

[19]Boyd, *God of the Possible*, p. 95. Note also the statement of David Basinger: "Those who affirm the open model believe the status of petitionary prayer within this model to be one of its most attractive features" ("Practical Implications," in *Openness of God* [Downers Grove, Ill.: InterVarsity Press, 1994], p. 162).

rence, our questioning, even our protests and our petitions. He enlists our input because he wants it, not because he needs it. He treats us as responsible agents with whom he has a dynamic relationship. Prayer validates the open view of God because it is so revealing of the interactive relationship.[20]

The attractiveness of the open model with respect to petitionary prayer can be seen most clearly when it is compared to those that advocate exhaustive divine foreknowledge. These models, it is argued, render petitionary prayer superfluous and irrelevant in the end. This is because of the certainty and fixity of the future that exists if God's foreknowledge is in fact exhaustive and infallible. And if God exhaustively and infallibly knows the future, he knows every prayer that will ever be lifted up to him and exactly how he will respond to that prayer. It is all part of his eternally foreknown plan. Pinnock argues that this will eliminate the relevance and the urgency of petitionary prayer.

> People pray passionately when they see purpose in it, when they think prayer can make a difference and that God may act because of it. There would not be much urgency in our praying if we thought that God's decrees could not be changed and/ or that the future is entirely settled. Then we would pray more out of obedience than hope. Why pray if nothing depends on our praying or not praying?[21]

David Basinger argues that intercessory prayer in the classical view is never truly efficacious in the sense that it is "an activity that can initiate unilateral divine activity that would not have taken place if we had not utilized our God-given power of choice to request his assistance."[22] Or, in other words, petitionary prayer in classical theism can never be truly "impetratory," defined by Sanders as "receiving something *because* one asks for it."[23]

---

[20]Pinnock, *Most Moved Mover,* pp. 171-72.

[21]Ibid., p. 172.

[22]Basinger, "Practical Implications," p. 162. Basinger does allow that classical theists who affirm not only God's exhaustive foreknowledge but also his specific sovereignty can affirm intercessory prayer to be a means God chooses to use to carry out his preordained plan, being, in the words of Pinnock, "a predestined means to a predestined end" (*Most Moved Mover,* p. 174).

[23]John Sanders, *The God Who Risks* (Downers Grove, Ill.: InterVarsity Press, 1998), p. 268. He concludes that "the God of specific sovereignty is not actually prevailed upon by prayer. God never responds to us or does anything because of our prayers because this would imply contingency in God. . . . Consequently, proponents of specific sovereignty may rightfully claim that petitionary prayer is justified because God has decreed that he would perform a certain action after the request is made. Moreover, in this model it makes sense to say that God has ordained such prayers for therapeutic benefit to those who pray as well as to those who are aware that others are praying for them. But proponents of the no-risk model cannot legitimately claim that God responds to our prayers or does something because we prayed. There is no room for impetratory prayer in this model" (ibid., pp. 270-71).

Open theists affirm, on the other hand, that their view of God genuinely allows petitionary prayer to be efficacious and impetratory. Contrary to process theism, the open view believes God can unilaterally act in the world, so he can answer our prayers and "use petitionary prayer to bring about desired ends."[24] And contrary to classical theism, the open view believes that the future is, in part at least, open and undecided. This is demonstrated by the experience of prayer, in which God has graciously and lovingly decided to take our concerns, wishes, and desires into account in deciding what he will or will not do. Thus Pinnock argues:

> God promises to hear and answer our prayers. . . . Prayer can change things. Because of prayer things can be different than they would have been without it (James 4:2; Matt 7:7). This must mean that God summons us into partnership with himself in running the universe. His plan is open. God actually accepts the influence of our prayers in making up his mind. Prayer proves that the future is open and not closed. It shows that future events are not predetermined and fixed. If you believe that prayer changes things, my whole position is established.[25]

Because of the intensely personal relationship that God has freely and lovingly entered into with his children, our prayers genuinely affect him.[26] Thus for open theists what we bring to God in prayer can truly make a difference in what happens in the future. Pinnock argues, "In prayer God makes himself dependent on us, in a certain sense, and allows himself to be affected by our praying. What happens on earth affects what happens in heaven."[27]

As biblical examples of cases in which God is conditioned by and genuinely responds to the prayers of his people, Sanders cites the following texts: Exodus 8:13, 31 in which God removed a plague at the request of Moses; Exodus 32:10-14, in which God changed his mind in response to the prayer of Moses and did not destroy the Israelites after their sin with the golden calf; and 2 Kings 20:1-6,

---

[24]Basinger, "Practical Implications," p. 160.

[25]Pinnock, "God Limits His Knowledge," in *Predestination and Free Will*, ed. David Basinger and Randall Basinger (Downers Grove, Ill.: InterVarsity Press, 1986), p. 152.

[26]Thus Sanders says, "Our prayers make a difference to God because of the personal relationship God enters into with us. God chooses to make himself dependent on us for certain things" (*God Who Risks*, p. 271).

[27]Pinnock, *Most Moved Mover*, p. 172. In support of this claim, Pinnock cites Mt 18:18 ("I tell you the truth, whatever you bind on earth will be bound in heaven, and whatever you loose on earth will be loosed in heaven"). However, the future perfect tense of these verbs (lit., "whatever you bind on earth will have been bound in heaven, and whatever you loose on earth will have been loosed in heaven") raises questions about Pinnock's statement that "what happens on earth affects what happens in heaven." The rare Greek verb tense communicates rather that what happens on earth reflects and declares what has already been done in heaven (see Leon Morris, *The Gospel According to Matthew* [Grand Rapids: Eerdmans, 1992], p. 426).

in which God changed his mind and granted Hezekiah fifteen additional years
of life in answer to his prayer. Sanders concludes, "If Moses and Hezekiah had
not prayed to God about these matters, biblical history would have been different."[28] Or as Boyd says, "The open view [alone] is able to declare, without qualification or inconsistency, that some of the future *genuinely depends on prayer*.[29]

But does biblical teaching on prayer support openness claims that it best accounts for the genuineness and efficacy of petitionary prayer? And specifically,
does a nonexhaustive view of divine foreknowledge better sustain a robust life
of prayer on the part of Christian disciples? I contend that the biblical data leads
us in the opposite direction.

Biblical teaching on divine foreknowledge and petitionary prayer. I
have already argued in chapter four that the genuinely "successful" intercessory
prayers of Moses in Exodus 32 and Hezekiah in 2 Kings 20 that lead to God's
repentance do not necessitate a less-than-exhaustive divine foreknowledge. The
very fact that God told both Moses and Hezekiah of his intentions beforehand
was an invitation from him designed to elicit his servants' pleas for mercy. God
first proposed to do one thing, and then having received the very prayers he
was eliciting, he did something else. In so doing God was graciously inviting
the participation of his servants. Their participation was not in the formation of
the divine intention, but in carrying it out.[30]

Does that mean that prayer makes no difference? Not at all. But we must be
clear about what kind of difference prayer does make. The reason prayer makes
a difference (so much so that Jas 4:2 says, "You do not have, because you do not
ask God") is not because our prayers actually present God with new information
he didn't know before or because they cause him to literally change his mind in
previously unforeseen directions. It is not because God has decided to wait to
determine his intentions until he receives input from us. No, our prayers make a
difference because God has decided to accomplish some of his purposes only as
we pray.[31] It seems that God graciously decided to do this to involve us in the

---

[28]Sanders, *God Who Risks*, p. 271. Pinnock concurs and argues on the basis of Jas 4:2 and Mt
7:7 that "It appears that God's actions can be conditioned by our praying and that our not
praying may thwart God's will" (*Most Moved Mover*, p. 172).

[29]Boyd, *God of the Possible*, p. 95. For a comprehensive and helpful description of the open
view of petitionary prayer see Terrance Tiessen, *Providence and Prayer* (Downers Grove, Ill.:
InterVarsity Press, 2000), pp. 71-118.

[30]Bruce A. Ware, *God's Lesser Glory* (Wheaton, Ill.: Crossway, 2000), pp. 92-98.

[31]Ware writes, "The role of prayer, then, becomes necessary to the accomplishing of these certain purposes, and our involvement in prayer, then, actually functions to assist in bringing
these purposes to their fulfillment" (Bruce Ware, *Their God Is Too Small* [Wheaton, Ill.: Crossway, 2003], p. 98).

accomplishment of his purpose. In his love God desires to share bountifully with his children. He does not share with us the formation of his purposes; rather, he invites us to participate with him in carrying out his infinitely wise purposes through prayer. But this does not presuppose that God's will and his knowledge of it is not definite and fixed and certain. Just the opposite.

In the one place in the New Testament where God's knowledge of the future is explicitly linked with the prayers of believers, Jesus appeals to an exhaustive view of divine foreknowledge to support and sustain a bold and confident practice of petitionary prayer on the part of his disciples. Recall our earlier discussion of Jesus' teaching on prayer in Matthew 6 (see pp. 88-92). Two times in that chapter, Jesus appeals to the knowledge of God the Father in exhorting his disciples to pray. In Matthew 6:7-8, Jesus says, "And when you pray, do not keep on babbling like pagans, for they think they will be heard because of their many words. Do not be like them, for your Father knows what you need before you ask him." And in Matthew 6:31-32, he says, "So do not worry, saying, 'What shall we eat?' or 'What shall we drink?' or 'What shall we wear?' For the pagans run after all these things, and your heavenly Father knows that you need them."

My argument in chapter 3 was that the Father's knowledge of what we need before we ask him is indeed divine foreknowledge (see pp. 90-91). And it includes his knowledge of future free decisions of human beings. The point is that Jesus is appealing to the Father's exhaustive and infallible foreknowledge precisely to encourage his disciples and to motivate them to a robust and passionate life of prayer. For Jesus this kind of divine foreknowledge in no way makes petitionary prayer superfluous and irrelevant. Anything but.

At this point we might be tempted to simply say that this explicit teaching of Jesus settles the case and overrules the objections of open theists. But the openness questions are significant and deserve additional investigation. And when such investigation is undertaken, two major problems rise to the surface that are very problematic for the view that a nonexhaustive view of God's foreknowledge actually enhances our confidence in petitionary prayer.

Theological problems with the open view of petitionary prayer. The first major problem comes when we ask how the God of open theism decides whether he should answer my prayer in the way I asked. If God cannot know with certainty future free decisions, there is a vast amount of the situation that he does not and indeed cannot know. In addition, a very crucial part of what would make a particular answer to my prayer wise and loving and good or not depends on my response to his answer. To the extent that these responses are free, God cannot foreknow them with certainty either. For example, if I pray to God for a good job that will support my family, God cannot know for sure the response of a potential employer to my application for the job. Equally so, he cannot know for sure my own response to the job if I get it, or the responses of my supervisor and my coworkers on the job that will be such an important part of whether the job is a good one or not.[32]

It is clear in the New Testament that God delights to answer the prayers of his children. Jesus encouraged his followers to pray: "Ask and it will be given to you; seek and you will find; knock and the door will be opened to you. For everyone who asks receives; he who seeks finds; and to him who knocks, the door will be opened" (Mt 7:7-8). But it is equally clear that God does not always answer the prayers of his children in the way they ask. We can see this from God's refusal to grant Jesus' request in Gethsemane to have the cup taken from him (Mt 26:39-42) and from God's refusal to remove Paul's thorn in the flesh when Paul asked him to (2 Cor 12:7-10). There was nothing sinful in those requests.[33] So the question

---

[32]There is a significant debate at this point about what kind of foreknowledge would be most helpful in enabling God to know how to answer the prayer of one of his children for a good job. Many have argued that God's "simple foreknowledge" is of no benefit to him in enabling him to decide how best to answer the prayer. That is because the future he foreknows includes the prayer being prayed and the particular job being given in response to that prayer. Thus God's simple foreknowledge would allow him no opportunity to influence a human decision in ways other than the decision that God eternally foreknows will be made. So if the decision to be made will be a good one, God's foreknowledge recognizes that. But if the decision to be made will be an unwise and hurtful one, God cannot change the decision because the future God eternally foreknows is fixed. This "uselessness" of simple foreknowledge for God's providential action in the world is argued for by open theists William Hasker (*God, Time, and Knowledge,* [Ithaca, N.Y.: Cornell University Press, 1989], pp. 59-63) and David Basinger (*Case for Freewill Theism,* pp. 123-34). The contrary position, that God's simple foreknowledge does in fact provide him with a "providential edge," has been argued by David Hunt (e.g., "The Simple-Foreknowledge View," in *Divine Foreknowledge: Four Views,* ed. James K. Bielby and Paul R. Eddy [Downers Grove, Ill.: InterVarsity Press, 2001], pp. 96-101). Others have argued that for God's foreknowledge to be useful to him in answering prayer in the manner discussed in this chapter, it must include his foreknowledge of hypothetical states of affairs (e.g., "if Mary gets job x, she will have experience y"). This is true both for Molinists who view God's middle knowledge to be that of counterfactuals of libertarian freedom (e.g., William Lane Craig, *The Only Wise God* [Grand Rapids: Baker, 1987], p. 137), and for those who affirm middle-knowledge Calvinism (Tiessen, *Providence and Prayer,* pp. 289-362) or compatibilist middle knowledge (Bruce Ware, *God's Greater Glory* [Wheaton, Ill.: Crossway, 2004], pp. 110-30). As noted in n. 35 of chap. 1, my own position is consistent with the affirmation of such compatibilistic middle knowledge. But for our purposes the key truth to note is that various forms of exhaustive divine foreknowledge are indeed useful to God in determining his answers to our prayers in ways that the nonexhaustive, openness position by definition cannot be.

[33]We know that Jesus' request in Gethsemane was not sinful because of the consistent New Testament teaching about the absolute sinlessness of Jesus. And I believe we can reasonably infer that Paul's request that God remove his thorn was legitimate and not sinful from the context in 2 Corinthians 12. See Scott J. Hafemann, *2 Corinthians,* The NIV Application Commentary (Grand Rapids: Zondervan, 2000), p. 464.

for us remains, On what basis will God know whether to answer our prayer or not? If God does not know vast amounts of the future completely and certainly, how will he know if it is better to grant our request or not?

Jesus promises in Matthew 7:11 that the Father delights to give his children good gifts in response to their prayers: "If you, then, though you are evil, know how to give good gifts to your children, how much more will your Father in heaven give good gifts to those who ask him!" But this forces us to ask another question, How will a God with less-than-exhaustive foreknowledge know what will constitute a truly good gift to give us in response to our prayers?

It is clear that we are not in a position to advise God with infallible wisdom. Open theists affirm that God is far more knowledgeable and far wiser than we humans are. Yet they view it as a strength of their position that God will listen to us and make his decisions, in part at least, on the basis of what he hears from us in prayer. But is this really a strength? Ware notes:

> When one considers that *only* God (and not us) knows all that can be known, and *only* God (and not us) has unsurpassable wisdom to discern what is best in any situation, and *only* God (and not us) has purity of motives and freedom from the distortion of sinful perspectives and urgings, and *only* God (and not us) is in the optimal situation to judge the probable effects of a decision on other people, situations, future developments, and kingdom purposes, it begins to make one wonder why it is so wonderful that "divine activity is at times dependent on our freely offered petitions."[34]

In fact, the openness insistence that our prayers inform God and guide him in his decision making is contrary to the repeated teaching of Scripture. Consider, for example, Isaiah 40:13-14:

> Who has understood the mind of the LORD,
>   or instructed him as his counselor?
> Whom did the LORD consult to enlighten him,
>   and who taught him the right way?
> Who was it that taught him knowledge
>   or showed him the path of understanding?

The clearly implied answer to these rhetorical questions is "no one."[35] These

---

[34]Ware, *God's Lesser Glory*, p. 168. The quotation Ware refers to is from Basinger, "Practical Implications," p. 160.

[35]If, as the next verse declares, "the nations are like a drop in a bucket" in comparison to the infinite greatness of God (Is 40:15), clearly we humans can contribute no wisdom or knowledge to God to guide him in his running of the universe (see Ware, *God's Lesser Glory*, p. 169). This same truth is taught in Job 15:8; 21:22; 36:22.

verses are so important to Paul that he quotes them in Romans 11:34 and 1 Corinthians 2:16. And the presumption that our wisdom and knowledge is such that we can indeed participate in the formation of God's purposes is the opposite of the kind of humility we are to have in prayer—humility modeled by Jesus in Gethsemane when he prayed "not what I will, but what you will" (Mk 14:36).

Sanders recognizes the force of this objection. He acknowledges that some might object to his view

> claiming that we have no business advising God, who possesses vastly superior wisdom. Is it not the epitome of hubris to think that we can counsel an omniscient God who already knows all the data? Such remarks may arise out of a sense of humility and a desire to be still before God. But the biblical record is more than a call to silence. It also calls us to make our requests known to God (Phil 4:6; 1 Jn 5:14-15) and to ask what we will in Jesus' name (Jn 14:13-14). . . . God wants this sort of conversation not because we have anything stupendous about which to advise him but simply because God decides to make our concerns his concerns. God wants us to be his partners not because he needs our wisdom but because he wants *our* fellowship. It is the *person* making the request that makes the difference to God. The request is important because God is interested in us. God loves us and takes our concerns to heart just because they are our concerns. That is the nature of a personal, loving relationship.[36]

Sanders, I believe, is helpful here. But his vision of the relationship of God's decisions to our prayers is very different from the kind of relationship that is argued for by most open theists from texts like Exodus 32 and 2 Kings 20, where God actually changes his mind in response to prayer. And if Sanders is right and God desires our prayers not for the sake of our wisdom but for our fellowship, it still must be asked how he will decide how best to respond to our prayers.

This situation is complicated further by the fact that the God of open theism can and at times does make mistakes in his beliefs about the future. Since he cannot know future free decisions with certainty, every belief he has about the future (including his belief about what would be the best response to my prayer) is potentially fallible. Once free decisions are made by humans, God's beliefs about the future may prove to be mistaken. Open theists point to texts like Jeremiah 3:6-7, 19-20 and 32:35 to argue that this does at times happen. And in addition, God may reassess what he has previously done and decide that it was not best (as with God's creation of humanity in Gen 6:6 and his making Saul king in 1 Sam 15:11). Given all this, what God believes to be the best answer to my prayer may not in fact turn out to be best. David Basinger admits

---

[36]Sanders, *God Who Risks*, p. 272.

this explicitly: "Since God does not necessarily know exactly what will happen in the future, it is always possible that even that which God in his unparalleled wisdom believes to be the best course of action at any given time may not produce the anticipated results in the long run."[37]

If this is true, it is hard to see how we are to pray with confidence and joy, as Jesus instructs us in Matthew 6:10, that God's will would "be done on earth as it is in heaven." This petition in the Lord's Prayer presupposes that God's will is already formed through his infinite wisdom. The purpose of this petition is not to seek to be involved in the process of forming God's will through the genuine give and take of our personal relationship with God, but rather to submit to God's preexisting will that we trust to be infinitely wise and perfectly loving.[38] But if God's will might well be based on his mistaken beliefs about the future, its accomplishment may not be the best thing at all. Surely this will erode our confidence and joy in prayer.[39]

Taken together, these considerations raise serious questions about the wisdom of God. It is hard to see how a God who makes decisions about whether and how to answer prayers based on incomplete information about the future, on input from beings who are less knowledgeable and wise and holy than himself, and in light of his own beliefs that are at least potentially fallible can be considered to be the all-wise God of Scripture.[40]

A second problem with the open view of prayer involves its relationship to God's knowledge of the present and the past. Open theists readily affirm their belief in God's exhaustive knowledge of the past and present. This certainly includes our present and past thoughts and feelings and actions.[41]

But this presents a problem for the open view of prayer. The fact is that everything we tell God in prayer is something that exists in the present. While our petitions might relate to future realities, our anxieties, fears, desires, hopes and

---

[37]Basinger, "Practical Implications," p. 165.

[38]Ware, *God's Lesser Glory*, p. 170.

[39]Millard Erickson combines this point with what I said earlier (that the God of open theism may not be able to answer our prayers because of his commitment to respect the functioning of libertarian free will): "This means that the prayers of a free will theist will be uttered without a great sense of assurance, either that God will know what is best to do or will be able to accomplish that in every instance, even if he knows what should be done" (*God the Father Almighty*, [Grand Rapids: Baker, 1998], p. 284).

[40]See the helpful assessment of the problems the open view of prayer has with the wisdom of God in Ware, *God's Lesser Glory*, pp. 167-72.

[41]As Boyd says, "Our omniscient Creator knows us perfectly, far better than we even know ourselves" (*God of the Possible*, p. 35). Specifically, Boyd asserts that God "knows the thoughts and intentions of all individuals perfectly" (ibid., p. 152). Presumably, Boyd means that God knows the *past and present* thoughts and intentions of all individuals perfectly.

dreams about them are present realities. And everything that goes into the formulation of our prayers, be it over the past minute or hour or day or decade, is something from the past. And therefore by definition all of these formative elements are perfectly known by a God who knows everything about the past and the present. The point is that there is nothing we can tell God in prayer that he does not already know. Our prayers contribute absolutely no new information to God. This makes it hard to see how our prayers can make a genuine contribution to God's decision-making process. In addition, this makes it hard to see how prayer becomes the hallmark of a genuine and mutually responsive relationship between God and his children. Ware argues:

> The open view makes much of the dynamic nature of this relationship. . . . [It affirms] that God waits to hear what we think, that he learns what our thoughts are when we come to him, that he adjusts his plans only after learning from us what our longings are, and so on. The truth is, however, this is not how it works at all! God never learns what we think when we tell him in prayer. Because he knows us perfectly, he knows every thought we ever have had, he knows all our feelings and desires, and he can anticipate fully what we will be bringing to him in prayer.[42]

Or even more bluntly, "The fact is that the God of open theism knows too much about me for his relationship with me to be 'genuine' and 'real.' "[43] The reality is that the kind of mutually interactive, mutually instructing relationship with God in prayer that is often promoted by open theists would seem to demand not only that God not have exhaustive foreknowledge but also that his knowledge of the present and past be limited as well.[44] This is a far greater modification of classical understanding of divine omniscience than has heretofore been advocated by open theists. But the logic of the openness conception of what constitutes a real and genuine divine-human relationship in prayer may well point in that direction.

Both of these problems arise when we consider the possibility of bringing our petitionary prayers to a God who possesses less-than-exhaustive foreknowledge. Other central theological tenets of open theism also cause problems for a

---

[42]Ware, *God's Lesser Glory,* p. 166.

[43]Ware, *Their God Is Too Small,* p. 102. But Ware goes on to note that because he lacks exhaustive, definite knowledge of the future, the God of open theism is also "not knowledgeable and wise enough to answer our most urgent and pressing prayers in the ways that are, in fact, best" (ibid., p. 105).

[44]Ware, *God's Lesser Glory,* p. 167. Ware asserts that the root problem is the openness assumption that for the divine-human relationship to be real and genuine, it must be very similar to a human model of personal relationships. Ware affirms, on the other hand, that we must rather let God be God and let him define the parameters of the divine-human relationship in the unique and distinctive way he designed it to function.

robust understanding of and commitment to a life of intercessory prayer. Consider, for example, God's commitment to respect libertarian human freedom and in the vast majority of cases to allow it to function. This means that with regard to prayers whose answers depend in one way or another on free human decisions, God has limited himself as to whether and how he will answer those prayers. In my earlier example of praying for a good job (see pp. 241-42), God can answer by appealing to a prospective employer and seeking to persuade him or her to hire me. But only in the rarest of circumstances could he render it certain that this will actually happen. Similarly, he could only very rarely guarantee that other coworkers will not harass me so much that I will feel I need to quit. And the list could go on and on. The point is that there are many needs an open theist could not pray about with full assurance that God will be able to grant the request, even if he should decide to do so.

In addition, we must consider the relationship of the open view of prayer to God's love. Open theists are insistent that God's love is central to the nature of God, and by definition this divine love is universal and impartial.[45] Yet problems arise when this kind of divine love is held together with the openness conception of the efficacy of petitionary prayer. Specifically, how is a God of love justified in withholding a good gift from his children simply because they have not asked him for it? It is understandable that God would want to teach his children the value and necessity of prayer by withholding some benefits until they ask him. Yet it becomes harder and harder to justify this divine withholding the longer it continues and the more desperately his children need the good gift. The dilemma is even more severe when it comes to the case of God withholding a benefit for one person because *someone else* has failed to intercede for him or her. Can God legitimately withhold the good that he knows one person needs

---

[45]For example, Richard Rice says, "From a Christian perspective, *love* is the first and last word in the biblical portrait of God. According to 1 John 4:8: 'Whoever does not love does not know God, because God is love.' The statement *God is love* is as close as the Bible comes to giving us a definition of the divine reality. . . . The statement *God is love* embodies an essential biblical truth. It indicates that love is central, not incidental, to the nature of God. Love is not something God happens to do, it is the one activity that most fully and vividly discloses God's inner reality. Love, therefore, is the very essence of the divine nature. Love is what it means to be God" ("Biblical Support for a New Perspective," in *Openness of God* [Downers Grove, Ill.: InterVarsity Press, 1994], pp. 18-19).

Basinger cites as one of his five summary points of the basic tenants of open theism the following statement: "God *always* desires our highest good, both individually and corporately" ("Practical Implications," p. 156, emphasis added). In another article Basinger argued that "an omnibenevolent God is obligated to maximize the quality of life for those beings he chooses to create" ("In What Sense Must God be Omnibenevolent?" *International Journal for Philosophy of Religion* 14 [1983], p. 3).

just because another person is negligent or disobedient? Sanders affirms that this can happen:

> What God decides to do for others sometimes seems to depend on my prayers. That is, God might sometimes refrain from acting beneficially in one person's life because others have failed to pray. This may not sound fair to those of us in the West with our high value on individualism, but God values community and desires that it be fostered, in part, by our concern for one another and by our manifesting this concern in intercessory prayer for others.[46]

This understanding places a high value on the efficacy of intercessory prayer, but it is hard to see how it is consistent with a God of genuinely universal and impartial love for his children as individuals and not only as members of a community.

David Basinger, on the other hand, argues that "God would never refrain from intervening beneficially in one person's life simply because someone else has failed to request that he do so."[47] This understanding certainly does more justice to the universal, impartial character of God's love, but it seems in turn to jeopardize the efficacy of intercessory prayer. Ware summarizes the dilemma that open theists face:

> Either God's impartial and perfect love is maintained without compromise at the cost of the efficacy of prayer (for God will do what is best regardless of whether or not people pray); or it really does matter whether or not we pray for others (i.e., petitionary prayer is efficacious), but only at the expense of compromising the impartial and perfect love of God for all.[48]

Conclusion. We have seen significant problems that arise from the assertion that the God to whom we pray does not infallibly foreknow free human decisions or any element of the future causally dependent on those free decisions. But when we go back to the teaching of Jesus in Matthew 6, we find that he did not teach such a view. He told his praying disciples that "your Father knows what you need before you ask him." In so doing, he appeals to God's knowledge of all of our needs, present and future, and of all the free decisions that would be involved in meeting those needs. And he does so precisely to encour-

---

[46]Sanders, *God Who Risks,* p. 274. Basinger cites Hasker along with Sanders as proponents of the openness model who "see no necessary incompatibility in affirming both that God always seeks what is best for each of us and that God may at times wait to exert all the noncoercive influence that he can justifiably exert on a given person until requested to do so by another person" ("Practical Implications," p. 161).

[47]Basinger, "Practical Implications," p. 161. See also Basinger, "Petitionary Prayer: A Response to Murray and Meyers," *RelS.* 31 (1995): 482-83.

[48]Ware, *God's Lesser Glory,* p. 173.

age his disciples (and us) to pray and to keep on praying. He intentionally grounds our confidence in prayer in God's exhaustive knowledge of the future. This divine foreknowledge in no way renders our prayers meaningless or should lead us to pray with less passion and urgency. In reality, if we are to pray as Jesus would have us pray, we too must be confident that our God does in fact know what we need before we ask him. And equally so, if our view of God's foreknowledge is to function in our lives in the way it does in Scripture, it must lead us to the kind of confidence in prayer that is hard to come by in open theism.

GOD'S GUIDANCE

Christians throughout the centuries have taken great delight in God's promise that as the great Shepherd, God "guides [his people] in paths of righteousness for his name's sake" (Ps 23:3). They have rejoiced that

> good and upright is the LORD;
>> therefore he instructs sinners in his ways.
> He guides the humble in what is right
>> and teaches them his ways. (Ps 25:8-9)

And so they have sought to heed the admonition of Proverbs 3:5-6:

> Trust in the LORD with all your heart
>> and lean not on your own understanding;
> in all your ways acknowledge him,
>> and he will make your paths straight.

But isn't it necessary for God to have an exhaustive, definite knowledge of the future for him to guide us in what is right and to make our paths straight? For a high level of confidence in the guidance of God to be warranted for us as Christians, isn't it necessary for God to possess exhaustive foreknowledge?

The open view of divine guidance. Open theists say this is not the case. They argue that we must rightly understand the nature and goal of God's guidance. God is not seeking to guide his children according to a preordained blueprint of the future. On the contrary, Sanders argues, "God has a goal for our lives, but there are numerous open routes to its achievement."[49] This is not to say that God never desires a specific person to do a specific act. Sometimes he does, and in those cases he guides the person in the way he desires.[50] But this

---

[49]Sanders, *God Who Risks,* p. 276.
[50]As an example of this, Sanders cites God's asking Gideon to tear down the altar of Baal in Judges 6:25 (ibid).

is relatively rare. "For most of us there is no such specific guidance. The will of
God for our lives is not a list of activities regarding vocation, marriage and the
like. Rather, it is God's desire that we become a lover of God and others as was
exemplified in God's way in Jesus."[51] God is seeking a loving partnership with
us in determining the course of our lives. According to Sanders:

> It is God's desire that we enter into a give-and-take relationship of love, and this
> is not accomplished by God's forcing his blueprint on us. Rather, God wants us to
> go through life together with him, making decisions together. Together we decide
> the actual course of my life. God's will for my life does not reside in a list of specific
> activities but in a personal relationship. As lover and friend, God works with us
> wherever we go and whatever we do. To a large extent our future is open and we
> are to determine what it will be in dialogue with God.[52]

And when God does give specific guidance, we should understand it to be
more for the present rather than for the long-range future. David Basinger says:

> Since we believe that God can know only what can be known and that what hu-
> mans will freely do in the future cannot be known beforehand, we believe that God
> can never know with certainty what will happen in any context involving freedom
> of choice. We believe, for example, that to the extent that freedom of choice would
> be involved, God would not necessarily know beforehand exactly what would
> happen if a couple were to marry. Accordingly, we must acknowledge that divine
> guidance, from our perspective, cannot be considered a means of discovering ex-
> actly what will be best in the long run—as a means of discovering the very best
> long-term option. Divine guidance, rather, must be viewed primarily as a means of
> determining what is best for us now.[53]

For Basinger this understanding of God's guidance is very positive. It can free
Christians from the frantic need to determine whether they are within God's will
at any given moment, and if they are not, to figure out how they can "re-enter"
God's will or cope with what is obviously "second best."

> Since we do not believe that God has exhaustive knowledge of the future, it makes
> no sense for us to think in terms of some perfect, preordained plan for our lives
> and, hence, to worry about whether we are still within it. Accordingly, we need
> never feel—no matter what has happened in the past—that we must now settle for
> "second best" in this rigid sense.[54]

---

[51]Ibid. Sanders writes, "The way of Jesus is a way of life not concerned about blueprints but
about being the kind of person God desires" (ibid).

[52]Ibid., pp. 276-77.

[53]Basinger, "Practical Implications," p. 163.

[54]Ibid., p. 164.

This becomes especially important in the difficult and painful situations of life. So argues Boyd in an extended real-life illustration of a woman he calls "Suzanne." She approached Boyd angrily after a sermon on how God directs our paths. As she told her story, her pain was evident, intense and heartbreaking. Suzanne was a committed Christian woman with a heart for missions. She had prayed fervently for God to bring to her a husband who would share her passion, especially for missions in Taiwan. In college she met such a man and fell in love with him. After 3 1/2 years of seeking God's will, a period filled with prayer, fasting and the seeking of much godly counsel, they married. Suzanne was fully confident that God had brought them together. Boyd writes, "While in prayer, she was overwhelmed by a supernatural sense of joy and peace wrapped up with a very clear confirmation that this marriage was, in fact, God's design for her life."[55] But two years into their missionary training, Suzanne learned that her husband was involved in an adulterous relationship. She confronted him, and he repented (or so it appeared). But after several months he returned to this relationship, and this pattern repeated itself over the next three years. During that time Suzanne's husband became spiritually uninvolved, emotionally distant and at times physically and emotionally abusive. He ended up filing for divorce and moving in with his lover. Two weeks later, Suzanne discovered she was pregnant, leaving her emotionally and spiritually devastated. Boyd writes:

> Understandably, Suzanne could not fathom how the Lord could respond to her life-long prayers by setting her up with a man he *knew* would do this to her and her child. Some Christian friends had suggested that perhaps she hadn't heard God correctly. But it if wasn't God's voice that she and everyone else had heard regarding this marriage, she concluded, then no one could ever be sure they heard God's voice.[56]

As Boyd sought to give pastoral care to Suzanne in an attempt to help her cope with her pain, loss and sense of betrayal, he began by assuring her that her situation was in fact her ex-husband's fault, not God's. But Suzanne countered by saying that if God knew in advance all that her husband would do, then God would in fact bear responsibility for leading her into a marriage he knew would be so incredibly painful. Boyd had to agree and sought to offer her a different way to view the situation.

I suggested to her that God felt as much regret over the confirmation he had given

---

[55]Boyd, *God of the Possible*, p. 104.
[56]Ibid., p. 105.

Suzanne as he did about his decision to make Saul king of Israel (1 Sam 15:11, 35; see also Gen 6:5-6). Not that it was a bad decision—at the time, her ex-husband was a good man with a godly character. The prospects that he and Suzanne would have a happy marriage and fruitful ministry were, at the time, very good. Indeed, I strongly suspected that he had influenced Suzanne and her ex-husband toward this college with their marriage in mind.

Because her ex-husband was a free agent, however, even the best decisions can have sad results. Over time, and through a series of choices, Suzanne's ex-husband had opened himself up to the enemy's influence and became involved in an immoral relationship. Initially, all was not lost, and God and others tried to restore him, but he chose to resist the prompting of the Spirit and consequently his heart grew darker. Suzanne's ex-husband had become a very different person from the man God had confirmed to Suzanne to be a good candidate for marriage. This, I assured Suzanne, grieved God's heart at least as deeply as it grieved hers.[57]

Boyd asserts that helping Suzanne understand her trauma within the framework of an open future was of great help to her. As a result, "she didn't have to abandon all confidence in her ability to hear God and didn't have to accept that somehow God intended this ordeal 'for her own good.' Her faith in God's character and her love toward God were eventually restored and she was finally able to move on with her life." Boyd concludes, "Without having the open view to offer, I don't know how one could effectively minister to a person in Suzanne's dilemma."[58]

Responding to the open view of guidance. While I do not want at all to diminish the agonizing heartache of Suzanne, I respectfully disagree with Boyd and argue that his conception of divine guidance is neither biblically accurate nor pastorally the most helpful.

It is important to note that Boyd did not respond to Suzanne in terms of Sanders's insistence that God is more concerned about the kind of people we are becoming than he is about who we will marry. He did not tell Suzanne that God's guidance was never designed to be specific about who her husband should be. No, Boyd agreed with Suzanne that God had specifically guided and directed her to marry the very person who would hurt her so deeply. The way Boyd's counsel differed from Suzanne's prior understanding was not in its specificity, but in the nature of the knowledge that guided God's direction.

I must admit to being very sympathetic to Sanders's view that God is far more interested in the kind of people we are becoming than in a specific list of activities we are and are not to engage in. That seems to be the thrust of Paul's teach-

---

[57]Ibid., pp. 105-6.
[58]Ibid, p. 106.

ing in 1 Thessalonians. Two times in this letter Paul explicitly describes God's will for his children. And in both cases, God's revealed will is that his children grow in moral conformity to the likeness of Christ.[59] In 1 Thessalonians 4:3, the progressive sanctification that is God's revealed will specifically involves the area of sexual purity, while in 1 Thessalonians 5:16-18, the will of God is that his children rejoice always, pray continually and give thank in all circumstances.[60] But in neither case is the revealed will of God primarily concerned with specific decisions concerning marriage and career and the like. The priority God places on our growth in holiness must be the starting point for us as Christians when we are seeking his guidance for decisions we need to make. Far too often, I fear, we Christians become overly worried about making the "right" decisions in the specific issues of life when God's revealed priority is the godliness of our character.

But the fact that God's *revealed* will in Scripture prioritizes moral Christlikeness and the fact that God longs for us to make decisions in our lives based on this revealed priority, does not mean that God doesn't have a *sovereign* will that he is guiding and directing his children toward in all areas of life.[61] I believe that Scripture points to this kind of sovereign will of God that oversees the flight of every sparrow (Mt 10:29); seemingly random events like the casting of lots (Prov 16:33); the history and geography of every people group (Acts 17:26); the leadership of nations (Dan 4:25) and human decision making in areas of politics (Prov 21:1), economics (Jas 4:13-15), and the day-in, day-out planning of our lives (Prov 16:19; 19:21); and salvation (Rom 9:16). This is also true of suffering and evil. Scripture repeatedly testifies that in ways that are admittedly filled with mystery, not even evil is outside of God's sovereign design. This is true of disasters, whether they are natural or inflicted by humans (e.g., Is 45:7; Lam 3:37-38; Amos 3:6), and of issues of sickness, disease and death (e.g., Ex 4:11; Deut 32:39). Even when the free evil actions of Satan are involved, God reigns su-

---

[59]Gene L. Green, *The Letters to the Thessalonians*, Pillar New Testament Commentary (Grand Rapids: Eerdmans, 2002), p. 189. Green cites Mt 7:21; 12:50; 21:31; Mk 3:35; Lk 12:47; Jn 7:17; 9:31; Acts 13:22; Rom 12:1-2; Eph 6:6; Heb 10:36; 13:21; 1 Jn 2:17 in support of this moral sense of the revealed will of God.

[60]Green cites the neuter *touto* ("this") as indicating that the antecedent most likely is all three imperatives rather than just the latter one (*Letters to the Thessalonians*, p. 260). Charles A. Wanamaker cites the parallel imperatival structures of the three commands in 1 Thess 5:16-18 to argue that all three are the will of God for his children (*The Epistles to the Thessalonians*, New International Greek Testament Commentary [Grand Rapids: Eerdmans, 1990], pp. 200-201).

[61]For a classic presentation of moral decision making based on the revealed will of God, see Garry Friesen, *Decision Making and the Will of God* (Portland: Multnomah Press, 1980).

preme (e.g., Job 1—2).[62] And with respect to the sinful decisions of human beings, Genesis 50:20 affirms that the selling of Joseph into slavery was at the same
time an evil decision of his brothers and a part of the good purpose of the sovereign God. Acts 2:23 and Acts 4:27-28 describe the crucifixion of Jesus as both
the sinful act of wicked humans and the eternal redemptive purpose of the holy
God. We will grapple more with questions of suffering and evil in the next section (see pp. 258-68), but my purpose at this point is to affirm the biblical teaching that evil does not exist outside the sovereign purpose of God. He reigns supreme over it and uses it for his own wise and holy and good purposes. Indeed
Scripture as a whole affirms the kind of universal and exhaustive understanding
of God's sovereign will that Paul argues for in Ephesians 1:11, where he says that
God "works out everything in conformity with the purpose of his will."[63] And for
our purposes it is important to note that this is true whether or not God reveals
what his specific, sovereign will is through prayer and the counsel of others.

But when God does guide and direct his children in a specific direction, as
Boyd understood God to have done in Suzanne's life, the relationship of his
guidance to his foreknowledge is crucial.

Bruce Ware helpfully sums up the essence of the openness understanding of
the guidance God specifically gives to his children, saying that it must be understood "as *evolving,* not fixed; and as *relative* in its level of accuracy, not uniform."[64] And he argues, and I concur, that in the end both of these aspects of
the open view of God's guidance serve to weaken our confidence in it.

Consider, first, the evolving nature of God's guidance. If God is constantly gaining new information, learning of free decisions as they are made, then the possibility always exists that his counsel to us will have to be revised in light of this new
information. Under open theism, any guidance God gives to his children must of
necessity be provisional, for it is given without definite knowledge of crucial elements of the future. As a result, God may end up giving guidance that turns out

---

[62]In Job 1—2 we see Satan actively working, bringing horrifying evil to Job and his family. Yet
after all his children were killed, Job said in Job 1:21, "The LORD gave and the LORD has taken
away; / may the name of the LORD be praised." Thus Job attributed the taking away of his
children ultimately to God (Satan is clearly the immediate cause, but God is the ultimate
cause), and he affirms that even in this God is to be praised, not blamed. Similarly, after Satan
had afflicted Job with painful boils, he responded to his wife in Job 2:10, "Shall we accept
good from God, and not trouble?" And the author of Job gives his inspired commentary on
Job's responses in Job 1:22 and 2:10, indicating that Job was right in what he said (including
viewing God as the ultimate cause of his suffering).
[63]On this distinction between God's sovereign will and his revealed moral will, see John Piper,
"Are There Two Wills in God?" in *Still Sovereign,* ed. Thomas R. Schreiner and Bruce A. Ware
(Grand Rapids: Baker, 2000), pp. 107-31.
[64]Ware, *God's Lesser Glory,* p. 180.

not to be best. This is illustrated by Boyd's understanding of Suzanne's experience. And this is admitted very honestly by Basinger: "Since God does not necessarily know exactly what will happen in the future, it is always possible that even that which God in his unparalleled wisdom believes to be the best course of action at any given time may not produce the anticipated results in the long run."[65]

Thus whenever Christians receive what they perceive to be guidance from God, they may rightly ask, Is this direction from God the very best? And at every point subsequently, Christians who are serious about following God's direction for their lives will need to ask, Has God's will in this matter changed? Has it evolved from my initial sense of his guidance, as God has learned new information? The sense of uncertainty, both initial and ongoing, is evident under this conception of God's guidance.

Linked to the evolving nature of God's guidance is its relative accuracy. Remember, Basinger argued that God is relatively more accurate with this guidance in the short run rather than in the long run. The further into the future we look, the greater the risk that God's guidance might prove not to be the best. But isn't it the case that the most important issues in our lives, the issues we would most want to seek God's guidance on, have long-run implications? Questions of education, marriage, vocation, child-raising, ministry and service not only have present significance but also long-range implications. In all of these areas, we come to God and ask, What is the best decision to make now in light of my long-range future? The issues that have no long-range significance at all, those things that affect the present moment only, tend to be relatively insignificant: What should I have for breakfast? What color shirt should I wear this morning? The weightiness of these questions pales in comparison with questions that carry significant long-range implications. But it is precisely the long-range questions that Basinger says God is not all that good at answering. It may well be the case, according to openness understandings, that God's present counsel will prove to be disastrous in the future (as it did in Suzanne's case). And the consequences of such a lack of accuracy are rightly devastating for our Christian lives. Ware says:

> To say that God is pretty good at short-range guidance but can't really handle long-range direction is to say that, concerning the *weightiest decisions we make* in our lives, God has little if any solid help to give. Surely this only discourages what the Bible commends throughout: trusting God implicitly with all of our lives.[66]

How different the situation is if we are guided by a God whose knowledge of

---

[65]Basinger, "Practical Implications," p. 165.
[66]Ware, *God's Lesser Glory,* p. 182.

the future is exhaustive and infallible. Scripture calls us to make wise decisions that pursue God's agenda, which is revealed in Scripture. And God calls us to make these kinds of decisions regardless of how strong or weak or even potentially fallible our own subjective sense of his guidance might be.[67] But our ultimate trust as we make decisions is that God will guide us for his glory and for our own good in light of his complete knowledge of every dimension of the future.

What about Sanders's conception that what God desires most of all is a partnership of genuine give-and-take love in which "we are to determine what [our future] will be in dialogue with God"?[68] I gladly affirm God's loving and gracious desire for partnership with his children. But the partnership God seeks with us is not one of *determining* the course of my life but in *accomplishing* his purpose for my life. It is interesting that Jesus, the eternal Son of God, did not seek to determine the course of his life in partnership with the Father. Rather he came to do the will of his heavenly Father. John's Gospel gives eloquent testimony to the nature of the relationship Jesus had with the Father. Jesus says, "The Son can do nothing by himself; he can only do what he sees his Father doing, because whatever the Father does the Son also does" (Jn 5:19). "I do nothing on my own but speak just what the Father has taught me" (Jn 8:28). "I did not speak on my own accord, but the Father who sent me commanded me what to say and how to say it" (Jn 12:49). "I do exactly what my Father has commanded me" (Jn 14:31). Indeed on the night before he died, Jesus summed up his life as he prayed to the Father: "I have brought you glory on earth by completing the work you gave me to do" (Jn 17:4).[69] And that reached its climax later that

---

[67]In my own experience, and I strongly suspect this is not unusual, I have sometimes sensed God's guidance very strongly and clearly. Other times I have not had anything close to a clear sense of God's direction. If that is the case with regard to a decision that must be made now, I need to make the wisest decision I can. I do so trusting in the God who knows and directs the future to lead me, either through my decision or by redirecting it, closing doors and so forth. I am also aware that my own subjective sense of God's guidance is not infallible. Sometimes I can misinterpret what I think God is saying to me. This means that it is very wise and practically essential to seek to confirm my own subjective sense of God's guidance with the counsel of other wise and godly people, circumstantial factors, and the like.

[68]Sanders, *God Who Risks,* p. 277.

[69]The subordination of the Son to the Father expressed in these verses is clearly in the realm of function. With respect to what Jesus says and what he does, Jesus says in Jn 14:31, "The Father is greater than I." But with respect to the divine essence, Jesus says in Jn 10:30, "I and the Father are one." The question of whether the functional subordination of God the Son to God the Father is eternal or operates only during the earthly life and ministry of Jesus Christ is hotly debated among some evangelicals today. For a presentation of the eternal subordination position, see Stephen D. Kovach and Peter R. Schemm, "A Defense of the Doctrine of the Eternal Subordination of the Son," *Journal of the Evangelical Theological Society* 42, no. 3 (1999): 461-76. For an argument for the temporary subordination of the Son, see Kevin Giles, *Trinity and Subordinationism* (Downers Grove, Ill.: InterVarsity Press, 2002).

evening in Gethsemane, when during an agonizing season of prayer Jesus poured out his heart in prayer, "My Father, if it is possible, may this cup be taken from me." Yet in the final analysis, Jesus ultimately submitted his own will to that of the Father, "Yet not as I will, but as you will" (Mt 26:39). In this way, as Paul puts it, Jesus "became obedient to death—even death on a cross" (Phil 2:8). The picture is not one of mutual collaboration in determining the direction of Jesus' life but rather of willing and even joyful (Heb 12:2) obedience to the will and the plan of the Father for his life.[70]

And this is the portrait of the Christian life we are to follow as we seek to "walk as Jesus did" (1 Jn 2:6). In the Lord's Prayer, Jesus taught us to pray that God's will would be done on earth (in our own lives first and foremost) as it is in heaven (Mt 6:10). This petition has primary reference to God's revealed moral will, but I also believe that it involves our willing and eager submission to God's sovereign will. But God's will, in both senses of the word, is something that already exists. Our partnership with him through prayer and active obedience in all the dimensions of life involves the carrying out of God's will, not determining what it will be.

What then could someone like me who believes in the exhaustive foreknowledge of God say to Suzanne in response to her situation? Boyd claims that God never had any particular and specific good purposes in the ordeal he guided her into, and that what happened to her was in no way "for her own good" (see p. 252). But is the view of God's guidance that Boyd presents to Suzanne pastorally wise and helpful? Clearly Boyd's desire is to exonerate God from moral responsibility for the suffering that Suzanne has undergone. And according to Boyd's testimony, his counsel was indeed helpful. "Her faith in God's character and her love for God were eventually restored and she was finally able to move on with her life."[71] But as she moves on, there will undoubtedly be countless other decisions Suzanne will have to make in her life. Will she be able to trust God in the process of making decisions in the future? Will she be able to make decisions confident that God will indeed "guide [her] in what is right" (Ps 25:9)? Wouldn't Boyd's account of God's involvement in her former life lead Suzanne to turn away from God in the big decisions of life rather than entrust them to him? Whatever gains might be had in exonerating God from moral responsibility for Suzanne's suffering, the cost is very great. While Suzanne might have been restored to confidence in the loving character of God's heart, she is in no position to believe that he will be able to guide her in the future any better than he

---

[70]On the example of Jesus in this regard, see Ware, *God's Lesser Glory,* pp. 184-85.
[71]Boyd, *God of the Possible,* p. 106.

did in the past. This is certainly one way to "move on with one's life," but we must ask if this is the lifestyle that Scripture points the children of God to. Is this the kind of confidence God wants us to have in him and his good purposes as we make decisions in life? Not only is the pastoral counsel offered by Boyd inconsistent with the teaching of Scripture on the extent of God's foreknowledge (as I have tried to argue throughout this book), but it also leaves people with far less confidence in the guidance of God in the future and thus far less reason to entrust their futures to God.

A belief in the exhaustive foreknowledge of God certainly does not answer all the questions that Suzanne raises—in fact it raises the very ones she is grappling with most. Why would a God who knew what her ex-husband would do specifically guide them to marry? We will grapple with these questions in the section titled "Grappling with Suffering and Evil," but my point for now is that the denial of God's exhaustive foreknowledge raises another question that is every bit as big and every bit as crucial from a practical standpoint: Why should I continue to trust God in the future? Why should I take him into account when making the big decisions of life?

Conclusion. God has promised to guide his children (Ps 23:4; 25:8-9). He promises to order their lives for his glory and for their eternal good (Rom 8:28). He longs for us to have confidence in these precious promises. Yet our confidence in these promises is directly tied to our convictions about God's knowledge of the future. To the extent that God does not possess exhaustive, definite foreknowledge, he is potentially fallible in the way he guides and directs our lives. His providence is called into question, and our confidence in his guidance as we make decisions is weakened. This would be a significant loss as we seek to live our lives following the guidance and direction of our Shepherd.

GRAPPLING WITH SUFFERING AND EVIL

Open theists believe that their model provides substantial theological and practical advantages over classical views in grappling with suffering and evil. The importance of this issue can be seen from the fact that Sanders begins *The God Who Risks* by describing the death of his brother in a car accident. This led Sanders, as a young boy, to ask the question, "Why did God kill my brother?" And indeed over the years, Sanders affirms, it was this question and the discussions which followed that spurred his thinking on the nature of divine providence.[72] We have already seen the shaping influence of the story of Suzanne for Boyd in his book *God of the Possible.* And Boyd has written extensively on the problem

---

[72]Sanders, *God Who Risks*, p. 1.

of evil from an openness perspective in his books *God at War* and *Satan and the Problem of Evil.*[73]

The openness understanding. Central to the open view is the conviction that evil and suffering are never the explicit intention of God. Evil is always and only the result of creaturely freedom being used in ways God never intended. God neither knows in advance that a particular evil event will happen nor wills it to occur. He does not have some specific divine purpose that somehow justifies the suffering. Sanders, for example, argues that

> the overarching structures of creation are purposed by God, but not every single detail that occurs within them. Within general providence it makes sense to say that God intends an overall purpose for the creation and that God does not specifically intend each and every action within the creation. Some evil is simply pointless because it does not serve to achieve any greater good. Thus God does not have a specific divine purpose for each and every occurrence of evil. The "greater good" of establishing the conditions of fellowship between God and creatures does not mean that gratuitous evil has a point. Rather, the possibility of gratuitous evil has a point but its actuality does not. . . . When a two-month-old child contracts a painful, incurable bone cancer that means suffering and death, it is pointless evil. The Holocaust is pointless evil. The rape and dismemberment of a young girl is pointless evil. The accident that caused the death of my brother was a tragedy. God does not have a specific purpose in mind for these occurrences.[74]

Pinnock concurs:

> Unlike conventional theism with its much stronger doctrine of divine control, we can say that God does not want horrors like the Holocaust to happen. They are genuine tragedies that God did not will and which are not part of some greater good. He did not ordain them and, in fact, weeps over them. We too are entitled to be outraged by them. Practically speaking it means that we can fight evil without fighting God. Though God can bring good out of evil, it does not make evil itself good and does not even ensure that God will succeed in every case to bring good out of

---

[73]Gregory Boyd, *God at War* (Downers Grove, Ill.: InterVarsity Press, 1997), and *Satan and the Problem of Evil* (Downers Grove, Ill.: InterVaristy Press, 2001). Boyd begins *God at War* by recounting the story of Zosia, a young Jewish girl living in Warsaw during the Nazi occupation whose eyes were cruelly gouged out by sadistic Nazi soldiers before she was killed (pp. 33-34). This story serves as a framework for Boyd's work.

[74]Sanders, *God Who Risks,* pp. 261-62. David Basinger also affirms that we "need not assume that some divine purpose exists for each evil that we encounter. We need not, for example, assume when someone died that God 'took him home' for some reason, or that the horrors many experience in this world in some mysterious way fit into God's perfect plan. We can justifiably assume, rather, that God is often as disappointed as are we that someone's earthly existence had ended at an early age or that someone is experiencing severe depression or that someone is being tortured" ("Practical Implications," p. 170).

it. Greater goods do not arise out of every occurrence of evil. In reference to evil, God is not the author of it but is a very present help in time of trouble. Though not the cause of our suffering, God is always alongside, helping us through it.[75]

Thus the blame for suffering and evil goes not to God but rather to those who actually caused it—to human and angelic beings who used their libertarian freedom in ways God never intended. God cannot control these free decisions in such a way as to guarantee that creatures never sin.[76] God freely chose to give the gift of libertarian freedom to the moral beings he created, knowing full well of the possibility of their misuse.[77] He did so because of the benefits that could only come through free choices.[78] Supremely this involves love—a loving relationship with himself that God created human beings for. But this love must be freely chosen. Sanders writes:

> God made human beings capable of responding to the divine love with love of their own. God is solely responsible for bringing this possibility about, yet what God desires is a reciprocal relationship of love. Love is vulnerable and does not force itself on the beloved. Thus there is the risk that the beloved may not want to reciprocate love. In creating such conditions God takes the implausible risk that his creatures may reject him.[79]

This primacy of love is why Sanders argues that his grappling with the problem of evil should rightly be called the "logic-of-love defense," rather than as it has traditionally been called the "free-will defense." Freedom is a necessary prerequisite for the achieving of God's ultimate goal—a genuinely mutual relationship of love with his human image-bearers.[80]

There are two other crucial factors involved in the openness understanding of God's relationship to suffering and evil. The first is the fact that God in his sov-

---

[75]Pinnock, *Most Moved Mover*, p. 176.

[76]Such divine determination of free human and angelic actions, understood in the sense of libertarian freedom, would be logically self-contradictory. Openness theologians understand God's omnipotence as enabling him to do all things, but only those things that are logically possible to do (see Pinnock, *Most Moved Mover*, p. 252, and his "Systematic Theology," in *Openness of God* [Downers Grove, Ill.: InterVarsity Press, 1994], pp. 113-17).

[77]Unlike classical Arminians, who argue that God actually knew of the misuse of freedom that would come in history, open theists argue that God merely knew of the possibility (and no doubt the probability) that such libertarian freedom would be misused.

[78]Pinnock quotes from C. S. Lewis: "Why did God give [human beings] free will? Because free will, though it makes evil possible, is also the only thing that makes possible any love or goodness or joy worth having. A world of automata—of creatures that worked like machines—would hardly be worth creating" (*Mere Christianity* [New York: Macmillan, 1952], p. 49; quoted in Pinnock, "God Limits His Knowledge," p. 148).

[79]Sanders, *God Who Risks*, p. 258.

[80]Ibid. See also chap. 4 of David Basinger's *Case for Freewill Theism*.

ereignty reserves the right to intervene unilaterally in human affairs. He can and at times does intervene, even to the point of overruling human freedom if need be. Basinger maintains that "God does retain the right to intervene unilaterally in earthly affairs. That is, we believe that freedom of choice is a gift granted to us by God and thus that God retains the power and moral prerogative to inhibit occasionally our ability to make voluntary choices to keep things on track."[81]

Hasker compares God's "control" over the lives of people with the "control" that parents exercise in the lives of their small children. He argues that God retains "coercive power . . . in reserve" should "the deliberate and intensive application of 'persuasive power' " not prove sufficient.[82] God in his wisdom decides when he should do this. Sanders says, "There are some things that the almighty God retains the right to enact unilaterally in the future. If the divine wisdom decides it is best to bring about some specific event in history, then God can do so."[83]

Yet it must be said that God only very rarely overrides human freedom in this way. His goal is to preserve the full exercise of human freedom whenever possible.

Second, open theists are quick to affirm that God is present with us in the midst of suffering and evil. He grieves over evil. Being genuinely relational, God is affected by what affects us. Thus he suffers with us.[84] And being a God of love, he comforts us and cares for us when we suffer. Pinnock says, "In reference to evil, God is not the author of it but is a very present help in time of trouble. Though not the cause of our suffering, God is always alongside, helping us through it."[85]

Open theists see substantial theological and practical advantages in their view when it comes to grappling with the problem of evil. Theologically, they hold that their view successfully avoids making God the author of evil. The ultimate moral responsibility for the evil in the world does not rest with God, as it does in any view that holds to exhaustive divine foreknowledge linked with God's specific sovereignty. And even views such as classical Arminianism, which reject such divine determination but hold to his exhaustive foreknowledge, run the risk of making God the author of evil. For if God infallibly foreknows the evil to be committed by a particular person, why would God create

---

[81]Basinger, "Practical Implications," p. 159.
[82]William Hasker, "A Philosophical Perspective," in *Openness of God* (Downers Grove, Ill.: InterVarsity Press, 1994), p. 142.
[83]Sanders, *God Who Risks*, p. 234.
[84]Pinnock, *Most Moved Mover*, pp. 55-59.
[85]Ibid., p. 176.

him or her? Only a denial of God's specific sovereignty and exhaustive foreknowledge successfully places moral responsibility for evil at the feet of human
and angelic beings rather than God. Practically, open theists argue that this enables us to trust in the goodness of God's character and to experience his love
and care even as we suffer.

How advantageous is the openness account? But is it in fact the case that
the openness construction is the most theologically helpful in dealing with the
problem of evil? And is it the most practically and pastorally helpful? I say no
on both counts.

First, consider the issue of God's knowledge and its relationship to suffering
and evil. Open theists argue that God's lack of exhaustive foreknowledge means
he cannot infallibly know in advance of evils that will occur. But the God of
open theism does know everything about the past and the present. Thus he is
intimately aware of all the thoughts and feelings, all the deliberation and planning that would go into a sinful decision that would inflict evil and suffering on
another person. Consider, for example, the Holocaust, cited by both Sanders
and Pinnock as an example of gratuitous evil that has no greater good that
would justify it in particular. Clearly the open God did not and indeed could not
have known the specific free decisions involved in the Holocaust before they
were made. But knowing the present perfectly, God would have been aware of
every step of the planning of the Nazi final solution as it happened—even before this planning was implemented. He would know intimately all of the hate-
ful prejudices of Hitler and other Nazi leaders and all of their thinking and deliberations even before they were put into murderous practice. And once the
extermination of the Jews began, God certainly knew about it long before all
six million Jews were killed. So the question remains, Why didn't God do something about it?[86] Open theists insist that God retains the right and the power to
unilaterally intervene. And sometimes he does intervene. So why didn't he in
this case?

It is no solution to argue that God only rarely intervenes out of respect for

---

[86]Ware gives another illustration that makes the same point—the example of a murder. "While
the openness God does not and cannot know the future free action by which a murder will
take place, he does fully know the character of the would-be murderer. He knows all of his
thoughts, plans, meditations, discussions, motives, and intentions. And further, he sees perfectly as each situation (in the present) unfolds. Given this, would not God be in an ideal
position to anticipate the likelihood of the murder occurring? Would not God observe the plot
of the murder unfolding in exact detail (e.g., the man packing the weapon he plans to use,
driving to the location where he intends to commit the murder, mulling over his strategy)?"
(*Their God Is Too Small*, pp. 77-78). The question then is why God wouldn't intervene to stop
the murder.

his gift of libertarian freedom. Even if we argue that in order to promote the full exercise of the gift of freedom, God intervenes only 0.1 percent of the time, the question can still be raised: Why this 0.1 percent and not some other? Why not intervene before the Holocaust to prevent it or even in its earliest stages so as to minimize the suffering and death? Why not intervene in the case of Suzanne?

Sanders appeals to the wisdom of God at this point: "If *the divine wisdom* decides it is best to bring about some specific event in history [or to prevent some event], then God can do so."[87] But on what basis will God's wisdom decide which evils to prevent and which to permit? Certainly it is not on the basis of his infallible foreknowledge of human decisions. And since God's probabilistic anticipations about the future can be wrong (e.g., Jer 3:6-7, 19-20), how can God be confident that any particular occasion is decisive enough to call for his unilateral intervention? And he cannot know for sure the ultimate impact of his intervention because he cannot know how humans will choose to respond to it. Thus God is forced to make his decisions about whether and how to intervene based on incomplete knowledge. This hardly seems to be the exemplary exercise of divine wisdom.

But far more serious is the lack of any specific divine purpose behind suffering and evil. This openness conviction is sharply different from historic understandings of God and his relationship to suffering. Nonopenness views affirm that, whether by reason of God's exhaustive foreknowledge or his sovereign control over all of history, God specifically permits what he knows will ultimately serve a greater purpose. While admittedly the precise nature of this greater purpose and its relationship to any specific occasion of suffering and evil are shrouded in mystery, God does have such an ultimately good purpose. As a result, suffering is not pointless, because God can see what purpose is being served by all the suffering in the world. And because he knows the end from the beginning, he can oversee history to ensure that his good purposes do in fact come to pass.[88]

But according to open theism there is no necessary greater good that is served by any specific occurrence of suffering and evil. This is not to say that there is not some ultimate greater good that operates in a general sense. God is committed to the preservation of libertarian freedom and the love that it makes

---

[87]Sanders, *God Who Risks*, p. 234, emphasis added.
[88]Ware, *Their God Is Too Small*, pp. 78-79. Again, many would argue that God's ability to oversee history in such a way that his ultimate good purposes are accomplished is enhanced to the extent that his exhaustive foreknowledge also includes his knowledge of hypotheticals (as opposed to a purely simple foreknowledge).

possible.[89] But that general purpose does not account for specific occurrences of gratuitous evil. Sanders argues that "God does not have a specific divine purpose for each and every occurrence of evil. The 'greater good' of establishing the conditions of fellowship between God and creatures does not mean that gratuitous evil has a point. Rather the possibility of gratuitous evil has a point but its actuality does not."[90]

Pinnock goes even further, arguing that the fact that God *can* bring good out of evil "does not even ensure that God will succeed in every case to bring good out of it."[91] In this Pinnock is not representative of open theists as a whole, but they are united in denying a necessary connection between every specific occurrence of suffering and evil and a specific greater purpose of God. Yet at this point it is crucial for us to note that even though the God of open theism is unalterably opposed to evil and knows that a specific occurrence may well serve no greater purpose, and that he may not be able to bring good out of it, he allows such suffering to occur in his universe when he could have prevented it.[92] How, may I ask, does this theology exonerate God from moral responsibility for the evil in the world?

The end result, I believe, is that the God of open theism is not as distant from responsibility for evil as it is claimed. He knows every evil plan as it unfolds and can certainly anticipate evil decisions that are coming. He possesses the right to intervene unilaterally but in the vast majority of cases chooses not to. Thus the evils in the world occur because God specifically permitted them to happen—though there is no greater good that would justify them. In short, he is intimately involved in the occurrence of evil. And thus the supposed theological advantage of open theism in grappling with the problem of evil evaporates. This is certainly not to say that there aren't huge questions that advocates of exhaustive divine foreknowledge must grapple with regarding the problem of evil. But it is apparent that open theists are in no better position.[93]

---

[89]For example, Sanders says, "God has a reason for not preventing gratuitous evil—the nature of the divine project" (*God Who Risks*, p. 262).

[90]Ibid.

[91]Pinnock, *Most Moved Mover*, p. 176.

[92]Thus open theists end up asserting some type of permissive will of God. To be sure, Sanders argues strenuously against any kind of view that asserts "two wills in God" (*God Who Risks*, pp. 217-20). Yet whenever there are evil acts that God chooses to allow rather than intervening to stop, God is in fact exercising a form of permissive will.

[93]See Paul Helm, "The Philosophical Issue of Divine Foreknowledge," in *The Grace of God, the Bondage of the Will*, ed. Thomas R. Schreiner and Bruce A. Ware (Grand Rapids: Baker, 1995), pp. 485-97. I would go a step further and argue that open theists are in a worse position, precisely because of their insistence on the absence of any greater good that would justify the evil that God specifically permits.

And when it comes to God's relationship with us as we suffer, we must also ask whether God really is as close to us and as caring for us as open theists affirm. God could have intervened to prevent the suffering or to stop it as soon as it begins, yet he chooses not to for no good reason and with no necessary guarantee that anything good will come out of it. Is this truly a picture of God's loving care for his children? Or is it rather a picture of a God who stands aloof and distant from us in our suffering? The God of open theism does not want this suffering; he has not willed it; he grieves over it and wishes it weren't happening. And yet he will not stop it from happening.[94] Again, I ask, is this a picture of a God who cares for us intimately and lovingly when we suffer? I am not persuaded that it is.

A preferable account of the biblical picture. Biblical teaching, I believe, presents a very different picture of suffering. The Bible clearly and unambiguously asserts God's moral holiness and his freedom from every taint of evil (e.g., "You are not a God who takes pleasure in evil" [Ps 5:4], "Your eyes are too pure to look on evil; / you cannot tolerate wrong" [Hab 1:13], "When tempted, no one should say, 'God is tempting me.' For God cannot be tempted by evil, nor does he tempt anyone" [Jas 1:13]). But Scripture also teaches that God does ordain and use suffering to accomplish his good purposes. In other words, suffering is not an *essential* good. It is not a part of the very nature of God or the world he initially created (cf. Gen 1:31) or the new heavens and the new earth that is God's ultimate goal (cf. Rev 21:3-4). But suffering is used by God as an *instrumental* good. In his eternal divine wisdom, God uses suffering—every occasion of it—to accomplish his good purposes.[95] And while the specifics of exactly how any particular experience of suffering fits into the good and glorious purposes of God are in the vast majority of cases shrouded in mystery (cf. Deut 29:29), nevertheless Scripture gives examples of the kind of instrumental goods that God wills to accomplish through suffering. Thus God ordains that some suffering (not all) is a punishment for sin and God's means of bringing his judgment on those who are opposed to him (e.g., Is 10:5-19; 2 Thess 1:6). On other occasions pain can be part of God's loving fatherly discipline that he uses to mold his children in holiness (Heb 12:5-11). Suffering can at times be appointed by God for the strengthening and purification and growth of the faith of his children (e.g., Rom 5:3-5; Jas 1:2-4). Suffering and pain can also expose human frailty and weakness so that the strength of God shines all the more gloriously (e.g., 2 Cor 4:8-12; 12:8-10), and it can equip believers to more effectively minister to others in their

---

[94]Thus Ware says that if suffering believers cry out in their pain "Where is God in all this?" open theists can only reply, "He's not here" (*Their God Is Too Small,* p. 81).
[95]Ibid., pp. 69-70.

pain (e.g., 2 Cor 1:3-7).[96] This list is not comprehensive, but it does illustrate the kind of instrumental goods that God may be pleased to accomplish through suffering and evil. But no matter what instrumental good (or combination of instrumental goods) God is seeking, the point is that in and through every experience of suffering and evil, God is at work to accomplish his good purposes.

This is why Paul makes the astounding and very precious promise of Romans 8:28, "We know that in all things God works for the good of those who love him, who have been called according to his purpose."[97] Through his inspired apostle, God assures his children that nothing comes into their lives (including the kinds of suffering that Paul mentions in Rom 8:35—"trouble or hardship or persecution or famine or nakedness or danger or sword") that is not foreseen by God and ordered and used by him for their ultimate good. The next verse clearly defines the "good" that God is working for in and through every circumstance of the lives of his children—their moral conformity to the likeness of his Son, the Lord Jesus Christ.[98] But the comfort of this verse is precious beyond imaging. God does have a good purpose for all that occurs in the lives of his children, as opposed to the possibility of gratuitous evil without a specific good purpose affirmed by open theists. And this good purpose is one that God actually accomplishes.

Sanders, on the other hand, argues that even though God seeks to work in our lives for good purposes in the midst of our trials, his good purposes are not always accomplished: "Tribulations do not always strengthen people's trust in God. Just because God is at work in our lives does not assure his victory. . . . The purposes of God meet with resistance, and even God does not always get what he desires."[99]

---

[96]Ibid.

[97]There is considerable controversy about the proper translation of Rom 8:28. At issue is the subject of the verb *synergei* ("work together"). The traditional rendering of the KJV ("all things work together for good") takes *panta* to be the subject of the verb. This is followed by the ESV ("And we know that for those who love God all things work together for good . . ."). Alternately, the NIV and NRSV take the understood he from the verb *synergei* to refer to God (in continuity with the divine subject of vv. 29-30). For arguments in support of each translation, see Schreiner, *Romans*, p. 449, and Leon Morris, *The Epistle to the Romans* (Leicester: Inter-Varsity Press and Grand Rapids: Eerdmans, 1988), pp. 330-31.

[98]Schreiner argues that this moral good that God is working for in and through every circumstance in the lives of believers is eschatological. "It will be evident and fully realized only at the end time." Yet knowing this final outcome now, believers are strengthened and filled with courage in facing any and every situation in life (*Romans*, p. 450).

[99]Sanders, *God Who Risks*, p. 128. To be sure, Sanders does argue that in an ultimate and cosmic sense God will win in the end. So in the most universal sense God will "get what he desires." But Paul's concern in Rom 8:28 is with God's good purposes not for the cosmos as a whole but for the specific believers he was writing to—and by extension all those "who love [God] and are called according to his purpose."

But this is exactly the opposite of what Paul is arguing in this passage. He argues that those God foreknew, he predestined to be conformed to the likeness of his Son. And those he predestined, he called, justified and will ultimately glorify (Rom 8:29-30). There is no doubt that God will actually accomplish his ultimate purpose of glorifying everyone he foreknows, conforming them to the likeness of his Son. Paul continues to argue that since God has already given his people his greatest and most costly gift of all, his Son, he will most assuredly give to them "all things" as well (Rom 8:32). And finally Paul argues that nothing can ultimately separate God's people from his love in Christ, not even all the sufferings of this life (Rom 8:33-38). Nothing in this passage signifies uncertainty as to whether God's ultimate good purposes in the lives of these believers will be accomplished. Thus there can be and indeed should be an ultimate sense of hope and confidence that can sustain Christians through all the ups and downs of life. But, on the other hand, the openness teaching about the lack of divine purpose for suffering and evil and the uncertainty of whether God can bring good out of it ends up robbing Christians of the very hope and confidence that Scripture intends for them to have.

Indeed believers must have confidence in God's good purposes in and through our suffering if we are ever to obey Scripture:

> Not only so, but we also rejoice in our sufferings, because we know that suffering produces perseverance; perseverance, character; and character, hope. And hope does not disappoint us, because God has poured out his love into our hearts by the Holy Spirit, whom he has given us. (Rom 5:3-5)
>
> Consider it pure joy, my brothers, whenever you face trials of many kinds, because you know that the testing of your faith develops perseverance. Perseverance must finish its work so that you may be mature and complete, not lacking anything. (Jas 1:2-4)

Both of these texts command us to rejoice when we suffer—not because of any essential goodness in the suffering itself but because of our confidence in the instrumental good God promises to bring about through our suffering. But if we were persuaded that our suffering might in fact be utterly gratuitous, with no divinely ordained good purpose in it, or that a good purpose that God does have might not necessarily be accomplished in our lives, how could we rejoice? Those theological convictions of open theism would lead us away from a confident rejoicing, even in the midst of pain, to uncertainty, anxiety and perhaps even despair.[100]

---

[100]Ware makes a similar point with regard to the biblical commands for believers to give thanks in all circumstances (1 Thess 5:18) and to give thanks for everything (Eph 5:20)—including suffering. This makes sense only if God has promised to be at work in and through every

My conclusion is that the only genuine source of comfort and hope for believers who are grappling with suffering and evil is a God who knows the future
exhaustively, who can thus know exactly when to intervene to take away the
suffering, and who is assuredly working out his eternal good purposes wisely
and efficaciously for his children.[101] In this God, and this God only, we can rejoice and put our ultimate hope—even when we suffer.

Hope in the Ultimate Triumph of God

Especially when we suffer, we need hope. In the midst of the worst of suffering,
we instinctively cry out, Will this ever end? Will my suffering have the last word
in my life? And more broadly, we ask, Will God win in the end? Will his kingdom
be ultimately and finally victorious? To this issue we turn our attention now.[102]

The open view and eschatological confidence. Open theists consistently
affirm a high degree of confidence that God's ultimate purposes will be
achieved in the end. Though the future is in part open and indeterminate, the
eventual outcome of history does not remain in doubt. God's kingdom will ultimately triumph over the powers of evil. For example, Pinnock confidently asserts, "Evil may have its day, but it will not finally triumph."[103] At first glance this
high level of ultimate eschatological confidence seems unwarranted in light of
openness understandings of God's nonexhaustive foreknowledge; the general,
not specific nature of his sovereignty; and his willingness to take risks to enable
the full functioning of libertarian freedom. But nonetheless open theists insist
that we can be confident of the final triumph of God's kingdom and his ultimate
victory over sin and evil.

There are two primary reasons for this high degree of ultimate eschatological
confidence. We have already seen the first: God in his sovereignty retains the right

---

circumstance to accomplish his good purpose. But how different would the situation be if
the teaching of open theism were correct. "If the suffering that comes into our lives is pointless, if God has no good intent for it, and if all that it does is cause harm, then there is no
reason to give thanks *in* the suffering, and certainly not *for* the suffering. You cannot genuinely give thanks in the suffering if you think that there is simply nothing about this that can
possibly be a basis for giving thanks, that God is not in it (that in fact he feels badly about
it and wishes it weren't happening), that Satan is chuckling over this, and that there is no
assurance that the suffering will end any differently than it began—pointless, meaningless,
and void of any and all possible good purpose. If that is how we think of suffering, we can
only (rightly) despair *in* it and *for* it" (*Their God Is Too Small,* p. 71).

[101]Paul's confidence in God's wisdom and love in this regard is what enabled him to rejoice
contentedly when God said no to his prayer to remove his thorn in the flesh (2 Cor 12:7-10).

[102]Much of the material in this section is taken from Steven C. Roy, "God as Omnicompetent
Responder? Questions about the Grounds of Eschatological Confidence in Open Theism," in
Looking to the Future, ed. David W. Baker (Grand Rapids: Baker, 2001), pp. 263-80.

[103]Pinnock, "Systematic Theology," p. 116.

to intervene in human history and on rare occasions to overrule human freedom coercively if necessary to ensure the ultimate accomplishment of his purposes.[104]

The second reason for eschatological confidence in open theism is that God is viewed as "omnicompetent" or "omniresourceful" in his ability to anticipate what his creatures will freely choose to do and to respond appropriately. It is God's omnicompetent response in every circumstance that guarantees the accomplishment of his ultimate purposes. An example of this kind of argument comes from Richard Rice:

> The open view of God does not render God helpless before a dark and mysterious future. Nothing can happen that He has not already envisioned and for which He has not made adequate preparations. Consequently, although God does not know the future absolutely, He nevertheless anticipates it perfectly. . . . God knows what could happen as the result of creaturely decisions. And He knows just what course of action He will take in response to each eventuality.[105]

Pinnock agrees that God is able to bring his will to pass in the ultimate sense even in a world in which finite agents are free to resist him. "He can do it because of his ability to anticipate the obstructions the creatures can throw in his way and respond to each new challenge in an effective manner. . . . Nothing

---

[104]Recall the comparison made by Hasker of God's "control" over the lives of people with the "control" parents have over their small children: "Their policy could well be described as the deliberate and intensive application of 'persuasive power'—though to be sure, coercive power is there in reserve, should the child start to run out into a busy roadway. Should not a similar account be given of God's control over us?" ("A Philosophical Perspective," p. 142). Erickson notes perceptively, "If I understand Hasker correctly, he seems to be suggesting that, in a situation of extremity, God may use 'coercive power' to exercise his 'control over us.' But is this not the very thing, which the free will [i.e., open] theists have charged the classical view: of holding that God coerces, or works irresistibly, thus robbing humans of their freedom? If he is actually suggesting this, however, then the difference between this view and the classical view is one of degree, not of kind" (*God the Father Almighty*, pp. 91-92). God's willingness to overrule libertarian freedom in extreme situations to keep his program on track raises a crucial problem for open theists. If Hasker is correct and God is willing at times to use coercive control to insure his ultimate triumph, then at those decisive points in history, humans are no longer exercising libertarian freedom. A coercively determined action is not free. And thus the human agents are no longer morally accountable because libertarian freedom is the necessary prerequisite for moral responsibility. The implications of this are indeed staggering. At the most crucial points in all of human history, where the key decisions have to be made that will be decisive for the final outcome, God effectively takes humans out of the picture, turning them into "robots," as it were, devoid of freedom and moral responsibility in these decisions. Ultimately, then, open theism, which seeks to elevate the reality and the importance of libertarian human freedom and of human moral responsibility, ends up minimizing these realities. At the crucial decisive moments in human history, God is willing to dispense with both freedom and moral responsibility.

[105]Richard Rice, *God's Foreknowledge and Man's Free Will* [Minneapolis: Bethany House, 1985], p. 58.

can happen which God has not anticipated or cannot handle."[106]

Often cited in support of this position is Peter Geach's illustration of a chess game played between a Grand Master, who represents God, and a novice, who represents humans in their freedom. While not being able to determine every move the novice makes, the Grand Master has sufficient skill and resourcefulness to respond to whatever the novice does so as to guarantee victory. Geach explains the illustration:

> God and man alike play in the great game. But God is the supreme Grand Master who has everything under control. Some of the players are consciously helping his plan, others are trying to hinder it; whatever the finite players do, God's plan will be executed. . . . God cannot be surprised or thwarted or cheated or disappointed. God, like some grand master of chess, can carry out his plan even if he has announced it beforehand. "On that square," says the Grand Master, "I will promote my pawn to Queen and deliver checkmate to my adversary": and it is so. No line of play that finite players may think of can force God to improvise: his knowledge of the game already embraces all the possible variant lines of play, theirs do not.[107]

Open theists agree with Geach that no matter what humans choose to do, individually or collectively, God will still win in the end. Thus Boyd pictures God as a master chess player who is supremely confident of her ability to ensure ultimate victory.

> Her confidence is rooted in her ability to wisely anticipate all *possible* future moves her opponent might make together with all possible responses she may make to each of these possible moves. She does not know exactly how many moves she will make, or what these moves will be, before the match begins, for she does not know exactly how her opponent will move his pieces. If her opponent is formidable, she may even have to place certain pieces "at risk" in order to finally checkmate him. But *by virtue of her superior wisdom* she is certain of victory.[108]

Because of this, Rice argues that "the final outcome of history is a practical certainty. God's objectives for mankind will be realized, whatever the actual course of events may be. Because God's resources are infinitely superior to those of His creatures, He can respond to all their decisions with complete adequacy."[109]

---

[106]Pinnock, "God Limits His Knowledge," p. 146. Hasker argues in the same vein, saying that "we certainly should not underestimate the tremendous resourcefulness of God in adapting his responses to human actions—even willful and disobedient human actions—so as to achieve his wise and loving purposes" ("Philosophical Perspective," p. 153).

[107]Peter Geach, *Providence and Evil* (New York: Cambridge University Press, 1977), p. 58.

[108]Boyd, *Satan and the Problem of Evil*, p. 113.

[109]Rice, *God's Foreknowledge and Man's Free Will*, pp. 66-67.

Sanders is less confident, however, that the Grand Master analogy can adequately illustrate the personal nature of the relationship between God and his
human creatures.[110] He argues that future reality is not as closed as Geach seems
to suggest and that the reality of libertarian human freedom eliminates the kind
of total and complete control of the game that Geach postulates (down to the
very square on which God will win the game). Indeed, Sanders says that "God
cannot win every move on account of human sin and evil."[111] Thus Sanders argues that we must distinguish between God's overall goal in creation and his
specific desires for specific individuals. God's specific desires for individuals
may not be accomplished. "If God does not force the creatures to reciprocate
his love, then the possibility is introduced that at least some of them may fail to
enter into the divine love, and thus certain of God's specific desires might be
thwarted."[112] But when Sanders looks to the ultimate fulfillment of God's overall
goals and objectives, he argues that we may rightly trust the living God for the
fulfillment of his promises. There is substantial hope for this ultimate victory because God is the omnicompetent responder.

> We should not underestimate God's ability or overestimate our own in this enter-
> prise. God is omnicompetent, resourceful and wise enough to take our moves into
> account, mighty enough to act and faithful enough to persist. If one of God's plans
> fails, he has others ready at hand and finds other ways of accomplishing his objec-
> tives.[113]

Thus for both of these reasons—God sovereignly retaining the right to unilaterally intervene in human history if need be, and God being an omnicompetent responder to everything his creatures will freely choose to do—open theists
argue for a strong sense of eschatological confidence. Whether this eschatological confidence is "guaranteed" (Boyd) and rises to the level of "practical certainty" (Rice) or remains at the level of confident hope (Sanders), they are united
in the conviction that God will ultimately win in the end. Jesus Christ will return

---

[110]Sanders, *God Who Risks*, pp. 229-30. Sanders suggests that better analogies include that of
the leader of a climbing-party, who is responsible to plan for routes and supplies but who
on the journey has to make ad hoc decisions along with the other members of the party, and
that of a theater director directing actors and actresses in a play who also play a significant
part in how the play goes [ibid., pp. 216-17, 230].
[111]Ibid., p. 230.
[112]Ibid., p. 229. Sanders argues that "God's overarching intentions cannot fail in that God estab-
lishes the boundaries in which the world will operate; but God's detailed or particular desires
can fail in that God may not achieve all he wants for every individual. . . . Unless one affirms
either universalism or double predestination, it must be concluded that God's project ends
in failure for some" (ibid., p. 230).
[113]Ibid., p. 234.

and will bring the kingdom of God to its ultimate and eternal triumph.

How much confidence is truly warranted under the open view? It is my conviction that this level of eschatological confidence cannot be coherently sustained within the open model. Given its central theological assumptions (e.g., libertarian human freedom, God's actions being contingent on and responsive to free human decisions, and God's nonexhaustive foreknowledge), a high level of eschatological confidence cannot stand. In fact, I believe that there is an inverse relationship between eschatological confidence and these central, core doctrines of the open view. The more strongly these are affirmed, the less eschatological confidence is warranted. Conversely, the greater the level of eschatological confidence, the more compromises will need to be made in these core doctrines.

We have already considered the difficulties raised by a nonexhaustive view of divine foreknowledge for the effectiveness of the openness argument from God's ability to unilaterally intervene in human history. How will such a God know whether a particular circumstance is crucial enough to warrant his intervention? How will such a God know the best time to intervene and how his intervention should take place? We understand that openness proponents affirm that God will intervene in this way only rarely (perhaps only 0.1 percent of the time). But on what basis will God decide which 0.1 percent of the time to intervene? This has great implications for the problem of evil. But now we ask, How can a God with less than exhaustive foreknowledge guarantee that his intervention will be precisely at the most needed points in history and in the most effective ways so as to insure his ultimate victory?

The only way available to the open theist at this point, as I see it, would be to affirm that God will choose to act in a final display of divine omnipotence that will bring about ultimate eschatological victory at a time of his own choosing. This final dramatic, omnipotent act would be utterly independent of any and all human decisions. God will act at the time of his choosing to bring human history to an end and to usher in the fullness of his kingdom—whether this divine act is in continuity with what he has been doing in responsive relationship with his people or whether it is utterly disparate from his previous activities. This conviction would truly allow open theists to rightly have a high level of eschatological confidence. But it would come, I argue, at a high cost for open theists. This conception of God's final eschatological victory would end up minimizing any intrinsic continuity between the final eschatological act of God and the mutually responsive partnership that God desires to have with his children. For when the time comes for the ultimately decisive and triumphant act, God will act with or without his children. The partnership may rightly be ignored if need be. This will bring about final victory, but the essential role of the divine-human partnership will be minimized. Equally so, questions remain about how the open God, possessing nonexhaustive foreknowledge, will know when the right time will be for his final omnipotent act of triumph. If, as 2 Peter 3:8-9 indicates, God's patience in delaying final judgment is designed to allow for more time for humans to repent, how will the open God know the very best time to end his patience and bring about his final judgment? If he waits longer, would more people repent? The open God cannot know for sure. So how will he know when to act?

The point of all this is that the openness convictions of God's sovereign right to intervene unilaterally and omnipotently in human history does not in itself warrant a high level of eschatological confidence for open theists. Other crucial elements of the openness model, most notably a nonexhaustive understanding of the extent of divine foreknowledge, minimize the eschatological conviction that God's omnipotence may rightly bring.

A similar argument can be made with respect to the openness view of God as the omnicompetent responder. One of the reasons why Rice believes that God can omnicompetently respond to everything humans freely choose to do is that he is able to perfectly anticipate their actions in the future: "Although God does not know the future absolutely, He nevertheless anticipates it perfectly."[114]

Yet it is not clear how God's perfect anticipation of future human decisions is different from the classical view of divine foreknowledge. Rice acknowledges that practically the results of God's perfect anticipation look to be identical with his having exhaustive foreknowledge. But with respect to creaturely freedom, Rice argues there is a world of difference. Exhaustive divine foreknowledge would eliminate the possibility of genuine human freedom, while God's anticipation, even if it is perfect, gives room for freedom to function.[115]

Yet to me Rice seems to want to have both sides of an incompatible combination. To ensure that the future is not definite and fixed in such a way as would eliminate the reality of libertarian human freedom, Rice downgrades God's beliefs about the future from that of certain and infallible knowledge to "anticipations" that are potentially fallible. Their fallibility could be illustrated by Jeremiah 3:6-7, 19-20. But if God's "anticipation" of the future could be mistaken and wrong in this case, couldn't it be wrong in other more serious cases as well?

---

[114]Rice, *God's Foreknowledge and Man's Free Will*, p. 58.

[115]Rice says, "The open view of God, then, views the future as partly definite and partly indefinite from God's perspective. His relation to the future is one of perfect anticipation. This understanding allows for creaturely freedom" (ibid., p. 59).

It is hard to see how this kind of fallible anticipation can enable God to omni-competently respond to whatever humans freely decide to do. (How could a false anticipation help God cope with the future challenges of human history?)

On the other hand, if God's anticipation of the future is perfect enough and accurate enough to provide the basis for God to make adequate preparations for his future responses, it implies just as great a fixity of future events as does exhaustive divine foreknowledge. In the end this would undermine libertarian human freedom and the contingency of God's responsiveness to it.

Unfortunately for Rice it is impossible to have both sides of this incompatible combination. He and other open theists can have a future that is open enough for libertarian freedom to flourish but which lessens the level of eschatological confidence that is warranted, or they can have a high degree of ultimate confidence at the cost of the fullest flourishing of libertarian freedom. But they cannot have both.

A second concern about God as omnicompetent responder turns on the nature of human freedom. If, as open theists argue, human freedom truly is libertarian, how can God guarantee that he will be able to respond to every move freely made by humans in the cosmic chess game? Sanders seems to grant the force of this objection is his statement: "God cannot win every move on account of human sin and evil."[116] But if God cannot win every move, how can we be sure that he will inevitably win the decisive moves that determine the outcome of the game? Granted, God's wisdom, skill and resourcefulness are infinitely greater in comparison to ours (much like that of the greatest Grand Master compared to the novice chess player), but what guarantee is there that by blind chance the novice will make the one in a million move that the Master cannot respond to? As long as humans have libertarian freedom, that is always possible.

Consider, for example, God's judgment of the world through the flood. When the Lord saw the depth and pervasiveness of human evil, he "was grieved that he had made man on the earth, and his heart was filled with pain" (Gen 6:5-6). The openness argument is that for God's repentance here to be real and genuine, the depth and pervasiveness of human sin must not have been foreseen and certainly not planned by God. Thus in Genesis 6, God genuinely responds to unforeseen and freely chosen human decisions and undertakes a new and different course of action (judging the world through the flood).

But what would necessarily prevent another future degeneration of the human race into sin that is even greater than that which precipitated the flood? What is to prevent an outbreak of human sin and evil great enough and perva-

---

[116]Sanders, *God Who Risks*, p. 230.

sive enough such that God will respond by abandoning his prior plans and destroying the human race completely in his judgment? Most open theists argue that this kind of universal judgment will not happen because God has promised in the Noahic covenant that it never will (Gen 8:21-22). While God does not foreknow the free decisions of creatures possessing libertarian freedom, he can and does know what he will unilaterally choose to do in the future.

But again we ask, Can the open God really know that? If God is indeed genuinely responsive to humans and if he cannot infallibly know their future free decisions, then it is in principle impossible for God to know infallibly what he will do in the future as well. Couldn't there be a future, unforeseen occurrence that would lead God to reconsider his previously planned and previously announced course of action? God could not infallibly know such an eventuality in advance. And should it occur, it is certainly possible that a genuinely responsive God would decide to change his plans. This is what happened when God reconsidered his announced intention to destroy Nineveh after the Ninevites had repented in response to the preaching of Jonah. God's statement of impending judgment on Nineveh included an implicit, though unstated, condition. But how do we not know that God's promise to never again destroy all living creatures (Gen 8:21-22) does not contain a similar implicit condition? The point is that the mere statement of the open God that he will never do something in the future (or a positive statement that he will most assuredly do something in the future) cannot be taken as an absolute guarantee. There is always the possibility that some unforeseen event in the future would move this genuinely responsive God to change his announced plans and do things differently. Thus even God's knowledge of his own actions in the future is at best probabilistic.[117] And so God's statement that he will ultimately triumph over sin and evil is no necessary guarantee. As Wayne Grudem says:

> How can we be sure that God will triumph over [evil] in the end? Of course, God
> *says* in Scripture that he will triumph over evil. But if he was unable to keep it out
> of his universe in the first place and it came in against his will, and if he is unable
> to predict the outcome of any future events that involve free choices by human,

---

[117]Recall the argument of Richard Swinburne that God cannot infallibly know what he will do in the future. He grounds this, however, not in God's responsiveness to unforeseen, freely chosen actions of humans but rather in the nature of God's own libertarian freedom. Just as exhaustive divine foreknowledge is incompatible with libertarian human freedom, so it is incompatible with libertarian divine freedom. "I conclude that it seems doubtful whether it is logically possible that there be both an omniscient person and also free men; but that it is definitely logically impossible that there be an omniscient person who is himself perfectly free" (*Coherence of Theism*, p. 177).

angelic, and demonic agents, how then can we be sure that God's declaration that he will triumph over all evil is itself true? Perhaps this is just a hopeful prediction of something that . . . God simply cannot know.[118]

And finally, we must consider the distinction that Sanders draws between God's overall goals and objectives for his creation project and his specific desires for individual persons. This distinction is necessary, in my opinion, if a person seeks to hold both to overall eschatological confidence and to the libertarian freedom of individual human beings. But it comes with a very heavy price. Sanders's distinction assumes that it is possible for God's ultimate purposes in history to be fulfilled even while many individuals reject God's grace in Christ and end up in hell. If this is the case, then God's ultimate purposes must be separated from the welfare of individual human beings. God's ultimate purposes must be cosmic and racial rather than individual, tied not to his love for specific individuals but only to general purposes, such as giving libertarian freedom to each person and then respecting his or her choice. But this reality, I believe, ultimately goes against the claim that open theism magnifies the love of God for individuals. In reality, it seems to do the opposite.

All of these considerations lead to the conclusion that neither the argument from God's sovereign and unilateral intervention nor the argument from God as omnicompetent responder warrants the level of eschatological confidence claimed by open theists. In the end I affirm that there is an inverse relationship between the level of eschatological confidence that is rightly warranted and the central, core theological convictions of open theism. To the extent that one is elevated, the other is diminished.[119] In the final analysis they can either rightly enjoy a high degree of eschatological confidence or they can allow key theological elements of their position to flourish. But once again, they cannot have both.

Is there a better alternative? I wholeheartedly agree with the desire of open theists to be eschatologically confident. It is biblical. Scripture teaches the importance of eschatological confidence for us at a personal level. Our confident hope as believers is that God and his grace will have the last word in our lives. He will be ultimately and eternally victorious in our lives. And that hope is regularly appealed to in Scripture to encourage us to persevere in faith and obedience. One example of this is Romans 8. The chapter begins with the confident hope that all believers can rightly have because of Christ in God's verdict in the final judgment: "Therefore, there is now no condemnation for those who

---

[118]Grudem, *Systematic Theology* (Grand Rapids: Zondervan, 1994), p. 350.
[119]Erickson argues that in the end open theists are confronted with "either the loss of human freedom or of certainty of the ultimate outcome" (*God the Father Almighty,* p. 92).

are in Christ Jesus" (Rom 8:1). The chapter speaks of our confident hope in the glory of our future inheritance with Christ, a hope that will sustain us in times of suffering: "Now if we are children, then we are heirs—heirs of God and co-heirs of Christ, if indeed we share in his sufferings in order that we may also share in his glory. I consider that our present sufferings are not worth comparing with the glory that will be revealed in us" (Rom 8:17-18). And Romans 8 concludes with Paul's triumphant hope that nothing will ever be able to separate him from God's love in Christ.

> Who shall separate us from the love of Christ? Shall trouble or hardship or perse-cution or famine or nakedness or danger or sword? As it is written:
>
>> "For your sake we face death all day long;
>> we are considered as sheep to be slaughtered."
>
> No, in all these things we are more than conquerors through him who loved us. For I am convinced that neither death nor life, neither angels nor demons, neither the present nor the future, nor any powers, neither height nor depth nor anything else in all creation, will be able to separate us from the love of God that is in Christ Jesus our Lord. (Rom 8:35-39)

But Scripture also intends for us to have hope in God's triumph in history, his cosmic and eternal triumph over all the powers of evil. The book of Revelation is certainly intended to foster and strengthen such confidence for God's people, especially when they suffer. Robert Mounce, for example, argues that as a result of the book of Revelation, "We know that the persecuted church will witness the victorious return of Christ and share in his subsequent reign. We also know that the forces of evil will be totally defeated and Satan and his hordes will forever be destroyed."[120]

And this cosmic eschatological confidence influences how we live here and now (cf. Rev 13:10, following a vision of the beast coming out of the sea, "This calls for patient endurance and faithfulness on the part of the saints").

But I contend that such biblical confidence in the ultimate triumph of God, both personally and cosmically, requires the exhaustive foreknowledge of God. Only a God who knows the end from the beginning—exhaustively and infalli-bly—can know how to order and rule our own lives and indeed all of history to insure that his purposes of grace will be ultimately victorious. Only a God of exhaustive foreknowledge can infallibly know whether and how to answer our prayers to maximally contribute to his glory and to our eternal good. Only such

---

[120]Robert H. Mounce, *The Book of Revelation,* rev. ed. New International Commentary on the New Testament (Grand Rapids: Eerdmans, 1998), p. 33.

a God can guide us as believers and guide history to his appointed end. And the good news is that this is in fact the God of Scripture. Scripture shows consistently and pervasively that God does indeed foreknow future free decisions. And so we can have hope.

CONCLUSIONS

Throughout this chapter we have examined the practical implications of our understanding of the extent of God's foreknowledge. We have looked at five areas—worship, petitionary prayer, God's guidance in our lives, our grappling with suffering and evil, and our hope in the ultimate triumph of God and his kingdom. And in each of these areas we have found the theological model of exhaustive divine foreknowledge to be much more satisfying than its openness, nonexhaustive counterpart. In each area this understanding produces a greater degree of confidence in life and ministry than the openness alternative. Exhaustive divine foreknowledge enables a level of expectation and practice that much more closely corresponds to the vision of the Christian life portrayed in Scripture.

While the primary burden of this book has been to demonstrate that the model of exhaustive divine foreknowledge best accounts for the data of Scripture and thus is to be preferred on biblical and theological grounds, this chapter shows that exhaustive divine foreknowledge also passes the adequacy criterion far more successfully than its openness alternative.

7

CONCLUSION

God knows the future—exhaustively and definitely and infallibly! Such has been the burden of this book. Throughout I have sought to demonstrate that this understanding of divine foreknowledge, which has been the majority position throughout the history of Christian theology, is indeed the most biblically accurate model. While admittedly there are no doctrinal passages in Scripture that explicitly and conclusively deal with this issue in the form of succinct theological propositions, I have sought to establish that Scripture does in fact teach God's exhaustive, definite foreknowledge. It does so, I have argued, widely and pervasively. Both quantitative and qualitative evidence have been put forward to support this claim.

I have made my argument through an examination of Old Testament evidence (chap. 2) and New Testament evidence (chap. 3). In both Testaments we have seen a vast and wide biblical portrayal of a divine foreknowledge that does in fact include free human decisions (e.g., Ps 139, the promise and fulfillment motif of 1-2 Kings, Old Testament messianic prophecy, the New Testament language of foreknowledge, the foreknowledge of Jesus, and God's foreknowledge of his own plan of redemption). Not only is this portrayal numerically significant in both testaments, we also find that God placed tremendous weight on his knowledge of future free decisions. This is seen most clearly in the Old Testament in Isaiah 40—48, where Yahweh specifically and repeatedly appeals to his unique ability to know and predict the future, including future free decisions (esp. those of Cyrus), to show his utter and complete superiority over all the gods of the surrounding pagan nations. A corresponding New Testament statement of the vital importance of exhaustive divine foreknowledge comes from the teaching of Jesus in John 13:19. In the context of his predictions of the future free decisions of Peter and Judas, Jesus said to his disciples that he was telling them in advance what would happen so that when it did happen they would believe that "I am he." Thus in a way strikingly similar to Isaiah 40—48, Jesus sought to strengthen the faith of his disciples by pointing to his ability to know and predict the future free decisions of two of his apostles. As Yahweh did, so

Jesus points to his foreknowledge as evidence of his deity.

We then turned our attention in chapter four to biblical texts claimed to support an open, nonexhaustive view of God's foreknowledge. Many of these texts involve the repentance of God. We sought to understand them in light of their nature as anthropomorphic metaphors, concluding that biblical statements of divine repentance are reality-depicting metaphors; that is, they portray a genuine similarity between the divine and the human experience of repentance. But as metaphors, these texts also speak to the differences that exist between divine and human repentance. Scripture asserts that when God repents, he does not do so in every sense as humans do (Num 23:19; 1 Sam 15:29; Hos 11:8-9). The question then becomes whether the relationship between God's repentance and his foreknowledge is one of the similarities or one of the differences inherent in the metaphor. That question cannot be answered from the divine-repentance texts themselves; but in light of the quantitative and qualitative biblical evidence for exhaustive divine foreknowledge presented in chapters two and three, I concluded that the repentance of God does not argue against his exhaustive foreknowledge. Toward the end of chapter four, we looked more briefly at God's testing of Abraham and the knowledge he gained from it (Gen 22:12). I argued that God's statement to Abraham did not indicate a movement from ignorance to knowledge on God's part but rather a statement that Abraham's fear of God had now been demonstrated in experience. And finally, we looked at examples of texts in which God says "perhaps," texts in which God asks nonrhetorical questions, and texts in which it is claimed that God's beliefs about the future are mistaken. My analysis led us to the conviction that none of these texts necessarily demanded a less-than-exhaustive divine foreknowledge.

In chapter five we examined two crucial hermeneutical questions that have been raised by openness proponents: (1) Has our understanding of the biblical evidence been so shaped by Greek philosophy that we have not read these texts fairly? And (2) is it possible that the Bible teaches a twofold understanding of the future and God's knowledge of it? Could it be the case that the Bible teaches that a portion of the future is definite and fixed, and thus can be known by God with infallible certainty, while another portion of the future is indefinite and open, and thus can be known by God only as possibilities? Our examination of each of these questions did not diminish our confidence in the conclusions of our exegetical study. My conviction remains that the exhaustive foreknowledge of God is in fact the theological model that best accounts for the evidence of Scripture.

While this study has been primarily a biblical and theological one, we turned our attention in chapter six to the practical implications of our understanding of the extent of God's foreknowledge. We looked at five areas of practical implications: worship of God, petitionary prayer, God's guidance, suffering and evil, and hope in the ultimate triumph of God and his kingdom. In each area I contrasted the practical implications of a nonexhaustive understanding of God's foreknowledge (combined as it so often is with the other elements of the open view of God) with those flowing from an understanding of exhaustive divine foreknowledge. And we found that holding to God's foreknowledge of free human decisions enabled the kind of confidence in God and Christian practice that is commended in Scripture. In short, I concluded that the theological model of God's exhaustive, definite foreknowledge passes the adequacy test better than its open, nonexhaustive counterpart.

To be sure, I have not demonstrated the biblical correctness of this model of divine foreknowledge with absolute certainty. No doubt our openness brothers and sisters will arrive at different conclusions from the texts of Scripture. But our conclusion is that a very strong case can be made that the view of exhaustive divine foreknowledge is the best model to deal with the teaching of all of Scripture. Thus I believe we can honestly affirm that the God who is "perfect in knowledge" (Job 37:16), the almighty God whose "understanding has no limit" (Ps 147:5), the great God who "knows everything" (1 Jn 3:20) does indeed possess full and absolute and infallible knowledge of all future events—including all actions freely chosen by human beings. God's foreknowledge is one of many attributes that make him qualitatively different and infinitely superior to us, and thus it redounds to his great glory.

By design, the scope of this study has been limited. It is focused on *whether* the God of Scripture foreknows future free decisions. The question of *how* God foreknows these decisions is one of many questions that is deserving of more study and analysis. But though limited in scope, my prayer is that this study will be a significant piece of our ongoing search for understanding of the nature of God and his relationship to his human creation. May it deepen our knowledge of the great God who is our Creator and Redeemer, and may it intensify our love and worship of him and our desire to serve him with all our hearts.

> I am God, and there is no other;
> > I am God, and there is none like me.
> I make known the end from the beginning,
> > from ancient times, what is still to come.
> I say: My purpose will stand,
> > and I will do all that I please. (Is 46:9-10)

To this great God be glory and honor forever and ever!

BIBLIOGRAPHY

Allen, Leslie C. *The Books of Joel, Obadiah, Jonah and Micah*. New International Commentary on the Old Testament. Grand Rapids: Eerdmans, 1976.

———. *Psalms 101-150*. Word Biblical Commentary 21. Waco, Tex.: Word, 1983.

Allen, Ronald B. *Numbers*. Expositor's Bible Commentary 2. Grand Rapids: Zondervan, 1990.

———. "The Theology of the Balaam Oracles." In *Tradition and Testament: Essays in Honor of Charles Lee Feinberg,* edited by John S. Feinberg and Paul D. Feinberg. Chicago: Moody Press, 1981.

Andersen, Francis I., and David Noel Freedman. *Amos: A New Translation with Introduction and Commentary*. Anchor Bible 24A. New York: Doubleday, 1989.

Anderson, Bernhard W. "When God Repents." *Bible Review* 121 (1996).

Brother Andrew. *And God Changed His Mind*. Grand Rapids: Chosen Books, 1999.

Aquinas, Thomas. *Summa Contra Gentiles* 1, translated by the Dominican Fathers. London: Burns, Oates, & Washborne, 1924.

———. *Summa Theologiciae:* Vol. 2, *Existence and Nature of God,* translated by Timothy McDermott. London: Blackfriars, 1964.

———. *Summa Theologiciae:* Vol. 4, *Knowledge in God,* translated by Thomas J. Gornall. London: Blackfriars, 1964.

Archer, Gleason L. *A Survey of Old Testament Introduction*. Rev. ed. Chicago: Moody Press, 1974.

Argyle, Aubrey W. "God's 'Repentance' and the LXX." *Expository Times* 75 (1964).

Aristotle. *The Categories of Interpretation,* translated by Harold P. Cooke. Loeb Classical Library. Cambridge, Mass.: Harvard University Press, 1967.

Arminius, James. "Friendly Conversation of James Arminius with Francis Junius About Predestination." In *The Works of James Arminius,* translated by James Nichols and William Nichols. Vol. 3. Grand Rapids: Baker, 1991.

Auffret, Pierre. "O Dieu, connais mon coeur: Etude structurelle du Psaume CXXXIX." *Vetus Testamentum* 47 (1997).

Augustine. *The City of God,* translated by M. Dods and J. J. Smith. In *Basic Writings of St. Augustine*. Vol. 2. Edited by Whitney J. Oates. Grand Rapids: Baker, 1980.

———. *The Confessions,* translated by J. G. Pilkington. In *Basic Writings of St. Augustine*. Vol. 1. Edited by Whitney J. Oates. Grand Rapids: Baker, 1980.

———. *De Libero Arbitrio,* translated by John H. S. Burleigh. In *Augustine: Earlier Writings.* Library of Christian Classics 6. Philadelphia: Westminster, 1953.

Aune, David E. *Revelation 6-16.* Word Biblical Commentary 52B. Nashville: Thomas Nelson, 1998.

Austel, Hermann J. *"shāqar."* *Theological Wordbook of the Old Testament,* edited by R. Laird Harris, Gleason L. Archer Jr. and Bruce K. Waltke. Vol. 2. Chicago: Moody Press, 1980.

Auvray, Paul. "Cyrus, instrument du Dieu unique." *Bible et vie Chretienne* 50 (1963).

Baldwin, Joyce G. *Daniel: An Introduction and Commentary.* Tyndale Old Testament Commentary. Downers Grove, Ill.: InterVarsity Press, 1978.

———. *1 and 2 Samuel: An Introduction and Commentary.* Tyndale Old Testament Commentary. Downers Grove, Ill.: InterVarsity Press, 1988.

———. "Jonah." In *The Minor Prophets: An Exegetical and Expository Commentary.* Vol. 2. Edited by Thomas E. McComiskey. Grand Rapids: Baker, 1993.

Ballentine, Samuel E. "Isaiah 45: God's 'I Am,' Israel's 'You Are.' " *Horizons in Biblical Theology* 16, no. 2 (1994).

Barr, James. *The Semantics of Biblical Language.* 1961. Reprint, London: SCM Press, 1983.

Barrett, C. K. *The Gospel According to St. John: An Introduction with Commentary and Notes on the Greek Text.* 2nd ed. Philadelphia: Westminster Press, 1978.

Barth, Markus. *Ephesians.* Anchor Bible. New York: Doubleday, 1974.

Basinger, David, and Randall Basinger, eds. *Predestination and Free Will.* Downers Grove, Ill.: InterVarsity Press, 1986.

Basinger, David. "Can an Evangelical Christian Justifiably Deny God's Exhaustive Foreknowledge of the Future?" *Christian Scholar's Review* 25, no. 2 (1995).

———. "Human Freedom and Divine Providence: Some New Thoughts on an Old Problem." *Religious Studies* 15, no. 4 (1979).

———. *The Case for Freewill Theism: A Philosophical Assessment.* Downers Grove, Ill.: InterVarsity Press, 1996.

———. "Divine Control and Human Freedom: Is Middle Knowledge the Answer?" *Journal of the Evangelical Theological Society* 36, no. 1 (1993).

———. *Divine Power in Process Theism: A Philosophical Critique.* Albany, N.Y.: SUNY Press, 1988.

———. "In What Sense Must God be Omnibenevolent?" *International Journal for Philosophy of Religion* 14 (1983).

———. "Middle Knowledge and Divine Control: Some Clarifications." *International Journal for Philosophy of Religion* 30 (1991)

———. "Petitionary Prayer: A Response to Murray and Meyers." *Religious Studies* 31, no. 4 (1995).

———. "Simple Foreknowledge and Providential Control." *Faith and Philosophy* 10, no. 3 (1993).

Bavinck, Herman. *The Doctrine of God,* translated and edited by William Hendricksen. Grand Rapids: Baker, 1979.

Bayer, Hans F. "Predictions of Jesus' Passion and Resurrection." In *Dictionary of Jesus and the Gospels,* edited by Joel B. Green and Scot McKnight. Downers Grove, Ill.: InterVarsity Press, 1992.

Beale, G. K. *The Book of Revelation: A Commentary on the Greek Text.* New International Greek Testament Commentary. Grand Rapids: Eerdmans, 1999.

Beasley-Murray, George R. *John.* Word Biblical Commentary 36. Waco, Tex.: Word, 1987.

Becker, Ulrich. "βίβλιος," *New International Dictionary of New Testament Theology.* Vol. 1. Grand Rapids: Zondervan, 1986.

Beckwith, Francis J. "Limited Omniscience and the Test for a Prophet: A Brief Philosophical Analysis." *Journal of the Evangelical Theological Society* 36, no. 3 (1993).

Beilby, James K., and Paul R. Eddy, eds. *Divine Foreknowledge: Four Views.* Downers Grove, Ill.: InterVarsity Press, 2001.

Berkhof, Hendrikus. *Christian Faith: An Introduction to the Study of the Faith,* translated by Sierd Woudstra. Grand Rapids: Eerdmans, 1979.

Bloesch, Donald G. *God the Almighty: Power, Wisdom, Holiness, Love.* Christian Foundations. Downers Grove, Ill.: InterVarsity Press, 1995.

Blomberg, Craig L. *Matthew.* The New American Commentary 22. Nashville: Broadman, 1992.

Blum, Edwin A. *1 Peter.* Expositor's Bible Commentary 12. Grand Rapids: Zondervan, 1981.

Boethius. *The Consolation of Philosophy,* translated by V. E. Watts. New York: Penguin, 1961.

Botterweck, G. Johannes. "*yādaʿ.*" *Theological Dictionary of the Old Testament,* edited by G. Johannes Botterweck and Helmer Ringgren. Vol. 5. Grand Rapids: Eerdmans, 1986.

Boyd, Gregory A. "Christian Love and Academic Dialogue: A Reply to Bruce Ware." *Journal of the Evangelical Theological Society* 45, no. 2 (2002).

———. *God at War: The Bible and Spiritual Conflict.* Downer's Grove, Ill.: InterVarsity Press, 1997.

———. *God of the Possible: A Biblical Introduction to the Open View of God.* Grand Rapids: Baker, 2000.

———. *Satan and the Problem of Evil: Constructing a Trinitarian Warfare Theodicy.* Downers Grove, Ill.: InterVarsity Press, 2001.

———. *Trinity and Process: A Critical Evaluation and Reconstruction of Hartschorne's Di-polar Theism Towards a Trinitarian Metaphysics.* New York: Peter Lang, 1992.

Boyd, Gregory A., and Edward K. Boyd. *Letters From a Skeptic.* Colorado Springs: ChariotVictor, 1994.

Brady, David. "The Alarm to Peter in Mark's Gospel." *Journal for the Study of the New Testament* 4 (1979).

Braithwaite, R. B. *Scientific Explanation: A Study of the Function of Theory, Probability and Law in Science.* Cambridge: Cambridge University Press, 1953.

Bray, Gerald. *The Doctrine of God.* Downers Grove, Ill.: InterVarsity Press, 1993.

Bright, John. *Jeremiah: A New Translation with Introduction and Commentary.* Anchor

Bible 21. Garden City, N.Y.: Doubleday, 1965.

Bromiley, Geoffrey W. "Foreknowledge." In *Evangelical Dictionary of Theology,* edited by Walter A. Elwell. Grand Rapids: Baker, 1984.

Brown, Harold O. J. *Heresies: Heresy and Orthodoxy in the History of the Church.* 1984. Reprint, Peabody, Mass.: Hendrickson, 1998.

Brown, Raymond E. *The Gospel According to John, I-XII.* Anchor Bible 29. Garden City, N.Y.: Doubleday, 1966.

———. *The Gospel According to John, XIII-XXI.* Anchor Bible 29a. Garden City, N.Y.: Doubleday, 1970.

———. "How Much Did Jesus Know? A Survey of the Biblical Evidence." *Catholic Biblical Quarterly* 29, no. 3 (1967).

Bruce, F. F. *The Acts of the Apostles: The Greek Text With Introduction and Commentary.* 3rd ed. Grand Rapids: Eerdmans, 1990.

———. *Romans.* Rev. ed. Tyndale New Testament Commentary. Grand Rapids: Eerdmans, 1987.

Brueggemann, Walter. *The Book of Exodus.* In *The New Interpreter's Bible.* Vol. 1. Nashville: Abingdon, 1994.

———. *Genesis.* Interpretation. Atlanta: John Knox, 1982.

———. *To Build, To Plant: A Commentary on Jeremiah 26-52.* Grand Rapids: Eerdmans, 1991.

———. *To Pluck Up, To Tear Down: A Commentary on Jeremiah 1-25.* Grand Rapids: Eerdmans, 1988.

Brümmer, Vincent. *The Model of Love: A Study in Philosophical Theology.* Cambridge: Cambridge University Press, 1993.

———. *Speaking of a Personal God: An Essay in Philosophical Theology.* Cambridge: Cambridge University Press, 1992.

Budd, Philip J. *Numbers.* Word Biblical Commentary 5. Waco, Tex.: Word, 1984.

Bultmann, Rudolph. *"γινώσκω,γνῶσις."* *Theological Dictionary of the New Testament,* edited by Gerhard Kittel and Gerhard Friedrich. Translated by Geoffrey W. Bromiley. Vol. 1. Grand Rapids: Eerdmans, 1964.

Caird, G. B. *A Commentary of the Revelation of St. John the Divine.* New York: Harper, 1966.

———. *The Language and Imagery of the Bible.* 1980. Reprint, Grand Rapids: Eerdmans, 1997.

Calvin, John. *Commentary on the Book of Psalms.* Vol. 1. Translated by James Anderson. Grand Rapids: Eerdmans, 1948.

———. *Commentaries on the Epistle of Paul to the Romans,* translated and edited by the Rev. John Owen. Grand Rapids: Baker, 1979.

———. *Commentaries on the First Book of Moses Called Genesis,* translated by John King. Grand Rapids: Baker, 1979.

———. *Institutes of the Christian Religion,* edited by John T. McNeil; translated by Ford Lewis Battles. Philadelphia: Westminster Press, 1960.

Caneday, A. B. "The Implausible God of Open Theism: A Response to Gregory A. Boyd's *God of the Possible.*" *Journal of Biblical Apologetics* 1 (2000).

————. "Putting God at Risk: A Critique of John Sanders's View of Providence," *Trinity Journal* 20NS (1999).

Carasik, Michael. "The Limits of Omniscience." *Journal of Biblical Literature* 119, no. 2 (2000).

Carson, D. A. *The Difficult Doctrine of the Love of God.* Wheaton, Ill.: Crossway Books, 2000.

————. *Divine Sovereignty and Human Responsibility: Biblical Perspectives in Tension.* 1981. Reprint, Grand Rapids: Baker, 1995.

————. "God, the Bible, and Spiritual Warfare: A Review Article." *Journal of the Evangelical Theological Society* 42, no. 2 (1999).

————. *The Gospel According to John.* Grand Rapids: Eerdmans, 1991.

————. *How Long, O Lord? Reflections on Suffering and Evil.* Grand Rapids: Baker, 1990.

————. *Matthew.* Expositor's Bible Commentary 8. Grand Rapids: Zondervan, 1984.

Charnock, Stephen. *Discourses upon the Existence and Attributes of God.* 1853. Reprint, Grand Rapids: Baker, 1996.

Childs, Brevard S. *Biblical Theology in Crisis.* Philadelphia: Westminster Press, 1970.

————. *The Book of Exodus: A Critical, Theological Commentary.* Philadelphia: Westminster Press, 1974.

Chisholm, Robert B., Jr. "Does God 'Change His Mind'?" *Bibliothecra Sacra* 152, no. 3 (1995).

Cicero. *De Fato,* translated by H. Rackham. In *De Oratore III.* Loeb Classical Library. Cambridge, Mass.: Harvard University Press, 1960.

————. *De Senectute, De Amicitia, De Divinatione,* translated by William Armistead Falconer. Loeb Classical Library. Cambridge, Mass.: Harvard University Press, 1964.

Clines, David. "Yahweh and the God of Christian Theology." *Theology* 83, no. 695 (1980).

Clowney, Edmund. *The Message of 1 Peter.* Downers Grove, Ill.: InterVarsity Press, 1988.

Cobb, John B., Jr., and David Ray Griffin. *Process Theology: An Introductory Exposition.* Philadelphia: Westminster Press, 1976.

Cobb, John B., and Clark H. Pinnock, eds. *Searching for an Adequate God: A Dialogue Between Process and Free Will Theists.* Grand Rapids: Eerdmans, 2000.

Cole, R. Alan. *Exodus: An Introduction and Commentary.* Tyndale Old Testament Commentary. Downers Grove, Ill.: InterVarsity Press, 1973.

Cottrell, Jack. *What the Bible Says About God the Creator.* Joplin, Mo.: College Press, 1983.

Craig, William Lane. *The Problem of Divine Foreknowledge and Future Contingents from Aristotle to Suarez.* New York: E. J. Brill, 1988.

————. *The Only Wise God: The Compatibility of Divine Foreknowledge and Human Freedom.* Grand Rapids: Baker, 1987.

Craigie, Peter C. *Psalms 1-50.* Word Biblical Commentary 19. Waco, Tex.: Word, 1983.

Craigie, Peter C., Page H. Kelley and Joel F. Drinkard Jr. *Jeremiah 1-25.* Word Biblical Commentary 26. Waco, Tex.: Word, 1991.

Cranfield, C. E. B. *A Critical and Exegetical Commentary on the Epistle to the Romans.* Vol. 1. Edinburgh: T & T Clark, 1975.

————. *The Gospel According to Saint Mark: An Introduction and Commentary.* Cambridge: Cambridge University Press, 1963.

Dahood, Mitchell. *Psalms I: 1-50: Introduction, Translation, and Notes.* Anchor Bible. Garden City, N.Y.: Doubleday, 1965.

————. *Psalms II: 51-100: Introduction, Translation, and Notes.* Anchor Bible. New York: Doubleday, 1968.

————. *Psalms III: 101-150: Introduction, Translation, and Notes, with an Appendix on the Grammar of the Psalter.* Anchor Bible 17A. Garden City, N.Y.: Doubleday, 1970.

Davies, Eryl W. *Numbers.* The New Century Bible Commentary. Grand Rapids: Eerdmans, 1995.

Davis, Marvin S. "An Investigation of the Concept of the Repentance of God in the Old Testament." Th.D. diss., New Orleans Baptist Theological Seminary, 1983.

Davis, Stephen T. "Divine Omniscience and Human Freedom." *Religious Studies* 15, no. 3 (1979).

————. *Logic and the Nature of God.* Grand Rapids: Eerdmans, 1983.

Davis, William C. "Does God Know the Future? A Closer Look at the Contemporary Evangelical Debate." *Modern Reformation* 8, no. 5 (1999).

Delitzsch, F. *Psalms,* translated by Francis Bolton. Grand Rapids: Eerdmans, 1980.

Derrett, J. D. M. "The Reason for the Cock-Crowings." *New Testament Studies* 29, no. 1 (1983).

Dillard, Raymond B. "Joel." In *The Minor Prophets: An Exegetical and Expository Commentary,* edited by Thomas E. McComiskey. Grand Rapids: Baker, 1992.

Edwards, Jonathan. *The Works of Jonathan Edwards.* Carlisle, Penn.: Banner of Truth Trust, 1974.

Edwards, Paul, ed. *The Encyclopedia of Philosophy.* New York: Macmillan, 1967.

Eichrodt, Walther. *Theology of the Old Testament.* Translated by J. A. Baker. Vol. 1. Philadelphia: Westminster Press, 1961.

Enns, Peter. *Exodus.* The NIV Application Commentary. Grand Rapids: Zondervan, 2000.

Erickson, Millard. *Christian Theology.* 2nd ed. Grand Rapids: Baker, 1998.

————. *The Evangelical Left: Encountering Postconservative Evangelical Theology.* Grand Rapids: Baker, 1997.

————. "God, Foreknowledge, Bethel, and the BGC." www.desiringgod.org/media/pdf/booklets/bgc_foreknowledge_booklet.pdf .

————. *God the Father Almighty: A Contemporary Exploration of the Divine Attributes.* Grand Rapids: Baker, 1998.

————. *What Does God Know and When Does He Know It? The Current Debate over Divine Foreknowledge.* Grand Rapids: Zondervan, 2003.

Farley, Benjamin Wirt. *The Providence of God.* Grand Rapids: Baker, 1988.

Fee, Gordon D. *1 and 2 Timothy, Titus.* New International Bible Commentary. Peabody, Mass.: Hendrickson, 1988.

————. *The First Epistle to the Corinthians.* New International Commentary on the New Testament. Grand Rapids: Eerdmans, 1987.

Feinberg, Charles L. *Jeremiah.* Expositor's Bible Commentary 6. Grand Rapids: Zondervan, 1986.

Feinberg, John S. *No One Like Him: The Doctrine of God.* Wheaton, Ill.: Crossway, 2001.

Feldman, Seymour. "The Binding of Isaac: A Test-Case of Divine Foreknowledge." In *Divine Omniscience and Omnipotence in Medieval Philosophy: Islamic, Jewish and Christian Perspectives,* edited by Tamar Rudavsky. Boston: Reidel, 1985.

Fischer, John Martin, ed. *God, Foreknowledge, and Freedom.* Stanford, Calif.: Stanford University Press, 1989.

Flint, Thomas P. *Divine Providence: The Molinist Account.* Ithaca, N.Y.: Cornell University Press, 1998.

Ford, J. M. *Revelation: Introduction, Translation and Commentary.* Anchor Bible 38. New York: Doubleday, 1975.

Forster, Roger T., and V. Paul Marston. *God's Strategy in Human History.* Wheaton, Ill.: Tyndale, 1973.

Frame, John M. *Worship in Spirit and Truth.* Phillipsburg, N.J.: Presbyterian & Reformed, 1996.

Fretheim, Terence E. "The Book of Genesis." In *The New Interpreter's Bible.* Vol. 1. Nashville: Abingdon, 1994.

————. "Divine Foreknowledge, Divine Consistency, and the Rejection of Saul's Kingship." *Catholic Biblical Quarterly* 47 (1986).

————. "Jonah and Theodicy." *Zeitschrift für die alttestamentliche Wissenschaft* 90 (1978).

————. *The Message of Jonah: A Theological Commentary.* Minneapolis: Augsburg, 1977.

————. "The Repentance of God: A Key to Evaluating Old Testament God-Talk." *Horizons in Biblical Theology* 10, no. 1 (1988).

————. "The Repentance of God: A Study of Jeremiah 18:7-10." In *Hebrew Annual Review,* edited by Reuben Ahroni. Vol. 11. Columbus, Ohio: Department of Judaic and Near Eastern Languages and Literatures, 1987.

————. *The Suffering of God: An Old Testament Perspective.* Philadelphia: Fortress, 1984.

————. "Suffering God and Sovereign God in Exodus: A Collision of Images." *Horizons in Biblical Theology* 11, no. 2 (1989).

————. "yada'." *New International Dictionary of Old Testament Theology and Exegesis,* edited by Willem A. VanGemeren. Vol. 2. Grand Rapids: Zondervan, 1997.

Fuller, J. William. "'I Will Not Erase His Name from the Book of Life' (Rev 3:5)." *Journal of the Evangelical Theological Society* 26, no. 3 (1983).

Ganssle, Gregory A. "God's Knowledge of the Future." Paper given at the Evangelical Theological Society Annual Meeting. Danvers, Massachusetts. November 18, 1999.

————. ed. *God and Time: Four Views.* Downers Grove, Ill.: InterVarsity Press, 2001.

Geach, Peter. *Providence and Evil.* New York: Cambridge University Press, 1977.

Geisler, Norman L. *Creating God in the Image of Man?* Minneapolis: Bethany House, 1997.

Giles, Kevin. *The Trinity and Subordinationism: The Doctrine of God and the Contempo-

rary Gender Debate. Downers Grove, Ill.: InterVarsity Press, 2002.

Glenn, Donald R. "An Exegetical and Theological Exposition of Psalm 139." In *Tradition and Testament: Essays in Honor of Charles Lee Feinberg,* edited by John S. Feinberg and Paul D. Feinberg. Chicago: Moody Press, 1981.

Godet, Frederick. *Commentary on the Epistle to the Romans,* translated by A. Cusin; edited by Talbot W. Chambers. Reprint, Grand Rapids: Zondervan, 1956.

Goppelt, Leonhard. *A Commentary on 1 Peter,* translated by John E. Alsup; edited by Ferdinand Hahn. Grand Rapids: Eerdmans, 1993.

Gray, George Buchanan. *A Critical and Exegetical Commentary on Numbers*. International Critical Commentary. Edinburgh: T & T Clark, 1903.

Gray, John. *I and II Kings: A Commentary*. Philadelphia: Westminster Press, 1963.

Green, Gene L. *The Letters to the Thessalonians*. Pillar New Testament Commentary. Grand Rapids: Eerdmans, 2002.

Green, Joel B. *The Gospel of Luke*. New International Commentary on the New Testament. Grand Rapids: Eerdmans, 1997.

Grudem, Wayne. *1 Peter*. Tyndale New Testament Commentary. Grand Rapids: Eerdmans, 1990.

———. *Systematic Theology: An Introduction to Biblical Doctrine*. Grand Rapids: Zondervan, 1994.

Guleserian, Theodore. "Can God Change His Mind?" *Faith and Philosophy* 13, no. 3 (1996).

Gundry, Robert H. *Mark: A Commentary on His Apology for the Cross*. Grand Rapids: Eerdmans, 1993.

———. *Matthew: A Commentary on His Handbook for a Mixed Church Under Persecution*. 2nd ed. Grand Rapids: Eerdmans, 1994.

———. *The Use of the Old Testament in St. Matthew's Gospel with Special Reference to the Messianic Hope*. Leiden: E. J. Brill, 1967.

Gundry Volf, Judith M. *Paul and Perseverance: Staying in and Falling Away*. Tübingen: J. C. B. Mohr, 1990.

Guthrie, Donald. *The Pastoral Epistles*. Grand Rapids: Eerdmans, 1957.

Hafemann, Scott J. *2 Corinthians*. The NIV Application Commentary: Grand Rapids: Zondervan, 2000.

Hahn, Ferdinand. *The Titles of Jesus in Christology: Their History in Early Christianity*. London: Lutterworth, 1969.

Halas, Roman B. *Judas Iscariot: A Scriptural and Theological Study of His Person, His Deeds and His Eternal Lot*. Washington, D.C.: Catholic University of America Press, 1946.

Hamilton, Victor P. *The Book of Genesis: Chapters 1-17*. New International Commentary on the Old Testament. Grand Rapids: Eerdmans, 1990.

———. *The Book of Genesis: Chapters 18-50*. New International Commentary on the Old Testament. Grand Rapids: Eerdmans, 1995.

———. "*shāba*ʿ." *Theological Wordbook of the Old Testament*. Edited by R. Laird Harris,

Gleason L. Archer Jr. and Bruce K. Waltke. Vol. 2. Chicago: Moody Press, 1980.

Hartshorne, Charles. *Omniscience and Other Theological Mistakes*. Albany: State University of New York Press, 1984.

Hasker, William. *God, Time, and Knowledge*. Ithaca, N.Y.: Cornell University Press, 1989.

Hay, David M. *Glory at the Right Hand: Psalm 110 in Early Christianity*. SBL Monograph 18. Nashville: Abingdon, 1973.

Helm, Paul. *The Providence of God*. Downers Grove, Ill.: InterVarsity Press, 1994.

Helseth, Paul Kjoss. "On Divine Ambivalence: Open Theism and the Problem of Particular Evils." *Journal of the Evangelical Theological Society* 44, no. 3 (2003).

Heschel, Abraham. *The Prophets*. New York: Harper & Row, 1962.

Highfield, Ron. "The function of Divine Self-Limitation in Open Theism: Great Wall or Picket Fence?" *Journal of the Evangelical Theological Society* 45, no. 2 (2002).

Hobbs, T. R. *2 Kings*. Word Biblical Commentary 13. Waco, Tex.: Word, 1985.

Hodge, Charles. *Systematic Theology*. Grand Rapids: Eerdmans, 1979.

Holladay, William L. *Jeremiah 1: A Commentary on the Book of the Prophet Jeremiah, Chapters 1-25*. Philadelphia: Fortress, 1986.

Horton, Michael S. "Hellenistic or Hebrew? Open Theism and Reformed Theological Method." *Journal of the Evangelical Theological Society* 45, no. 2 (2002).

Hoskyns, E. C. *The Fourth Gospel*. Edited by Francis Noel Davey. London: Faber & Faber, 1947.

Hunt, David P. "Divine Providence and Simple Foreknowledge." *Faith and Philosophy* 10, no. 3 (1993).

Jacobs, P., and H. Krienke. *"proginōskō."* *New International Dictionary of New Testament Theology*. Vol. 1. Grand Rapids: Zondervan, 1986.

Jerome. *The Dialogue Against the Pelagians,* translated by John N. Hritzu. In *The Fathers of the Church* 53. Washington, D.C.: Catholic University of America Press, 1965.

Jewett, Paul. *Election and Predestination*. Grand Rapids: Eerdmans, 1985.

Jones, Gwilym H. *1 and 2 Kings*. New Century Bible Commentary. Grand Rapids: Eerdmans, 1984.

Jones, Major J. *The Color of God: The Concept of God in Afro-American Thought*. Macon, Ga.: Mercer University Press, 1987.

Kaiser, Christopher B. *The Doctrine of God: An Historical Survey*. Westchester, Ill.: Crossway Books, 1982.

Kaiser, Walter C., Jr. *Back Toward the Future: Hints for Interpreting Biblical Prophecy*. Grand Rapids: Baker, 1989.

———. *Exodus*. Expositor's Bible Commentary 2. Grand Rapids: Zondervan, 1990.

———. *The Messiah in the Old Testament*. Grand Rapids: Zondervan, 1995.

Keener, Craig S. *A Commentary on the Gospel of Matthew*. Grand Rapids: Eerdmans, 1999.

Kelly, J. N. D. *A Commentary on the Epistles of Peter and Jude*. Blacks New Testament Commentaries. London: Adam & Charles Black, 1969.

———. *A Commentary on the Pastoral Epistles*. Grand Rapids: Baker, 1963.

Kenny, Anthony. *The God of the Philosophers*. Oxford: Clarendon, 1979.

Kidner, Derek. *Psalms 1-72: An Introduction and Commentary.* Tyndale Old Testament Commentary. Downers Grove, Ill.: InterVarsity Press, 1973.

Klassen, William. *Judas: Betrayer or Friend of Jesus?* Minneapolis: Fortress, 1996.

Klein, Ralph W. *1 Samuel.* Word Biblical Commentary 10. Waco, Tex.: Word, 1983.

Klein, William W. *The New Chosen People: A Corporate View of Election.* Grand Rapids: Zondervan, 1990.

König, Adrio. *Here Am I! A Christian Reflection on God.* Grand Rapids: Grand Rapids: Eerdmans, 1982.

———. *The Eclipse of Christ in Eschatology: Toward a Christ-Centered Approach.* Grand Rapids: Eerdmans, 1989.

———. *New and Greater Things: Re-evaluating the Biblical Message on Creation,* translated by D. Roy Briggs. Pretoria: University of South Africa, 1988.

Kovach, Stephen D., and Peter R. Schemm. "A Defense of the Doctrine of the Eternal Subordination of the Son," *Journal of the Evangelical Theological Society* 42, no. 3 (1999).

Kvanvig, Jonathan. *The Possibility of an All-Knowing God.* New York: St Martin's Press, 1986.

Knight, George A. F. *Theology as Narration: A Commentary on the Book of Exodus.* Grand Rapids: Eerdmans, 1976.

Knight, George W., III. *The Pastoral Epistles: A Commentary on the Greek Text.* New International Greek Testament Commentary. Grand Rapids: Eerdmans, 1992.

Köhler, Ludwig. *Old Testament Theology,* translated by A. S. Todd. Philadelphia: Westminster Press, 1957.

Köstenberger, Andreas J. *John.* Baker Exegetical Commentary on the New Testament. Grand Rapids: Baker, 2004.

Ladd, George E. *A Commentary on the Revelation of John.* Grand Rapids: Eerdmans, 1972.

Lane, William L. *The Gospel According to Mark: The English Text with Introduction, Exposition and Notes.* New Interantional Commentary on the New Testament. Grand Rapids: Eerdmans, 1974.

Lewis, C. S. *Mere Christianity.* New York: MacMillan, 1960.

Lewis, J. P. *"yāda*ʿ.*" Theological Wordbook of the Old Testament.* Edited by R. Laird Harris, Gleason L. Archer Jr. and Bruce K. Waltke. Vol. 1. Chicago: Moody Press, 1980.

Long, A. A. *Hellenistic Philosophy: Stoics, Epicureans, Sceptics.* New York: Charles Scribner's, 1974.

Long, V. Philips. *The Reign and Rejection of Saul: A Case for Literary and Theological Coherence.* SBL Dissertation Series, No. 118. Atlanta: Scholars Press, 1989.

Luther, Martin. *The Bondage of the Will,* translated and edited by Philip S. Watson. In *Luther and Erasmus: Free Will and Salvation.* The Library of Christian Classics 17, Philadelphia: Westminster Press, 1969.

Marshall, I. Howard. *The Acts of the Apostles.* Tyndale New Testament Commentary. Grand Rapids: Eerdmans, 1986.

———. *The Gospel of Luke: A Commentary on the Greek Text.* New International Greek Testament Commentary. Grand Rapids: Eerdmans, 1978.

Mauchline, John. *1 and 2 Samuel*. New Century Bible. London: Marshall, Morgan & Scott, 1971.

Mays, James Luther. *Amos: A Commentary*. Philadelphia: Westminster Press, 1969.

———. *Hosea: A Commentary*. Philadelphia: Westminster Press, 1969.

McCabe, L. D. *Divine Nescience of Future Contingencies a Necessity*. New York: Phillips & Hunt, 1882.

———. *The Foreknowledge of God and Cognate Themes in Theology and Philosophy*. 1887. Reprint, North St. Paul, Minn.: American Reformation Project, 1987.

McCarter, P. Kyle, Jr. *1 Samuel: A New Translation with Introduction, Notes, and Commentary*. Anchor Bible 8. Garden City, N.Y.: Doubleday, 1980.

McComiskey, Thomas E. "Hosea." In *The Minor Prophets: An Exegetical and Expository Commentary,* edited by Thomas E. McComiskey. Grand Rapids: Baker, 1992.

McFague, Sallie. *Metaphorical Theology: Models of God in Religious Language*. Philadelphia: Fortress, 1982.

———. *Models of God: Theology for an Ecological, Nuclear Age*. Philadelphia: Fortress, 1987.

McKane, William. *I and II Samuel: Introduction and Commentary*. Torch Bible Commentaries. London: SCM Press, 1963.

McKenzie, John L. *Second Isaiah: Introduction, Translation, and Notes*. Anchor Bible. Garden City, N.Y.: Doubleday, 1968.

Michaels, J. Ramsey. *I Peter*. Word Biblical Commentary 49. Waco, Tex.: Word, 1988.

Molina, Luis. *On Divine Foreknowledge: Part IV of the Concordia*. Translated by Alfred Freddoso. Ithaca, N.Y.: Cornell University Press, 1988.

Moo, Douglas. *The Epistle to the Romans*. New International Commentary on the New Testament. Grand Rapids: Eerdmans, 1996.

Morris, Leon. *The Epistle to the Romans*. Leicester: Inter-Varsity Press and Grand Rapids: Eerdmans, 1988.

———. *The Gospel According to John*. New International Commentary on the New Testament. Grand Rapids: Eerdmans, 1971.

———. *The Gospel According to Matthew*. Grand Rapids: Eerdmans, 1992.

———. *Revelation*. Tyndale New Testament Commentary. Rev. ed. Grand Rapids: Eerdmans, 1987.

Morris, Thomas V. *Our Idea of God: An Introduction of Philosophical Theology*. Downers Grove, Ill.: InterVarsity Press, 1991.

Motyer, J. Alec. *The Prophecy of Isaiah: An Introduction and Commentary*. Downers Grove, Ill.: InterVarsity Press, 1993.

Mounce, Robert H. *The Book of Revelation*. Rev. ed. New International Commentary on the New Testament. Grand Rapids: Eerdmans, 1998.

Murray, John. *The Epistle to the Romans*. New International Commentary on the New Testament. Grand Rapids: Eerdmans, 1968.

Nash, Ronald H. *The Concept of God*. Grand Rapids: Zondervan, 1983.

———, ed. *Process Theology*. Grand Rapids: Baker, 1987.

Nicholls, Jason A. "Openness and Inerrancy: Can They Be Compatible?" *Journal of the Evangelical Theological Society* 45, no. 4 (2002).

Nicole, Albert. *Judas the Betrayer.* Grand Rapids: Baker, 1957.

Niehaus, Jeffrey. "Amos." In *The Minor Prophets: An Exegetical and Expository Commentary,* edited by Thomas E. McComiskey. Grand Rapids: Baker, 1992.

North, Christopher R. "The 'Former Things' and the 'New Things' in Deutero-Isaiah." In *Studies in Old Testament Prophecy: Festschrift for T. H. Robinson,* edited by H. H. Rowley. Edinburgh: T & T Clark, 1950.

———. *The Second Isaiah: Introduction, Translation, and Commentary to Chapters 40-55.* Oxford: Clarendon, 1964.

Noth, Martin. *Numbers: A Commentary,* translated by James D. Martin. London: SCM Press, 1968.

Oden, Thomas C. *The Living God.* Systematic Theology 1. San Francisco: Harper & Row, 1987.

Origen. *Against Celsus.* In *The Ante-Nicene Fathers* 4, edited by Alexander Roberts and James Donaldson. Buffalo: Christian Literature, 1887.

Osborne, Grant R. *Revelation.* Baker Exegetical Commentary on the New Testament. Grand Rapids: Baker, 2002.

Oswalt, John N. *The Book of Isaiah: Chapters 1-39.* New International Commentary on the Old Testament. Grand Rapids: Eerdmans, 1986.

———. *The Book of Isaiah: Chapters 40-66.* New International Commentary on the Old Testament. Grand Rapids: Eerdmans, 1998.

———. *'kāzab."* Theological Wordbook of the Old Testament,* edited by R. Laird Harris, Gleason L. Archer Jr. and Bruce K. Waltke. Vol. 1. Chicago: Moody Press, 1980.

Owen, H. P. *Concepts of Deity.* New York: Herder & Herder, 1971.

Packer, J. I. *Evangelism and the Sovereignty of God.* Downers Grove, Ill.: InterVarsity Press, 1961.

———. *Knowing God.* Downers Grove, Ill.: InterVarsity Press, 1973.

Pannenberg, Wolfhart. "The Appropriation of the Philosophical Concept of God as a Dogmatic Problem of Early Christian Theology." In *Basic Questions in Theology.* Vol. 2. Translated by George H. Kehm. Philadelphia: Fortress, 1971.

Parunak, H. Van Dyke. "A Semantic Survey of *NHM.*" *Biblica* 56 (1975).

Payne, J. Barton. *Encyclopedia of Biblical Prophecy.* New York: Harper & Row, 1973.

Peterson, David. *Engaging with God: A Biblical Theology of Worship.* Downers Grove, Ill.: InterVarsity Press, 1992.

Peterson, Michael. *Evil and the Christian God.* Grand Rapids: Baker, 1982.

Philo. *Quod Deus Immutabilis Sit* in *Philo.* Vol. 3. Translated by F. H. Colson and G. H. Whitaker. Loeb Classical Library. Cambridge, Mass.: Harvard University Press, 1968.

Piciarilli, Robert E. "An Arminian Response to John Sanders's *The God Who Risks: A Theology of Providence.*" *Journal of the Evangelical Theological Society* 44, no. 3 (2001).

Pinnock, Clark H. "Between Classical and Process Theism." In *Process Theology,* edited by Ronald Nash. Grand Rapids: Baker, 1987.

———. *Grace Unlimited.* Minneapolis: Bethany Fellowship, 1975.

———. *Most Moved Mover: A Theology of God's Openness.* Carlisle: Paternoster; Grand Rapids: Baker, 2001.

———. "There Is Room for Us: A Reply to Bruce Ware." *Journal of the Evangelical Theological Society* 45, no. 2 (2002).

———. *A Wideness in God's Mercy: The Finality of Jesus Christ in a World of Religions.* Grand Rapids: Zondervan, 1992.

Pinnock, Clark H., ed. *The Grace of God; the Will of Man.* Grand Rapids: Zondervan, 1989.

Pinnock, Clark H., et al. *The Openness of God: A Biblical Challenge to the Traditional Understanding of God.* Downers Grove, Ill.: InterVarsity Press, 1994.

Piper, John. "Answering Greg Boyd's Openness of God Texts." May 11, 1998. www.ondoctrine.com/2pip1201.htm

———. *A Godward Life.* Sisters, Ore.: Multnomah Press, 1997.

———. *A Godward Life: Book Two.* Sisters, Ore.: Multnomah Press, 1999.

———. *The Pleasures of God: Meditations on God's Delight in Being God.* Portland, Ore.: Multnomah Press, 1991.

———. "Why the Glory of God is at Stake in the 'Foreknowledge' Debate." *Modern Reformation* 8, no. 5 (1999).

Piper, John, Justin Taylor and Paul Kjoss Helseth, eds. *Beyond the Bounds: Open Theism and the Undermining of Biblical Christianity.* Wheaton, Ill.: Crossway, 2002.

Plantinga, Alvin. *The Nature of Necessity.* Oxford: Oxford University Press, 1974.

Plato. *Laws.* Translated by R. G. Bury. Loeb Classical Library. Cambridge, Mass.: Harvard University Press, 1961.

———. *The Republic.* Translated by Francis MacDonald Cornford. New York: Oxford University Press, 1966.

Polhill, John B. *Acts.* The New American Commentary 26. Nashville: Broadman, 1992.

Pratt, Richard L. "Historical Contingencies and Biblical Predictions." Inaugural Address presented to the faculty of Reformed Theological Seminary, November 23, 1993.

Reumann, John H. "Psalm 22 at the Cross: Lament and Thanksgiving for Jesus Christ." *Interpretation* 28, no. 1 (1974).

Rice, Richard. *God's Foreknowledge and Man's Free Will.* Minneapolis: Bethany House, 1985.

Robertson, O. Palmer. *The Christ of the Covenants.* Phillipsburg, N.J.: Presbyterian & Reformed, 1980.

Roy, Steven C. "God as Omnicompetent Responder? Questions About the Grounds of Eschatological Confidence in Open Theism." In *Looking into the Future: Evangelical Studies in Eschatology,* edited by David Baker. ETS Studies. Grand Rapids: Baker, 2000.

———. *How Much Does God Foreknow? An Evangelical Assessment of the Doctrine of the Extent of the Foreknowledge of God in Light of the Teaching of Open Theism.* Ph.D. diss., Trinity Evangelical Divinity School, 2001.

———. "Your Father Knows What You Need Before You Ask: The Implications of Matthew 6 for the Open View of Petitionary Prayer." Paper given at the Evangelical Theological Society Annual Meeting. Colorado Springs. November 16, 2001.

Sanders, John E. "Be Wary of Ware: A Reply to Bruce Ware." *Journal of the Evangelical Theological Society* 45, no. 2 (2002).

——. *The God Who Risks: A Theology of Providence.* Downers Grove, Ill.: InterVarsity Press, 1998.

——. *No Other Name: An Investigation into the Destiny of the Unevangelized.* Grand Rapids: Eerdmans, 1992.

Schmitz, E. D. *"ginōskō."* New International Dictionary of New Testament Theology. Vol. 2. Grand Rapids: Zondervan, 1986.

Schreiner, Thomas R. *Romans.* Baker Exegetical Commentary on the New Testament. Grand Rapids: Baker, 1998.

Schreiner, Thomas R., and Bruce A. Ware, eds. *The Grace of God; The Bondage of the Will.* Grand Rapids: Baker, 1995.

Schrenk, Gottlob. "βουλή." *Theological Dictionary of the New Testament,* edited by Gerhard Kittel and Gerhard Friedrich; translated by Geoffrey W. Bromiley. Vol. 1. Grand Rapids: Eerdmans, 1964.

Seesemann, Heinrich. "οἶδα." *Theological Dictionary of the New Testament,* edited by Gerhard Kittel and Gerhard Friedrich; translated by Geoffrey W. Bromiley. Vol. 5. Grand Rapids: Eerdmans, 1979.

Selwyn, Edward Gordon. *The First Epistle of St. Peter: The Greek Text with Introduction, Notes, and Essays.* Grand Rapids: Baker, 1981.

Shank, Robert. *Elect in the Son: A Study of the Doctrine of Election.* Springfield, Mo.: Westcott, 1970.

Snaith, Norman H. "The Language of the Old Testament." *The Interpreter's Bible.* Vol. 1. New York: Abingdon, 1952.

Stott, John R. W. *The Cross of Christ.* Downers Grove, Ill.: InterVarsity Press, 1986

——. *Guard the Gospel: The Message of 2 Timothy.* Downers Grove, Ill.: InterVarsity Press, 1973.

——. *Romans: God's Good News for the World.* Downers Grove, Ill.: InterVarsity Press, 1994.

——. *The Spirit, the Church, and the World: The Message of Acts.* Downers Grove, Ill.: InterVarsity Press, 1990.

Strimple, Robert B. "What Does God Know?" In *The Coming Evangelical Crisis,* edited by John H. Armstrong. Chicago: Moody Press, 1996.

Stuart, Douglas. *Hosea-Jonah.* Word Biblical Commentary 31. Waco, Tex.: Word, 1987.

Swinburne, Richard. *The Coherence of Theism.* Rev. ed. Oxford: Clarendon, 1993.

Taylor, Vincent. *The Gospel According to St. Mark: The Greek Text with Introduction, Notes, and Indexes.* New York: St. Martin's Press, 1959.

Thompson, J. A. *The Book of Jeremiah.* New International Commentary on the Old Testament. Grand Rapids: Eerdmans, 1980.

Tiessen, Terrance. *Providence and Prayer: How Does God Work in the World?* Downers Grove, Ill.: InterVarsity Press, 2000.

Tödt, H. E. *The Son of Man in the Synoptic Tradition,* translated by Dorothea M. Barton. Philadelphia: Westminster Press, 1965.

Torrance, James B. *Worship, Community, and the Triune God of Grace.* Downers Grove, Ill.: InterVarsity Press, 1996.

Tozer, A. W. *The Knowledge of the Holy.* San Francisco: Harper & Row, 1961.

VanGemeren, Willem A. *Psalms.* Expositor's Bible Commentary 5. Grand Rapids: Zondervan, 1991.

Vasholz, Robert. "Isaiah Versus 'the Gods': A Case for Unity." *Westminster Theological Journal* 42 (1980).

Vischer, Wilhelm. "Words and the Word: The Anthropomorphisms of the Biblical Revelation," translated by John Bright. *Interpretation* 3 (1949).

Waltke, Bruce K. "Micah." In *The Minor Prophets: An Exegetical and Expository Commentary.* Vol. 2. Edited by Thomas E. McComiskey. Grand Rapids: Baker, 1993.

Wanamaker, Charles A. *The Epistles to the Thessalonians: A Commentary on the Greek Text.* New International Greek Testament Commentary. Grand Rapids: Eerdmans, 1990.

Ware, Bruce A. "Defining Evangelicalism's Boundaries Theologically: Is Open Theism Evangelical?" *Journal of the Evangelical Theological Society* 45, no. 2 (2002).

———. "Eschatological Hope in Classical and Openness Theologies." Paper given at Evangelical Theological Society Annual Meeting, Danvers, Mass., November 17, 1999.

———. "An Evangelical Reformulation of the Doctrine of the Immutability of God." *Journal of the Evangelical Theological Society* 29, no. 4 (1986).

———. *God's Greater Glory: The Exalted God of Scripture and the Christian Faith.* Wheaton, Ill.: Crossway, 2004.

———. "God's Lesser Glory: Open Theism's Diminutive Conception of Divine Providence." Bueerman-Champion Lectureship. Western Seminary. Portland, Oregon, October 5-7, 1999.

———. *God's Lesser Glory: The Diminished God of Open Theism.* Wheaton, Ill.: Crossway, 2000.

———. "Rejoinder to Replies by Clark H. Pinnock, John Sanders, and Gregory A. Boyd." *Journal of the Evangelical Theological Society* 45, no. 2 (2002).

———. *Their God Is Too Small: Open Theism and the Undermining of Confidence in God.* Wheaton, Ill.: Crossway, 2003.

Watts, John D. W. *The Books of Joel, Obadiah, Jonah, Nahum, Habakkuk and Zephaniah.* The Cambridge Bible Commentary. New York: Cambridge University Press, 1975.

———. *Isaiah 34-66.* Word Biblical Commentary 25. Waco, Tex.: Word, 1987.

Wellum, Stephen J. "Divine Sovereignty-Omniscience, Inerrancy, and Open Theism." *Journal of the Evangelical Theological Society* 45, no. 2 (2002).

———. "The Importance of the Nature of Divine Sovereignty for our View of Scripture." *Southern Baptist Journal of Theology* 4 (2000).

Wenham, Gordon J. *Genesis 1-15.* Word Biblical Commentary 1. Waco, Tex.: Word, 1987.

Wenham, John W. "How Many Cock-Crowings? The Problem of Harmonistic Text-

Variants." *New Testaments* 25, no. 4 (1979).

Westerman, Claus. *Genesis 1-11: A Commentary.* Translated by John J. Scullion. Minneapolis: Augsburg, 1984.

———. *Genesis 12-36: A Commentary.* Translated by John J. Scullion. Minneapolis: Augsburg, 1985.

———. *Isaiah 40-66: A Commentary.* Translated by David M. G. Stalker. Philadelphia: Westminster Press, 1969.

Whybray, R. N. *Isaiah 40-66.* New Century Bible. London: Marshall, Morgan, & Scott, 1975.

Williams, David John. "Judas Iscariot." In *Dictionary of Jesus and the Gospels,* edited by Joel B. Green and Scot McKnight. Downers Grove, Ill.: InterVarsity Press, 1972.

Willis, John T. "The 'Repentance' of God in the Books of Samuel, Jeremiah, and Jonah." *Horizons in Biblical Theology* 16, no. 2 (1994).

Wolff, Hans Walter. *Hosea: A Commentary on the Book of the Prophet Hosea,* translated by Gary Stansell; edited by Paul D. Hanson. Philadelphia: Fortress, 1974.

———. *Joel and Amos: A Commentary on the Books of the Prophets Joel and Amos,* translated by Waldemar Janzen, S. Dean McBride Jr. and Charles A. Muenchow; edited by S. Dean McBride Jr. Philadelphia: Fortress, 1977.

Wright, R. K. McGregor. *No Place for Sovereignty: What's Wrong with Freewill Theism.* Downers Grove, Ill.: InterVarsity Press, 1996.

Yamauchi, Edwin M. "Anthropomorphism in Ancient Religion." *Bibliotheca Sacra* 125 (1968).

———. "Anthropomorphism in Hellenism and in Judaism." *Bibliotheca Sacra* 127 (1970).

Young, E. J. *The Book of Isaiah.* Grand Rapids, Eerdmans, 1972.

———. *Psalm 139: A Devotional and Expository Study.* London: Banner of Truth, 1965.

Zagzebski, Linda Trinkaus. *The Dilemma of Freedom and Foreknowledge.* New York: Oxford University Press, 1991.

Name Index

Albert the Great, 115
Alexander, Paul, 88
Allen, Leslie C., 28, 30, 141-43, 147, 282
Allen, Ronald B., 149-50, 282,
Andersen, Francis I., 128-29, 131, 133, 136-38, 143, 15-52, 282
Anscombe, G. E. M., 199
Anselm of Canterbury, 210
Aquinas, Thomas, 207-8, 210, 215, 218, 282
Archer, Gleason L., 282
Argyle, Aubrey W., 165, 282
Aristotle, 164, 198-99, 204, 207-8, 211, 218, 282
Arius, 206
Arminius, James, 14, 17, 282
Auffret, Pierre, 282
Aune, David E., 119, 283
Austel, Hermann J., 152, 283
Auvray, Paul, 283
Baldwin, Joyce G., 131, 283
Ballentine, Samuel E., 283
Barr, James, 127, 205, 283
Barrett, C. K., 60, 283
Barth, Karl, 83, 85
Barth, Markus, 283
Basinger, David, 16, 18, 130, 209, 237-39, 242-45, 247-48, 250, 255, 259-61, 283
Basinger, Randall, 283
Baugh, S. M., 75-76, 81, 86-88
Bavinck, Herman, 12, 166, 283
Bayer, Hans F., 93-94, 284
Beale, Gregory K., 118-22, 284
Beasley-Murray, George R., 106, 284

Becker, Ulrich, 33, 284
Beckwith, Francis J., 284
Bentzen, A., 58
Berkhof, Hendrikus, 284
Biddle, John, 182
Bloesch, Donald G., 284
Blomberg, Craig, 89, 104, 284
Blum, Edwin A., 88, 284
Boethius, 14, 169, 202, 207, 284
Botterweck, G. Johannes, 284
Boyd, Gregory, 16, 19, 33-34, 37, 53, 64, 70, 77, 82-83, 99-101, 105, 109-10, 117, 121, 129, 131, 135, 138, 145-47, 155, 169-70, 173, 175, 177-79, 181-83, 186, 190-92, 197-98, 209, 213, 215, 217, 219-23, 227-28, 232-33, 237, 240, 245, 251-52, 254-55, 257-59, 270-71, 284
Brady, David, 97, 284
Braithwaite, R. B., 163, 284
Bray, Gerald, 203, 284
Bright, John, 192, 284
Bromiley, Geoffrey W., 285
Brother Andrew, 282
Brown, Harold O. J., 205-6, 285
Brown, Raymond E., 94, 96, 105, 107-10, 112-13, 285
Bruce, F. F., 76, 285
Brueggemann, Walter, 128, 134-35, 179, 185, 285
Brummer, Vincent, 159, 161-63, 285
Budd, Philip J., 150, 285
Bultmann, Rudolf, 81, 285
Caird, George B., 121, 159, 161, 163, 168, 285
Calvin, John, 58, 85, 90, 165, 172, 285
Caneday, A. B., 286
Carasik, Michael, 286
Carson, D. A., 15, 56, 60-61, 89, 102-13, 232, 235, 286
Charnock, Stephen, 12, 30, 37, 46, 286
Childs, Brevard S., 136-37, 205, 286
Chisholm, Robert, 127, 148-49, 151-55, 286

Cicero, 12, 200-201, 211, 286

Clines, David, 164-65, 286

Cobb, John B., Jr., 215, 286

Cole, R. Alan, 286

Cottrell, Jack, 80, 86-87, 286

Craig, William Lane, 15-16, 30, 34, 67, 131, 199, 213, 242, 286

Craigie, Peter C., 58-59, 286

Cranfield, C. E. B., 85, 94-95, 97, 287

Cratylus, 200

Dahood, Mitchell, 30, 58, 147, 287

Davies, Eryl W., 287

Davis, Marvin S., 128, 134, 136, 138, 143-44, 147, 149, 152-53, 287

Davis, Stephen T., 287

Delitzsch, F., 58, 287

Derrett, J. D. M., 97, 287

Dillard, Raymond B., 141-43, 287

Dongell, Joseph B., 17

Edwards, Jonathan, 15, 114, 200, 287

Edwards, Paul, 287

Eichrodt, Walther, 170-71, 287

Enns, Peter, 140, 287

Erickson, Millard J., 18, 169, 182, 199, 202-4, 206, 208-9, 213, 220, 245, 269, 276, 287

Erigena, John Scotus, 210

Farley, Benjamin Wirt, 16, 201, 287

Fee, Gordon D., 116-17, 287

Feinberg, Charles L., 288

Feinberg, John S., 15, 69-70, 173, 187, 196, 209, 288

Feldman, Seymour, 288

Fischer, John Martin, 288

Flint, Thomas P., 15, 288

Forster, Roger T., 75, 77, 86, 288

Frame, John, 16, 235, 288

Freedman, David Noel, 128-29, 131, 133, 136-38, 143, 151-52, 282

Fretheim, Terence, 27, 32, 70, 125-26, 132-35, 137-38, 144-45, 154-55, 159-62, 167-69, 174, 178, 185-91, 288

Friesen, Garry, 253

Fuller, J. William, 17, 122, 288

Ganssle, Gregory A., 213, 224

Geach, Peter, 270-71, 288

Geisler, Norman, 180, 210, 288

Giles, Kevin, 206, 256, 289

Glenn, Donald R., 28-30, 33-34, 289

Godet, Frederick, 289

Goppelt, Leonhard, 88, 289

Gray, George Buchanan, 150, 289

Gray, John, 37, 289

Green, Gene L., 253, 289

Green, Joel B., 98, 104-5, 113, 289

Grider, J. K., 17

Griffin, David Ray, 215, 286

Grudem, Wayne A., 7, 67, 87, 131, 169, 208-9, 275-76, 289

Guleserian, Theodore, 289

Gundry, Robert, 89-90, 93, 95, 102, 104, 113, 289

Gundry Volf, Judith M., 81-82, 85, 289

Gunton, Colin E., 115

Guthrie, Donald, 289

Hafemann, Scott J., 242, 289

Hahn, Ferdinand, 94, 289

Halas, Roman B., 101, 107, 109-10, 289

Hamilton, Victor, 129, 148, 177-78, 289

Harris, Murray J., 86

Harrison, R. K., 48

Hartshorne, Charles, 214-16, 218, 290

Hasker, William, 18-19, 31, 131, 201, 213-15, 217, 220, 242, 248, 261, 269, 270, 290

Hay, David M., 147, 290

Helm, Paul, 15, 123, 174, 264, 290

Helseth, Paul Kjoss, 16, 290, 294

Hengstenberg, E. W., 58

Heraclitus, 200

Heschel, Abraham, 290

Highfield, Ron, 290

Hobbs, T. R., 290

Hodge, Charles, 290

Holladay, William, 134, 290

Horton, Michael S., 290

Hoskyns, E. C., 60, 290
Hunt, David P., 242, 290
Jacobs, P., 290
Jeremias, Joachim, 94-95
Jerome, 12, 290
Jewett, Paul K., 85, 290
Jones, Gwilym H., 37, 139, 290
Jones, Major, 20, 290
Kaiser, Christopher, 290
Kaiser, Walter C., Jr., 34-35, 55, 57-59, 290
Kane, William, 153
Keener, Craig S., 90-91, 290
Kelly, J. N. D., 88, 117, 290
Kenny, Anthony, 198-99, 291
Kerferd, G. B., 200
Kidner, Derek, 58, 291
Klassen, William, 102, 104-5, 108-9, 291
Klein, Ralph W., 130, 152, 291
Klein, William, 83, 291
Knight, George A. F., 291
Knight, George W., III, 117, 291
Köhler, Ludwig, 163-65, 291
König, Adrio, 62-64, 164-65, 291
Köstenberger, Andreas J., 291
Kovach, Stephen D., 256, 291
Krienke, H., 290
Kvanvig, Jonathan, 15, 291
Ladd, George F., 118-19, 122, 291
Lane, William L., 93-94, 97, 113, 291
Lewis, C. S., 12, 260, 291
Lewis, J. P., 291
Long, A. A., 199-200, 291
Long, V. Philips, 130, 153-54, 170, 291
Luther, Martin, 12-13, 291
Marshall, I. Howard, 74-75, 98, 104, 291
Marston, V. Paul, 75, 77, 86, 288
Mauchline, John, 292
Mays, James Luther, 158, 171, 189, 292
McCabe, L. D., 77-78, 95, 292
McCarter, P. Kyle, Jr., 152, 154, 292
McComiskey, Thomas E., 158-59, 189, 292

McFague, Sallie, 159-62, 292
McKane, William, 170, 292
McKenzie, John L., 44, 292
Michaels, J. Ramsey, 87, 292
Molina, Luis de, 287
Moo, Douglas, 80-82, 84-85, 292
Morris, Leon, 61, 89-90, 105-7, 109-11, 113, 239, 266, 292
Morris, Thomas V., 210, 292
Motyer, J. Alec, 51, 190, 292
Mounce, Robert H., 119, 277, 292
Murray, John, 80-81, 93, 292
Nash, Ronald H., 196, 209, 292-93
Newman, Robert C., 34-35
Nicholls, Jason A., 293
Nicole, Albert, 101, 293
Niehaus, Jeffrey, 293
North, Christopher R., 52, 293
Oden, Thomas C., 204, 209, 293
Olson, Roger, 17
Origen, 14, 203, 293
Ortlund, Raymond C., Jr., 30
Osborn, Grant R., 118-20, 293
Oswalt, John N., 43-46, 48-52, 54, 139, 151, 190, 293
Owen, H. P., 196, 293
Owen, John, 182
Packer, J. I., 236, 293
Pannenberg, Wolfhart, 196, 293
Parunak, H. Van Dyke, 127, 157, 293
Patterson, R. D., 37
Payne, J. Barton, 55, 293
Peterson, David, 230-31, 235, 293
Peterson, Michael, 293
Philo, 165, 201-2, 293
Piciarilli, Robert E., 293
Pinnock, Clark H., 16-20, 64, 66, 68-70, 80, 83, 126, 131, 135, 138, 147, 162, 169, 179, 197, 208, 211-17, 220, 229, 237-40, 259-62, 264, 268-70, 286, 293-94
Piper, John, 16, 37, 47, 98, 112, 116-18, 171, 173, 175-76, 181, 186, 190, 193, 236, 254, 294

Plantinga, Alvin, 15, 294
Plato, 164, 197-98, 202-3, 294
Plotinus, 203
Polhill, John B., 74, 294
Pratt, Richard L., 224, 294
Rad, Gerhard von, 35-36
Reichenbach, Bruce, 13, 17, 212
Reumann, John H., 58-59, 294
Rice, Richard, 17, 20, 53, 64-69, 83, 85,
   103, 112, 123, 126, 135, 143, 147, 154-
   55, 214, 217, 220, 222-23, 247, 269, 270-
   71, 273-74, 294
Robertson, O. Palmer, 35-36, 294
Roy, Steven C., 34, 268, 294
Sanders, John E., 16-18, 22, 26, 31, 53,
   62-65, 67-68, 70, 77-78, 83, 94-95, 99,
   101-2, 105, 108, 113, 115, 119-20, 125-
   26, 128-31, 137, 139, 144-45, 147, 155-
   63, 166-67, 172, 179-80, 182, 184, 186,
   191, 196-97, 200-201, 207, 209-10, 219-
   20, 222-23, 225, 238-240, 244, 248-50,
   252, 256, 258-64, 266, 271, 274, 276,
   295
Schemm, Peter R., 256, 291
Schmitz, E. D., 295
Schreiner, Thomas R., 80-82, 84-85, 230,
   266, 295
Schrenk, Gottlob, 75-76, 295
Scotus, John Duns, 115
Seesemann, Heinrich, 90, 295
Selwyn, Edward Gordon, 295
Seneca, 200
Shank, Robert, 83, 87, 295
Snaith, Norman H., 53, 127, 295
Socrates, 198
Sproston, W., 109
Stokes, Michael C., 200
Stott, John R. W., 74, 117, 204, 295
Strimple, Robert B., 295

Stuart, Douglas, 142-43, 158, 295
Swinburne, Richard, 19-20, 167, 220,
   223, 275, 295
Taylor, Justin, 16, 294
Taylor, Vincent, 94, 295
Thompson, J. A., 192, 295
Tiessen, Terence, 240, 242, 295
Todt, H. E., 92-94, 296
Torrance, James B., 160, 296
Tozer, A. W., 236-37, 296
VanGemeren, Willem A., 58-59, 147-48,
   296
Vasholz, Robert, 44, 296
Vischer, Wilhelm, 165-67, 172, 174, 296
Walls, Jerry, 17
Waltke, Bruce K., 56-57, 296
Wanamaker, Charles A., 253, 296
Ware, Bruce A., 7, 15-16, 23, 30, 32, 75,
   126, 146, 155-57, 159, 169-70, 172, 175,
   181, 209, 240, 242-43, 245-46, 248, 254-
   55, 257, 262-63, 265, 267, 295-96
Watts, John D. W., 49, 132, 139, 296
Wellum, Stephen J., 296
Wenham, Gordon J., 128, 296
Wenham, John W., 97, 297
Westermann, Claus, 43, 49, 129
Whybray, R. N., 297
Williams, David John, 101, 297
Willis, John T., 134, 297
Wolff, Hans Walter, 127, 142-43, 157,
   297
Wright, R. K. McGregor, 297
Xenophon, 198
Yamauchi, Edwin M., 163-65, 297
Young, E. J., 28-31, 45, 47, 49, 52, 138,
   297
Zagaebski, Linda Trinkaus, 297
Zimmerli, Walter, 95

Subject Index

anthropomorphism, 29, 163-68, 280
    appropriateness, 166
    in church history, 164-65
    degrees of correspondence, 167-68
    metaphors, 166-67
    in the New Testament, 164
    in the Old Testament, 163-64
    personal/relational value, 165
    reality-depicting, 167-68
    repentance of God, 168-76, 280
Arianism, 206
classical theism, 196
eternity of God, 14, 115, 209
foreknowledge of God, 12, 281
    compatible with freedom, 13-15,
        19-20, 32
    connected with God's set purpose,
        75-77
    of death of Christ, 74-79, 87
    of fall of humanity, 114-23
    of God's plan of redemption, 114-23
    importance of, 12
    New Testament language, 73-88,
        123
    Old Testament language, 27, 71
    of persons, 79-88
    prayer, 88-92, 123, 237-249
    view of Thomas Aquinas, 207-8
freedom of humans
    compatibilist, 15-16, 24
    libertarian, 13, 19-20, 211-13, 218
    role in argument of book, 24-25
future, 219-28, 280
    Boyd's view, 219-20
    fixed vs. open, 219-28
    open God's knowledge of, 222-26
    Sanders's view, 219-20
God's nonrepentance, 147-59
    divine decree, 148-49, 141, 152-53
    open view, 155, 156-57
    parallel to lying, 151, 152, 156
    specific not universal focus, 149,
        141, 154-59
Greek philosophy, 195-219, 280
    causal influence, 202-4, 218
    perfect-being theology, 209-11, 218
    positive/negative influence, 204-6,
        217-18
    role in open understanding, 195-98
    selective appropriation, 206-9, 218
    varied view of God's
        foreknowledge, 198-202, 218
guidance of God, 9-10, 249-58, 281
    and God's foreknowledge, 9-10,
        257-58
    and God's will, 252-53
    open view, 249-52, 254-56
hope, 10-11, 268-78
    and God's foreknowledge, 276-78
    open view, 268-72, 281
    warrant, 272-76
intercessory prayer, 9, 237-49, 281
    open view, 237-40
    problems with open view, 241-49
    teaching of Jesus, 88-92, 241
metaphors, 159-63
    reality-depicting, 160
    similar/dissimilar, 160-61
middle knowledge of God, 14, 23, 242
omniscience of God, 11, 17-18, 220-21
open theism, 16-17
open view of God's foreknowledge,
    17-21
    biblical support, 20-21, 125
    of the death of Christ, 77-79
    enhances God's greatness, 232-33

God's guidance, 249-52, 254-56
intercessory prayer, 237-40
in Isaiah, 53
potentially fallible, 65-66, 70, 129-
  30, 191-93, 244-45, 255, 280
predictive prophecies, 61-71, 72
repentance of God, 144-47
suffering and evil, 259-62
predictive prophecy
  conditional propheciesm, 66-67, 70-
    71, 131
  of Cyrus, 44-46, 48-50, 71
  displays God's glory, 46, 54-55
  distinguished from predictions, 62-
    64
  evidence of deity of Yahweh, 46-47,
    50, 52, 55, 71-72, 174, 227, 279
  of free human decisions, 36-41, 42-
    43, 44-45
  importance of, 34-35, 46, 50, 55, 71-
    72
  in Isaiah 40—48, 43-55, 71-72, 279
  Jesus predicts his Passion, 92-96
  Jesus predicts Judas' betrayal, 101-
    11
  Jesus predicts Peter's denial, 96-101
  in 1-2 Kings, 35-43, 71, 279
  numerical frequency, 34
  purpose of Jesus' predictions, 111-
    12, 174, 227, 279-80
  Old Testament messianic
    prophecies, 55-61, 71
  open view, 61-71, 72
  potentially fallible in open view, 65-
    66, 70, 129-30, 191-93, 244-45, 255,
    280
  shows God's guidance of history, 36
  wide range of events predicted,
    226-27
process theism, 211-17, 218
questions asked by God, 187-91, 280
repentance of God, 20-21, 126-76
  anthropomorphic metaphor, 168-76

biblical language, 127-28, 153-54
common-sense view of, 173, 175
controlling metaphor, 126, 144
in creedal statements, 139-44
different from human repentance,
  169-76, 193-94, 280
divine flexibility, 126, 134-35
divine-human contrast, 150, 152,
  156-59, 169-72
exhaustive foreknowledge view,
  174-76, 211
freedom of God, 132, 135, 142-43
importance of, 126-27
open view, 144-47
to repentance of any nation, 133-35,
  145-46, 175
to repentance of Nineveh, 131-33,
  175
in response to human sin, 128-31
response to prayer of Hezekiah,
  138-39, 146-47, 175
response to prayer of Moses, 135-
  38, 175
response to sin leading to the flood,
  128-30, 145, 175-76
response to sin of Saul, 130-131,
  145, 175-176
similar to human repentance, 168-
  69, 176, 193, 280
universal, 133, 135, 143-44
suffering and evil, 258-68, 281
  exhaustive foreknowledge view,
    265-68
  open view, 259-62
  problems with open view,
    262-65
testing of God, 177-85, 280
  knowledge of experience, 180-81
  open view, 177, 178-80
  problems with open view, 184-85
  straightforward understanding, 182-
    84
theological models, 22, 161-63

criteria for evaluation, 22-23, 163,
   229, 281
theologically necessary events,
   224
time, nature of in the open view, 213,

218
worship, 230-37, 281
   importance of, 230, 236-37
   linked to greatness of God, 231-34
   linked to truth of God, 234-36

Scripture Index

Old Testament

Genesis
1—11, *297*
1—15, *128, 296*
1:1, *52*
1:23, *73*
1:26-27, *166*
1:31, *265*
3, *177, 183*
3:9, *187*
3:9-13, *182, 183*
3:11, *187*
3:13, *187*
3:16-17, *128*
4:8, *128*
4:19, *128*
4:23-24, *128*
6, *128, 135, 136, 176, 274*
6:1-3, *128*
6:5, *128, 129*
6:5-6, *175, 252, 274*
6:6, *172, 175, 224, 244*
6:6-7, *20, 128, 131, 132, 135, 136, 144, 145, 165*
8:21, *129*
8:21-22, *275*
9:9-11, *129*
10:19, *158*
12—36, *297*
12:3, *178, 179, 180*
14:2-8, *158*

15:13-14, *54, 226*
15:16, *151*
17:6, *178*
17:8, *142, 151*
18, *183*
18:17-22, *125*
18:19, *27, 80, 180*
20:6, *27*
21:1-5, *178*
21:12, *178*
22, *177, 179, 180, 182*
22:1, *27*
22:12, *21, 27, 178, 180, 181, 182, 183, 184, 185, 221, 280*
22:16, *148*
22:16-18, *184*
22:17, *51, 151*
22:18, *148*
25:22, *84*
38:9-10, *66*
50:20, *254*

Exodus
3:7, *27*
3:12, *231*
3:14, *111*
3:16—4:9, *65*
4:11, *253*
4:22-23, *231*
7:16, *231*
8:1, *231*
8:13, *239*
8:20, *231*
8:31, *239*
9:1, *231*
9:13, *231*
9:13-19, *138*
9:29-30, *138*
10:3, *231*
10:25-26, *231*
16:4, *177*
19:4-6, *231*
20:3, *236*
20:4-6, *236*

20:5-6, *139*
20:20, *177, 178*
32, *136, 224, 240, 244*
32:4-5, *236*
32:5, *236*
32:7-8, *136*
32:7-14, *125*
32:10, *21, 136*
32:10-14, *239*
32:11-13, *137*
32:11-14, *20, 131, 135, 136*
32:11-15, *144*
32:12, *127*
32:14, *127, 138, 143, 175*
32:19-20, *140*
32:25-29, *140*
32:30-32, *140*
32:32, *118*
32:33, *34, 121*
32:35, *140*
33:1-3, *140*
33:12, *27*
33:14, *140*
33:16-17, *140*
33:18, *140*
33:19, *84, 140, 142*
34:5-7, *141*
34:6, *142*
34:6-7, *139, 140, 142*

Leviticus
26:12, *142*
26:44, *159*

Numbers
2, *140*
13:19, *154*
14:18, *140*
21, *149*
23:3, *149*
23:7-10, *149*
23:8, *150*
23:18-24, *149*

23:19, *127, 147, 149, 150, 151, 152, 153, 154, 155, 156, 157, 159, 169, 170, 171, 172, 173, 222, 280*
23:20, *151*
24:3-9, *149*
24:15-19, *149*
24:20, *149*
24:21-22, *149*
24:23-25, *149*
25:11, *144*

Deuteronomy
2:5, *149*
2:7, *27*
2:9, *149*
2:25, *149*
4:34, *170*
5:9-10, *139*
7:7-8, *83*
8:2, *27, 177*
10:16, *142*
13:1-3, *177*
13:3, *27*
13:14, *28*
13:17, *144*
18:15, *92*
29:23, *158*
29:29, *265*
30:6, *142*
31:21, *27*
32:36, *127*
32:39, *253*
34:10, *27*

Joshua
6:26, *41*
7:26, *144*

Judges
2:18, *127, 136*
2:21-22, *177*
3:4, *27, 177*
6:15, *56*

6:25, *249*
18:2, *28*

Ruth
2:14, *107*

1 Samuel
2:2, *158*
2:3, *72*
2:31-34, *138*
10:19, *56*
12:14-15, *145*
12:22, *82*
13:8-10, *130*
13:8-14, *175*
13:13-14, *130, 152,*
155
14:24, *130*
14:44, *130*
15, *130, 145, 153,*
154, 155, 170
15:1-9, *175*
15:11, *20, 130, 131,*
135, 144, 151,
153, 159, 170,
172, 173, 175,
244, 252
15:28, *130*
15:28-29, *152*
15:29, *127, 131,*
147, 151, 153,
154, 155, 156,
157, 159, 169,
170, 171, 172,
174, 176, 222, 280
15:35, *20, 125, 130,*
131, 135, 144,
151, 153, 170,
175, 252
16:1, *125*
23:10-14, *23*
23:23, *56*
30:6, *58*

2 Samuel
7, *35*
7:5-16, *35*

7:12, *56*
7:20, *27*
24:16, *127*

1 Kings
2:2-4, *35*
8:19-20, *35*
8:27, *169*
9:5, *35*
11, *36*
11:29-30, *64*
11:34-37, *36*
12:15-20, *64*
12:20, *36*
13, *43*
13:1-2, *64*
13:2, *37, 226*
13:2-3, *37*
13:5, *41*
14:1-6, *64*
14:5, *42, 226*
14:6, *42*
14:10, *138*
14:18, *64*
15:19, *64*
16:1-4, *64*
16:2-4, *38*
16:11-12, *64*
16:34, *41*
17, *43*
17:9, *38*
17:13-14, *38*
17:15-16, *38*
18:26-29, *89*
19, *82*
19:16-17, *39*
20, *43*
20:22, *42*
20:26, *42*
21:17-24, *64*
21:19, *37, 39, 226*
21:23, *39*
22:17, *64*
22:22, *42*
22:28, *42*
22:29-37, *64*
22:29-38, *39*

22:29-40, *42*
22:34, *42*

2 Kings
1:2-4, *138*
1:16, *41*
1:17, *41*
2:21, *41*
2:22, *41*
3:18-19, *42*
3:24-25, *42*
4:43, *41*
4:44, *41*
6:24-29, *40*
7, *43*
7:1, *226*
7:1-2, *40*
7:2, *37*
7:6-7, *40*
7:16-20, *40*
8:13, *42*
8:19, *37*
9—10, *64*
9:6-9, *39*
9:6-10, *39*
9:10, *37, 226*
9:35-36, *39*
10:17, *39*
10:30, *41*
15:12, *41*
18—19, *138*
19, *43*
19:15-16, *139*
19:32-34, *43*
19:35-36, *43*
20, *136, 240, 244*
20:1, *138*
20:1-6, *20, 136,*
138, 144, 175, 239
20:3, *139*
20:5-6, *139*
20:17-18, *41*
21:26, *37*
22:8-13, *37*
23, *43*
23:3, *37*
23:15-16, *38*

23:15-20, *64*
23:16, *144*
23:16-18, *37*
24:12-14, *41*

1 Chronicles
16:29, *231*
21:15, *127*

2 Chronicles
32:31, *27, 177*

Ezra
1:1, *57*

Nehemiah
9:17, *139*

Job
1—2, *254*
1:21, *254*
1:22, *254*
2:10, *254*
15:8, *243*
21:22, *243*
28:3, *28*
28:24, *11*
36:22, *243*
37:16, *11, 72, 220,*
281

Psalms
1—50, *58, 59, 286*
1—72, *58, 291*
1:6, *27*
4:2, *151*
5:4, *265*
8:4, *150*
14, *27*
17:8, *170*
18:2, *161*
19:1-6, *204*
19:14, *161*
22, *79*
22:1, *59*
22:1-18, *59*
22:5, *59*

22:7, *59*
22:8, *59*
22:13, *59*
22:15, *59*
22:17, *59*
22:18, *59, 226*
22:22, *59*
23:3, *249*
23:4, *258*
25:8-9, *249, 258*
25:9, *257*
29:2, *231*
31:2-3, *168*
31:7, *27*
40:9, *27*
41:9, *107*
44:21, *28*
69:19, *27*
69:25, *110*
69:28, *118*
78:38, *144*
86:15, *139*
89:35, *148*
90:13, *127, 136, 137*
95:6-7, *232*
96:7, *231*
100:2, *231*
100:2-3, *232*
101—150, *30, 147, 282*
103, *27*
103:8, *139*
106:23, *144*
106:44-45, *136*
106:45, *127, 144*
109:8, *110*
110, *147*
110:4, *127, 147, 149, 154*
111:4, *140*
112:4, *140*
135:14, *127*
139, *32, 279*
139:1, *29*
139:2, *30*
139:2-4, *180*

139:4, *27, 31*
139:6, *159*
139:16, *33, 34*
139:17-18, *11, 159, 220*
139:23, *27*
142:3, *27*
145:3, *159*
145:5, *232*
145:8, *139*
147:5, *11, 72, 159, 180, 220, 232, 281*

Proverbs
1:7, *52*
3:5-6, *249*
16:19, *253*
16:33, *253*
17:14, *52*
19:21, *253*
21:1, *57, 253*
25:2, *28*

Isaiah
2, *138*
4:4, *111*
5:1-7, *190, 192*
5:4, *125, 188*
5:25, *144*
7:18, *168*
10:5-19, *265*
11:1, *56*
22:11, *30*
25:1, *30*
34—66, *49, 139, 296*
35:4, *109*
38, *224*
38:1, *138*
38:1-5, *34*
38:1-6, *138*
38:5-6, *139*
40—48, *35, 43, 44, 55, 62, 70, 71, 72, 112, 113, 174, 226, 227, 234, 279*
40—66, *43, 297*

40:12-15, *174*
40:13-14, *243*
40:15, *243*
40:25, *158*
41:2, *46*
41:2-5, *43*
41:4, *112*
41:14-20, *66*
41:21-23, *45*
41:21-29, *43, 45*
41:24, *44, 45*
41:25-28, *46*
41:29, *46*
42—53, *104*
42:8-9, *46*
42:9, *47*
42:18-25, *43*
43:1, *44*
43:8-13, *43*
43:9-12, *47*
43:10, *111, 112*
44:1, *44*
44:6-20, *43*
44:7-8, *48*
44:24, *44, 49*
44:26—45:6, *48*
44:27, *49*
44:28, *37, 48, 49, 57, 226*
44:28—45:1, *44, 71*
44:28—45:4, *66*
44:28—45:6, *44*
45, *283*
45:1, *37, 48, 49, 57, 226*
45:7, *253*
45:9—46:13, *51*
45:18-19, *44*
45:20-21, *51*
45:20-25, *43*
46:4, *111*
46:9-10, *53, 64, 281*
46:9-11, *52, 220*
46:10, *64, 180*
46:10-11, *53, 66*
46:11, *64, 69*
47:12, *185*

48, *54*
48:3, *64*
48:3-5, *53*
48:6-11, *54*
50:2, *125, 188*
50:6, *94*
53, *79*
53:1, *168*
53:6, *95*
53:10, *176*
55:8-9, *11, 159*
57:4, *109*
57:6, *127*
60:22, *56*
62:8, *148*

Jeremiah
1, *290*
1—25, *286*
1:5, *27, 80*
2:14, *138*
2:32, *125, 188*
3, *21, 70, 184, 191, 193*
3:6-7, *21, 65, 70, 191, 192, 227, 244, 263*
3:7, *125, 192*
3:19, *125, 192*
3:19-20, *21, 191, 192, 227, 244, 263*
4:8, *144*
4:28, *127, 147*
5:7, *125, 188*
5:9, *125, 188*
5:29, *125, 188*
7:5, *125*
7:23, *142*
8:5, *125, 188*
8:19, *125, 188*
9:7, *125, 188*
9:9, *125, 188*
9:25, *142*
12:3, *27*
15:6, *127*
17:1, *134*
17:9, *134*

17:10, *28, 180*
17:16, *27*
18, *133, 135*
18—19, *70*
18:4, *133*
18:6, *133*
18:7-8, *135, 143, 175, 185*
18:7-10, *20, 133, 134, 135, 143, 144, 145, 155, 197*
18:8, *127*
18:9-10, *175*
18:10, *127, 135*
18:11, *133, 135*
18:20, *144*
18:23, *27*
19—20, *65*
20:16, *147*
26, *138*
26:2-3, *125, 185, 186*
26:3, *127, 144, 157*
26:13, *127, 157*
26:18, *138*
26:19, *127, 138, 157*
29:11, *27*
30:6, *125, 188*
32:4, *67*
32:18, *140*
36:3, *185*
36:7, *185*
37:6-10, *65*
44:26, *148*
51:8, *185*
52:12-14, *67*

Lamentations
3:37-38, *253*

Ezekiel
10:22, *144*
11:5, *27*
12:1-3, *185*
24:14, *127, 147*
24:24, *111*

26:1-21, *66*
29:17-20, *66*

Daniel
4:25, *253*
9:26, *104*

Hosea
2:2, *170*
5:2, *164*
5:4, *142*
5:12, *168*
5:14, *164, 168*
6:4, *125, 157, 188*
11, *157, 172*
11:1, *168*
11:5-6, *157*
11:8, *125, 172, 188, 189*
11:8-9, *157, 158, 159, 171, 172, 222, 280*
11:9, *171, 172, 174*
11:10, *164*
13:4-5, *27*
13:14, *147*
14:2, *142*

Joel
2, *143*
2:12-13, *135, 155*
2:12-14, *141, 143, 144*
2:13, *142, 144*
2:13-14, *127*
2:14, *142, 185*
2:21, *139*
2:28-32, *63*

Amos
3:2, *27, 80, 81*
3:6, *253*
5:4, *142*
5:21-24, *142*
7—8, *136*
7:1-3, *136*
7:1-6, *20, 131, 175*

7:3, *127, 157*
7:4-6, *136*
7:6, *127, 157*
7:7-9, *136*
8:1-3, *136*
9:11-12, *63*

Jonah
1:6, *132*
1:14, *132*
3, *224*
3:4, *21, 67, 131, 147*
3:5, *132*
3:5-9, *132*
3:5-10, *175*
3:6-10, *135*
3:7-9, *132*
3:9, *132, 142, 175, 185*
3:9-10, *20, 127, 131, 144*
3:10, *67, 132*
4, *143*
4:2, *127, 139, 141, 142, 143, 144, 155*

Micah
1:13, *52*
3:9-12, *66*
3:12, *138*
4:11-13, *56*
5:1, *56*
5:2, *56, 57, 61, 69, 72, 226*

Nahum
1:3, *140*

Habakkuk
1:13, *265*

Zechariah
8:14, *127, 147*
11, *102*
11:12-13, *110*
13:7, *96*

Malachi
1:2-3, *84*
3:6, *159*

New Testament

Matthew
2:4-6, *57*
2:6, *56*
4:10, *231*
6, *88, 90, 237, 241, 248, 294*
6:7-8, *89, 241*
6:8, *9, 91*
6:10, *230, 245, 257*
6:11, *90*
6:25, *90*
6:31, *90*
6:31-32, *88, 241*
6:32, *90, 91*
6:34, *90, 91*
7:7, *240*
7:7-8, *242*
7:7-11, *9, 90*
7:11, *243*
7:13, *109*
7:21, *253*
10:4, *103*
10:23, *113*
10:29, *253*
11:21-24, *23*
12:50, *253*
16:21, *93*
16:23, *102*
16:28, *113*
17:22-23, *93*
17:27, *113*
18:15-20, *102*
18:18, *239*
19:16-30, *92*
20:1-16, *92*
20:17-19, *92, 93*
20:19, *93*
21:31, *253*
22:37, *230*
22:44, *147*
23:15, *109*

24:2, *66, 113*
24:29-51, *113*
25:34, *114*
26:2, *103*
26:5, *101*
26:12, *102*
26:14-16, *74, 99,*
    101
26:20-25, *103*
26:21, *107*
26:21-25, *99*
26:23, *110*
26:24, *104, 105*
26:25, *103, 104*
26:31, *96*
26:33-35, *96, 226*
26:35, *99*
26:39, *78, 257*
26:39-42, *242*
26:40-41, *99*
26:47-50, *102*
26:50, *108*
26:51, *96*
26:64, *104, 147*
26:69-74, *96, 226*
26:75, *98*
27:3-10, *110*
27:18, *74*
27:26, *74*
27:35, *59*
27:39, *59*
27:43, *59*
27:46, *59*

Mark
3:19, *103*
3:35, *253*
8:31, *93*
8:38, *113*
9:1, *113*
9:12, *59*
9:31, *93, 94*
10:33, *94*
10:33-34, *93, 94*
10:34, *94*
10:45, *92*
12:36, *147*

13:2, *113*
13:24-36, *113*
14:2, *101*
14:10-11, *99, 102*
14:18, *107*
14:18-21, *99, 103*
14:21, *59, 105, 110*
14:27, *96*
14:29-31, *96, 97*
14:30, *97*
14:31, *99*
14:36, *244*
14:43-44, *94*
14:43-45, *102*
14:50, *96*
14:62, *147*
14:64, *94*
14:65, *94*
14:66-72, *96*
14:72, *98*
15:1, *94*
15:15, *94*
15:15-20, *94*
15:19, *94*
15:20, *94*
15:24, *59, 94*
15:29, *59*
15:31, *94*
15:34, *59, 60*
16:6, *94*
16:19, *147*

Luke
2:1-3, *57*
2:4-7, *57*
6:16, *103*
7:30, *75, 78*
9:22, *74, 93*
9:27, *113*
9:44, *93*
9:56, *102*
10:20, *118*
12:47, *253*
17:3, *102*
17:4, *98*
17:25, *74*
18:8, *113*

18:31-33, *93*
18:35-43, *92*
19:44, *113*
20:42-44, *147*
21:6, *113*
21:25-36, *113*
22:2, *101*
22:3, *108*
22:3-6, *99, 102*
22:10-11, *226*
22:21, *107*
22:21-22, *99*
22:21-23, *103*
22:22, *104, 105*
22:24, *99*
22:31, *99*
22:31-32, *98*
22:31-34, *96*
22:33, *99*
22:37, *74*
22:47-48, *102*
22:53, *108*
22:54-62, *96*
22:62, *98*
22:69, *147*
23:2, *74*
23:4-5, *74*
23:20-23, *74*
23:25, *74*
23:34, *59*
23:35, *59*
23:51, *74, 75*
24:19-26, *94*
24:26, *74*
24:27, *59*
24:44, *74*
24:46, *74*

John
1:14, *235*
1:18, *235*
1:33, *235*
1:47, *113*
2:4, *113*
2:19-22, *92*
4:17-18, *113*
4:21-24, *234*

4:23-24, *235*
4:24, *169, 235*
4:25-26, *235*
5:19, *256*
5:23, *235*
6, *105*
6:64, *105, 110*
6:70, *106*
6:70-71, *105, 110*
7:16, *92*
7:17, *253*
7:29, *113*
7:42, *56*
8:24, *111*
8:28, *92, 111, 256*
8:55, *113*
8:58, *111*
9:3, *113*
9:4, *108*
9:31, *253*
10:14, *113*
10:15, *113*
10:27, *113*
10:30, *256*
11:4, *113*
11:11, *113*
11:14, *113*
12:4, *106*
12:4-8, *102*
12:6, *102*
12:49, *256*
12:49-50, *92*
13, *106, 110, 112,*
    227
13:1, *107*
13:2, *99, 106, 107,*
    108
13:3, *113*
13:10, *107*
13:10-11, *106, 110*
13:18, *106, 107,*
    110, 111
13:19, *101, 111,*
    112, 113, 174,
    227, 234, 236, 279
13:20, *112*
13:21, *107*

13:21-26, *110*
13:21-27, *99, 111*
13:21-30, *107*
13:26, *104, 107*
13:27, *102, 108*
13:27-28, *104*
13:27-29, *107*
13:30, *108*
13:36-38, *96*
13:37, *99*
13:38, *111*
14:6, *235*
14:13-14, *244*
14:16, *235*
14:24, *92*
14:31, *256*
16:7, *235*
17, *110*
17:4, *256*
17:12, *105, 108, 109, 110*
17:25, *113*
18:1-2, *101*
18:2-4, *102*
18:2-5, *108*
18:4, *108, 113*
18:15-18, *98*
18:17-27, *96*
18:25-27, *98*
19:23-24, *60*
19:24, *59*
19:28, *59*
21:15-17, *98*

Acts
1:6-18, *105*
1:16, *110*
1:16-20, *110*
1:24, *180*
2, *74*
2:23, *73, 74, 75, 76, 77, 78, 79, 80, 86, 88, 104, 105, 111, 176, 254*
2:25, *73*
2:30, *58*
2:31, *73*

2:34-35, *147*
3:17-18, *75*
3:18, *76*
3:19, *98*
3:22, *92*
4:17-18, *105*
4:27-28, *76, 105, 254*
4:28, *73, 76, 78, 79, 81*
7:37, *92*
8:20, *109*
9:35, *98*
10:42, *104*
11:21, *98*
11:29, *104*
13:22, *253*
13:29, *59*
14:15, *98*
15:15-18, *63*
15:19, *98*
17:3, *74*
17:26, *104, 253*
17:28, *204*
17:31, *104*
20:27, *75*
21:29, *73*
26:5, *73*
26:18, *98*
26:20, *98*
27:12, *75*
27:42, *75*

Romans
1, *204*
1:5, *87*
1:19-21, *204*
5:2, *10*
5:3-5, *265, 267*
5:5, *59*
8, *79, 276, 277*
8—9, *117*
8:1, *277*
8:17-18, *277*
8:28, *258, 266*
8:28-29, *84*
8:28-30, *79*

8:29, *10, 73, 79, 80, 81, 82, 83, 86, 87, 88, 114*
8:29-30, *73, 114, 180, 267*
8:29-39, *84*
8:32, *74, 267*
8:33-38, *267*
8:34, *147*
8:35, *266*
8:35-39, *277*
8:38-39, *84*
9, *84*
9:6-9, *84*
9:6-29, *84, 85*
9:12, *84*
9:13, *84*
9:15, *84*
9:16, *84, 253*
9:18, *84*
9:19, *84*
9:20-21, *134*
9:21, *84*
9:22, *109*
9:30—10:21, *85*
11, *82*
11:1, *79, 85*
11:1-2, *81*
11:2, *73, 80, 81, 82, 83, 85, 86, 87, 88*
11:2-4, *82*
11:5, *84*
11:28, *85*
11:33, *11*
11:33-34, *159*
11:34, *244*
12:1, *230*
12:1-2, *253*
16:26, *87*

1 Corinthians
1:2, *116*
1:24, *116*
1:26, *116*
2:2, *116*
2:7, *73, 81, 114,*

116, 117
2:16, *244*
8:3, *81*
13:12, *10*
15:25, *147*
15:33, *204*

2 Corinthians
1:3-7, *266*
4:8-12, *265*
4:18, *203*
12, *242*
12:7-10, *242, 268*
12:8-10, *265*

Galatians
2:20, *74*
3:8, *73, 148*
3:16, *63, 148*
3:29, *63*
4:9, *81*

Ephesians
1, *85, 115*
1—3, *116, 117*
1:3-14, *116*
1:4, *80, 114, 117, 119, 123*
1:4-5, *85*
1:4-6, *116*
1:5, *73, 81, 85*
1:7, *115, 116*
1:11, *73, 75, 81, 86, 171, 254*
1:20, *147*
2:1-5, *116*
2:5, *116*
2:8, *116*
2:11-22, *116*
3:11, *114, 116*
5:20, *267*
6:6, *253*

Philippians
1:28, *109*
2:8, *257*
3:19, *109*

4:3, *118*
4:6, *244*
4:15, *105*

Colossians
3:1, *147*

1 Thessalonians
4:3, *253*
4:17, *66*
5:16-18, *253*
5:18, *267*

2 Thessalonians
1:6, *265*
2:3, *109*

1 Timothy
6:9, *109*

2 Timothy
1:9, *79, 114, 117,*
  118, 123
1:9-10, *117*
2:13, *156*
2:19, *81*
3:16-17, *22*
4:17, *59*

Titus
1:2, *114, 117, 156*
1:12, *204*

Hebrews
1:3, *147*
1:13, *147*
2:12, *59*
4:13, *11, 180*
5:6, *147*
6:18, *156, 191*
7:17, *147*
7:21, *147*
8:1, *147*
10:12-13, *147*
10:36, *253*
10:39, *109*
11:17-19, *178*
12:2, *147, 257*
12:5-11, *265*
12:23, *118*
13:21, *253*

James
1:2-4, *265, 267*
1:13, *265*
4:2, *239, 240*
4:13-15, *253*
1 Peter
1, *86*
1:1, *87*
1:2, *73, 80, 86, 87,*
  88, 114
1:11, *59*
1:18-19, *115*
1:18-20, *119*

1:19-20, *79, 87, 123*
1:20, *73, 80, 88,*
  114, 115
2:7-8, *87*
2:9, *83, 87*
5:8, *59*
2 Peter
2:1, *109*
3:7, *73, 109*
3:8-9, *273*

1 John
2:6, *257*
2:17, *253*
2:18, *109*
2:22, *109*
3:20, *11, 220, 232,*
  281
4:2, *169*
4:3, *109*
4:8, *247*
5:14-15, *244*

Revelation
1:5-6, *231*
2—3, *121*
3:1, *122*
3:4, *122*
3:5, *34, 121, 122,*
  288
3:8, *114*
4, *230, 232*

4:10-11, *232*
5, *122, 230, 232,*
  235
5:5-6, *232*
5:9-10, *118, 120,*
  232
5:10, *231*
5:13, *230*
6—16, *119, 283*
7:10, *230*
7:15, *231*
12:9, *119*
13:8, *79, 118, 119,*
  120, 122, 123
13:10, *277*
13:14, *119*
15:4, *158*
17:8, *109, 114, 119,*
  120, 121, 122
17:11, *109*
18:23, *119*
19:10, *231*
19:20, *119*
20:12-13, *118*
21—22, *10*
21:1-2, *63*
21:3-4, *265*
21:27, *118*
22:3, *230, 231*
22:9, *231*
22:19, *121*

Predictive Prophecies in Scripture About Future Free Human Choices Or Events Involving Free Human Choices

In a comprehensive survey I have identified a total of 4,017 predictive prophecies in canonical Scripture. Of these, 2,323 are predictive prophecies concerning future free human decisions or events that in one way or another involve such free decisions. From this survey I have created a list of the 2,323 prophecies by reference only. I have also created a list with 300 representative prophecies, 157 from the Old Testament and 143 from the New Testament, to illustrate the number, variety and precision of such biblical predictions. Taken together they form a strong quantitative argument for God's foreknowledge of free human decisions. Both of these lists can be accessed online by going to InterVarsity Press's website at www.ivpress.com and typing in the title of this book.